Joseph L. Mankiewicz

Joseph L. Mankiewicz

Critical Essays with an Annotated Bibliography and a Filmography

by CHERYL BRAY LOWER
and R. BARTON PALMER

McFarland & Company, Inc., Publishers
Jefferson, North Carolina, and London

Frontispiece: Mankiewicz directing a scene from *The Barefoot Contessa* (1954), with the movie's editor, Bill Hornbeck, at the right.

All photographs in this book are from the personal collection of Rosemary Mankiewicz and are used by permission.

Library of Congress Cataloguing-in-Publication Data

Lower, Cheryl Bray.
    Joseph L. Mankiewicz : critical essays with an annotated bibliography and a filmography / by Cheryl Bray Lower and R. Barton Palmer.
       p.   cm.
    Includes bibliographical references and index.
    ISBN 0-7864-0987-8 (library binding : 50# alkaline paper) ∞
    1. Mankiewicz, Joseph L.—Criticism and interpretation.
    2. Mankiewicz, Joseph L.—Bibliography.   I. Palmer, R. Barton,
    1946–   II. Title.

PN1998.3.M35[L...]   2001
791.43'0233'092—dc21

                               2001018055

British Library cataloguing data are available

Manufactured in the United States of America

McFarland & Company, Inc., Publishers
  Box 611, Jefferson, North Carolina 28640
    www.mcfarlandpub.com

To the three people who have nurtured my love of film: my mother, Gerry Bray, whose love of movies rubbed off on me at an early age; Rosemary Mankiewicz, who opened the door to the Mankiewicz treasure trove; and my husband, Bob Lower, whose enthusiasm and encouragement helped me stay focused when inundated with more material than I ever imagined.

—*Cheryl Bray Lower*

To my uncle and aunt, Gilbert A. and Pauline G. Barton, who took me along on their Saturday nights at the movies and taught me to love Hollywood films as much as they did.

—*R. Barton Palmer*

Contents

Introduction

The career of writer, director, and producer Joseph L. Mankiewicz spanned the rise and the fall of the Hollywood studio system. He entered the business with talkies and always felt that because films could talk they had an obligation to say something. His films say quite a lot about Hollywood, about people, and about social conventions. Ironically, this highly respected, articulate man had no press agent and detested interviews. Therefore, he was not only someone who refused to play by Hollywood's rules, but was also a conundrum to many in the film business and to those who chose to write about him.

Appreciated more in foreign countries than at home, Mankiewicz thought of himself as a forgotten man in America during his declining years. He died in 1993, just as several of his films were being released on video.

Not only did Mankiewicz address issues of gender and the aging professional woman as far back as 1950 in *All About Eve*, that same year he exposed racial prejudice in a frightening film, *No Way Out*. In 1957, he undertook a close examination of British and American involvement in Vietnam in *The Quiet American*. His *Julius Caesar* (1953) is considered by many to be one of the most faithful adaptations of Shakespeare on film. His work is revered in France and is still being written about today. But until now there has been no definitive guide to his work.

With this book of critical essays and a guide to resources, it is our hope that we might stimulate an interest for those to whom most of Mankiewicz's films are yet unknown. With the field of film scholarship burgeoning, the works of Joseph L. Mankiewicz deserve a fresh look because he was a writer-director years ahead of his time.

—*Cheryl Bray Lower* and *R. Barton Palmer*

1

PART I

Joseph L. Mankiewicz:
Notes on His Life and Career

A Biographical Sketch

by Cheryl Bray Lower

Intellectual discourse is the cornerstone of the films of Joseph L. Mankiewicz. The spoken word drives the visual image in his work as director because he maintained that ever since sound came to films, they had an obligation to *say* something.[1]

Joseph Mankiewicz is a curious product of the Hollywood studio system. Though he championed the high culture of East Coast theatre and fine arts, he flourished in the West Coast world of movies and low-brow entertainment. Throughout his career, he sustained this dichotomy. His most honored work was done in Hollywood, yet he abandoned the West in the early fifties for New York, maintaining all the while that he preferred writing for the theatre—yet he rarely did.[2] Hollywood continued to lure him back to the film world for the rest of his life, but New York was Mankiewicz's oasis in the desert. It promised him independence from the studio moguls, whom he had outgrown, and it offered him acceptance by the intellectual elite.

It is this constant psychological conflict of the metaphorical good (New York) and evil (Hollywood) that is the undercurrent of the biting satire of a Mankiewicz film. His work is the product of his own life's struggle—to be accepted in the world of the intelligentsia, while working in the world of common tastes. To understand the professional conundrum of Joseph L. Mankiewicz one merely has to look at his family background and upbringing.

The last of three children, Joseph was an unexpected addition to the family of Frank and Johanna (Blumenau). He was born February 11, 1909, in Wilkes-Barre, Pennsylvania. His father was an academician for whom intellectual rigor was a way of life. A demanding and very frugal man, he frequently moved the family to new locations, not only to better orchestrate his career goals, but save a few dollars on rent. By the time Joseph was five, they had moved to New York, where Frank took a new teaching position and began the graduate work that eventually would land him the college professorship he desired.

Because the family moved so often, young Joseph never developed a sense of belonging. To compensate for having no friends as a child, he turned inward and began a lifelong pursuit of understanding what motivates human behavior. In a rare in-depth interview at the height of his career, Mankiewicz addressed the subject of his isolation as a child:

> I became skillful at taking on the color of my environment without absorbing it, at participating in almost everything without becoming part of anything. I acquired an awareness of people the way an animal knows the woods in which he lives. I made no friends. I have no contact today with anyone who knew me as a child. I escaped into fantasies—thousands of fantasies. It isn't surprising that I ended up as a writer and in show business [*140*, 163*].

The Mankiewicz children were quick studies. Joseph, sister Erna (8 years older), and brother Herman (12 years older) advanced through the public school system at a record rate. Always a man ahead of his time, Joseph finished his first eight grades of school by age 11 but then was deemed too young to attend high school. While waiting until he was old enough to enroll, he was sent to study in Berlin for one year. He then returned to enter the prestigious Stuyvesant High School in New York where he graduated three years later at the age of 15. It was in high school that Mankiewicz began his writing career as editor of the school newspaper, *Caliper*. Ironically, it was a 1923 interview with one of his theatrical idols, W. C. Fields, that represented his first writing about Hollywood. Little did he know that at age 14 he would interview the man for whom he would eventually write the famous phrase, "my little chickadee."

Mankiewicz continued his writing at Columbia. But he entered Columbia as a premed major interested in psychiatry. Had he not had a

---

*In references in this chapter, the first number (in *italics*) refers to the source listed by that number in the Annotated Bibliography. The second number cites the page from that source.

bad experience with one of his science classes, he might have gone on to a career in medicine. Instead, he changed majors, opting for the fine arts and an English degree. He delighted in telling the story about how terribly he performed in biology:

> I took a pre-med course at Columbia. Then came the part where you disembowel frogs and earthworms; which horrified and nauseated me. But what really finished me was physics. I got an F-minus. There is no such grade. I went to Professor Farwell and protested. He said "I feel that I must distinguish between mere failure and total failure such as yours" [*149*, 164].

He went on to be the youngest member of his class at Columbia University when he received a Bachelor of Arts degree in 1928. While not graduating with a major in psychiatry, he maintained his interest in the subject and was a friend of Karl Menninger and other leaders in the field.

As a college graduate of 19, Mankiewicz was once again sent abroad, to read literature. He returned to Berlin with intentions of undertaking further studies. His father had hoped that he would pursue a degree in education, but instead it was in Berlin that he got his first real taste of popular culture. He worked as a stringer for *Variety*, as well as an assistant correspondent for the *Chicago Tribune*, but it was his work at the German film studio UFA (translating subtitles from German to English) that gave him his first experience in the film business. By this time, brother Herman had established himself in Hollywood and was put in charge of recruiting other New York writers to try their hands at scenario writing (*435*, 715). Herman's assurance of bountiful success brought Joseph back to the United States to begin his Hollywood career.

Joseph L. Mankiewicz came to Hollywood in March of 1929, not long after his twentieth birthday. He began as a junior writer at Paramount, writing subtitles for sound films that played in movie houses not yet equipped with sound systems. Talking pictures were taking the country by storm and Mankiewicz never forgot that his career began with sound. He always felt an obligation for his words to mean something. He used his clever mind and sharp wit to bring life to his work, and as a result, he was an immediate success.

After two years as a journeyman writer at Paramount, his first screenplay, *Fast Company* (1929), was produced by David O. Selznick. He received his first Academy Award nomination for *Skippy* in 1931, when he was just 22 years old. In 1932 he wrote the original story and screenplay *Million Dollar Legs*, a hilarious satire on the Olympic Games, and in

Mankiewicz, aged 20, Paramount's youngest dialogue writer (1929)

1933, he ventured away from comedy to write the dialogue for the Depression saga, *Our Daily Bread*, for his friend, independent producer-director, King Vidor.

At age 24, Mankiewicz jumped at the chance to write for Metro-Goldwyn-Mayer. His first project was *Manhattan Melodrama* (1934), the movie made famous by John Dillinger who was gunned down by police outside Chicago's Biograph Theatre after watching the film for two consecutive showings. By 1934 Mankiewicz was writing full-time but he wanted to direct as well. So he approached his boss, Louis B. Mayer, about the possibility. Mayer refused because he wanted Mankiewicz to succeed Irving Thalberg as Metro's second-in-command. However, this was a job that the young man neither sought nor wanted. Instead of allowing him to write and direct, Mayer offered him the chance to produce, saying, "You have to learn to crawl before you walk." Mankiewicz often remarked that this statement was the best definition of a producer he had ever heard (*149*, 25).

To Mankiewicz, a man who wanted to have creative control over his words on screen, being a producer was agony. "I felt completely uncomfortable as a producer. I felt useless and sterile and pretentious" (*140*, 168). He considered this period "the black years" of his career and later would refer to himself as "the oldest whore on the beat" because of his years as a producer (*333*, 8). But it was during this nine-year stint at MGM that he produced the first collaboration of Spencer Tracy and Katharine Hepburn in *Woman of the Year* (1942). He also was responsible for nine Joan Crawford films, including *The Gorgeous Hussy* (1936) and *Strange Cargo* (1940), and he gave Mickey Rooney his first starring role in *The Adventures of Huckleberry Finn* (1939). Likewise, his skills as a producer were demonstrated in the success of other MGM products, including Fritz Lang's first American film, *Fury* (1936). Mankiewicz also was instrumental in the revival of the screen career of an actress considered box-office poison, Katharine Hepburn, in *The Philadelphia Story* (1940).[3]

While he produced 20 films at MGM, he always kept his hand in the writing process, often cowriting or rewriting screenplays for which he received no credit. Much to his dismay, the Screen Writers Guild, a union he helped create, had laid down what he called "draconian" provisions for on-screen credits: no producer's name was permitted to appear in the writing credits (*38*, 4). His most famous "anonymous" contribution to screen dialogue was on *Three Comrades* (1938), a screenplay written by F. Scott Fitzgerald. "If I go down at all in literary history, in a footnote, it will be as the swine who rewrote Fitzgerald," recalled Mankiewicz, who believed Fitzgerald to be a wonderful novelist but quite unacceptable as a writer of screen dialogue (*435*, 716).

Indeed, Joseph L. Mankiewicz was always a force in the creative process of the films on which he worked, but it was not until 1943, when he moved to 20th Century–Fox, that he got his wish to write *and* direct. It was at this studio that he attained the most recognition, and he considered it his "most fruitful period" (*40*, 1). During this time, he received

Mankiewicz in his middle years

his highest critical acclaim and won back-to-back double Oscars for screenwriting and directing *A Letter to Three Wives* (1949) and *All About Eve* (1950).

Mankiewicz's success was foreshadowed by his early work at Fox, which began with his serving, once again, in the capacity of producer. His first project was *The Keys of the Kingdom* (1944), a story he and Nunnally Johnson adapted from the best selling novel by A. J. Cronin. Mankiewicz wrote the screenplay and produced the film that gave Gregory Peck his first starring role and costarred Mankiewicz's wife, Viennese actress, Rosa Stradner.[4]

Delighted to give up the producing reins following *Keys*, Mankiewicz quickly moved to writing and directing his own films. His directorial debut—the 1946 gothic thriller *Dragonwyck*—starred Gene Tierney and Vincent Price. Mankiewicz's longtime friend and mentor, Ernst Lubitsch, served as producer on the film.

Mankiewicz first met Lubitsch during his days at Paramount. He recalled in a 1989 interview, "[Lubitsch] took me right under his wing. God, he was divine to me" (*447*, 74). Lubitsch was originally scheduled to direct *Dragonwyck* but ill health took him off the project. When Lubitsch approached him about directing the film, Mankiewicz felt unprepared since he had only directed screen tests thus far. But he recalled telling himself, "Schmuck, if Lubitsch is the producer, that's like having the world-champion chess player as your teacher for a few months" (*447*, 74).

As screenwriter-director on *Dragonwyck*, not only did Mankiewicz begin to learn his craft as a director, but he finally heard his script as he had intended it. His adaptation of Anya Seton's novel capitalized on the male-female relationship in the story and laid particular emphasis on the strong-willed woman. This was the first of many Mankiewicz films in which the primary action revolves around character motivation, not plot events.

The body of Mankiewicz's work looks for explanations of why people act the way they do. Drawing on his psychology background and a lifelong interest in the workings of the mind, he delves into the psyche of his characters, and their motivation is what drives the plot. In *Dragonwyck*, the female protagonist, Miranda Wells, is also a model for the headstrong women to follow in other Mankiewicz films.

It was at 20th Century–Fox that he honed his craft, in large part due to his collaboration with Darryl F. Zanuck, who was in charge of production at the studio. Zanuck appreciated Mankiewicz's intelligence and wit and gave him a considerable amount of free rein over his films by hiring him as writer, director, and producer. But the Napoleonic Zanuck was soon upstaged by his young director when he won four Oscars in two years for writing and directing. By the time Mankiewicz began work on *People Will Talk* (1951), Zanuck felt overshadowed by Mankiewicz's glory and petulantly refused to place his own name on the credits as producer of the film, complaining that Mankiewicz was receiving all the attention now and no longer needed his endorsement. He recanted, however, and the name Darryl F. Zanuck prominently appears on screen as producer.

The fifties were an exciting time for Mankiewicz. Not only was his career moving in the direction he had hoped as a "film-author" (a term he used in a 1947 article to denote the writer and director of a film), but he also was president of the Screen Directors Guild (SDG) at the height of blacklisting.

He never considered himself a political animal, but he was drawn into political controversy nonetheless. No event would haunt Hollywood more than the Communist witch-hunts of Sen. Joseph McCarthy and the House Un-American Activities Committee (HUAC). Like it or not, Mankiewicz was caught up in the political name-calling because of his stand on a voluntary signing of the loyalty oath for members of the SDG. This seemingly innocent act brought down the wrath of ultraconservatives in the guild led by director Cecil B. DeMille, who with his political cohorts attempted to oust Mankiewicz from his post as president. In secret, they set off to rally support of like-minded politicos to impeach him and remove him from office while he was abroad scouting locations for his next picture. Word leaked out and his supporters rallied sufficient steam to quash the effort. He retained his leadership, thanks in large part to directors such as George Stevens and John Ford who supported his presidency and spoke vehemently against the right-wingers who sought to empower themselves at the expense of others.[5]

That Mankiewicz made a name for himself in Hollywood's political circles was more the result of an accident than an attempt at grandstanding. He was much more focused on turning out films in the fast-paced world of the studio system. In six years, he directed an eclectic group of 11 films, eight of which he wrote as well.[6] After writing and directing the gothic romance, *Dragonwyck* (1946), he tried his hand with the popular film noir genre of the time by writing and directing *Somewhere in the Night* (1946). Here he turned out a moody and complex psychological tale of an amnesiac who tries to uncover the truth about himself.

Deciding to focus on learning the skills required to make a successful transition from writer to director, he then turned to studio colleagues Philip Dunne and Nunnally Johnson for scripts for his next three films: *The Late George Apley* (1947), a delightful comedy of manners and mores in the changing social world of Boston at the turn of the century; the whimsical romance *The Ghost and Mrs. Muir* (1947); and *Escape* (1948), a haunting tale of a man wrongly accused of a crime. These were the years of directorial apprenticeship for Mankiewicz.

Always a fast study, Mankiewicz quickly returned to writing his own films. Working within the studio system, he went on to accomplish something no one ever had before (or has since): he won double Academy Awards for screenwriting and directing in two successive years.[7] With *A Letter to Three Wives* (1949), he delivered a social discourse on marriage in post-war suburbia. At a time when gender issues were considered merely the battle of the sexes, he elevated the "battle" to examine social mores, the working woman, and classism. His uncanny ability to discern the plight of the working woman is demonstrated in the character of Rita (convincingly played by Ann Sothern), who is caught in the middle of the dilemma of the working mother. This is also the first of many Mankiewicz tirades on the high culture–low culture debate, wherein Rita's academician husband (a character loosely modeled after Mankiewicz's father) personifies the dignity of the fine arts, while his wife exemplifies the grittiness of popular culture—all packaged in high comedy.

On the heels of the critical success of *Letter*, came two intensely dark films: *House of Strangers* (1949) and *No Way Out* (1950), both of which continued the Mankiewicz examination of the iconoclast in society. *House of Strangers* explored social change, loyalty, and familial responsibilities in a Sicilian immigrant family, while *No Way Out* tackled the larger family of man by exploring racial prejudice. It garnered critical acclaim from African-American publications such as *Ebony*, which called it the "first out-and-out blast against racial discrimination in everyday American life" (*123*, 31).

That Mankiewicz was at ease writing in any genre is evident in this diverse assortment of films made during his early years at Fox. However, it is in *All About Eve* (1950) that he found his most articulate voice in the genre of social satire. Here, he explores his favorite topics—the theatre, and the complexities of women—all revealed in a style that was to become his trademark: the flashback. He most successfully uses the device which became his signature to slowly unfurl the facade of the ambitious actress who stops at nothing to achieve stardom. Mankiewicz, who loved to write about women because he viewed them as more complex and thus more interesting than men, is in his element in *Eve* as he dissects the personalities of the aging actress, the wife of the famous playwright, the ingenue, and the aggressive up-and-comer. This is also a film that dares to compare the cultural worlds of New York and Hollywood, and if ever Joseph L. Mankiewicz appeared in one of his films, he does so in the character of Addison DeWitt, the theatre critic played by George Sanders. DeWitt serves as the voice of authority on the culture-war debate while Mankiewicz was merely a pawn in the game. Ironically, *Eve* was made only two years before Mankiewicz left Hollywood for the East Coast, perhaps convincing himself that the theatre was a more viable environment for his talents.

With four Academy Awards on his mantel, he finished this phase of his work on the West Coast with two films. *People Will Talk* (1951) was a diatribe against the medical profession with veiled references to the HUAC hearings, and *Five Fingers* (1952) was a marvelous spy thriller based on a true story of a valet to the British ambassador who sold state secrets to the Germans during World War II.

After completing his contract with Fox in the fall of 1951, Mankiewicz moved his family from the "intellectual fog belt" of Los Angeles to New York City (*84*, 173). There he would raise his children in the East Coast educational system for which he had such high regard while also allowing for his wife to resume her stage career.

He moved to New York with the thought of writing for the theatre, but before he could explore that possibility, he returned to the film world with his personal vision of a Shakespearean play, *Julius Caesar* (1953). Approaching the film as though it were a play, he assembled the cast for three weeks of rehearsals (prior to filming) with one goal in mind: "I wanted to show in *Julius Caesar* that Mr. Shakespeare could be played exactly as if he were our contemporary" (*313*, 35). Mankiewicz chose to make his film a character study in black and white to avoid the dominance of a grizzly Technicolor scene of the death of Caesar (*460*, 244). He also made a risky casting choice for the role of Marc Antony by selecting Marlon Brando, an actor with an on-screen persona as a lowbrow street thug. The film was a success, according to producer John Houseman, because of Mankiewicz's intelligence and devotion to dialogue:

> The freshness of his approach to Shakespeare's tragedy, his sure sense of the dynamics of a movie scene, and his insistence at all times that every resource of motion picture technique be employed to enhance the clarity and energy of Shakespeare's dramatic text—these proved a strong unifying force [*180*].

In 1953, Mankiewicz entered the world of independent film production when he formed Figaro, Inc. He would make only two films for this company as writer, director, and producer: *The Barefoot Contessa* (1954), and *The Quiet American* (1957). But before he embarked on any independent projects he took a brief respite from filmmaking to stage the 1952 production of *La Bohème* for the Metropolitan Opera. This would be his only realized work for the stage.

His first independent film, *The Barefoot Contessa*, starred screen sensations Ava Gardner and Humphrey Bogart. As writer, director, and producer of this dark fairy tale about a Hollywood Cinderella, Mankiewicz had the freedom to express his long-held views on some of the more unseemly characters that haunt the film world. *Contessa* was filmed in Italy under what seemed like his complete control. But the censors defused his original concept of a homosexual Prince Charming, and although he was skilled at working under the rigors of the Production Code, he was never completely satisfied with the end result.

Between his two independent productions, he made a film for Samuel Goldwyn which showed that his diversity knew no bounds. *Guys and Dolls* (1955) was Mankiewicz's one and only musical. Adapting the critically acclaimed Broadway musical comedy, he took another chance casting Brando—this time in a singing role. Trying to convince the skeptical Brando, who had just completed *On the Waterfront*, that he could handle the part, he wired him, saying, "Understand you don't want to do *Guys and Dolls* as you've never done a musical. You have nothing to worry about as I haven't done one either" (*400*, 13). Brando agreed and Mankiewicz succeeded in bringing another stage play to life on the big screen. The confidence Mankiewicz showed in Brando was not wrongly placed; the film was a success and Mankiewicz chalked up another hit in his multi-faceted *oeuvre*.

Following *Guys and Dolls*, Mankiewicz returned to the role of independent filmmaker when he ventured to Vietnam to make *The Quiet American*, a film loosely based on the novel by Graham Greene. In this film, war-hero Audie Murphy plays an idealistic American in Indochina in the 1950s, and Michael Redgrave portrays a cynical British reporter who struggles to maintain, at all costs, his relationship with a Vietnamese woman who comes to prefer the American.

Hitherto known for a keen wit, Mankiewicz's *The Barefoot Contessa* and *The Quiet American* were departures from the biting satire of his earlier films. These were tragedies filmed during a tragic time in his life. Prior to the premiere of *Julius Caesar*, his brother, Herman, died of uremic poisoning at the age of 55.

Herman was a powerful influence in Joseph's life on a personal as well as professional level. Being 12 years his senior, he often saw himself as young Joseph's surrogate parent. He helped him land a job at Paramount where the extroverted Herman was an influential writer. A friend of the Mankiewicz brothers recalled how difficult it was for Joseph when he first came to Paramount:

> Joe was the kid brother all right. Herman rode him, patronized him, did everything but send him out for cigarets [*sic*]. Well, that was understandable. Herman was a god among the writers, Joe was strictly nobody. Even people who knew him, when they bumped into him around the studio, would say, 'Hello, Herm—I mean Joe.' One day Joe said, 'I know now what will be on my tombstone. It'll say, "Here lies Herm—I mean Joe—Mankiewicz."' But at the same time Herman did a lot for him. He showed him the ropes, gave him advice, steered him around, did all sorts of things [*140*, 164].

In the early fifties, as Joseph was achieving critical acclaim, Herman remarked:

> I suppose—in fact, I'm sure—I've been an influence in Joe's life, but it's been mostly negative. Like Shaw said, "Parents should be a warning to their children instead of an example." Nobody can deny I've been a good bad example. Otherwise I make no claims: I helped him at first, but he learned fast [*140*, 164].

As Joseph's career was taking off, Herman's was falling, in large part due to his lifelong battle with addictions to gambling and alcohol. Joseph did not speak publicly about his brother's failed potential; instead he qui-

Mankiewicz shooting an exterior night scene on *The Barefoot Contessa* **(1954)**

etly supported him financially whenever his gambling debts grew out of hand (*382*, 177).

The inevitable sibling rivalry existed to the end, as the younger brother recalled: "I remember vividly the last time I saw Herman. He was full of praise about *Julius Caesar*, which he loved. Quite understandably, he found it much easier to like my direction than to like my writing" (*380*, 236).

Coming on the heels of the move to New York and his brother's death was the failing mental health of his wife, Rosa Stradner. A long-time sufferer from severe depression, Rosa attempted to take her own life several times, often having to be hospitalized for extended periods. She finally committed suicide in 1958 in a summer home in upstate New York while Mankiewicz was working in Manhattan. He later acknowledged that those years of personal struggle showed in his work:

> *The Barefoot Contessa* was a tragedy. Even the very bad film I made during a very muddled part of my life, *The Quiet American*, was. During this unhappy phase I became a sort of Angry Old Man. I was bitter. I think I started using a club where I previously used a very sharp knife on things that upset me. I got angry at them rather than exposing and ridiculing [*239*, 33].

Even though Mankiewicz (and most American critics) were unhappy with *The Quiet American*, French critic-filmmaker, Jean-Luc Godard, called it the best film of the year (quoted in *330*, 23).

One more intensely serious film would occupy Mankiewicz's attention, but this time he bypassed the writing process to direct a movie version of Tennessee Williams' play, *Suddenly, Last Summer* (1959). Working with Elizabeth Taylor, Montgomery Clift, and Katharine Hepburn, Mankiewicz directed the Williams–Gore Vidal screenplay about a mother who so idolizes the memory of her dead son that she is willing to lobotomize her niece to silence the truth about her son's homosexuality. This powerful drama not only was a box office success, but landed Oscar nominations for Taylor and Hepburn, and led to the lifelong mutual admiration of Mankiewicz and Taylor.

With his personal life returning to normal and his professional reputation once again flourishing, Mankiewicz signed a contract to return to Fox as a writer-director. Always fascinated with complex psychological stories about women, he worked diligently on condensing Lawrence Durrell's four novels *Justine, Balthazar, Mountolive*, and *Clea* (known as *The Alexandria Quartet*) into a film treatment that he proudly presented to Durrell, who wholeheartedly endorsed the project. While vacationing and working on the screenplay, entitled "Justine," Mankiewicz received a frantic call from Fox president, Spyros Skouras, beseeching him to come to the rescue of a failing picture. "It was a matter of life and death," he would recall Skouras as pleading. Would he please fly to London for just a few weeks to check out some of the problems on the film? He did, and the result was the greatest regret of his career—he never got to make "Justine" because he became entangled in the process of saving *Cleopatra* (*295*, 27).

"*Cleopatra*," according to Mankiewicz in the few times he ever mentioned the work, "was conceived in emergency, shot in hysteria and wound up in blind panic" (*271*, 8). Yet when he was called to London—with the assurance that he could make his "Justine" for Fox if he would just consider helping get *Cleopatra* back on track—he was hooked:

> There was this unreadable script and these impossible little sets and everybody standing around waiting for the English fog and rain to turn suddenly into Egyptian sunshine. Of course I was hooked. I couldn't resist it. I started writing [*295*, 27].

Following the resignation of the previous director, Rouben Mamoulian, Mankiewicz resurrected the film by completely taking over the project from the writing to the directing. He scrapped the few minutes of film shot by Mamoulian, rewrote the script and, except for Elizabeth Taylor, completely recast the film. The most expensive movie made up to that point (approximately $40 million) was constantly scrutinized in the press, not only from a financial viewpoint but because of the real-life extramarital romance of its stars, Elizabeth Taylor and Richard Burton.

It was more taxing than he ever imagined. He spent his days directing the scenes he had stayed up writing the previous night. He coped with Taylor's near-fatal illness, unpredictable weather, incomplete sets, the nervous behavior of the 20th Century–Fox board of directors, and the misconception that he was making two films, not just one. With the blessing of Skouras, who was willing to give him anything he wanted to have him direct the picture, Mankiewicz conceived of *Cleopatra* as two separate movies. One film, to be titled, *Caesar and Cleopatra*, and the other, *Antony and Cleopatra*, would be an exhaustive character study of the power of this intelligent and beautiful woman over the men in her life (*366*). However, with all of the hoopla over the escalating budget, producer Walter Wanger was fired from the film and eventually even Skouras would fall victim, being sacked as president of Fox. Replacing him was Mankiewicz's former boss, Darryl F. Zanuck, whose first act was to fire him from the project during the editing process. Mankiewicz was soon rehired to shoot some retakes and work on postproduction, but the film was no longer as he had conceived it. Zanuck took over the editing and merged Mankiewicz's two sagas about one of the world's most powerful women into a weak, overly long film that fell on its face before the critics and the public at large. Devastated by the outcome of the final product, Mankiewicz remarked, "They [the two films] were taken over and butchered into the most beautiful and expensive banjo picks in the world" (*367*, 4).

This film that should have taken just a few months to make, in fact, took nearly two years of Mankiewicz's life. After its release, he felt he could no longer trust those in power at Fox and would not work for them again. Much to his despair, his "Justine" script went unused. "I am more bitter about that than anything else that happened during *Cleopatra*," he recounted many years later when he succumbed to answering questions on the film from which he tried to have his name removed (*366*).

One good thing did come out of the agony of *Cleopatra*. Mankiewicz fell in love with the woman with whom he would share the rest of his life. Rosemary Matthews, a production assistant on the movie, was a highly intelligent and supremely competent young Englishwoman who had first worked with Mankiewicz on *The Barefoot Contessa* in 1954. They were married December 14, 1962.

Cleopatra and the loss of his pet project "Justine" took an immense toll on Mankiewicz's creative psyche. After a lengthy respite, he directed a made-for-television film in honor of the United Nations, *A Carol for Another Christmas* (1964), which was a modern-day apocalyptic vision by screenwriter Rod Serling, based on Dickens's *A Christmas Carol*. Also, Mankiewicz continued to work on several projects that he had undertaken over the years. He wrote a play for Broadway based on Friedrich Durrenmatt's *The Meteor*, a screen adaptation of John Updike's *Couples*, and another play based on Carl Jonas' *Jefferson Selleck*. Unfortunately, none of these projects ever materialized on stage or screen.

Mankiewicz's first feature film following *Cleopatra* was not until 1967 when he wrote, directed, and co-produced *The Honey Pot*. Returning to the genre of social satire, he cast Rex Harrison in the leading role. This would be the fourth time he had called on Harrison to star in one of his films, having used him in *The Ghost and Mrs. Muir* (1947), *Escape* (1948), and most recently, *Cleopatra* (1963).

Following all of the press coverage of the exorbitant costs and high finance involved with *Cleopatra*, it may have been no coincidence that Mankiewicz was drawn to the theme of avarice for his next screenplay. He reflected on the story's appeal in an interview in *Cahiers du Cinéma*:

> It is a new version of the sempiternal story of human greed and concupiscence. The eternal desire to obtain something without giving anything in exchange. Since I make films on the moral weaknesses of man that seem indeed to motivate his conduct almost entirely, I thought that it would be appropriate for me to take up greed [*313*, 37].

The Honey Pot drew praise from film critics for its eloquent dialogue. Calling it "a literary trampoline," *Newsday* writer Joseph Gelmis welcomed back the Mankiewicz touch, noting, "[Mankiewicz] playfully bounces metaphors, morals and mystification off the screen" (*471*, 3).

Abruptly changing genres, but with his tongue firmly placed in his cheek, he directed his one and only Western, *There Was a Crooked Man* (1970). Turning to *Bonnie and Clyde* screenwriters, Robert Benton and David Newman, he chose the prison–Western genre to poke fun at Wild West mythology. *Crooked Man* was Mankiewicz's first film in Hollywood after a 14-year absence, and reunited him with some of his old friends from the early days: Kirk Douglas, Burgess Meredith, Henry Fonda, and Hume Cronyn. This tall tale takes full advantage of the demise of the Production Code, by displaying nudity on screen, portraying a blatantly homosexual character, and even letting the bad guys win.

By this time, Mankiewicz was tiring of the exhausting process of writing and directing his own movies. "It's difficult for me to find material I can write quickly," he recalled during the filming of *Crooked Man*. "If I write and direct a film, it takes me the better part of two years" (*330*, 22).

He knew his career as a film author was coming to an end. Times and tastes were changing in Hollywood, where filmmaking was becoming increasingly dependent on special effects and action adventure stories. "My particular type of writing," he recalled in a 1970 interview, "is concerned with the manners and mores of our time, and it demands an audience which is patient with *the word*" (*330*, 22). And thus, the end of an era of literate filmmaking in America was upon us.

Always highly esteemed abroad, Mankiewicz decided to film his next project in Great Britain. His last filmed-theatre piece, *Sleuth* (1972), was shot in England with British actors and based on Anthony Shaffer's award-winning play. Mankiewicz directed Laurence Olivier and Michael Caine in a tour de force that captured Academy Award nominations for the director and his two stars.

Even though Mankiewicz never made another film, his work continued to grow in renown with foreign film critics during the rise of the auteur theory. French theorists dubbed his work "le théâtre film," a term Mankiewicz embraced (*313*, 31). "I write plays for the screen," he once noted. "I write essentially for audiences who come to listen to a film as well as to look at it" (*239*, 9). But his era of filmmaking—that of high comedy, witty dialogue, and complex character development—was coming to an end. What emerged in its place were the glitzy computer-generated visuals of *Star Wars* and the easily digestible story lines geared to the short attention span of a Sesame Street generation. Gone was an appreciation for the Mankiewicz type of literate filmmaking. What audiences wanted were special effects, car chases, and blatant sex on the screen. Mankiewicz recalled in a 1975 interview, "My thing is to develop characterizations, to direct actors instead of special effects. A recurrent theme in my films is how life louses up the script we write for ourselves each day" (*371*, 27).

Life loused up the Mankiewicz script when he flew to London to check on *Cleopatra*. The humiliation he faced over that film would stifle his writing, and even though he never made another film after *Sleuth*, he continued to work on projects that were never realized. His personal favorite, a screenplay entitled "Jane," was unceremoniously taken away from him in the summer of 1975 by Columbia producer Joe Janni, who claimed Mankiewicz was taking too long to deliver a finished script. This seemed to be the last straw. Mankiewicz soon suffered a debilitating writer's block that lasted nearly ten years.

Although his name never again appeared on the motion picture screen, Mankiewicz received copious praise throughout the world for the remainder of his life. Awards were bestowed on him from American film institutions, but the greatest affection for his work came from abroad. Toward the end of his life he thought of himself as a forgotten man in America, but foreign film festivals treated him like royalty. He gave very few in-depth interviews in the United States, but he spoke freely with the foreign press who seemed to appreciate and understand him more than their American counterparts.

Joseph L. Mankiewicz lived a comfortable life in upstate New York with his wife Rosemary until he died of heart failure on February 5, 1993, less than a week before his 84th birthday. He was the father of four children, Eric Reynal, Christopher, Tom, and Alexandra Kate.[8]

Mankiewicz hoped he would live long enough to write his memoirs, but he never got around to it. However, he did publish a lengthy discussion of his screenplay *All About Eve* in a 1971 book, *More About All About Eve*.

Few books have been written about him. Only two exist by American writers, and both are out of print. One is a look by a scholar at Mankiewicz's individual films; the other is a gossipy biography.[9] The most serious work to date on Hollywood's most literate writer-director can be found in the few documentaries by foreign filmmakers and a handful of biographies by foreign writers who recognize the power of the Mankiewicz touch.[10]

Mankiewicz wrote the following, not long before he died:

I have a good mind.

I have read much.

I have done and seen much.

I have done many things that were wrong without being called to account for them. I have done many good, generous and helpful things without recognition, much less acknowledgement and reward.

I have pondered values, principles and the behavior of man in general for many more of my waking hours than most similarly equipped persons.

I am convinced that this knowledge of himself and control of that knowledge (inherent in) man is to be his ultimate, and only salvation—and that the cultivation of man's intellect has fallen into dangerous neglect.

I want my reflections upon such matters to be seriously considered. How can I go about it—in the few years I have left? [526, 16].

A new generation of viewers is now being exposed to Mankiewicz films through the release of his works on video or their airing on classic movie channels on television. There is no doubt that Joseph L. Mankiewicz succeeded in creating films for the thinking public. His critical acclaim ranges from high praise to concern for the wordiness of his work. Some critics have called him a "genius" (*148*), "a pioneer in independent production" (*223*, 8), and "the master of flashbacks" (*463*, 1). Godard called him, "the most intelligent man in all contemporary cinema" (quoted in *463*, 28). Still others fault him for his static camera work or the excessive length of his films. But none have questioned the intelligence of his product.

Mankiewicz has left a legacy of films that are highly literate character studies. They champion strong female characters and extol his love for a cleverly turned phrase. In the final analysis, there is little doubt that a Mankiewicz film always has something to say.

NOTES

1. Biographical information was gleaned from the personal papers of Joseph L. Mankiewicz. The most accurate and useful published biographical data are found in Gow (*330*), Coughlan (*140*) and Wakeman (*435*).

2. Mankiewicz spent considerable time on several theatrical projects that were never realized. For example, *The Meteor* which was an ongoing project during the sixties that even got to the point of casting. The other play was *Maiden Voyage*, to be produced by Billy Rose. This too never occurred. See Appendix A.

3. See note in filmography on *The Philadelphia Story* for further details.

4. Mankiewicz's first marriage to Elizabeth Young in 1934 ended in divorce in 1937. In 1939, he wed Viennese-born actress, Rosa Stradner. She died in 1958. Mankiewicz married Rosemary Matthews in December, 1962.

5. Mankiewicz details these times in *428*, 219–224.

6. *Dragonwyck* (sc) (1945), *Somewhere in the Night* (sc) (1946), *The Late George Apley* (1947), *The Ghost and Mrs. Muir* (1947), *Escape* (1948), *A Letter to Three Wives* (sc) (1949), *House of Strangers* (sc) (1949), *No Way Out* (sc) (1950), *All About Eve* (sc) (1950), *People Will Talk* (sc) (1951), *Five Fingers* (uncredited sc) (1951).

7. *Letter to Three Wives* (1949), *All About Eve* (1950)

8. Eric, born in 1936, was from the marriage to Elizabeth Young. Christopher (born 1940), and Tom (born 1942), were from the marriage to Rosa Stradner. Alexandra, the only daughter, born in 1966, was from the marriage to Rosemary Matthews.

9. Bernard Dick (*404*) and Kenneth Geist (*380*).

10. See *414*, *419*, and *514*.

Film Chronology

a–actor; d–director; dia–dialogue; o–original story; p–producer;
s–screenwriter; t–titles; *–uncredited

The Dummy (1929) Famous Players-Lasky-Paramount (t)
Close Harmony (1929) Famous Players-Lasky-Paramount (t)
The Man I Love (1929) Famous Players-Lasky-Paramount (t)
The Studio Murder Mystery (1929) Famous Players-Lasky-Paramount (t)
Thunderbolt (1929) Famous Players-Lasky-Paramount (t)
River of Romance (1929) Famous Players-Lasky-Paramount (t)
Dangerous Curves (1929) Famous Players-Lasky-Paramount (t)
The Mysterious Dr. Fu Manchu (1929) Famous Players-Lasky-
    Paramount (t)
The Saturday Night Kid (1929) Famous Players-Lasky-Paramount (t)
The Virginian (1929) Famous Players-Lasky-Paramount (t)
Fast Company (1929) Famous Players-Lasky-Paramount (dia)
Woman Trap (1929) Paramount (a)
Slightly Scarlet (1930) Famous Players-Lasky-Paramount (s, dia)
The Social Lion (1930) Paramount-Publix Corp. (s, dia)
Only Saps Work (1930) Paramount-Publix Corp. (dia)
Paramount on Parade (1930) Paramount (s*)
Sap from Syracuse (1930) Paramount (s*)
The Gang Buster (1931) Paramount-Publix Corp. (dia)
Finn and Hattie (1931) Lasky-Paramount-Famous Players (s, dia)
June Moon (1931) Paramount-Publix Corp. (s, dia)
Skippy (1931) Paramount-Publix Corp. (s, dia)
Forbidden Adventure / Newly Rich (1931) Paramount-Publix Corp. (s, dia)
Sooky (1931) Paramount-Publix Corp. (s, dia)

Dude Ranch (1931) Paramount (s*)
Touchdown (1931) Paramount (s*)
This Reckless Age (1932) Paramount-Publix Corp. (s, dia)
Sky Bride (1932) Paramount-Publix Corp. (s, dia)
Million Dollar Legs (1932) Paramount-Publix Corp. (o, s, dia)
If I Had a Million (1932) Paramount-Publix Corp. (s)
Diplomaniacs (1933) RKO (o, s)
Emergency Call (1933) RKO (s)
Too Much Harmony (1933) Paramount (s)
Alice in Wonderland (1933) Paramount (s)
College Humor (1933) Paramount (s*)
Manhattan Melodrama (1934) Metro-Goldwyn-Mayer (s)
Our Daily Bread (1934) A Viking Production/United Artists (dia)
Forsaking All Others (1934) Metro-Goldwyn-Mayer (s)
I Live My Life (1935) Metro-Goldwyn-Mayer (s)
After Office Hours (1935) Metro-Goldwyn-Mayer (s*)
Three Godfathers (1936) Metro-Goldwyn-Mayer (p)
Fury (1936) Metro-Goldwyn-Mayer (p, s*)
The Gorgeous Hussy (1936) Metro-Goldwyn-Mayer (p)
Love on the Run (1936) Metro-Goldwyn-Mayer (p)
The Bride Wore Red (1937) Metro-Goldwyn-Mayer (p)
Double Wedding (1937) Metro-Goldwyn-Mayer (p)
Mannequin (1938) Metro-Goldwyn-Mayer (p)
Three Comrades (1938) Metro-Goldwyn-Mayer (p)
The Shopworn Angel (1938) Metro-Goldwyn-Mayer (p)
The Shining Hour (1938) Metro-Goldwyn-Mayer (p)
A Christmas Carol (1938) Metro-Goldwyn-Mayer (p)
The Adventures of Huckleberry Finn / Huckleberry Finn (1939) Metro-
    Goldwyn-Mayer (p)
Strange Cargo (1940) Metro-Goldwyn-Mayer (p)
The Philadelphia Story (1940) Metro-Goldwyn-Mayer (p)
The Wild Man of Borneo (1941) Metro-Goldwyn-Mayer (p)
The Feminine Touch (1941) Metro-Goldwyn-Mayer (p)
Woman of the Year (1942) Metro-Goldwyn-Mayer (p)
Cairo (1942) Metro-Goldwyn-Mayer (p*)
Reunion in France (1942) Metro-Goldwyn-Mayer (p)
The Keys of the Kingdom (1944) 20th Century–Fox (p, s)
Dragonwyck (1946) 20th Century–Fox (d, s)
Somewhere in the Night (1946) 20th Century–Fox (d, s)
The Late George Apley (1947) 20th Century–Fox (d)
The Ghost and Mrs. Muir (1947) 20th Century–Fox (d)

Escape (1948) 20th Century–Fox (d)

A Letter to Three Wives (1949) 20th Century–Fox (d, s)

House of Strangers (1949) 20th Century–Fox (d, s*)

No Way Out (1950) 20th Century–Fox (d, s)

All About Eve (1950) 20th Century–Fox (d, s)

People Will Talk (1951) 20th Century–Fox (d, s)

Five Fingers (1952) 20th Century–Fox (d, dia*)

Julius Caesar (1953) Metro-Goldwyn-Mayer (d)

The Barefoot Contessa (1954) Figaro Inc./United Artists (p, d, s)

Guys and Dolls (1955) Samuel Goldwyn/Metro-Goldwyn-Mayer (d, s)

The Quiet American (1958) Figaro Inc./United Artists (p, d, s)

Suddenly, Last Summer (1959) Horizon Pictures/Columbia Pictures (d)

Cleopatra (1963) 20th Century–Fox (d, s)

Carol for Another Christmas (1964) ABC-TV/Telsun Foundation Inc. (p, d)

The Honey Pot (1967) Feldman/Famous Artists Productions/United
    Artists (p, d, s)

King: A Filmed Record ... Montgomery to Memphis (1970) MLK Film
    Project, Inc. (d)

There Was a Crooked Man (1970) Warner Brothers–Seven Arts, Inc. (p, d)

Sleuth (1972) Palomar Pictures International/20th Century–Fox (d)

PART II

Essays

Mankiewicz's Dark Cinema

by R. Barton Palmer

In the late thirties and early forties, Joseph L. Mankiewicz was climbing with deliberate speed the ladder of Hollywood success, moving from screenwriting and producing to directing. At the time, such an apprenticeship was hardly unusual, though there were other routes to the coveted director's chair, as the careers of Orson Welles and Elia Kazan, to take two obvious examples, remind us. Work as a screenwriter, so the studio wisdom went, was useful preparation for assuming control over the actual mounting of a script. Someone who could write good movies and had demonstrated the requisite organizational skills (as Mankiewicz certainly had as a producer) should be able to oversee their creation on the set.

Ironically, however, changes within the industry made irrelevant in part the specific skills Mankiewicz had honed in writing social realist films like *Our Daily Bread*, wacky comedies such as *Million Dollar Legs*, and dramas such as *Manhattan Melodrama*. In the immediate postwar era, a new kind of movie, quickly dubbed film noir or "dark film" by French journalists who were eager observers of the Hollywood scene, rose to prominence. American producers and consumers were disinclined to recognize film noir as a separate type, though some used the term crime melodrama to describe these films. This emerging series was a complex amalgam of already existing genres (most particularly, the detective story, the thriller, the woman's picture, and even the gothic romance) and was now given a darker, more pessimistic, often socially radical or critical dimension.

At first, many of these noir films were rather faithful adaptations of bestsellers from the so-called "hard-boiled" school of American crime fiction writers: notably James M. Cain, Raymond Chandler, Dashiell Hammett, and Cornell Woolrich. Though this kind of fiction had achieved a limited popularity in the twenties and thirties, it enjoyed much wider and more enthusiastic acceptance in the forties. Chandler, Hammett, and Cain profited from more celebrity than they had found earlier in their novel-writing careers. Woolrich switched from churning out short stories for pulp magazines to producing hardcover bestsellers for reputable publishers.

This new fashion in the commercial fiction market showed that a radical shift in popular taste had occurred. In accordance with industry practice, Hollywood did its best to capitalize on the trend by transferring it to the screen. For a variety of reasons, the adaptation process proved complicated, producing a very rich and multilayered result. In its visual form, for example, film noir was heavily influenced by German Expressionism, brought to Hollywood by a number of émigré directors. Fritz Lang, Robert Siodmak, Billy Wilder, Otto Preminger, Rudolph Maté, and Anatole Litvak, the most notable of these, came to specialize more or less in film noir.

The same directors brought an interest in the more pessimistic and world-weary varieties of European naturalism to their work in this new series. Lang's *Human Desire*, for example, is an adaptation of the same Zola novel brought to the French screen by Jean Renoir as *La Bête Humaine*, but the American version shares much in common with a number of Cain novels and films, particularly *The Postman Always Rings Twice* and *Double Indemnity*. Likewise, Lang's version of Graham Greene's *The Ministry of Fear* showed the compatibility of a staple Expressionist theme—the paranoid nightmare of subjective experience—with the destinal twists and turns of the Christian thriller. The result is a noir vision of how irresistible grace transforms characters inhabiting a Manichaean world dominated by evil materiality. In that film, moreover, Lang's protagonist moves through a bizarre and threatening urban landscape—London during the blitz—quite reminiscent of Raymond Chandler's viperish Los Angeles.

Films noirs, in short, offered a potent mixture of American crime story and European artiness. They limned a despairing portrait of a seedy and treacherous urban America dominated by chiaroscuro images of cheap diners, transient hotels, and low-class bars. These were the appropriate settings for violent encounters and illicit romance, for lives doomed to failure by the irrepressible flaws of human nature. This collective vision of a culture in crisis contested the pattern for successful storytelling adopted officially by the studios in the early thirties. The Production Code emphasized poetic justice and the triumph of goodness or innocence over evil, while the film noir provided few if any "happy endings," preferring instead the often fatal attractions of unrepentant venality, adulterous couplings, and unrelieved paranoia. The traditional Hollywood genres were dominated at the time by a Victorian aesthetic based on the rhetorical principle of moral uplift. The film noir offered an alternative regime of representation, one more in line with the grim commitment to truth telling of latter day naturalism. It is easy to see why many of the sophisticated and worldly Europeans among Hollywood's directorial cadre found it a congenial form to work in. Given Mankiewicz's intellectual and literary interests, his attraction to this series hardly requires a special explanation either.

As he moved into directing, moreover, the film noir provided an ideal vehicle for one of Mankiewicz's most dominant and obvious artistic intentions. His films show that as an artist he was obsessed with exposing, through a detached yet trenchant irony, the false pieties and dubious values of respectable society (an aim achieved with different tactics in his comedies). In fact, of his first eight films, five are films noirs of different subtypes, each of which is socially critical to some degree. *A Letter to Three Wives* and *All About Eve*, prestige productions, are perhaps better described as melodramas. (They will be discussed elsewhere in this volume.) But even these films contain important noir elements, especially the director's refusal in each case to offer a reassuring happy ending to ameliorate his penetrating critiques of middle-class life, especially the sanctity of marriage and the drive for economic success and upward mobility.

To some small degree, Mankiewicz's work for Fritz Lang on *Fury*— often considered a film noir before that phrase was coined—prepared him for the new fashion in filmmaking he found so congenial. *Fury* shares much with Lang's more noirish, later Hollywood productions. (*The Big Heat* is a particularly good example, with its central confrontation between an isolated, virtuous man and a corrupt establishment.) But with its pointed criticism of social ills, especially mob violence, *Fury* finally resembles more closely the social realist problem film so popular in the period. Dominated by a tendentious representation of social injustice and strident call for reform, the film is much like the more famous *I Am a Fugitive from a Chain Gang*. In any event, Mankiewicz's work on the screenplay (he also served as producer) was subordinate to the more central contributions of Bartlett Cormack and Lang himself. Perhaps more significant, Mankiewicz gained valuable experience in writing what was to become a sine qua non of most noir productions: sharp, wisecracking dialogue spiced with sophisticated double entendre. The screenplay he had previously written with Oliver H. P. Garrett for the racy *Manhattan Melodrama* provides ample evidence of the expertise Mankiewicz was quickly developing in this area.

Dragonwyck

Mankiewicz's first directorial assignment, however, was not to afford him the opportunity to try his hand at a contemporary crime melodrama with a witty and rapid-fire urban argot. Instead, the management at Fox offered him a gothic romance set in early nineteenth century America, Anya Seton's *Dragonwyck*, the screen possibilities of which he had previously minimized when asked for his opinion by studio executives. Even though the property, as Mankiewicz correctly argued, suffered from an unsophisticated handling of historical elements, particularly politics, the studio had every reason to expect that a successful film could be made from it. The modern gothic, a time-honored form reinvented by Daphne Du Maurier, was enjoying much popularity with the public at the time. The film version of Du Maurier's most famous work, *Rebecca*, became outstandingly successful at the box office after being brought skillfully to the screen by Alfred Hitchcock. The American version of a similar British screen hit, retitled *Gaslight* and directed superbly by George Cukor, also proved extremely popular. *Dragonwyck* had received substantial acclaim from middlebrow readers when serialized in *Ladies' Home Journal* and when later published in book form. Seton's novel, lacking Du Maurier's flair for compelling mystery, was obviously no *Rebecca* (though it appealed to the same readership). Still, it was undeniably a "presold" property whose appeal ought to transfer readily enough to the screen. Furthermore, the modern gothic shared much in common with the hard-boiled fiction whose screen versions had proved so successful at the box office during the early 1940s. In fact, the two narrative types were similar enough to be combined, as a number of interesting hybrids produced at the time attest (most notably, *Sorry, Wrong Number*, *The Spiral Staircase*, *Suspicion*, and *The Two Mrs. Carrolls*).

Like hard-boiled fiction, the modern gothic features a negative view

of romance, at the very least a partial rejection of conventional Hollywood happy heterosexual coupling. The plot emphasizes the husband's
possibly murderous intentions toward the woman whom he had once so
ardently wooed. His scheme to kill her, if such it is, generally unfolds in
an opulent mansion, which is initially the most striking image of his
attractiveness and power but becomes her prison as it is shown to conceal
his dangerous obsessions or past transgressions. Two kinds of endings pre-
dominate in the genre, neither of which recuperates entirely the fearful
threat around which the story is structured. The husband may be proved
innocent, as in *Rebecca*, and a new life for the reunited couple may be
predicated upon the destruction of his ambiguous past (i.e., the burning
of the mansion in that film and the death of the housekeeper so loyal to
the husband's faithless first wife). Or the husband acts out the desire to
murder his wife, the direction the plot takes in *Gaslight*. In the noir
inflections of this narrative, most notably *Sorry, Wrong Number*, the wife,
failing to find anyone to save her, falls victim to the husband's plotting,
despite her frantic attempts to defeat it. This variety of the formula, however, normally features a former male admirer or friend who rescues the
woman at the last possible moment. The implication is that the friend
will resume his romantic relationship with her once the husband is properly disposed of (he often self-destructs in some spectacular fashion).

In terms of how they represent sexual politics, the modern gothic
and the hard-boiled thriller are more similar than different. The noir films
made from hard-boiled novels and stories usually feature femme fatales
whose evil machinations justify a fearful vengeance exacted by betrayed
protagonists, the men who are attracted to these alluring sirens, whom
they must destroy in order to save themselves. The modern gothic offers
a different twist on this misogynistic theme: the spectacle of a woman
schemed against, oppressed, even tortured by the man who has promised
to love and protect her. This "homme fatal" may be the villain, but the
genre derives its emotional power from detailing the dangerous and hurt-
ful predicament in which the helpless heroine finds herself, thus turning
into compelling spectacle a sinister violence against women.

Dragonwyck presents a husband who murders one wife when he tires
of her and is frustrated by her inability to provide him an heir. Marrying
a younger and quite naïve woman, his behavior toward her becomes threatening when she proves too independent and willful after the son she bears
him dies prematurely. Seton's novel thus belongs to the more common type
of gothic in which the husband is proven guilty. However, Seton has obviously borrowed much from the most famous example of the other sub-
type of the genre, *Rebecca* (particularly the central motif of the lower class

woman suddenly elevated in society by the surprising attentions of a fabulously rich man).

In the typical fashion of the genre, Seton's *Dragonwyck* develops its plot in a somewhat leisurely fashion, embellishing the story of domestic terror with lengthy evocations of the customs, mores, and political issues of the period (1840s New York and Connecticut). In their film adaptations of *Rebecca* and *Gaslight*, Alfred Hitchcock and George Cukor each realized that these elements of the gothic would not translate well to the screen because film art offers no useful analogue for extended verbal description. Any overlong dramatic portrayal of the social milieu, moreover, would simply distract attention from the fascinating enigma posed by the husband's ambiguous behavior. The gothic's psychological effect, dependent upon a gradually unfolding threat of violence, would then be diluted. The screen versions of both *Rebecca* and *Gaslight* thus wisely reduce "atmosphere" to a bare minimum. Developing interest in and sympathy for the woman's terrifying situation, Hitchcock and Cukor fashion riveting narratives of entrapment and narrow, improbable escape.

Unfortunately, Mankiewicz was not so wise in his approach to Seton's novel. The film loses focus and energy because the director attempts to present a too detailed social background. The novel's political theme, its opposition of a fundamentalist and democratic Yankee ethic to an aristocratic Dutch life of self-indulgence, does of course connect closely to the main gothic plot in an important way. The aggrieved heroine, having found boring her stern father's devotion to hard work and the good book, is charmed into marrying a distant, immensely rich relative who can offer her comfort and ease. The problem with Seton's conception, however, is that the political opposition the aristocratic husband faces and is ultimately destroyed by does not involve the heroine directly, even though she displays a natural sympathy for the oppressed farmers, who remind her of her own family. The more expansive form of the novel permits an effective counterpointing of the separate predicaments the farmers and the wife find themselves in because the "poltroon" will brook no opposition to his desire and no threat to his hereditary rights. But this simply could not work for any film version of conventional length.

An adapter of this property is thus forced to make a hard choice. He could opt for a historical film in which the personal life of the main character (who would have to be the poltroon) parallels his public one. Or he could construct a gothic (with the woman as main character) in which the husband's murderous plotting is explained by the social circumstances that have made him inflexible and maniacally obsessed with siring an heir to his estates. Mankiewicz managed to do neither. His *Dragonwyck* fails at being either a period piece (the suspense plot distracts attention from the political themes) or a truly terrifying gothic (subplots and exposition dilute the building of suspense).

It is easy to imagine why he approached the novel in this way. Mankiewicz's later films reveal an abiding interest in representing complex social relations (this is indulged to good effect in *All About Eve* and *A Letter to Three Wives*). Such portrayal is inappropriate in the case of *Dragonwyck* and would also prove so in *Cleopatra*, whose source materials posed similar problems. Condensing the expansiveness of its fictional source, the successful screen gothic deals in flat characters and exaggerates psychological effects (suspense and identification) in order to cover the superficiality, abruptness, or inconsequence of its flimsily developed narrative. For some directors, this approach to adaptation was congenial. Most notably, Alfred Hitchcock found subliterary sources like *Rebecca* much easier to work with than honored and valued texts because the implausibilities and infelicities of the former could easily be masked by a treatment that concentrated on involving the spectator.

Faced with adapting a mediocre novel, Mankiewicz mistakenly attempted to heighten its value with spectacle and detail in the Ernst Lubitsch manner. This was not entirely a bad idea and was perhaps an inescapable consequence of the film's production circumstances. Fox initially designated Lubitsch, then working for the studio, as producer, and he picked Mankiewicz for the project, undoubtedly recognizing the young man's wit and sophistication. The inexperienced former screenwriter may have thought that together they could produce something like *The Merry Widow* or *Design for Living*, films that with the famed Lubitsch touch actually improved upon the limited artistic value of their mediocre sources. But Lubitsch and the surprisingly feisty Mankiewicz often disagreed during the initial phases of shooting. The director found the famed producer, then quite ill with the heart condition soon to kill him, difficult to work with. Lubitsch eventually withdrew from the project and refused to have his name associated further with the film. The release print of *Dragonwyck* credits no producer, only Mankiewicz as writer and director. But Mankiewicz could not make a Lubitsch film without Lubitsch's help.

Closely resembling *Rebecca*, the film begins with a promising situation. Miranda Wells (Gene Tierney) is the beautiful daughter of a fundamentalist Yankee farmer with more morals than money who works hard to keep his Connecticut farm going. Out of the blue, she is invited to become part of the household of her mother's rich cousin, Nicholas Van Ryn (Vincent Price). Impressed by Nicholas's sophistication and wealth when they meet at the Astor Hotel in New York City, she then journeys up the Hudson with him. From the deck of the steamer, she catches sight of a glamorous life that has thus far eluded her: the manor house of Dragonwyck set majestically on cliffs overlooking the river. Like the unnamed heroine of Du Maurier's novel and Hitchcock's film, Miranda (obviously named for the wide-eyed innocent in Shakespeare's *The Tempest*) is over-awed by her initial experience of this new world. Her misplaced wonder motivates the narrative of marriage, disillusionment, and betrayal to follow.

Mankiewicz errs in presenting these initial sequences in too objective a fashion, mostly offering the characters as groups or twosomes often posed in tableaux compositions. It would have been more effective to develop Miranda as a main character by emphasizing single compositions and subjective forms of characterization, especially point of view editing. Thus the director wastes the opportunity to emphasize Gene Tierney's not inconsiderable attractiveness, a contradictory mix of innocence and womanliness that had been exploited more effectively—and recently—by other directors (notably Otto Preminger in *Laura* and John Stahl in *Leave Her to Heaven*).

In contrast, the political context of her cousin's offer is well established by a family dinner scene in which her father's puritanical scorn for the gentry and their high life is given considerable and effective emphasis (aided by Walter Huston's fine performance in the role). As Mankiewicz evidently understood, this scene develops a social contrast that is important for understanding the anachronistic position of Van Ryn as a hereditary landlord with little respect for individual rights. By showing the father's inability to redirect the social aspirations of his daughter, Mankiewicz here also anticipates the too easy surrender Miranda makes to what proves to be the merely superficial gentility of her cousin.

Van Ryn's character and social position are symbolized by the huge manor house on the cliffs. This opulent mansion indexes the husband's hereditary wealth but later becomes the oppressive, threatening setting for his murderous plottings and reckless self-indulgence. Mankiewicz's use of fluid camera movements as the pair enter the house emphasizes its grandeur and size. The portrait of a long-dead female ancestor over the mantel piece as well as the narration of her sad history by the housekeeper makes clear at once that all is not right and happy in *Dragonwyck*. Not only is the house thought to be haunted, the dead woman's ghost has also, it is believed, vowed to exact a terrible vengeance on her descendants.

Initially, Van Ryn is solicitous about Miranda, to whom he is obviously attracted. Soon, however, he reveals himself as inflexible and even cruel toward his wife and the tenant farmers dependent upon him, who are eager to shed his now outlawed control over their lives. The handsome and young Dr. Jeff Turner (Glenn Langan) supports the farmers in their resistance to the haughty overlord and is quickly smitten with Miranda. The director handles these details of exposition economically but with proper dramatic emphasis. Yet he was unable to extract much of a performance from the lackluster Langan and hammy Price.

Van Ryn easily outclasses the young doctor in the pursuit of the beautiful woman's hand, flaunting his affection for her in full view of his family and the assembled gentry by waltzing with her at an evening celebration. This is yet another sequence handled effectively by Mankiewicz with fluid camera movement in the style pioneered by Jean Renoir and William Wyler. Attracted to Miranda, and desiring an heir his now barren wife cannot provide, Van Ryn poisons his unfortunate spouse so that he may be free to possess the young woman legally.

It is at this point that the film begins to lose energy and focus. The murder scene is handled in an indirect, distanced, and somewhat unclear fashion; an excellent opportunity for developing Van Ryn's psychopathology as well as an atmosphere of threat and terror is wasted. Initially, the viewer is left in the dark about the way Van Ryn kills his wife. It later becomes clear that he somehow uses the leaves of a plant growing in her room, but this important exposition is bungled. Similarly, the growing bitterness between the poltroon and his new wife, who rejects his godlessness and lack of values, is not given an effective emotional heightening with subjective techniques. Even the stock sequence where Miranda discovers his secret room and other life (he is an opium addict) is developed with scant attention to suspense. (Compare the similar sequences, handled expertly, in Hitchcock's *Rebecca*.) Dr. Turner's arrival on the scene when Van Ryn turns violent is neither anticipated nor particularly timely. That Miranda is actually threatened is not clear; nor does Mankiewicz use parallel editing to show Turner's realization that all is not right at Dragonwyck. This is exposition necessary to set up his discovery of the husband and wife in the secret room. The subsequent pursuit and killing of Van Ryn is hastily presented and not well dramatized. Once again Mankiewicz declines to use parallel editing; the result is that the embittered farmers who play an important role in the poltroon's demise are not pictured until late in the sequence. Even the ending is flawed. The implied union between Miranda and the now heroic Turner satisfactorily concludes the young woman's personal troubles, but the political plot is more or less jettisoned with no dramatization of the effect the poltroon's death has on his former tenants.

In sum, *Dragonwyck* shows that Mankiewicz at the beginning of his career was unable to exploit the kind of material that a Hitchcock or Lubitsch might have made sparkle. Even so, the film offers substantial evidence of his knack for the effective dramatization of character, his flair for identifying the right social nuance despite having to work with a cast that was far from ideal. And he was soon to learn how to create a mysterious and threatening atmosphere and sustain a suspenseful narrative. The inadequacies of *Dragonwyck* furnish useful benchmarks for judging the substantial success of his later dark films.

Somewhere in the Night

After a contentious and unprofitable collaboration with Ernst Lubitsch on *Dragonwyck*, Mankiewicz was understandably eager for more control on his next project. Thus he was rather easily persuaded to do a contemporary thriller with producer Anderson Lawler, a minor Hollywood player and friend of notables such as Tallulah Bankhead. Mankiewicz had met Lawler, then an actor, while he was doing the screenplay fifteen years earlier for *Only Saps Work*. Lawler was now eager to make a screen version of "The Lonely Journey," a pulp magazine story by unknown writer Marvin Borowsky, a not too skillful imitator of Raymond Chandler and Cornell Woolrich.

After perusing the property, Mankiewicz agreed with the informal assessment of Somerset Maugham, then resident in Hollywood, that the story could make a successful film. At the time, he was not much interested in doing thrillers (subsequent projects show Mankiewicz later had a change of heart about the genre). But the producer and this script offered him another chance to write and direct. Besides, the project promised every chance of success. Undoubtedly, Mankiewicz and Lawler hoped to capitalize on the developing popularity of hard-boiled detective films, one of the emerging noir genres. The trend had begun with John Huston's startling and hugely successful adaptation of Dashiell Hammett's *The Maltese Falcon* (1941). It was firmly established by Edward Dmytryk's version of Chandler's *Farewell, My Lovely* which, when released as *Murder, My Sweet* by Paramount some two years earlier, in 1944, had proven box office magic.

The new project also fit nicely into studio plans. The executives at Fox were by this time committed to a steady production of dark thrillers, a series they would continue to exploit into the early fifties. The most obvious prototype for what would become *Somewhere in the Night* was Henry Hathaway's *The Dark Corner*, already in production at Fox when

Lawler and Mankiewicz were in the final stages of planning. Mankiewicz's film is less well known than Hathaway's and has never enjoyed the same critical acclaim. Yet in a number of interesting ways *Somewhere in the Night* substantially improves on what was no doubt its model.

The Dark Corner more closely follows the profitable path marked out by *Murder, My Sweet*, with its returning veteran private eye skillfully ensnared as the fall guy in a murder scheme that is masterminded by an effete and conscienceless art gallery owner. Against great odds, the detective, Brad Galt, much like Chandler's Marlowe, succeeds in extricating himself from the trap laid for him and delivers his tormentor to justice. In *Murder, My Sweet*, Marlowe is hired to solve a case that soon threatens to destroy him. In *The Dark Corner*, by way of contrast, Brad Galt is not investigating a case but becomes, through no fault of his own, a random victim and has no choice but to save himself. The overwhelming sense of fatality and, for a time, helplessness, is not really a Chandler theme, but recalls instead the darker fiction of Cornell Woolrich (author of a then popular "black series" featuring innocently doomed protagonists). More than Dmytryk's, Hathaway's film limns a despairing and paranoid portrait of modern urban life, where forbidding cityscapes and strangers met on the street threaten sudden destruction to the innocent. Galt's unenviable task becomes to understand himself (that is, the part he has been forced to play) and figure out why he has been chosen as a victim.

Somewhere in the Night develops the conventions of the hard-boiled detective story further along the path marked out by Woolrich, even employing one of that author's signature themes: amnesia, the sudden lack of self-knowledge that makes everyone a potential enemy of the sufferer, every experience threateningly unfamiliar. Though persecuted and betrayed, Brad Galt and Philip Marlowe are otherwise traditional protagonists who struggle to preserve themselves and solve a mystery. Skillfully reshaped by Mankiewicz, Borowsky's story offers instead a main character who knows who he is but, having lost all memory, does not know what that means. He has no choice but to embark on what becomes a perilous quest to discover his past. That quest is ironically successful, for he learns that the name he now bears is a pseudonym. Borowsky's hero, it turns out, is a dishonest and heartless detective who gave up his identity to escape the consequences of a serious crime.

Somewhere in the Night, we might say, is more thoroughly and interestingly noir than its predecessors. Both *Murder, My Sweet* and *The Dark Corner* offer traditional Hollywood narratives whose protagonists struggle successfully against great odds to solve a mystery and establish their own innocence. Both films are noir to the extent that they are set in dark cities whose deceptively venal and deadly inhabitants threaten the detectives with disgrace and death. Yet the narrative in each case works to vindicate the hero, who emerges, if not unscathed, at least intact and uncorrupted by his experience. In other words, these two films ultimately conform to the protocol of moral uplift enshrined in the Production Code; virtue is rewarded, while evil is punished through the imposition of an unquestioned justice that vindicates traditional morality.

In contrast, Mankiewicz's hero solves the case to discover that he is in some sense the criminal. His successful feat of intellectual and physical courage becomes an act of ironic, Oedipal reversal. Even at film's end, when a more villainous villain has been punished for the crime, the hero has still endorsed his worst fears, uncovering the evil behind his only apparent goodness, an identity that is itself part of a plot to escape justice.

To some degree, the film's success must be attributed to Mankiewicz's fruitful partnership with producer Darryl Zanuck. It was Zanuck who suggested the outlines for the film's opening sequence, one of its most impressive. Without any establishing shots of either the setting or main character, the camera pans across a military hospital operating room that is revealed to be close to the battlefield by the sound of distant cannonfire. The images of the hospital then become subjective as a voice-over reveals the main character to be one of the patients, a soldier (John Hodiak) so badly wounded in the face he can talk only to himself. Thus the voice-over is not narration, but the spoken realization of silent speech, yet a further mark of the film's investment in the main character's subjectivity. Waking from what has evidently been extensive plastic surgery, his face swathed in bandages, the man has not merely forgotten his name: apparently the victim of a trauma-induced paranoia, he actually resolves not to reveal his condition to the doctor.

Somewhat recovered, the wounded man discovers that his name is George Taylor, an identity he cannot remember but pretends for the moment to "inhabit," fearing the discovery of the truth, which of course he does not himself know. By film's end, this fear is effectively explained by the revelation that Taylor is on the run from the law and would thus have every reason to avoid any investigation of his past. At this point in the story, his concerns seem unreasonable and unreasoning, a disproportionate reaction to the experience of pain and suffering on the battlefield.

After being invalided out of the service, Taylor follows the clues that chance provides. Checking into a Los Angeles hotel that was his last known address, he cannot find his name on the register. A trip to the railroad station to claim a footlocker soon follows, and he finds there a gun and a note from someone named Larry Cravat, presumably a friend, to the effect that $5000 has been deposited for him at a local bank. Attempting to claim the money, however, Taylor is thwarted by a nervous and overly inquisitive teller. Cravat's stationery leads him then to a local bathhouse where he is also met with a rebuff when mentioning his erstwhile friend's name. Told by the unfriendly attendant to check at a neighboring bar, Taylor quickly finds himself in real danger. Two toughs make their way toward him after he asks the bartender about Cravat, and he escapes by going into a dressing room where he meets Christy (Nancy Guild), the club singer. The sense in which the narrative follows a dreamlike illogic is here further strengthened as Taylor discovers in Christy's possession a postcard from a girlfriend that reads, "By the time you get this I'll be Mrs. Larry Cravat." Wary of his questions, Christy summons the two toughs, and Taylor barely makes his escape unharmed. Back at his hotel, he meets a seductively dressed woman who talks her way into his room and attempts to make love to him after admitting that she was waiting for Larry.

Now convinced that Larry Cravat holds the key to his identity, Taylor embarks in earnest upon a search to find him. But he soon becomes more the prey than the hunter as a local gangster named Anzelmo (Fritz Kortner) abducts him and tries to beat out the very information (Cravat's whereabouts) that Taylor himself is seeking. Near collapse, Taylor makes his way to Christy's apartment, and, taking pity on him, she agrees to help him locate Cravat.

In the Chandler style, the remainder of the narrative presents Taylor with a series of bizarre and dangerous encounters. He meets up with a lonely spinster who claims to have loved him but is obviously self-deceived; soon afterward a speeding truck just misses running him down in the street. He then pays a visit to the local mental hospital where one of the inmates provides a vital clue; afterward, he journeys at midnight to examine an abandoned dock, where the huge cache of money that Anzelmo and his compatriots think is in Cravat's possession is found. It is there too that Taylor discovers that he is in fact Cravat, a private investigator who got mixed up in a scheme to hijack some stolen Nazi money. Through a plot twist too complex to unravel here (and one a bit hard for a first-time viewer of the film to follow either), it turns out that Cravat, though implicated in the robbery, couldn't have been responsible for the murder that followed. But the threat of punishment did prompt his change of names and enlistment in the Marine Corps. Through a complex movement of affirmation and denial, Taylor/Cravat is both vindicated and convicted of serious crime.

The murderer, and last member of the gang, turns out to be the night club owner, Phillips (Richard Conte), the friend of Christy who was helping her and Taylor locate Cravat. In a final showdown, Cravat and Christy avoid death when the detective, Kendall (Lloyd Nolan), yet another friend of Christy's eager to help Taylor, arrives in time to thwart Phillips' plans to get rid of the pair.

Through an exchange-of-guilt plot twist as complex as any in a Hitchcock film, the narrative thus locates a villain who can be punished in Cravat's stead. And yet the former amnesiac in effect realizes the truth of his own worst and truly Oedipal fears, discovering that he is indeed the criminal he suspected he might be. Taylor/Cravat is not just a decorated veteran eager to solve a crime, but also the cheap crook who got involved in a robbery that cost several lives. He is the man who made Christy love him, but also the one who jilted Christy's friend Mary and is partially responsible for her subsequent accidental death. The narrative proves Taylor/Cravat to be a person of virtue and integrity; for even his initial guiltiness points to inner goodness since he rejects in effect what he used to be, but feels compelled to unmask the disguise he has adopted to conceal his identity. At the same time, his secretiveness and distrust of authority reveal a darker side that the ending, which punishes him by proxy, does nothing to alleviate, except to show that he is not as guilty as he might be. More than either *Murder, My Sweet* or *The Dark Corner*, Mankiewicz's initial foray into film noir connects more centrally to the moral ambiguity and the rejection of simple happy endings that later became such a central feature of Hollywood's dark cinema.

Escape

After *Somewhere in the Night*, Mankiewicz for a time avoided projects based on pulp magazine sources. Ironically, of course, two of his most praised films took shape from his skillful rewriting of stories originally printed in *Cosmopolitan*: not only *A Letter to Three Wives*, but also *All About Eve*. Unlike Alfred Hitchcock, however, Mankiewicz was always more comfortable with material of greater literary value. And this suited Darryl Zanuck's plans for him at Fox. His next three projects for the studio were all adaptations of works that had achieved some reputation with the educated reading public: *The Late George Apley* (from the Broadway play written by John P. Marquand and George S. Kaufman); *The Ghost and Mrs. Muir* (from the popular novel by R. A. Dick); and *Escape* (from the John Galsworthy play). This last allowed Mankiewicz the opportunity to revisit the thriller genre, but this time utilizing source material with more thematic richness.

However much he may have admired Mankiewicz's literary abilities, Zanuck did not afford the apprentice writer-director the chance to craft his own scripts or, indeed, exercise much control over the material at all beyond its effective realization for the screen. Instead, he was teamed on all three projects with veteran screenwriter Philip Dunne, a fellow Ivy Leaguer with whom he had much in common. Mankiewicz approached these three assignments (the first two urbane dramas and the third an intellectual thriller) as a more traditional *metteur en scène*. Freed from the demands of scriptwriting, he made the most of this opportunity to learn more about the intricacies of visual language. By the time the filming of *Escape* began, he had learned enough to make this project an interesting artistic, if not popular success.

Like *Somewhere in the Night*, *Escape* offers the episodic story of a man, guilty yet innocent, who desperately struggles to escape from oppressive circumstances in order to reestablish his own identity. In other words, both stories conform to the double pursuit plot initially made popular by John Buchan's novel *The Thirty-Nine Steps* (1914) and its subsequent transfer to the screen by Alfred Hitchcock (1935). Despite the superficial generic resemblance, however, the two Mankiewicz films could hardly be more different.

Galsworthy's play is more an allegorical Christian think piece than a thriller. Unlike Buchan or Hitchcock, Galsworthy was not interested in the opportunities to build excitement and suspense afforded by the double pursuit element of the thriller plot. Instead, for Galsworthy the hero's random but significant encounters with strangers become a metaphor for the Christian life, where the oppressive burden of individual guilt can be alleviated by the selfless kindness of others; the hero passes through experiences that only seem directionless, but in fact are structured by the workings of divine grace.

Heavy with obvious symbolism and often invoking the inevitability of original sin, *Escape* is not a property Mankiewicz would likely have himself chosen to direct. However he was able to make it his own. The film, though inevitably betraying its theatrical origins, depends more on the connection between socially significant dialogue and visuals that explore the depth of or extend the dialogue's emotional and intellectual range. Here is an approach Mankiewicz would again try several years later with *No Way Out*, but in that instance substantially shaping his own screenplay. He shows no little brilliance in making *Escape* an effective film rather than simply a competently screened play. Galsworthy's material, even as astutely transformed by Dunne, could have resulted in a film of tiresome staginess if the spoken word had been overemphasized (compare, among a host of examples, the screen version of *The Petrified Forest* [1936]). Or the director's intentions could have been undone by pretty images that, lacking the balancing influence of well-staged dialogue, could not advance a complex intellectual theme (the classic example here is John Ford's *The Fugitive* [1947], an incoherent version of Graham Greene's Christian thriller *The Power and the Glory*).

Mankiewicz neatly avoided both traps despite his lack of control over key aspects of production. He had to remain fairly faithful to Dunne's version of Galsworthy's play because star Rex Harrison had strongly influenced Zanuck's choice of this source material. Harrison, it seems, had always liked the initial 1930 British film version; the good and bad nature of the main character appealed to him. *Escape*, then, was to be not only an adaptation, but also a star vehicle. Under Mankiewicz's careful direction, Harrison made a compelling hero whose egotism and occasional self-righteousness neatly balance his character's basic sense of decency. *Escape* provided the actor with useful training in this kind of layered role, which he was afterward often called upon to play (probably most effectively as the apparently solicitous but really cold-blooded husband in *Midnight Lace* who accepts with grace and wit his failure to scare his wife to death).

As a project, *Escape* faced an additional challenge in the unusual circumstances of its production. Unlike the first two films with Dunne, *Escape* was to be shot in England where, under a recently signed agreement with the Hollywood studios, frozen assets that could not be transferred out of the country were used for Hollywood productions there. It was the first film of this kind produced in Britain, then suffering through worse deprivation and austerity than the war itself had caused. Food, clothing, and other necessities were all in short supply. An even more difficult problem for Mankiewicz was posed by the British craft unions, whose newly found power (under a Labour government) sometimes wreaked havoc with production schedules and requirements. Location shooting during a rainy fall on the Devonshire moors proved nightmarish at times, especially with an obstreperous crew who had a penchant for going on strike. The documentary look of the exteriors, however much a postwar cliché, neatly serves Mankiewicz's plan to transform Dunne's very literary screenplay into a truly cinematic film, heavily dependent on telling images.

Mankiewicz's contributions to the project are probably most evident in the opening sequence. *Escape* begins with an establishing shot in which no human figures are initially visible: the camera moves across the desolate landscape of the west country moors until it locates a prison. An epigraph (actually a quote from another Galsworthy text) fixes the symbolic meaning of this grim landscape: "There is nothing more tragic in life than the utter impossibility of changing what you have done." Mankiewicz then cuts to a shot of a grim Harrison who, framed by the shadows the bars on the windows throw across his body, stares intently toward the sky. He is looking at birds gliding effortlessly in the air, a shot that cues, through a well handled visual match, his flashback memory. As the present becomes the past, the birds change into an airplane that Harrison pilots and lands with ease. He is revealed to be Matt Denant, an obviously successful and very patrician figure (and a former RAF pilot).

The plot's *in medias res* beginnings result from Dunne's restructuring of the play. Mankiewicz makes this change work through the right kind of visuals—the forbidding landscape, the symbolic prison, the twin images of transcendence, bird and airplane. No dialogue accompanies these images, for none is needed. The enigmatic epigraph, with its emphasis on the impossibility of changing the past, encourages the spectator to give them a symbolic or abstract significance, one connected to the impossibility of undoing what one has done. And yet Matt's intent fixation on the birds, who become the very image of his own powerful drive for freedom, suggests otherwise. The flashback generated by this moment of desire (the "escape" defined by the film's title), then, is interestingly ambivalent. On the one hand, it gives movement and impetus to the character, who is pictured making choices after he descends from the clouds to rejoin the world of men; thus his desire to "escape" is actualized through an act of will. On the other hand, the flashback ironically exemplifies the very unchangeability of experience. What we are about to see is a flashback, a dynamic imaging of the past that, as the past always does, absolutely lacks contingency.

The images, in other words, have two values: even as they appear to be happening, they have already happened, already resulted in the imprisonment of the protagonist. Matt wishes to escape from his past and its present consequences, but the memories that desire awakens expose the very unattainability of that desire. He remembers the descent from the heavens and the fall into sin. The very urge for transcendence thus connects to what it is in human experience that makes transcendence impossible. As the epigraph has it, changing what you have done is utterly impossible. Flashbacks may be a conventional element in the dark thrillers of this period, but the particular use of the device here is a stroke of genius (Mankiewicz uses flashbacks brilliantly in a number of his films). For the flashback generated by Matt's present moment of crisis not only expresses the heavy fatality of desire and action (as Billy Wilder's use of narrated flashback does in *Double Indemnity*, for example). Here, framed effectively by the initial visuals, the subjective flashback also exemplifies Galsworthy's main point about experience, which is traditionally Christian. Impelled by the possibility of heavenly transcendence, each of us strives to escape the prison house of sin, which is nothing less than the weight of our own experience.

This sin is "original" in the sense that it results from the impossibility of conforming to the law yet remaining fully human. The play opens appropriately with a reenactment of the Fall in a scene that is dramatically effective, if not thematically profound. The version designed by Mankiewicz and Dunne is much richer, not the least because it makes full use of specifically cinematic devices: a panoramic establishing shot, a point-of-view editing sequence, and a flashback that is imaged but not narrated, the "realization" of memory.

The flashback suggests the impossibility of escaping the past. This theme is complexly developed by the narrative it introduces, full of effective dramatic moments contributed by Dunne's rewriting. Walking in a London park, Matt meets a lonely lady, with whom he begins a conversation about Adam, Eve, and original sin. Her pessimism about the possibility of human goodness intrigues him, though he is obviously law-abiding and she is a prostitute. Matt walks on, and the narrative shifts to the woman, who is rousted by a passing patrolman. Coming to her rescue, Matt tries to restrain the policeman, who is attempting to arrest her. A fight ensues, the policeman falls and strikes his head, and the lady flees as Matt tries to help the injured man. Other policemen arrive and arrest him. The injured man dies, and Matt is put on trial. Convicted, he tells the judge: "I cannot submit to that verdict." Matt's impulse toward charitable protection of the weak, enacted in a world of moral ambiguity, results in the unwilled and unmerited death of another.

Galsworthy's conception raises interesting moral questions, some of which are explored at length in the play through dialogue. Aided by Dunne's streamlining of the playscript, Mankiewicz's adaptation of these materials takes another direction, one much more cinematic. Matt's desire for transcendence and moral perfection are not debated but projected in effective action. The middle part of the film treats Matt's escape into the moors, emphasizing not only the power of his will but the inhospitability of the environment. As in Hitchcock's *The Thirty-Nine Steps*, this guilty man who is also innocent meets a girl who, persuaded of his innocence, agrees to help him. Her charity, like his, involves her in crime.

A series of attempts to escape follow (including a visit to the airfield to reclaim his plane, foiled by the venality of his erstwhile mechanic friend, who betrays him to the police). At the very end, he takes refuge in a church whose minister is faced with the dilemma of giving him up to the police or lying. Matt surrenders rather than force the man to compromise his principles. He returns to the prison from which he can never escape.

If *Escape* did not achieve the popularity with audiences that Hitchcock's similar thrillers did, the blame should not be assigned to Mankiewicz. With its heavy emphasis on religious themes, Galsworthy's play offers material that is ultimately unappealing to popular audiences. Though it reshaped that material into an effective narrative, Dunne's screenplay still emphasizes these themes, including the idea of "original sin," which is mentioned over and over again by the characters. In films such as *Shadow of a Doubt*, Hitchcock showed that a thriller could effectively embody that same theme (ideally suited to its generic concern with pursuit, guilt, and flight) without mentioning it every five minutes. Dunne's screenplay falls into the trap of an overreliance on "significant" dialogue, a fault that Mankiewicz could only partially remedy through a bravura design and use of images.

No Way Out

In the late 1940s, race relations became an urgent item on the national agenda. Among other examples of worsening friction between blacks and whites, a destructive race riot erupted during the war in Detroit, where many southern blacks had moved to work in the booming defense industries. Many Americans, Joseph Mankiewicz among them, became convinced by such events that fundamental change in American society must come. Agitation against the continuing segregation of the armed forces was spearheaded by the NAACP, then enjoying its largest membership (including many whites) and political power. Under the benevolent direction of President Harry Truman, the desegregation of all branches of the military was accomplished with surprising ease and swiftness by 1948. Desegregation of major league baseball began about the same time with the signing of a prominent player from the Negro leagues, Jackie Robinson, to the Brooklyn Dodgers. Suddenly the national pastime, perhaps the most hallowed of lily-white cultural institutions, opened its ranks to players of color.

Encouraged by these successes and by changes in public opinion, the

NAACP launched a legal assault against the late nineteenth century Supreme Court decision, Plessy versus Ferguson, which had established the doctrine of a "separate but equal" status under the law for the two races. Plessy versus Ferguson had for more than half a century provided sanction for the Jim Crow laws across the Old South and various forms of de facto segregation in the northern states. These institutions, these laws, formerly so monolithic, now faced powerful challenges. Once hotly debated, not only in the white but in the African-American community as well, integration of the races became a goal supported by an increasing proportion of the public. In the process, integration became an issue that Hollywood could safely make its own.

For the first time since *The Birth of a Nation* (1915), in fact, the commercial film industry found racial questions suitable material for entertainment. The late forties and early fifties saw the production and widespread exhibition of a number of commercially successful films about race and, more generally, ethnic prejudice. A liberal Jewish American, Zanuck broke industry silence on the issue of anti–Semitism with *Gentleman's Agreement* (1947), a film that won Oscars for best picture and best director (stage and screen sensation, Elia Kazan) while making a fortune for Fox at the box office. Interestingly, Zanuck and Kazan were beaten to the nation's screens that year by a less prominent film on the same subject: Edward Dmytryk's *Crossfire* (based on a novel about homophobia, a still taboo subject that had to be changed to anti–Semitism). Zanuck and Kazan teamed again to repeat their success two years later with *Pinky*, which provocatively (for the times at least) explored the color line and the phenomenon of "passing for white."

Much like the less noticed *Lost Boundaries*, also released in 1949, *Pinky* featured a "Negro" professional (played by a white actress, Jeanne Crain) who returns to her home in the South and there discovers—and is in a sense endowed with—her heritage. She rededicates herself to the service of "her people" after breaking her engagement to marry a white doctor and rejecting his offer to move out west where the color line won't trouble them. Praised at the time for its liberalism, *Pinky* is actually anti-integrationist, perhaps because it deals with the two most sensitive and inflammatory of American racial questions: the problematic identity of those with mixed blood; and intermarriage between the races (then still outlawed in a number of southern states). The narrative works to establish and fix a stable racial identity for the woman who "is" black but looks white. The film gives this identity institutional form in the Deep South "colored" hospital where the erstwhile "Pinky" agrees finally to work (reversing the historical pattern of migration to the North). There the sexual threat she poses to the established racial order is blunted when she is introduced to a handsome, unmarried black doctor as an apparent compensation for her ruptured engagement to his white counterpart.

Despite his profitable work on these themes with the famed Kazan, Zanuck was unsatisfied. He regarded *Pinky* as a lightweight effort that did not engage deeply with the issues then confronting America. Convinced that a profitable and more politically sophisticated film could be made about race prejudice and conflict, in 1950 he engaged longtime Hollywood professional Lesser Samuels (who had worked with Mankiewicz in the thirties) to produce a realistic and politically committed screenplay on the subject. The grimly titled *No Way Out* was the result. Though the writing assignment was farmed out to Samuels, Zanuck had Mankiewicz in mind from the beginning to direct the project (quite a compliment to him as, in a sense, he was supplanting the much celebrated Kazan in Zanuck's continuing series of "message" films). The producer knew that some effective rewriting would undoubtedly be needed, and he trusted that Mankiewicz would do an exceptional job shaping the final script. Zanuck was not disappointed.

In devising the plot, which makes an unmistakable reference to the Detroit riot, Samuels and Zanuck were apparently influenced by one of the most successful message pictures of the previous year (1949). *Home of the Brave*, a Stanley Kramer production directed by Mark Robson, was adapted from a successful Broadway play by Arthur Laurents. Originally featuring a Jewish protagonist, *Home of the Brave* was rewritten to focus on anti–Negro sentiment. In the South Pacific, a black soldier is temporarily assigned to an otherwise all white unit. Bullied and baited by a rabid Negro hater, he discovers during the mission that one of his other comrades, a childhood friend in fact, also harbors bigoted sentiments. When his friend is killed, the Negro soldier suffers a hysterical paralysis that is eventually cured only when a sympathetic and obviously Jewish psychiatrist makes him express his deep-seated anger against the whites who have mistreated him. Unlike Jackie Robinson, who in *The Jackie Robinson Story* (1950) is charged to exercise Gandhi-like patience in dealing with ill treatment, the victimized main character here is authorized to stand up for himself. He does so literally in fact, since feeling anger alleviates the psychosomatic paralysis and allows him to rise from his hospital bed and walk.

Samuels' script, mounted with bravura and sensitivity by Mankiewicz, who incorporated many of his own revisions, is far superior to *Home of the Brave* and the other race pictures mentioned above because of its uncompromising engagement with larger cultural issues. Such a focus is

unusual for a Mankiewicz project (note the contrast with the playfully apolitical treatment of the war in *Five Fingers*). *No Way Out*'s more strident
tone and approach are certainly explained by Zanuck's supervision (there
is no doubt, however, that Mankiewicz shared the producer's prointegra-
tionist sentiments). *Gentleman's Agreement* similarly attempts to place the
destructiveness of anti–Semitism within a wider social context, and the
two films make an interesting diptych.

   No Way Out's protagonist is a newly minted intern working emergency services at a northern hospital, where he is the first black to practice medicine. Dr. Luther Brooks (Sidney Poitier in his first featured role)
is unsure of his own abilities and so are many of the hospital staff, who
have never worked with a Negro doctor before. The chief resident, Dr.
Wharton (Stephen McNally), respects Brooks' ability and is in favor of
a color-blind hiring policy; Wharton does not believe in either quotas or
what subsequently became known as "affirmative action." The hospital
administrator, Dr. Moreland (Stanley Ridges), in contrast, plays Branch
Rickey to Luther Brooks' Jackie Robinson; because the good public relations of the hospital depend on a proper Negro presence, Moreland is
hopeful that Brooks will succeed, especially since he could well pave the
way for other helpful hires. The disagreement between Wharton and
Moreland over the proper way to judge Brooks—neutrally or "affirma-
tively"—is quite effectively written and staged. Samuels and Mankiewicz
do not simplify the political and ethical issues involved and are eminently
fair to these differing positions on integration.

   Doubts about Brooks' competence drive the narrative, as the film
engages with a dominant theme of the fifties race relations debate: the
uncertainties of whites, including integration supporters, about the abilities of aspiring black professionals. The young doctor is called upon to
treat two white-trash brothers, the Biddles, each wounded in the leg by
policemen's bullets during a bungled robbery attempt. George seems
overly disoriented and confused; suspecting a brain tumor, Brooks performs a spinal tap, but the patient suddenly dies. His brother Ray, a vocif-
erous and virulent Negro hater (a disturbingly effective performance by
Richard Widmark), witnesses the procedure and is convinced that Brooks
killed his brother as payback for the verbal abuse that the young doctor
earlier received at his hands.

   Shaken and filled with self-doubt, Brooks seeks the advice of Dr.
Wharton, who says he may have been right in his diagnosis. Only an
autopsy can clear his name and prevent the hospital's integration policy
from failing, but legal authorization from next of kin is required. Ray naturally refuses permission. The physicians then make their way to the white

slum where Biddle's ex-wife Edie lives, an urban hellhole appropriately named Beaver Canal. Linda Darnell plays Edie with great effectiveness as a less hopeful and resourceful version of Lora Mae, the slum girl on the make she had made so appealing in *A Letter to Three Wives*. Like her husband and neighbors, Edie is afraid of and prejudiced against Negroes. Can Brooks and Wharton persuade her to do the right thing? At first, she seems willing to agree, ironically in large part to foil her ex-husband. But talking to others in the community makes her unsure what course to follow.

Edie's inner turmoil, however, does not become the focus of attention. Samuels and Mankiewicz had no intentions of confining, in the manner of *Home of the Brave*, the film's treatment of the race issue to the protagonist victimized by prejudice. The unnamed northern city in *No Way Out* is no stranger to racial violence, and integration achieved by an emerging black professional class would offer no easy solution to the bitter feelings in the starkly divided community. Entering the hospital to assume his duties, Brooks finds that the elevator operator is an old friend named Lefty (Dots Johnson). Stuck in a dead-end job, Lefty feels that whites will not allow his people to succeed; he bears on his cheek a jagged scar, which he got, he says, when Beaver Canal "came over" the last time on a rampage. The suspicious death of Biddle's brother, in fact, encourages the hooligans of Beaver Canal to plan another raid. But Lefty gets wind of the plans and persuades the members of the black community to launch a preemptive strike, one that is carefully planned in a military fashion.

The sequences detailing the preparations for the riot, mounted with a carefully calculated balance between realism and noirish pessimism, are among the film's most effective. Mankiewicz's camera tracks among the ranks of whites assembled in a junkyard, where they are trying out on empty garbage cans and scrap metal their various weapons: baseball bats, chains, and steel pipes. The disquieting sounds of the exercise, and the sight of coolly planned impersonal violence, provide an unforgettable metaphor for the riot itself, which, in accordance with the Production Code, could not be shown directly. While the whites hammer and beat their practice targets (a mock image of the industrial assembly line), the blacks, divided into several groups, make their way through narrow, garbage-strewn passageways to assemble for the ambush. One of them carries a navy flare gun (an interesting symbol of democratic war aims gone astray), and he fires it at a prearranged time, bathing the junkyard in an otherworldly phosphorus light as the rioting starts. At this point, Mankiewicz's camera departs for the hospital, where the casualties begin to pour in.

In most "message" pictures, the drama involving the individual characters is so structured as to resolve, in a fashion that confirms the status quo, the larger cultural struggle of which it is a microcosm. *No Way Out*, in contrast, avoids such a simple melodramatic approach. Brooks and Biddle in some sense cause the riot, but they are not its principal focus, which is quite clearly established as the long-term, bitter hostility between the racial communities. The question of the black doctor's competence provides merely the latest excuse for a renewal of communal violence. Like the conflict between Wharton and Moreland over the proper ethos of an integrative politics, the disagreement between Lefty and Brooks over how to deal with anti–Negro sentiment replays a larger, national debate: roughly speaking, the argument between Booker T. Washington and W.E.B. Dubois. Lefty is not shown to be mistaken in his prediction of a Beaver Canal raid, but the violence he orchestrates in response, though justified to some degree, escalates and does not resolve the problem. In fact, no other solution is proposed within the world of the film, nor do any of the characters give voice to a hope that one might be found. Like the black community, the white population is confirmed in its prejudice. It turns out that the residents of Beaver Canal do have something to fear from the blacks on the other side of the boundary marker. Both communities harbor militants eager to raise the level of violence and destruction. The film passes no judgment on their similar urges for self-protection except to comment on their futility and wastefulness as the hospital fills with victims.

In the end, however, *No Way Out* does lay a symbolic burden for stopping the violence on Brooks, who, because of his Hippocratic Oath, must finally act with Jackie Robinson–like restraint. Eventually allied with Edie, the doctor finds his safety compromised when Biddle, despite his worsening condition, escapes from the hospital and confronts Brooks in his own home. His attempt to murder the pair foiled, Biddle is finally at the mercy of Brooks, who in a sense has the right to kill his tormentor in self-protection. Brooks, however, remains true to his doctor's creed and to his newly earned professional status—to finish Biddle off would be to slip to his enemy's level, in terms of both morals and social class. The film ends with Brooks' promise to keep Biddle alive and therefore able to suffer the punishment he has coming to him.

In *Gentleman's Agreement*, the specter of anti–Semitism is put to rest by the self-sacrifice of the good gentile, a crusading reporter who pretends to be Jewish, suffers discrimination as a result, and then goes on to publish a heartfelt and effective denunciation of this social evil. In *No Way Out*, a much less hopeful resolution emerges. Brooks resolves not only the issue of his competence, when the autopsy confirms his judgment; he also shows that he has the inner strength to confront prejudice without being destroyed in the process. Yet the rioting between the two communities only comes to an end because both sides are bloodied and wearied by their confrontation. The emergence of a good man and true does nothing to alter these racial politics. The narrative clearly shows that he can find "a way up" even if the community that he must inevitably leave behind discovers it possesses "no way out." Though the city hospital might find more and more room for black doctors on its staff, Lefty and the Beaver Canal hooligans will live to fight again yet another day, to defend the communities they lack the means to leave. With remarkable prescience, the film predicts both the happy result of integration—the flight of the black professional class to the suburbs—and its most troubling result as well—the creation of a hopeless and disaffected urban underclass. *No Way Out* thus exemplifies the kind of fruitful collaboration among writer, director, and producer that the traditional studio structure made possible. It is a far better film than Zanuck, Mankiewicz, or Samuels could have made on his own.

House of Strangers

Within the studio system, writer-directors like Joseph Mankiewicz often found that working under contract and hence by assignment could sometimes bring unexpected benefits. Such was certainly the case for Mankiewicz with the project that was to become *House of Strangers*.

Producer Sol C. Siegel was in 1948 desperate for new story material to fit the emerging series of bleak, tough contemporary dramas that French critics were beginning to label film noir. In particular, Fox producers like Siegel were interested in the hybrid form created by shooting conventional crime melodramas in actual urban locations. One of the earliest of these noir-documentary films was the studio's quite successful *House on 92nd Street* (1945), the exteriors of which were filmed in New York. By the late forties, this new series was achieving a good deal of popularity. Nineteen forty-eight, in fact, saw the appearance of three quite successful productions of this type: Universal's *Naked City*, and Fox's *Call Northside 777* and *Cry of the City*, the last two of which featured Richard Conte, who was fast developing a reputation for interestingly layered portrayals of ethnic toughs or schemers. The studio's producers were eager to make more of the same and found suitable material in short supply.

The genesis of *House of Strangers* shows how far they went to find a filmable story. Cannibalizing a popular Jerome Weidman novel, *I'll Never Go There Any More*, Siegel instructed screenwriter Philip Yordan to develop a screenplay from just a few pages of the book. The novel chronicles Italian-American immigrant life in New York's Lower East Side, and Siegel found most interesting the chapter devoted to Max Maggio, a famed criminal lawyer who falls afoul of the law and goes to jail for his father's crimes. Here was material ideal for development into a noir crime drama that would emphasize the poisoned destructiveness of family relations (a theme, interestingly enough, at the center of Mankiewicz's maiden directorial effort, *Dragonwyck*). The current project was quite likely conceived in part as a vehicle for Conte, who was slated for a fat role as the good-bad guy protagonist redeemed by love. Yordan, however, proved unable to construct on a hurried schedule anything suitable for filming. Darryl Zanuck, head of studio production, then asked Mankiewicz, who had just finished directing *A Letter to Three Wives* and was between assignments, to try his hand at doctoring or even rewriting the script. Zanuck picked the right man for the job. The plot's focus on Max's relationship with his father and brother, on the one hand, and with two women on the other, offered ideal opportunities for the kind of nuanced dramatic portrayals that Mankiewicz had carried off to perfection in *Letter*. The assignment offered him an excellent opportunity that he found exciting, and he made the most of it.

Turning to the task of scriptwriting, he retained little of what Yordan had completed, but remained quite faithful to the Weidman material. The witty hard-boiled dialogue is certainly all Mankiewicz and favorably recalls the effective script work he had had done for *Somewhere in the Night*, which featured a similar romantic plot. Like George Taylor, *House*'s Max Monetti (Conte had played a somewhat similar role as the morally ambiguous villain in the earlier film) is bent on redemption and revenge for the wrongs done to him. Both men are saved, in part, from a potentially self-destructive course of action by the enduring love of a good woman who is strong-minded and independent. Though he wrote nearly all the script, Mankiewicz fell victim to an unjust decision by the Screen Writers Guild, who insisted he share screen credit. Furious, he refused. Despite its official lineage, however, *House of Strangers* is a film that bears strong imprints of Mankiewicz's gifted touch throughout, both in its effectively structured screenplay and in the rich, often intricate visual style Mankiewicz developed to mount it. The film, perhaps, is not as brilliant as the witty, sophisticated *A Letter to Three Wives*, a story which, because it unfolds in a suburban, middle-class milieu, offered more opportunities for the kind of flashy repartee for which Mankiewicz is justly famous.

House of Strangers, however, is no slight effort and deserves more than the passing attention given it by most critics of Mankiewicz's work.

For reasons beyond the director's control, the film was given only limited distribution and had little chance to make an impression on the moviegoing public. Like *Citizen Kane*, *House of Strangers*, following Weidman's lead, used fictional characters to retell what was in part a true story: the founding of the Bank of America by the Giannini family. The bank's subsequent phenomenal success, like that of its fictional counterpart, was undone by the illegal and careless practices of its directors, forcing a foreclosure in the early years of the Depression. Perhaps hoping for a notoriety that would help at the box office, Zanuck shaped *House of Strangers* to sharpen its oblique reference to recent history. He even asked the Fox art department to construct a faithful copy of the Giannini bank (in San Francisco) that would be relocated in a fictionalized Manhattan. The studio weathered a mild storm of protest from the Gianninis, but, ironically, fell victim to an attack from an unexpected source. Spyros Skouras, head of Fox's operations in New York, thought that Zanuck intended the immigrant vulgarity of Gino Monetti (a fine characterization by Edward G. Robinson) as mockery of his thick Greek accent and ethnic ways. Like Monetti, Skouras presided somewhat uneasily over a family of contentious sons, further evidence, he supposed, of Zanuck's deliberate insult. To the chagrin of both Siegel and Mankiewicz, Zanuck capitulated to the protests of Skouras. The film, which was enjoying brisk business at Grauman's Chinese Theater in Hollywood, was suddenly yanked, and subsequent national distribution, Mankiewicz claims, was unfairly restricted. The director attributed *House*'s financial failure to this inadequate distribution. He never changed his view—and rightly so—that it was a good film.

We need look no further than the bravura opening sequences for confirmation of the director's judgment. These promise a complex drama that the film goes on to develop in quite sophisticated ways. Establishing shots of Manhattan and then the Lower East Side locate an energetic and determined man making his way down streets thronged with shoppers. A longish track emphasizes the contrast between the man and the everyday world from which he finds himself apparently estranged. Arriving at a bank, he bulls his way into the executive offices without waiting to be announced. A hollow greeting awaits him there from his brothers who, it turns out, were involved with him in a crime that only he had to pay for with a prison sentence. The man, revealed as Max Monetti, rejects the insincere offers of a celebratory dinner and a wad of cash; vengeance, it seems, is on his mind as he exits the office in a huff.

Max then makes his way to another destination, an upscale apartment whose obviously female occupant is then not at home; he makes himself comfortable on her bed. The woman (Susan Hayward) then returns; her initial puzzlement at an unexpected arrival turns at once to joy when she finds that it is Max. The contrast between the two "welcomes" could not be greater. Irene's joy, however, soon turns to distress when she realizes that Max is bent on vengeance. Max, she says, must choose between the alternatives that she and his brothers represent. If he is to opt for personal happiness, success, and upward mobility with her, he must reject the dark vendetta that a grim family past—the legacy of both his ethnic origins and a manipulative and lawless father—pulls him toward.

Unable to forgo his desire for revenge, Max storms out of Irene's apartment. But this time his journey, through a surprising straight cut, is over in an instant. Just as Irene predicted, the past can readily and quickly pull him away from what the present offers. Suddenly back in the Lower East Side, Max enters what is revealed as the family home. As a significant counterpoint to the bank office, the home is neither guarded nor securely locked. Its arrivistic and overdecorated living room, in fact, is empty of the living, but dominated by a huge portrait of his father Gino (Edward G. Robinson), who, we learned earlier, is now dead. Having reentered the space of the past, Max's relentless forward motion abruptly ends. Apparently in tribute to his father's tastes and his own heritage, he stands quietly by the mantle and puts on a record of an opera aria ("M'appari" from von Flotow's *Martha*). While he remains lost in thought, perhaps of the family past, the camera—in a move very unusual for Hollywood filmmaking at the time—leaves him behind, slowly tracks out of the room, and then ascends the stairs to the landing. Here a sound montage indicates a switch from the present to the past; the beautiful tenor voice of the recording artist gives way to the rough and inexpert singing of Gino, whom the camera locates in a bathtub, where he is attended by eldest son Joe. At this point in the past, seven years earlier it turns out, the flashback that constitutes the bulk of the film begins.

This masterful opening depends only partly on dialogue. The encounters between Max and Irene and Max and his brothers are set up expertly by silent sequences. Max respectfully and slowly enters his empty girlfriend's apartment, then makes his way immediately to the bedroom where he quite evidently feels at home. Irene's joyful reaction at discovering that her unexpected visitor is Max completes the initial portrayal of their relationship; no exposition is needed. Likewise, Max's scornful attitude toward his brothers is indicated initially by his aggressive, reckless forward motion; the subsequent dialogue simply confirms what has already been effectively communicated through expertly designed visuals.

Only apparently seamless, the opening actually consists of two separate parts, joined effectively by the camera's desertion of Max at the mantelpiece for a flashback that Max himself could neither remember nor narrate, not having been present at the scene of bathtub singing. While Max's energy, desires, and choices dominate the present frame, the flashback must belong to Gino, for the father represents the power from which Max must free himself. The movement back to the family home and to a past moment at which he is not even present is the visual and narrative correlative of the course of action which Irene warns Max against.

This break from one focused character to another is not typical of studio filmmaking, but in this case it is thematically required, for the present must belong to Max as surely and completely as the past belongs to his father. *House of Strangers* is correspondingly structured around a double, contradictory movement, one that depends artfully on a flashback entirely different from the ones so tellingly deployed in *Letter*. In that film, the three flashback sequences constitute moments of intense, separate subjectivity, for each flashback for each woman occupies itself with memories generated by a fear that cannot be spoken of to the other two. The flashbacks thus provide exposition that indexes the terrible isolation of the protagonists, an isolation overcome only by the final revelation, which is presented dramatically and in the present.

In *House*, by way of contrast, the initial and intensely narrative focus on Max is abandoned for an "objective" flashback that makes Gino the main character for some time, but this flashback is not developed in the same subjective fashion. The initial objectivity of the flashback, which paints a broad portrait of the family, then gradually, as the present moment with which the film began is regained, gives way once again to a domination by Max, who is reinstalled as the main character. Max's abandonment of Irene for the family is then made good by his progress away from them and back to her. The structure is masterful, and it makes the best of material that might otherwise be confusing because of its double concern with father and son. Mankiewicz's use of flashback gives shape to that double concern, making Max a main character who is only able to regain his position at the center of the narrative by, first in the past and then in the present, rejecting the world of his father and family for that of Irene.

Max can accept happiness with Irene, however, only after the family literally releases its stranglehold on his life. Thinking that he intends to send them to prison, his three brothers lure Max to a meeting in the bank office, then attempt to throw him out the window, hoping it will appear a suicide. Before they kill him, however, Max frantically reminds them that this kind of violence is what their father would condemn them to. Realizing that he is right, they release him.

House of Strangers features some uninspired performances in secondary roles, but the principals (Richard Conte, Edward G. Robinson, Susan Hayward, and Luther Adler, who plays Joe) are excellent, a testimony to Mankiewicz's skillful direction. Like *Letter*, this film depends on ensemble acting to a great degree, and Mankiewicz not only provided impressive dialogue to this end, but also mounted these scenes quite effectively. *House of Strangers* compares quite well to the other noir-realist films of the period, especially since it not only interestingly recycles conventional characters and themes but has something important to say as well about the stifling nature of family relations.

In this regard, *House of Strangers* recalls an important film outside the noir cycle, the screen version of Arthur Miller's *All My Sons* (Irving Reis, 1948). In this film, a domineering father (here too played by Edward G. Robinson) causes the death of army airmen by producing and supplying shoddy airplane parts to the government. At first trapped by his father's lies, the sole surviving son confronts him with the truth and saves himself as the father regains his honor by committing suicide. Though Reis' film had the benefit of superior source material (Miller's Pulitzer Prize winning drama), Mankiewicz's is far superior in the way that it fashions appropriate cinematic structures to express the connection between transgressing father and suffering son. By the time he came to make this film, Mankiewicz had obviously gained great skills as a director who knew how the film medium could best present a story and not just offer visuals that interestingly counterpoint effective writing.

Five Fingers

Anxious to complete his agreement with Fox (and hoping to launch a more lucrative career as an independent), Mankiewicz seized on a property that offered him excellent opportunities for exercising his skill as a writer-director. Here was a story worthy of the award-winning director of *A Letter to Three Wives* and *All about Eve*. It promised similar dramatic possibilities and box office success. Screenwriter Michael Wilson had just finished a fictionalized version of a best-selling wartime memoir, *Operation Cicero* by former German diplomat L.C. Moyzisch, and was hoping to sell it to an interested producer. The book details the notorious exploits of German agent "Cicero," a valet (given the name Diello in the film) who worked for the British ambassador in Turkey. Diello is an opportunist who uses his position to steal top secret documents and sell them to the Germans. A charming, talented, and conscienceless schemer, he pursues success with the same well-disguised ferocity of Eve Harrington. Like Mankiewicz's most famous protagonist, Diello is a social climber. He is eager to leave his life as a servant behind and become a respected member of the elite whose manners he so closely imitates.

Wilson's script not only had obvious appeal to Mankiewicz, but another significant advantage as well. A realistic war story would be attractive to producer Darryl Zanuck, who was obsessed by World War Two, as a number of his films, most notably *The Longest Day* (1962), testify. Zanuck was, in fact, easily persuaded to buy the rights to the screenplay, with Mankiewicz's proviso that some minimal rewriting was needed. Actually, much of Wilson's dialogue was scrapped as too prosaic; the witty exchanges between Diello and the countess, Moyzisch, and others are pure Mankiewicz. These changes are significant. The director had no intentions of making an ordinary war film full of high seriousness and conventional patriotism. *Operation Cicero* is a noirish tale of betrayal and anomie at the highest levels of society. It is more about human frailty, class distinctions, and endearing villainy than the winning of the war. In fact, it turns out that ultimate Allied victory depends on an ironic and fortuitous reversal, not just military might. Wilson's version abounds in ironies that called for and received a sophisticated Mankiewicz treatment. Principal among these is that the Germans do not trust their source and hence make no use of the information they purchase, even though it is absolutely genuine. Eventually given plans for Operation Overlord, the invasion of Normandy, they do not redeploy their forces, a decision that leads, so the film implies, to their eventual defeat.

Though his employers do nothing with their purchases, the spy succeeds in obtaining a huge sum for his last delivery of documents and escapes to freedom. But he does no better than the Nazis, whose lack of cunning and subtlety he scorns. Opting for pay in British sterling because he feels the Germans cannot win the war, Diello receives only worthless counterfeit thousand pound notes in return for his efforts; he take no precautions against this most elementary of deceptions. This is not the only betrayal to which the betrayer arrogantly and foolishly subjects himself. Eager to become a gentleman, he involves his former employer, the beautiful Countess Staviska, in the scheme. She is to provide cover for his transactions and the means to launder the proceeds. Diello, however, wants more than a partner in crime. Convinced that she has always found him attractive if socially untouchable, he thinks that his newfound wealth will move the countess to accept him as her lover. Desperate for money since the Germans have confiscated her estates, she agrees to the scheme. But Diello has no reason to trust her, especially when she has unfettered access to their funds, deposited in a local bank under her name. She absconds with their money after notifying both the British and Germans of her partner's betrayal, insulted by his boldness and presumption, if not by his lack of conscience and loyalty. Arrogant and supremely self-confident, Diello is taken completely by surprise, the victim of yet another miscalculation.

Ostensibly the upholders of the right, the British are shown to be as foolish as the Germans; they cannot equal Diello's sophistication, cunning, and resourcefulness. The British soon deduce that the spy works in their Turkish embassy. Blinded by class prejudice, however, they pay little attention to Diello, even though his job allows him to move in and out of the ambassador's office at any hour and without explanation. The result is that he easily steals secrets of immeasurable importance that they might have protected by the simplest of expedients: posting guards in the ambassador's office. Even when an alarm traps Diello with his hands in the safe that he opens with ease, he escapes unhampered, running out the front door past the security agents after saying he is chasing an imaginary intruder, a childish but effective ruse. His cover blown, he flees Ankara and then Istanbul though pursued by both British and German agents, all of whom are easily and thoroughly fooled. But this triumph is illusory. He escapes to South America where he buys a villa. He settles down to live a life of gentlemanly leisure only to be arrested for passing worthless currency. Though all his efforts to make a different life for himself prove in vain, he never loses his appreciation for life's ironies and absurdities. Informed that the other counterfeit notes have turned up in Switzerland, where he knows his erstwhile confederate has fled, Diello casts into the wind the meaningless paper he has worked so hard to obtain and laughs uproariously in the recognition that the countess has unwittingly suffered the same unrewarding fate.

Operation Cicero's bitter vision of greed and frustration perfectly suited Mankiewicz. With Wilson's artful plot (the countess, among other changes, is his invention) and his own snappy dialogue, the resulting film would rival John Huston's *The Maltese Falcon* (1941) in its cold, but fascinating portrayal of unremitting villainy. Zanuck saw the project differently, but was not disappointed by the result. He was persuaded that the exciting wartime story of Diello's escapades would make for good box office. True to his producer's expectations, Mankiewicz did a superb job with the exterior sequences, which involve a double pursuit on the model of Hitchcock's *The Thirty-Nine Steps* (1935) and *North by Northwest* (1959). Zanuck contributed judicious management of the project. He also carefully oversaw the final editing. Though the director thought that the producer ruined the last third of the picture, critics and audiences did not agree when it was exhibited. *Five Fingers*, despite the friction between director and producer, must be counted a highly successful collaboration. Zanuck even contributed the release title, a sly allusion ("five finger discount" in American slang) to the thievery at which Diello proves so expert. To his credit, he realized that the obvious wartime reference of Moyzsich's original title would misrepresent the quite different emphases Mankiewicz had given the material.

Five Fingers fit nicely into the semi-documentary dramas that during the late 1940s had become a profitable staple of Fox production. Like Mankiewicz's own *House of Strangers* and *No Way Out*, this new project would use authentic locations to provide realism, as well as occasional voice-over narration to reinforce the story's announced claim to be true. As a tale of international espionage, *Five Fingers* also resembled similar noirish films such as *Journey into Fear* (Norman Foster, Orson Welles, 1942), *Confidential Agent* (Robert Buckner, 1945), and, most successful of the subgenre, Carol Reed's acclaimed *The Third Man* (1949). Before interior work began, Mankiewicz and crew traveled to Turkey, where (using doubles) they shot the chase sequences, mostly in quite well-designed long shots. During the shoot, Mankiewicz met informally with the real Diello, Eliaza Bazna. True to Moyzisch's description of his character, Bazna tried to make the most of his now established notoriety by offering for sale at an exorbitant price the "real story" of his exploits. Mankiewicz shrewdly turned him down.

At the time, the studio was simultaneously producing another wartime espionage drama that traced the actual exploits of a turncoat, in this case a German soldier who spied successfully for the Allies. Directed by the stylish Anatole Litvak and released as *Decision Before Dawn* (1951), this film shows by comparison how different Mankiewicz's intentions were. Dropped behind German lines, "Happy" begins a long odyssey through the collapsing social fabric of his homeland. Now a stranger in a strange land because of his decision to betray the cause he had been fighting to uphold, Happy experiences the rootlessness and paranoia of the noir hero. One narrow escape after another leads at last to his moment of truth: he gives himself up to certain death in order to allow his partner to deliver needed information to the American command. The tone of *Decision before Dawn* is uniformly serious and ideologically correct (the only good

Germans are the ones who betray their own and ratify that decision
morally by sacrificing their lives). The film uses ruined European cities
for its exteriors and expressionistically designed studio interiors; the
emphasis is on atmosphere and suspense, effects not spoiled by the predictable dialogue and flat characters.

In contrast, Mankiewicz gives the ending away early, in a prologue
that attests to the story's historical accuracy; he directs spectator interest
toward the characters, not the political plotting in which they are somewhat indifferently embroiled. Diello's motives—greed and a desire for the
good life—are simply developed and occasion no profound examination.
As in *A Letter to Three Wives*, Mankiewicz is here much more deeply interested in the complex human transactions that drive the plot. By surrounding Diello and the countess with characters who are dull, foolishly
self-confident, or inept, he forces the spectator to identify with the couple's attempt to turn the suffering of war to their advantage. As Billy
Wilder does in *Double Indemnity* (1944), audience sympathy is carefully
developed for the villains, whose success and evasion of capture is sus-
pensefully presented.

In a letter to Zanuck, Mankiewicz confessed that he was intrigued
by the neat dramatic structure of Wilson's script and the "off-center,
provocative" characters. Both producer and director recognized that proper
casting was of the utmost importance. Charming, coldly handsome, and
arrogant, British actor James Mason made a perfect Diello. The year
before, he had convincingly incarnated German general Erwin Rommel
in *The Desert Fox*. What other Anglo-American actor at the time could
have played that part with any success? The arrogant and iconoclastic
Rommel was a character whose intensity, self-confidence, and calculating intelligence made him a perfect study for Diello. Mason suitably incarnated the valet who would be a gentleman and who had the cunning and
sang-froid to plot a betrayal that might cost thousands of lives besides
changing the course of history. Mankiewicz takes full advantage of one
of the actor's talents that had been largely unexploited in previous films:
his physical grace. Some of *Five Fingers'* most successful sequences depict,
with no dialogue of course, Diello hard at work stealing secrets. With ath-
letic deftness and rapidity, he opens the safe, removes the diplomatic
pouch, readies the documents for photographing, shoots them in succession, and replaces them as he reassumes his domestic duties. Interestingly, as Mankiewicz stages them, the valet's legitimate physical duties—
picking up after his master, arranging his wardrobe—merge almost
imperceptibly with his betraying thefts. These suspenseful sequences make
a wordlessly profound comment on Diello's character (the two "sides" of

his self really being one) and on his consummate skill (for the seamless integration of the licit and illicit is the perfect cover for his thefts).

To find an appropriate foil for Mason's Diello, Zanuck rejected casting well-known Hollywood actresses in favor of Danielle Darrieux. Not only does she, like Mason, bring an Old World sophistication and charm to the part of the countess, she was actually condemned for her self-serving collaboration during the German occupation of France. Darrieux had just the right star image for the role which, under Mankiewicz's expert direction, was her best in an English language film. The verbal dueling between Diello and the countess, developed in the three exquisitely scripted scenes that are the core of the film, results in his eventual, but ambiguous, victory. Her surrender to the ardent suitor's demands paradoxically reestablishes her superiority and control of her own destiny (always dependent on a smitten man's money). The countess' hauteur, which simultaneously attracts the valet's seduction and leads her to resist it, explains, perhaps makes inevitable, her ultimate betrayal of the low-born man too confident of his abilities and strengths. Diello can fool the ambassador, run circles around British security agents, and bamboozle the predictable Germans—but he cannot win the countess' affection or respect.

As often in the noir universe, there is a perverse sense of poetic justice in this. For Diello fools the ambassador and exploits his trust just as viciously and deftly with his pretended submission and self-abnegation; appropriately, his betrayal is itself betrayed. As tricksters, Diello and the countess are as convincingly deceptive as Eve Harrington. Indeed, much like *All about Eve*, *Five Fingers* offers a nuanced portrait of womanly self-possession and worldly wisdom, the perfect complement to Diello's physical and intellectual success in the equally cutthroat realm of "business." Yet it is the countess who in their confrontation and collaboration wields the upper hand. In the classic noir romance *Double Indemnity*, the scheming protagonist, yet another two-faced charmer, confesses that he was after money and a woman, but got neither. Diello might say much the same, but is too inclined, admirably in fact, toward self-derisive laughter. In terms of gender politics, *Five Fingers* yields yet another fascinating incarnation of the strong-minded woman who, from Eve to Cleopatra, energizes almost every Mankiewicz film.

There Was a Crooked Man

In the Hollywood of the studio and post-studio eras, most contract directors became, through choice or necessity, identified with certain genres. For urbane Joseph L. Mankiewicz, the western was not one of the story types he either sought out or was asked to direct (though he did produce John Ford's *Three Godfathers*). Mankiewicz shared little in common with those such as Ford, Anthony Mann, and Howard Hawks who did critically acclaimed and profitable work in the western during the fifties and sixties. These were two of the most important, productive decades in the genre's distinguished Hollywood history.

At the end of his career, then, it is surprising, to say the least, that Mankiewicz developed a genuine enthusiasm for the project that would finally be titled *There Was a Crooked Man*. The film turned out to be unconventional in a number of ways, including the fact that it is also a prison picture (yet another standard type that the Ivy League–educated New Yorker had avoided throughout his career). Yet *There Was a Crooked Man* was undeniably still a western, replete with heroes on horseback, six-gun shootouts, charismatic good bad guys, and a morally ambiguous lawman. Why did this script tickle Mankiewicz's fancy, particularly at a time in his career when recent disappointments, notably the poor reception given *The Honey Pot*, had damaged his once unassailable reputation for quality workmanship?

To some degree, the answer can be found in the evolving status of the genre in the period of independent, post-studio production that would come to be known as the Hollywood Renaissance. For at this time, the western had become a favored form for directors with artistic intentions, and Mankiewicz was undoubtedly influenced by this change. In the late sixties, the western was no longer the simple and exuberant horse opera it had been prior to the slow, steady demise of the studios, which began in 1947 and ultimately caused Hollywood to rethink its production categories. Series westerns, built around stars such as Roy Rogers, Gene Autry, and Hopalong Cassidy, had long been a regular item on the menu offered filmgoers: either as second features in urban houses or as first features in rural theaters. These films, in their many hundreds, were overwhelmingly quickly manufactured "B" productions that remained true to a very limited set of conventions, the legacy of the genre's emergence into prominence during the silent era. Series westerns were generally shunned by the majors and were produced at poverty-row shops, especially Republic and Monogram, both of which more or less specialized exclusively in the genre.

This state of affairs changed dramatically during the late forties. Faced with, among other ills, intense competition from the new medium of television, Hollywood was forced in the postwar era to develop new production strategies. The western proved to be extremely accommodating to the two most important of these initiatives: pushing the limits of the Production Code with "adult" dramas and exploiting the visual possibilities of wide-screen cinematography. Films such as John Ford's *The Searchers* and *The Man Who Shot Liberty Valance* or Anthony Mann's *Naked Spur* and *The Man from Laramie* gave new life to the genre by exploring its mythologizing role in American culture. Meanwhile, the conventional plots and themes of the old series western found a welcome home on the small screen where, by the middle sixties, western dramas constituted a substantial part of prime-time programming, with such popular shows as *The Virginian, Gunsmoke*, and *Bonanza* dominating the ratings.

The demise of the Production Code in 1966 and its replacement by a ratings system made it possible for westerns to become even more adult, even provocative in their representations of violence and sexual themes. The European-influenced "art" directors of Hollywood Renaissance found in the western a rich repository of historical themes and a genre whose deconstruction could provide startling insights into the nature of American life. Just to take the most obvious examples, Arthur Penn's *Little Big Man*, Robert Altman's *McCabe and Mrs. Miller*, and Michael Cimino's *Heaven's Gate* explored the political and social significance of the genre's timeworn conventions, its good bad guys, itinerant gamblers, golden-hearted prostitutes, fortune-hunting Easterners, Indian attacks, and bloody range wars. Shorn of the trappings of myth, this "new" western revealed a nineteenth century America that filmviewers had scarcely glimpsed before, despite the inescapable and constant presence of the genre on screens both small and large for more than two decades. Sam Peckinpah's *The Wild Bunch* even offers shocking commentary on the genre's preoccupation with righteous violence, predicting the demise of honorable, personal encounters and the rise of mechanized death; the six-gun is replaced by the Browning machine gun in an apocalyptic climax the likes of which the western had never before attempted to represent. And, like most of the other film westerns at the time, *The Wild Bunch* reproduced the raw, unglamorized reality of western life, not the sanitized violence and clean frontier living then portrayed on television. Alternatively, some westerns of the period played the genre's conventions for laughs, exposing their exclusion of realities both physical and social. Of these parodies, perhaps Mel Brooks' *Blazing Saddles* is the most notable. Mankiewicz's film would provide an uneasy, if occasionally quite effective combination of both these emergent types, comic and realistic.

Signed to a multiple picture deal at Warner-Seven Arts, Mankiewicz was teamed with producer Kenneth Hyman. Hyman's biggest success had been with the unconventional World War II drama *The Dirty Dozen*

(1966), a mission picture in the vein of *The Guns of Navarone* but with paroled convicts as the soldiers called upon to blow up a chateau full of German officers. At the time he teamed up with Mankiewicz, Hyman was interested in a script by Robert Benton and David Newman (whose first effort, *Bonnie and Clyde*, had been turned by Arthur Penn into one of the most successful American films of recent years). Hyman had originally suggested the subject of the script to the two writers: a western that features a prison setting. Their finished product climaxes in an escape, with the adventure elements of the story built up around a conflict between Paris Pitman, a charming malefactor, and Woodward Lopeman, his lawman alter ego, with a gallery of unusual secondary characters providing color and contrast.

Though the two versions of the script that Mankiewicz read would have posed problems for any director trying to make a 120-minute film with clearly focused main characters and an easily followed narrative, he was impressed. Perhaps he thought that the script's diffuseness might be turned to advantage, as Peckinpah had done with similar materials in the case of *The Wild Bunch*. *Bonnie and Clyde*, of course, depends for its effect on a picaresque narrative energized by successive encounters with unusual characters, but in that film Benton and Newman establish from the very beginning the structural importance of the outlaw couple. *There Was a Crooked Man* lacks such a focus. This problem might have been remedied, as it was by director Robert Aldrich in making *The Dirty Dozen*, by arousing the spectator's interest in the story's directionality, its preoccupation with a particular end (i.e., the successful completion of the group's assigned mission). Unfortunately, Benton and Newman's script takes more than 30 minutes of running time before it effectively assembles its motley cast of characters and fits them into a suitable plot. Mankiewicz had proved able to handle similar difficulties deftly in other projects (notably, *All About Eve* and *A Letter to Three Wives*, with their extended ensembles of more or less main characters). Unfortunately, he proved unable to work the same kind of magic with this script.

The problem, strangely enough, has most to do with the film's narration, normally a Mankiewicz forte. The initial sequences introduce the various characters who are eventually going to share accommodations at the state prison, including the sheriff who will become their jailer. Such sequences are, as here, ordinarily prenarrative, in that their primary purpose is to provide backstory and introduce motifs or themes that will be further developed. In *The Dirty Dozen* or, to take a western example, *The Magnificent Seven*, the narrative offers some explanation for this changing focus on a diverse group of characters, each of whom has, in some sense, his own story. Benton and Newman provide no such explanation, but one could easily have been provided (e.g., by using occasional voice-over narration to set up each new episode or by an *in medias res* beginning that allowed them to be handled with flashbacks). Without such explanation, the succession of episodes is confusing, especially since Mankiewicz, interested in their variations on a theme (which turns out to be the different circumstances that drive people into criminal behavior), lets each of them go on too long and become too unfocused.

The film's opening provides an excellent example. Shots of horses approaching a house with muffled hooves suggest an initial focus on showing what the riders have in mind. The film, however, cuts to the house's interior, where a black maid, about to serve dinner, is fixing her head rag—and also, as it turns out, her public face. She changes from glum to jolly in order to serve fried chicken to the white family who apparently expect an Aunt Jemima performance from their cook. Without another cut back to the riders, the family's dinner is then interrupted by those who have arrived unannounced, thanks to their quiet horses. Paris Pitman (Kirk Douglas at his most comically wicked) and his gang proceed, with wit and finesse, to rob the reluctant patriarch, a man named Lomax, of his money. The gang then make their escape, but are challenged by the family, who run to their guns.

In the shootout, several of the gang are killed, and Paris finishes off his sole surviving companion. Mankiewicz then cuts back to the interior of the house, where the maid enjoins her husband not to risk getting killed to save the money of some "white folks." A cut then returns us outside. There we see how, having wounded Lomax, Pitman escapes to the desert, where he hides the loot in a rattlesnake nest, keeping out some money which he, grinning, puts in his shirt. Instead of staying with Pitman, the narrative focus returns to Lomax, whose financial embarrassment makes it impossible for him to pay for the usual services he requires at a local brothel. The madam offers one of her best customers something on the house, a session in the peephole room where he can spy on the action taking place next door. Joining him at the peepholes is the local judge, who is accompanied by a bored prostitute. To Lomax's surprise and indignation, the man whose bedroom feats Lomax has decided to observe is Pitman, who is enjoying immensely the services of two women for whom he has evidently paid with Lomax's money. The wronged "pillar of the community" raises a hue and cry, with the result that Pitman is arrested for his crime. With further irony, Pitman is tried before the very judge whom he had entertained with his sexual antics. The unrepentant thief is found guilty and sentenced to prison.

In some ways, this part of the film is quite successful. Not only do these sequences explain how Pitman finds himself in prison, they also establish his character, which is ruthless, charmingly self-indulgent, and resourceful—he is, in short, the perfect hero for a picaresque narrative such as the one in which he finds himself. These sequences, in addition, establish some important themes: the social self as a (perhaps hypocritical) performance; society as a dubious body riven by class and racial inequities; the impossibility, therefore, of discriminating between "good" and "bad" characters; and the moral weakness or outright venality of even the most conventionally respectable. It is no wonder that Mankiewicz told Hyman that the script was "very Dickensian," for, like the novels of the English master, it portrays, with no little humor, the imperfections of a diverse social pageant, a west suddenly revealed as populated by oppressed former slaves, amoral businessmen, and dance hall girls who do more than cadge drinks. At the same time, Mankiewicz confusingly changes focus in order to make these thematic points. The maid's Aunt Jemima performance, for example, is not an integral part of the story. Yet Mankiewicz provides it with a good deal of detailed attention, and the result is that any suspense that might have been aroused by the horses' muffled approach is lost. Mankiewicz also thereby forfeits the opportunity to craft an extended—and perhaps just as thematically effective—contrast between the robbers and the robbed, in the way that Peckinpah manages with such bravura in the opening action of *The Wild Bunch*. But the shift in focus from Pitman back to Lomax at the end of the robbery does allow Mankiewicz to create an effective moment of recognition for the good citizen (because Pitman in effect has taken Lomax's place in bed with the local whores). However, the game is perhaps not worth the candle since the result is, in part, to dilute the film's concern with Pitman, who is, after all, destined to be a focused character long after Lomax is gone from the scene. The same kind of problem quite adversely affects the continuity of the prison and prison escape sequences; here once again Pitman's experience is only occasionally focused on effectively. What remains only inadequately developed then is the central contrast between the charmingly immoral crook and the lawman, turned warder, who must insist, despite his own doubts, that the rules be followed.

As a result, the film's superb casting is thus largely wasted. Kirk Douglas is excellent as Pitman. Though often used in standard leading man roles by Hollywood (sometimes even in his own productions such as *Spartacus*), Douglas was always more effective in slightly villainous parts: as an energetic con man with a conscience (*Ace in the Hole*), a voracious marauder with character and principles (*The Vikings*), or a selfish adven-

turer who respects the gods and loves his wife (*Ulysses*). His Pitman is
suitably evil without ever becoming obnoxious or boring—no mean acting feat. Somehow we don't hold it against him that he breaks the rules
western heroes usually live by, such as the injunction against shooting
friends in the back. As the liberal lawman who is offended by crime yet
sympathetic to criminals, Henry Fonda was likewise an inspired choice.
Though his darker side was at the time being exploited by Sergio Leone
in "spaghetti" westerns, Fonda remained most familiar to American audiences as the very incarnation of American virtue. Consider, by way of
example, just these performances for John Ford: *The Grapes of Wrath* (as
a virtuous everyman), *Young Mr. Lincoln* (embodying the central American myth of homespun good sense and plain living), and *My Darling
Clementine* (where, as Wyatt Earp, he fights the good fight to rid the west
of those opposed to its civilization).

As written by Benton and Newman, Lopeman is an intriguing and
unusual character. Arrogant and principled enough to think that he can
apprehend criminals without a gun, he is shot in the leg by a petty thief,
thus becoming the *Crooked Man* in the film's title (or perhaps the title
refers to Pitman, who is equally crippled by his lack of restraint). The
wound means he must give up his job as sheriff and become the warden
of the prison where Pitman winds up after the foolish spree at the brothel
results in his capture. Lopeman's desire for authority and control soon
conflicts with Pitman's hatred of hypocrisy. The warden has the prison-
ers build a mess hall to impress local politicians, but Pitman incites his
fellow inmates to riot against the man who would make them conform
to his image of virtue and cooperation. Yet the film ends on an ironic
reversal. Pitman escapes to reclaim his loot, but is fatally bitten by a rattlesnake in retrieving it. Lopeman discovers the body and the money, but
instead of returning it to Lomax, he rides off to Mexico where he will
apparently use these truly ill-gotten gains to finance a new life.

The connection drawn by the script between the two characters is
well conceived. Structured by that connection, the story makes an important, revisionist point about the west, where the line between virtue and
vice was often shifting. Unfortunately, the conflict between the two
equally good, equally bad guys develops too slowly to save the film from
the somewhat confusing muddle it has become by the time of the prison
break. Benton and Newman's conception, as Kenneth Hyman apparently
recognized, was excellent, but needed refinement and simplification.
Mankiewicz could not bring himself to prune the story of its distracting,
if interesting, secondary characters; his final cut ran 165 minutes, a length
that many exhibitors considered unprofitable, and 40 minutes had to be

excised for theaters to show the film. Thus, it is hardly surprising that the release version is marred by continuity problems. *There Was a Crooked Man*, in any case, remains one of the most intriguing of the new westerns of the period that witnessed a last flourishing of the western genre before it passed out of popularity, perhaps forever.

The Mankiewicz
Woman

by Cheryl Bray Lower

The films of Joseph L. Mankiewicz are a testament to his lifelong fascination with human nature, and in particular, his exploration of the diverse nature of Woman. Decades before feminism became a popular term in the lexicon, Mankiewicz valued the complexity of the female nature and understood the limitations society placed on women. Truly ahead of his time, in 1958 he noted in his personal diary that there were too few good scripts about women.[1] This was nearly 40 years before contemporary actresses began complaining of the scarcity of significant roles for them in Hollywood.

Mankiewicz created his greatest work during the conservative years of the postwar baby boom when motherhood and the home were revered, and happy endings were mandatory. Unlike many films dealing with women's issues, his work stands the test of time. His films endure because his female protagonists were given a literate, articulate voice to express their feelings and predicaments which are not so different from those women experience today.

The strong women characters in Mankiewicz films expressed their displeasure at deriving power from the hands of men just as female protagonists do now. Many wanted to work when it was more socially acceptable to be in the home. Some wanted to explore the world without the shackles of a male companion. And a few wanted it all—a career and a marriage and a family, some 50 years before this was a lifestyle taken for granted. Most importantly, the Mankiewicz female protagonist had a voice. Equipped with his gift for clever dialogue, she was able to express her dissatisfaction with the way things were, and to articulate her dreams for the way things should be.

Joseph L. Mankiewicz developed a reputation for working well with strong women when he was a writer-producer at Metro-Goldwyn-Mayer in the 1930s. Not only was he put in charge of nine Joan Crawford films, but he also collaborated with one of the only female directors on the lot, Dorothy Arzner, in *The Bride Wore Red* (1937). He was also given the ominous task of producing a film that starred a woman considered box office poison by theatre owners, Katharine Hepburn. The resulting project, *The Philadelphia Story* (1940), revitalized her career. But perhaps his greatest contribution to the transformation of the women's picture from a "weepy" to a "battle of the sexes" farce came when he introduced Hepburn to his friend Spencer Tracy. Soon after, he paired the two screen icons in their first of many collaborations, *Woman of the Year* (1942). Once he moved to 20th Century–Fox to pursue his long-awaited career as writer-director, Mankiewicz capitalized on his reputation for working well with strong women to bring to the screen many memorable performances of women who questioned their roles and the gender limitations placed upon them by the times. His most memorable work during these years produced some of his greatest awards: *A Letter to Three Wives* (1949) and *All About Eve* (1950) won him back-to-back double Academy Awards for screenwriting and directing in two consecutive years—a feat which has never been equaled.

Mankiewicz was a student of the psyche. His early academic interest in psychiatry never left him as he pursued a career in filmmaking. At the base of every Mankiewicz film is an examination of human behavior. Because of this strong interest in trying to understand what makes people tick, the films of Joseph L. Mankiewicz are character-motivated, not plot-driven. And he is at his best when he uses his mordant wit as a tool for commenting on societal manners and mores.

The mark of a Mankiewicz film is its biting satirical dialogue. Some of his films have been criticized for being static and having much too much dialogue, but it is through this dialogue that the psychological depth of the character is exposed to the viewer—especially the female character.

Captivated by the multifaceted behavior of women, Mankiewicz found writing for and about them infinitely more satisfying than writing about men:

[Women are] fantastic creatures put together by the wind. Men are simple. Simple component parts. They're raised to conquer something, to be rich, to win something. Women, by the time they're six years old know that physically they're no match for that fellow, that person over there with the different physical build. So that at the age of six they must find other ways to get what they want. And each one is different, and each one has a separate scheme, and they begin to develop their little tricks, their little wiles, and it's fascinating. My God, there's nothing I want to write about more.[2]

During the early years of his career as a writer-director, the clever Mankiewicz knew that the only way he could make a film about a strong woman who questioned societal dicta was to be accommodating to the Production Code Administration. He learned to live within the MPPA guidelines that extolled the virtues of marriage and motherhood (all the while tacitly limiting women's power by keeping them in the home) by exercising his skill for high comedy. By using witty dialogue, he enabled his strong female characters to verbalize their displeasure with cultural conventions in a palatable form of social satire. But even with such a pro-female writer-director as Mankiewicz, the conservatism of the Hollywood studio system usually prevailed, and his strong women inevitably succumbed to patriarchal prescriptions through the inevitable return to the conservative status quo—via a happy ending.

Even with the accommodations Mankiewicz had to make to get his films produced, he created some of Hollywood's most memorable women who are as interesting today as they were 50 years ago. What survives the generations is Mankiewicz's appreciation for the complex nature of a woman's struggle to find her own identity in a conservative patriarchal culture. While he did not resolve the conflicts that women faced in the postwar years, he did address them and voiced unusually astute opinions as to the struggles a woman faces when she oversteps the bounds of her societal role. It was not until the 1967 film, *The Honey Pot*, that he created a female protagonist who not only challenged but triumphed over a male-dominated system.

Mankiewicz films are good material for feminist analysis because he created strong women who were more complex than the one-dimensional stereotypes that abounded in the Hollywood films of the forties and fifties. This is not to say that he did not create his share of stereotypes, but they are few in number and usually in supporting roles. One such stereotypical creation enabled Marilyn Monroe to resurrect a faltering career when he cast her as Miss Caswell in *All About Eve*. In a part that capitalizes on the dumb-blonde stereotype, Monroe played a dimwitted actress fresh from the "Copacabana School of Dramatic Arts." But the majority of the women in his films are too complex to categorize.

How would one characterize the Linda Darnell character in *No Way Out*? Is she simply poor white trash? How is she able to come to understand the plight of a black man in a white person's world when she spends her life with a man who is a hateful bigot? Or take the Peggy Cummins character in *The Late George Apley* (1947). Is she just a rebellious young woman in a stodgy Boston Brahmin household who does not want to marry the man her father has chosen for her? Or is she a model of the turn-of-the-century progressive movement? Another example of a woman in a historical setting is the young widow, Lucy, in *The Ghost and Mrs. Muir* (1947), who refuses to capitulate to the demands of her late husband's family and strikes off on a life of her own making.

What makes Mankiewicz films so impressive to the woman viewer is that he succeeds in giving these diverse female protagonists a voice — a rare situation in a patriarchal culture, let alone from a male writer-director. He does this through a gifted use of cutting, highly intelligent dialogue. Typically, the strong woman in a Mankiewicz film works within the patriarchy while vocalizing her displeasure with the system — pushing the envelope to attain what other women traditionally have not gained. His women characters are not so much post–Rosie the Riveters or protofeminist archetypes, but overreachers with sharp tongues and strong desires. Except for Edie Johnson (Linda Darnell) in *No Way Out* (1950) and Maria Vargas (Ava Gardner) in *The Barefoot Contessa* (1954), Mankiewicz's female protagonists are in a position of wealth and prestige which enables them to question the gender restrictions of the patriarchy. (In *No Way Out* it is Edie's compassion that empowers her; in *The Barefoot Contessa* it is Maria's beauty and talent that give her power.) In his comedies, Mankiewicz uses moral outrage and indignation as tools for his female protagonists to express their displeasure with the system.

One need only look to his first film as a writer-director to see the pattern of a strong woman emerging from the confines of societal expectations. In *Dragonwyck* (1946), Miranda Wells beseeches her father to let her leave home to seek an adventurous life far away from the family farm. With support from her mother, Miranda persuades her deeply religious father to let her go because she believes it is God's will. Not only must she convince the male in the family that she has unusual urges to experience more of the world than a woman should, but she must explain this to her sister as well:

TABITHA (Miranda's sister): I'm sure there isn't anything *I* want that I can't find right here. *I'm* not anxious to leave my home.

MIRANDA: That's not fair! You know I love you and Pa, all of you, and my home. It's just that—well, I try to be like everybody else and want what I'm supposed to want—but then I start thinking about people I've never known and places I've never seen— maybe if this letter hadn't come—Oh, I don't know, I must be loony.

In *Dragonwyck* we see Mankiewicz establish a formula that he will continue to use throughout his career—that of a strong female protagonist who questions society's prescriptions for women, all the while knowing that she must indeed live within that same conservative society. His female characters grow stronger and more clearly defined throughout his years as a filmmaker—from the youthful Miranda in *Dragonwyck*, driven by naiveté, to the Machiavellian Eve Harrington in *All About Eve*; from the sensual powerhouse of Maria Vargas in *The Barefoot Contessa*, to the most memorable woman in history in *Cleopatra* (1963). But it is in his next-to-last film, *The Honey Pot*, that Mankiewicz encapsulates all the strong women who have come before—and this time one of them succeeds in beating the system.

The Ghost and Mrs. Muir

The Ghost and Mrs. Muir continues the Mankiewicz theme of a strong woman who confronts a conservative establishment. Unlike *Dragonwyck's* heavy, moody atmosphere, with its evil male protagonist, *The Ghost and Mrs. Muir* is a light-hearted romance with an appealing leading man.

The woman's picture genre that was so popular during the war years was designed to give wives of soldiers a little romance while their men were away. As cathartic an experience as these films were for women who expected their husbands to return from the war, light-hearted romances could be very painful for the young wife who had learned that her husband had died in battle. *The Ghost and Mrs. Muir* is a film for all who love romance, but it is an especially apt film for a young widow who must learn to live life on her own. The mystical nature of the film's love affair between a living woman and a dead man—whether real or fantasy—serves as an entry into the world of the imagination—the world of what could have been, and indeed, what might be.

Fantasy films with ghosts as pivotal characters were in vogue in the forties. *Here Comes Mr. Jordan*, the award-winning 1941 film starring

Robert Montgomery, was followed by the equally successful Frank Capra film, *It's a Wonderful Life* (1947). 20th Century–Fox produced its contribution to the genre in 1946 with *The Ghost and Mrs. Muir* which reunited director Mankiewicz with screenwriter Philip Dunne and producer Fred Kohlmar just a few months after their successful collaboration on *The Late George Apley*.

Following *Dragonwyck* and *Somewhere in the Night*, Mankiewicz took a self-imposed hiatus from writing and directing, to hone his skills as a director. *The Ghost and Mrs. Muir* was the second of three films he would direct based on screenplays by like-minded, east-coast intellectual Philip Dunne. Based on the novel by R. A. Dick (a pseudonym for author Josephine Aimee Campbell Leslie), *The Ghost and Mrs. Muir* lends itself to the ongoing interest Mankiewicz had in exploring the nature of strong women. It bears a faint resemblance to *Dragonwyck* in that it is a historic romance with an overreaching female protagonist. Unlike *Dragonwyck* however, *The Ghost and Mrs. Muir* does not concern itself with issues of classism but rather looks at death, change, and progress—also how one woman copes with these things—all packaged in a charming romance.

For nearly a year, the young widow, Lucy Muir, and her eight-year-old daughter, Anna, have lived in mourning with the mother and sister of her late husband. Within the first scene, Mankiewicz and Dunne unveil Lucy as an overreacher as she attempts to explain to her in-laws why she needs a life of her own making:

> LUCY: Please don't think I'm not grateful! You've both been so very kind to me. But I'm not really a member of the family, except for marrying your son. And now he's gone and I have my own life to live, and you have yours, and they simply won't mix. I've never had a life of my own. It's been Edwin's life—and yours—and Eva's. Never my own.

By shifting from dependent to independent woman, Lucy takes her first step as a challenger to the conservative status quo.

In moving away from the family, Lucy, like Miranda in *Dragonwyck*, strives to establish life on her own terms. Unlike Miranda, though, she is not whisked away into the lap of luxury. Lucy must learn to fend for herself once her meager inheritance dries up.

With the casting of Gene Tierney as both Miranda in *Dragonwyck* and Lucy in *The Ghost and Mrs. Muir*, it is as if Mankiewicz were exploring two different avenues of choice for women of this era. While both characters choose to leave the comfort and security of a known family environment, Miranda is seduced by the luxury of what she never had and loses sight of herself as she falls under the spell of a handsome man. Lucy Muir, on the other hand, gives up the economic security of her husband's family because she wants to end her dependent state. Lucy is ready to change—to end her mourning and strike out on a life of her own. Her eventual seductions are complementary to her needs, not challenges to her freedom.

In the first event in her new environment, she is confronted by a person who views her as incapable of making a decision because she is a woman. Her real-estate agent, Mr. Coombe—a stuffy, single-minded man—refuses to take her opinions seriously as she looks for a place to start her new life:

> LUCY: This house. Gull Cottage. It's exactly the sort of place I'm
>   looking for.
> COOMBE: Gull Cottage. Oh, no. It wouldn't suit you at all....
> LUCY: Why shouldn't it suit me?
> COOMBE: My dear young lady, you must let me be the judge of
>   that....
> LUCY: But if *I'm* going to live in the house, *I* should be the judge!

Mankiewicz delivers an amusing reversal of gender stereotypes when, in one scene, Coombe, the gruff male (who knows the cottage is haunted), is more frightened at the thought of encountering a ghost than is the seemingly delicate young widow.

Often overlooked by his critics, the visual skill employed by Mankiewicz is very convincing in this film. Especially well done is the introduction of the ghost. A high contrast shot illuminating only the face in a portrait creates the illusion of someone in suspended animation—a vision—a free-floating specter in a darkened room. This image is as startling and transfixing to Lucy Muir as it is to the filmgoer, and it successfully introduces a mystical aspect, not only to the character of the sea captain, but also to the film itself.

The underlying motif of *The Ghost and Mrs. Muir* is the issue of a woman struggling to find her own way in a world that prescribes that women should be passive, dependent, and attendant to matters of the home. The film specifically addresses the concept of private versus public spheres—and which is socially acceptable for women to inhabit. The conflict for Lucy comes when she realizes that she needs more than motherhood to feel fulfilled. In a brief encounter with her maid, Lucy expresses the frustration she feels at being confined to the private sphere:

LUCY: I feel so useless. Here I am nearly half-way through life, and what have I done?

MARTHA: I know what I done. Cooked enough beefsteaks to choke an 'ippopotamus....

LUCY: You've led a very useful life, haven't you? And I have nothing to show for all my years.

MARTHA: And I suppose Miss Anna is nothing?

LUCY: Heavens, I can't take any credit for *her*. She just happened.

Once Lucy verbalizes her need to be productive, she begins her journey to self-actualization, and in this process she encounters the ghost of Captain Daniel Gregg.

Other than the portrait, no personification of the ghost is evident until an umbra darkens Lucy's body as she naps in her bedroom. Mankiewicz quickly shifts the camera's point of view from omniscient observer to that of someone inspecting the room—and Lucy in particular. This scene mimics an earlier event in which Lucy stared at the portrait of the captain. However, in this scene, the inert image that serves as the object of the gaze is Lucy. Mankiewicz makes the object of the gaze both male and female in *The Ghost and Mrs. Muir*—a distinctively different approach than in most films of this era in which the female is traditionally the passive recipient of a man's aggressive eye. To further this dual-gaze perspective, the ghost must become real and endowed with stereotypical masculine traits to play against Mrs. Muir's femaleness.

The difficulty with this type of mystical-romance-comedy is how to introduce a ghost as a character that should be taken seriously. Initially, Mankiewicz toys with ghostly stereotypes when he introduces the sea captain as a prankster who delights in blowing out the matches Lucy uses to light a darkened room. Once the ghost determines that he and Lucy have a similar appreciation for his former home, he transforms from games-player to thoughtful coinhabitant of Gull Cottage.

A distinctive conflict in reading this film arises by the very nature of the movie itself. If viewed simply as a romance, the viewer must suspend disbelief only long enough to enjoy the camaraderie and banter between the two handsome stars. However, if one perceives the romance as an allegory, then Lucy's relationship with the captain becomes less of a romance with a ghost-man than a love affair with her own excitement at growing into independent womanhood. In this type of reading, the ghost becomes Lucy's alter ego. She learns from him what it is like to be a man in a man's world because she imagines herself in his place. She begins to talk like him and eventually writes a biography of what she imagines his life to have been. And thus her dream of the ghost serves as her door into the public sphere—the man's world into which she has no other entrée.

The ghost serves as an enabler for Lucy when she encounters obstacles to change. When her in-laws arrive to tell her that she is penniless, they find a different woman than the one who once lived in their home. Captain Gregg's derogatory words (heard only by Mrs. Muir) become Lucy's words as she tries to have two conversations at once: one with her nagging relatives who believe that she has lost her mind because she is talking to herself, and the other with the cantankerous ghost who will not keep quiet. This comic interchange underscores the brilliance of the Mankiewicz-Dunne collaboration in which humor is used to serve up a meaty message in a palatable form. It also illustrates the polarity of the gender debate among women themselves. Lucy is seen as a threat to these women because she makes them examine their own lives. Just as we saw in *Dragonwyck*, Mankiewicz once again highlights an unfortunate aspect for the overreaching woman—she is often dismissed as being crazy, even by members of her own sex.

Music and images of the sea are as vital to *The Ghost and Mrs. Muir* as are its characters. Mankiewicz combines Bernard Herrmann's masterful score with lengthy shots of the sea in its various states from roaring waves to gentle undulating tides to give nonverbal clues to Lucy's state of mind throughout the film. Not only does the sea serve as fodder for Captain Gregg's reminiscences of his exciting life but it becomes a metaphor for Lucy's quest. The sea is a symbol of the life Lucy has never been allowed to live, one of adventure, danger, and mystery.

As Lucy documents Daniel's life for the book, *Blood and Swash*, she is offered a glimpse into a world of freedom to do and be whatever one pleases. Mankiewicz creates an alliance of masculine and feminine traits during this creative process as Daniel's gruff exterior softens (allowing Lucy to correct his errors in speech) and her mild-mannered language becomes enriched with phrases picked up from his salty speech. Each character gradually assumes the other's strengths, and their weaknesses subside. This is the true romance of the story—the enchantment with becoming a more complete self.

When the book is finished, Lucy feels a great sadness. Fearing the end of a romantic collaboration, she asks the ghost, "What is to become of us?" She is, in fact, reckoning with the loss of the creative side of herself. Daniel assures her that there is more to life than ghostly ruminations. He suggests that she deserves a real man, not simply a figment of her imagination. However, Mankiewicz and Dunne are not suggesting that Lucy return to a state of dependence, but rather that one must live with a foot in both spheres to appreciate life at its fullest. Now that she is about to enter the public sphere of commerce she must also explore the sexual side of her life to become a complete person.

When Lucy plunges into the public sphere, Mankiewicz again illustrates the gender prescriptions of a conservative society. In a challenge to her newfound self-awareness, Lucy encounters a handsome writer, Miles Fairley, who is more interested in her posterior than her psyche. Dripping with condescension, he stares at her figure while feigning interest in her work: "Is it a cookbook? I hope not another life of Byron. Or is it a book of dreams?" He is the human personification of Daniel, a charming man who finds her attractive, but his motivation for helping her is far from ethereal, as was Daniel's. Miles is interested in the purely physical, and thus challenges Lucy to explore the repressed sexual dimension of her character.

In Lucy's encounters with her publisher, Mankiewicz and Dunne cleverly illustrate how gender assumptions must be accommodated by a woman who chooses to step out of her prescribed societal role. To be taken seriously by the publisher who has seen hundreds of women's novels, cookbooks, and guides to proper manners, Lucy must present the book under the pseudonym, Captain X. (Not unlike our author, Mrs. Leslie, who used the androgynous name, R. A. Dick.) Convinced that he could not be interested in a book such as hers unless it were written by a man— because a woman is incapable of thinking like a man—the publisher concludes that her work must have been written by her absent husband. Rather than risking further financial hardship, she capitulates and pretends that she is merely the author's emissary.

Once the book is published, Lucy becomes financially independent, but this success in the public sphere comes at a cost: Daniel leaves her to learn of the world on her own. When she awakens from what seems to her to be a dream, she does not remember Daniel and yet feels an absence that she cannot understand. To fill the void she allows herself to fall in love with Miles.

Dunne and Mankiewicz create a self-serving male stereotype in the dashing Miles Fairley, and in so doing they restructure Lucy's character into a more traditional womanly paradigm where her quest for love overpowers her ability to see things clearly. In her romantic euphoria, she is blinded to the fact that Miles does not have her best interests at heart. He cares nothing for her beyond her being the object of his desire, and it is only when she accidentally meets his wife that Lucy is startled back into a cautious, asexual state where she lives the rest of her life.

The inevitable Hollywood happy ending that concludes the film has an ironic twist that brings the narrative full circle. As an elderly woman, Lucy prepares to take a nap in the same chair she was in when she was first seen by the ghost many years before. As she grasps a glass of milk (an apt image of motherhood and nurture), it falls to the floor, and she dies peacefully in the chair in her bedroom. Immediately the perspective of the camera shifts to the point of view seen earlier, from omniscient observer to someone watching Lucy. As a man's hand reaches out to awaken her, the image of a tired old woman is transformed into that of a vibrant young beauty, the image of Lucy as she looked when she first came to Gull Cottage. Daniel has returned to walk with her arm-in-arm out of the front door and into the mist.

In *The Ghost and Mrs. Muir* Mankiewicz, Dunne, and Kohlmar offered postwar spectators another in a long line of woman's pictures, but this time with more substance than meets the eye. Lucy dies a happy woman not merely because she is reunited with her lost love, but also because she has led a full, self-actualized life. The reappearance of the ghost of Captain Daniel Gregg is a reunion with the side of herself that Lucy lost: her imagination, perhaps even her spirit.

A Letter to Three Wives

Mankiewicz went on a self-imposed directorial apprenticeship following *Somewhere in the Night*, which he directed and co-wrote with Howard Dimsdale. By forgoing the duties of writing *and* directing, Mankiewicz allowed himself the luxury of honing his skills as a director. Over the next 18 months, he directed three films based on screenplays by Philip Dunne. *The Late George Apley*, *The Ghost and Mrs. Muir*, and *Escape* offered Mankiewicz the freedom he needed to concentrate on technical directing matters even though he no doubt contributed to the screenplay dialogue, as was his nature. When he returned to directing his own screenplays, he had not only a keener visual sense but also a confidence that allowed him to create the first of his masterpieces of high comedy.

A Letter to Three Wives bears the hallmark of a distinctly new style for Mankiewicz. This critically acclaimed film incorporates many of the elements that he admired in the sophisticated comedies of Ernst Lubitsch (clever repartee, sexual innuendo, and moral superiority) with the addition of his own special touch—that of using voice-over narration and well-developed flashbacks to give an added dimension to his satirical voice.

This film cemented Mankiewicz's position as a force in Hollywood. With it he won the first of his double back-to-back Oscars for writing

A scene from *A Letter to Three Wives* (1949) with (left to right) Ann Sothern, Linda Darnell, and Jeanne Crain.

and directing. (He won the same dual honors the following year for *All About Eve*. This feat of winning double back-to-back Oscars has never been equaled.) But more importantly, it returned him to the job he liked most—that of directing his own screenplays.

The *Cosmopolitan* magazine short story, "A Letter to Five Wives" by John Klempner, was later adapted to "A Letter to Four Wives" by Fox writer Vera Caspary. Mankiewicz honed the concept down to a succinct analysis of three marriages when he wrote the screenplay for *A Letter to Three Wives* in 1948. This would be his first film of manners and mores. Its focus is on the home and in it he tackles the subject of marriage in general, and women and men in particular.

Once again, he proves a powerful advocate for the concerns of women. Each wife is an overreacher who challenges the patriarchal status quo established by her husband. However, while Mankiewicz gave voice to a number of women's issues—which are as current today as they were

50 years ago, especially the difficulties of the professional woman—there was still a societal limit as to how triumphant these women could be.

A Letter to Three Wives is a satirical look at the well-to-do—the upper class *sans* white telephones but with real problems. The time is postwar America, Anytown U.S.A., where white picket fences outline finely manicured lawns and train tracks serve as the dividing line between the haves and the have-nots. It is the first Saturday in May. Three couples are preparing for their day, which culminates in the first dinner dance of the season at the local country club. Deborah and Brad Bishop, Rita and George Phipps, and Lora Mae and Porter Hollingsway are the good friends who will spend the evening together. The women begin this auspicious day, as they have most years, by assisting in a daylong outing for an orphanage. The men, however, are acting strangely. Brad, who always plays golf on Saturday, is off to the office for a meeting that may keep him away overnight. George, who always goes fishing on the first Saturday in May, leaves the house dressed in a blue suit. And Porter is seen running for a train at the station. It is not until the three women arrive at the boat dock for their outing that they learn that their friend Addie Ross will not be joining them. She sent her regrets, however, in a letter that is delivered to the pier just as the boat is about to depart which will strand the three women at a far-away locale for the remainder of the day. In her letter, Addie tells her dear friends that she will not be joining them today because she has left town—for good. And as a token of their endearing friendship, she has taken something to remember them by—one of their husbands.

Mankiewicz places these three perplexed women on the deck of a boat that is leaving the shore (and the only telephone) behind. He then masterfully redirects the film into a series of flashbacks as each wife ponders her marriage and whether it could be her husband who has run away with Addie Ross. This highly successful narrative device transfers the tension that each of the women feels to the audience, as they (and we) must wait until the evening's festivities to learn the truth.

Mankiewicz delivers more stereotypical types of "woman" than usual in *A Letter to Three Wives*, but he does so by pitting them against traditional male-types which allows the spectator to focus more on the marital relationships than the individual characters. There is the naïve country girl, Deborah, who has been transported from the shelter of the family farm to military service and then to high society by her marriage to Brad Bishop. Another wife is Rita, the sharp, assertive mother of twins who supplements her teacher-husband's income by working as a writer of radio soap operas. Lora Mae is the social climber who uses her beauty and brains to cross from the wrong side of the tracks to a life of wealth and position as the wife of a successful merchant. In supporting roles are Lora Mae's gambling-loving mother, Mrs. Finney, and her best friend, the astute Sadie, a plain-speaking maid who serves as the voice of reason for everyone she meets. Topping off this cast of characters is the unseen Addie Ross—the divorced woman who is the ever-present topic of conversation.

The husbands in this high comedy are thinly drawn but represent three distinctively different male stereotypes: the supremely confident businessman, Brad Bishop; the ardent admirer of all things intellectual, teacher George Phipps; and the myopic, self-made man, Porter Hollingsway. Each husband has had some long-standing relationship with the inimitable Addie Ross. Brad gave Addie her first black eye as well as her first kiss. The two were "a couple" before Brad went off to war. George and Addie have known each other since school when they starred together in a Shakespearean play. And Porter has a picture of Addie in a silver frame displayed prominently on the grand piano in his living room.

In what will become one of his signature devices, Mankiewicz employs a voice-over narration (Addie played by Celeste Holm) to link the three subplots. Even though the viewer never sees Addie, she is a dominant force in the film. Not only is she the impetus for the dramatic action but she serves as the model of the perfect woman—at least by the standards of the male protagonists.

Addie represents a fundamental paradigm in a patriarchal culture— the ideal woman. The husbands in *Letter* refer to her with near reverence as one who always does "the right thing at the right time" (Brad), one who is "generous to a fault," and who is complete with "taste and discrimination" (George), and the epitome of "class" (Porter). The fact that the wives see the divorcée as a conniving threat and a woman who ran off her own spouse, positions them as petty and jealous rivals in the minds of their husbands. Addie is eventually demythologized through Mankiewicz's flashback episodes that enable the spectator to see the depth of each wife's character, as well as the shallowness of the men's appreciation for Addie.

Mankiewicz initiates each flashback with a supremely effective aural device—the cross-fade or sound dissolve. As Deborah tries to forget her early morning spat with Brad over the dress he selected for her to wear that evening (which was a replica of one seen recently on Addie Ross), she listens dreamily as a young girl reads aloud a fairy tale. Reflecting on her own true life fairy story of marrying a rich and handsome man, Deborah's pleasant thoughts are soon disrupted by the repetitive chugging of the boat's engine. Instantly she recalls her fear that it might be her husband who has run away with Addie Ross. By merging the ambient sound of the engine with Deborah's nonverbalized anxiety (expressed by Addie's voice repeating over and over again in Deborah's mind, "Is it Brad? Is it Brad?..."), Mankiewicz initiates the first flashback.

Deborah recalls her first night home as a civilian following her military service. As a new wife to a fellow officer, she is transported to a new home in a new town to meet his friends at the first dinner dance of the season (with only one old mail-order party dress to her name). She is worried that she will embarrass her husband because of her simple upbringing. To calm her fears, Brad offers her a pitcher of martinis that she drinks with unaccustomed abandon.

Representing more than an outsider who does not fit in with the tight-knit group of friends, Deborah is a symbol of the postwar resettlement of members of the military—but from a female perspective. Just as thousands of soldiers struggled to reacclimate to civilian life, Deborah too faced the uncertainty of life after the war. However, she reentered society as an overreacher clinging to the coattails of her upper-class husband. In a military uniform a poor farm girl such as she looked no different from her aristocratic husband, but now she feels lost without this anonymity. And unlike her military experience, where she rose to the head of her class on ability alone, her reentry into civilian life returns her to a subservient position in the culture. Her past accomplishments are insignificant in this socially astute culture. Now she is simply known as the wife of Bradbury Bishop. The fact that her husband is one of the wealthiest members of his clique affords Deborah a more privileged status than most, but her naïveté undermines her efforts to fit in with Brad's lifelong friends—especially once she learns that everyone had expected him to marry his old sweetheart, Addie Ross.

Deborah's self-fulfilling prophecy of embarrassing herself at the dance comes true as she not only becomes nauseated from being spun around on the dance floor by her husband, but also her tattered dress rips to expose her bare midriff. To top off her fears of not fitting in with her husband's tony friends, she reenters the ballroom to find her husband on the terrace having a grand time with another woman, a woman of poise and distinction, who has stolen Brad's attention—Addie has arrived.

This thinly developed episode introduces the viewer to the three couples, as well as exposes the cross that each wife must bear—that of living up to each husband's view of Addie Ross as the perfect companion. Brad wants Deborah to look like her and so he recommends that she buy a dress he saw recently on Addie. George wishes that Rita would appreciate the fine arts as he and Addie do whenever they meet and discuss classical music. And Porter wants Lora Mae to possess the charm of the upper class that she lacks from having been born into poverty.

As with any Mankiewicz film, *A Letter to Three Wives* can be read from a myriad of perspectives. Issues of classism permeate this film. Not only does each wife pale in comparison to her husband's perception of Addie Ross as the standard-bearer of charm and distinction, but the wives themselves regard Addie's ideals as important for their own lives—if only for maintaining their husbands' interest in them. In the case of Deborah and Brad Bishop, Deborah sees herself as a second-class citizen because of her lowly upbringing and therefore follows the suggestions her husband offers regarding her clothing style. Porter Hollingsway, the nouveau riche merchant who worships Addie from afar, not only belittles his wife in front of her peers, but also reminds them that even though Lora Mae may look good, she is from the wrong side of the tracks. And Rita, the mother of twins, wife of a teacher, and hard-working scriptwriter, juggles all of these tasks in an attempt to move up the social ladder. She feels a need to earn a large income because Addie told her that her wages are "the most restful shade of green in the world."

One does not have to look far for Mankiewicz's opinion on the high culture-low culture debate. This is personified in the Rita flashback episode which evolves from a deliberate highbrow to lowbrow cross-fade. As Rita wonders whether it is her husband who has run off with Addie Ross, she hears Addie's voice in her mind posing the question, "Why didn't George go fishing? And why the blue suit?" These questions merge into the opening theme from Brahms' second piano concerto, but then the scene makes an abrupt cut to a nerve-rattling commercial jingle that blares out of the radio in the Phipps' kitchen.

The clash of cultures that emanates from the Phipps household in this flashback stems from the fact that Rita has taken a job working as a writer of maudlin radio soap operas. It is not that she is a working woman that bothers her husband the teacher; it is that she devotes so much of her time and energy to writing pablum for the masses. To top things off, she is so preoccupied with preparations for a dinner party for her boss that she has completely forgotten that it is her husband's birthday. (Addie Ross did not forget, however; she sent him a copy of the Brahms piano concerto with the note, "If music be the food of love....")

George Phipps (appealingly played by a very young Kirk Douglas) verbalizes what Mankiewicz surely must have heard every night at the dinner table while growing up in a home with a father who was an educator—that the intellectual is mocked and jeered as obsolete in a society that relies on popular culture for entertainment. In *A Letter to Three Wives*,

Mankiewicz spins a persuasive tale about the backslide of a culture that prefers to believe the overblown hype of radio commercials than to think for itself (not unlike how many view television as a corrupting influence today).

This is the first film in which Mankiewicz delivers what will become a *cause juste* for him throughout the remainder of his career—a primordial assault on pretense. "Pretending" is like nails on a blackboard to him, and the drone of his hissing can be heard whenever one of his characters pretends to be something he or she is not. Most eloquent in the delivery of his barbs is the maid, Sadie (Mankiewicz's alter ego played to perfection by Thelma Ritter). In a scene reminiscent of a Marx Brothers comedy, the sweaty and very plain-looking Sadie is forced to wear a French maid's uniform, complete with a frilly little cap, as Rita attempts to impress her boss and her milquetoast husband who have come to the suburbs for dinner to discuss a potential job for George. Rita instructs Sadie to forego her traditional announcement of "Soup's on!" for the more elegant "Dinner is served." As George plays his new Brahms recording for the bored guests, Sadie crashes into the living room, wrestling to keep the cap on her head with one hand, while removing a large screen that unveils the dining table with the other. She gives up the pretentious display and grumbles "Soup's on!" to the startled guests. As Rita and her guests come to the table, Lora Mae mocks Sadie's "dolled up" appearance, but Sadie quickly chides Rita in return for her lousy idea. The irony of this scene is magnified when Rita realizes that all of her attempts to impress her big city boss are for naught when Mrs. Manleigh abruptly jumps up from the table in the middle of the first course to run to the living room to listen to her soap operas for the remainder of the evening.

The deflated festivities end with a Mankiewicz diatribe on the evils of low-brow culture, which George delivers with vitriolic abandon:

> GEORGE: The purpose of radio writing ... is to prove to the masses that a deodorant can bring happiness, a mouthwash guarantee success and a laxative attract romance!... Don't think says the radio, and we'll pay you for it! Can't spell cat? Too bad—but a yacht and a million dollars to the gentlemen for being in our audience tonight.... Use our product or you'll lose your husband, your job, and die! Use our product and we'll make you rich, we'll make you famous.

George may loathe the low-brow business Rita is in but he admires her success, especially when it comes to supplementing his income. What he fears most is that he has lost the independent, understanding woman he married because Rita has turned into groveling sycophant to an employer driven by commercialism.

Mankiewicz clearly appreciated the complexity of the issues surrounding a working woman. He created a character in 1948 who struggles with the same concerns as women today who juggle the maintenance of a home and a family with a job that requires them to work late into the night. But what makes this episode more astonishing for its time is that Mankiewicz drew a portrait of an accommodating husband who encourages his wife's individuality. This forward-thinking vision is but one example of why this film has had the capacity to maintain the interest of an audience over the fifty years since it was first released.

The Rita flashback is the height of Mankiewicz's high comedy style in this film that has a decidedly serious undertone. Each wife is found wanting in comparison to her husband's ideal—Addie Ross. Addie's supposed grace and thoughtfulness, as perceived by the husbands, is a myth, and Mankiewicz reveals the sham in the end.

The third episode examines the sobering consequences of living a life based on pretense. The serious undercurrent of this section is masked by the humor provided by its salty characters. Mankiewicz sets up this flashback as Lora Mae tells Rita that she does not care whether Porter is the one who has left town with Addie Ross. She insists that she wrote her own fairy tale: a poor girl from the wrong side of the tracks marries a rich man and lives in luxury. The only problem with Lora Mae's story is that she did not live happily ever after.

Mankiewicz initiates the final flashback through a segue of dripping faucets as Lora Mae's thoughts turn from triumph to sadness as she ponders her loveless marriage. On the surface this dissolve makes for an elementary transition from the present to the past. It is only at the completion of the flashback that we realize that the dripping water represents Lora Mae's tears.

Lora Mae Finney is a beautiful young salesclerk who works for the local department store owner, Porter Hollingsway. She lives in a ramshackle house so near the railroad tracks that all activity must cease every time a train rumbles past. Mrs. Finney, Lora Mae's down-to-earth poker playing, beer-swigging mother struggles to keep up the payments on her refrigerator while looking after her two daughters. Lora Mae has intentionally caught the eye of Hollingsway, who has been known to court a number of his shop clerks. But she has a loftier goal than her colleagues who have dated the boss in exchange for a promotion. Lora Mae has no intention of being another one of Porter's playmates. She expects him to ask her to marry him.

Porter Hollingsway is Mankiewicz's most complex male character in *A Letter to Three Wives*, a lowbrow lout who uses his wealth in a vain attempt to buy status (and potential happiness) for himself. He adores Addie Ross because she has the one thing he cannot buy—class. But Porter is a simple man who espouses a primordial philosophy with a twist of self-centered chauvinism:

> PORTER: It's a man's world. Yeah. See something you want, go after it. Get it. That's nature. Why we were made strong and women weak. Strong conquer, provide for the weak. That's what a man's for. Teach our kids more of that and there'd be more men.

Ironically, Porter is incapable of recognizing that these same traits are what makes his wife appealing to him. Lora Mae epitomizes a gender-reversal of Porter's philosophy, illustrating just how far ahead of his times Mankiewicz was when he conceived this feminist character in 1948.

As the strong member of her family, Lora Mae envisions a better life for herself and her mother. To achieve this improved status she uses her wits and beauty to position herself to be noticed by the boss. After a few dates, complete with Lora Mae playing hard to get, Porter realizes that he has met his match in Lora Mae. He wants sex with a beautiful woman. She wants marriage with a rich man. He wants a class act like Addie Ross but cannot get his mind off the irresistible Lora Mae. She wants money and improved social status. What appears to be social climbing is actually Lora Mae's method of taking care of the weak members of her family—even at the expense of her own happiness.

Even though she appears to be unrelentingly manipulative, Lora Mae reveals a vulnerable side once she sees a picture of Addie Ross prominently displayed in a silver frame on the piano in Porter's palatial living room. She admits that she wants to be in the position of being the image in the silver frame. Not only does she want a luxurious life, she wants to get married. In this revelation we learn that Lora Mae is a gold-digger with a crack in her heart of stone. She craves the adoration that Porter expresses for Addie—not because Addie has what Porter calls "class," but because Porter worships her. In this instance, the image of Addie Ross as Man's Ideal also serves as a paradigm for Lora Mae. She wants to be worshipped and adored by Porter, as is Addie, but Lora Mae understands the real struggles of a life of poverty and is willing to sacrifice love for improved social status.

When Porter proposes to her, it is the least romantic moment in her fairy tale. Lora Mae gets what she wants but it is as warm and heartfelt as a business transaction. Mankiewicz concludes this episode as Lora Mae tells her mother that she and Porter are getting married. But instead of tears of joy in Lora Mae's eyes, there are tears of sadness because there is no talk of love—only collaboration.

As the film returns to the present, the boat docks and the women leave for home to learn the fate of their husbands. Lora Mae concludes that it indeed is Porter who has left town with Addie Ross because he is very late returning home. Mrs. Finney opens her daughter's eyes to Porter's love for her just as he walks in the door. Rita also finds George at home. It is only Deborah who learns that a woman has called to say that her husband will not be home this evening.

Keeping up the pretense that nothing is wrong, Deborah stoically attends the evening's dinner dance under the impression that everyone knows about Brad and Addie. It is only when Porter learns that Deborah believes Brad left with Addie Ross that he admits that it was not Brad who left town with Addie, but he himself. He changed his mind, however, and returned. Porter then turns to Lora Mae and announces that he has given her everything she could ever want, including evidence that she can use against him in a divorce.

Mankiewicz unmasks all of the pretense in the final scene as Lora Mae and Porter finally admit that they love each other and willingly forget the past to forge a new future. Addie Ross has been run out of town by the one man who most believed her myth. She is revealed as the home-wrecker that she is, and everyone lives happily ever after. But do they? Many spectators wrote to Mankiewicz after the film's release asking for clarification of the ending. Some believed that Porter's admission of infidelity was only a ruse to help the young wife, Deborah, make it through the night until she learned the truth the next morning—that Brad did indeed run away with Addie Ross. But that seems an unlikely analysis because of the film's final image in which Mankiewicz hones in on a tee-tering champagne glass which falls and cracks as Addie sighs in acknowl-edgment of her failure to snare her prey.

In *A Letter to Three Wives*, Mankiewicz turned a clever comedy of manners into an astute observation of marriage in suburban America. By focusing on three different types of wives—the naïve farm-girl who mar-ries an aristocrat, the career-girl, and the social-climber—he limits his analysis to those women who occupy a small portion of society: the upper class. And yet, just because these women reside in comfortable sur-roundings does not signify that their problems are less acute than those of women generally. The problems that these wives explore, that of being judged and found wanting against an unattainable obstacle—the male

perception of a "perfect" woman—is something that women in all strata
of society must endure. In a patriarchal culture that shapes the concept
of a woman as being inferior to man, the only way for a woman to achieve
status is through a man's conception of what she should be. Her assessment of her own worth is largely predicated on the values these generic
husband-types express—those of charm, taste, and class. When such
superficialities are valued more than integrity and a loving heart, most
women will come up short. Mankiewicz succeeded in demythologizing
the perfect woman—the "Addie Ross" type that looks good on the outside but is corrupt on the inside—by returning each husband's attention
and appreciation to his own wife. But he did not leave it at that. Through
his use of the flashback sequences, he enables each wife to reevaluate her
own life in light of trying to please someone other than herself. Addie
Ross may be the symbol of the perfect woman for the husbands, but the
wives realize that they conspired in perpetuating this stereotype by valu-
ing those things that Addie found to be crucial to living a good life—chic
attire, excessive wealth, and conspicuous consumption.

A Letter to Three Wives is the first of a series of eloquent studies of
postwar manners and mores by Joseph L. Mankiewicz. In it he merges
his bracing wit with a litany of serious themes that will appear many times
throughout the remainder of his career as he shifts from merely celebrating the overreacher to evaluating just what it is he or she is really trying to accomplish.

People Will Talk

Mankiewicz was nearing the end of his contract with 20th Century–Fox when he began work on *People Will Talk*, his eleventh film in
eight years with the esteemed studio. He would make only one more
film—*Five Fingers*—before abandoning Hollywood (and the studio system that had nurtured his career) to return to the East Coast to begin his
new life as an independent filmmaker.

People Will Talk was the third consecutive project that Mankiewicz
wrote and directed in collaboration with Fox production chief, Darryl
Zanuck, who served as his producer. This highly successful team created
the controversial *No Way Out* in 1949 (released in 1950), the award-winning *All About Eve* in 1950, and *People Will Talk* over the course of approximately 20 months.

Zanuck had been a strong, positive influence in Mankiewicz's career
ever since he offered the younger man the opportunity he had always

wanted to direct his own screenplays. Mankiewicz flourished during these years at Fox, undoubtedly due to his association—at the high point of his creative development—with the powerful Zanuck. But following Mankiewicz's great acclaim for *All About Eve*, Zanuck realized that Mankiewicz no longer needed his input to create a successful film. As Mankiewicz was writing the screenplay for *People Will Talk*, Zanuck abruptly fired off a confidential memo to the writer-director in which he said that he would not put his own name on the credits as producer. Even though Zanuck intended to act in the capacity of the film's producer, in effect, he was admitting to Mankiewicz that he was unaccustomed to playing a subordinate role in the filmmaking process. Since Mankiewicz would be making the most significant contribution to this film, just as he had with *All About Eve*, Zanuck believed that he would be relegated to a secondary role in the process—a position with which he was not only unaccustomed, but also most uncomfortable. He was ready to cut Mankiewicz loose. He noted that *People Will Talk* would have to flourish or flounder on the Mankiewicz name alone. But the recalcitrant tycoon soon recanted, and the name of Darryl F. Zanuck is boldly emblazoned on the screen as producer.

People Will Talk would be to the medical profession what *All About Eve* was to the theatre—a stinging critique of some of the system's weaker inhabitants. But Mankiewicz did not employ the narrative devices that made *Eve* such a fascinating exposé. There is no voice-over narration in *People Will Talk*, nor is there a flashback sequence. In this film, Mankiewicz delivers a straightforward tale about a holistic doctor who takes on a jealous colleague who represents a medical system concerned more with self-aggrandizement than caring for the needs of the patient.

Mankiewicz was always fascinated with medicine and wanted be a psychiatrist as a young student at Columbia. *People Will Talk* was as close as he would come to illustrating what he would have been like as a doctor. The screenplay is loosely based on a German play, *Dr. Praetorius*, by Curt Goetz, but Mankiewicz significantly reshaped the narrative into one that served his own interests. Having recently had a bad experience in a hospital emergency room where he felt as though he was being treated as a number rather than a person, he dedicated *People Will Talk* (as noted in the opening sequence of the movie) to the one, without whom there would be no need for doctors—the patient.

People Will Talk became another venue for Mankiewicz's biting wit; however, it is a much more serious film than its lighter moments suggest. He debunks the notion that the needs of the patient pale in relation to those of the medical provider. His protagonist, Dr. Noah Praetorius is a humanist—a holistic medical practitioner with the unorthodox philosophy that a patient should be treated with dignity. He varies his methods of treatment from prescribing medicine to doling out pieces of candy. But most often he simply lets his patients talk about their problems. Praetorius is another in a series of Mankiewicz protagonists who are significantly ahead of their times. He also serves as a surrogate for Mankiewicz—a doctor who advocates the healing powers of the mind.

One of the most astonishing aspects of *People Will Talk* is that it was made at all. How could such a film get by the censors in 1951—a film that deals with illicit sex, unwed motherhood, attempted suicide, *and* a transgressive woman who not only is *not* punished at the end of the film, but gets to marry the handsome leading man? The mystery of this even baffled Mankiewicz, who years later proclaimed that he believed it was simply an oversight that let the film slip through the cracks. However, he was being modest.

He had a highly developed skill for working within the confines of the studio system that included the Breen Office which had the responsibility for monitoring offenses to the Production Code. He was well aware of the fact that no film that undermined the censor's strict moral code would be released. He learned early in his career not to belabor trivialities with Code administrators unless he was confident that he would win his point. Coming on the heels of his spectacular success with two highbrow comedies, *A Letter to Three Wives* and *All About Eve*, everyone (including the Breen Office) was curious to know what the brilliant Joe Mankiewicz planned for his next project. To the surprise of Zanuck and Mankiewicz, Joseph Breen was very accommodating when he learned that Mankiewicz was adapting the German play for American audiences. As long as the screenplay had a strong voice of morality that objected to the actions of the transgressive female, Mankiewicz could proceed. Of course, it did not hurt that everyone's favorite matinee idol, Cary Grant, was set to play the lead.

The casting of Cary Grant as Praetorius was an inspired decision for Zanuck and Mankiewicz. The highly successful Grant was an established leading man known for his light romantic comedies. Mankiewicz knew him well from their work together on *The Philadelphia Story* at MGM. He was certain that Grant would bring to *People Will Talk* the same air of grace and elegance that he employed in his past projects. Grant's on-screen persona was so positive that Zanuck and Mankiewicz believed he would lend an air of moral uprightness to a screenplay that, at its outset, violated the Code in a number of ways.

The character of Noah Praetorius was a more completely drawn role than Grant had portrayed to date. It required that he combine his warmth and charm, well-known to all of his adoring fans, with a very serious, almost preachy demeanor. This was true because *People Will Talk* was a thought-provoking drama, even if Mankiewicz did lighten its heavy message with moments of high comedy.

The comedic elements in this film are more sophisticated than the screwball comedies in which Grant made his name. Unlike his roles in *Bringing Up Baby* (1938), *The Philadelphia Story* (1940), *Arsenic and Old Lace* (1944), or *I Was a Male War Bride* (1949), Grant as Noah Praetorius would traverse the emotional spectrum from being charming and compassionate to being philosophical and intensely serious. In this role he would need the subtlety he used so successfully in his role as Dudley, the angel sent to earth in *The Bishop's Wife* (1947). For the good of the film and the message that Mankiewicz wanted to convey, Grant succeeded in delivering one of his best performances.

The principal theme developed by Mankiewicz in *People Will Talk* is the dehumanization of the medical profession. He addresses this subject through a character analysis of two different medical practitioners/educators. The kindly Dr. Praetorius, a well-beloved doctor who operates his own clinic and teaches at a large American university, is pitted against his colleague, Prof. Rodney Elwell, a menacing rat-like, little man (played by the marvelous character actor, and close friend of Mankiewicz, Hume Cronyn). This is a classic confrontation between good and evil, where professional jealousy leads Elwell on an obsessive quest to unmask Praetorius' mysterious past. Elwell believes that the mystery can be solved once he unveils the identity of Praetorius' constant companion, Shunderson.

Although this film revolves around a male protagonist, Mankiewicz maintains his interest in issues that are of concern to women. Only a writer-director who delights in the complexities of women would create a doctor whose area of practice is gynecology. By deftly merging the Praetorius-Elwell conflict with a female-related subplot of romance (and its consequences), Mankiewicz creates a fresh adult comedy that is of interest to both sexes.

The most controversial dimension of *People Will Talk* is its transgressive woman—the pregnant, unmarried female protagonist, Deborah. Mankiewicz knew that he needed a strong voice of morality to overcome the objections from the Breen Office about this aspect of the film. Instead of creating a morally righteous voice in any one character, Mankiewicz endowed Praetorius and his friends (Barker and Higgins) with such strength of character that their goodness rubbed off some of the tarnish of Deborah's sins. Since men were the arbiters of the Production Code, it appears that the Breen Office was mollified by the uprightness of these male characters—at least enough to distract them from the fact that Mankiewicz did not punish (or kill) the transgressor in the end. Not only did she get to live, she got to marry the handsome hero—quite a feat for 1951. No other film during the Production Code years allowed for such transcendence as experienced by Deborah in *People Will Talk*. Perhaps the comparison of the film's final trial scene to the real life HUAC hearings was enough to keep the Breen Office distracted.

Art certainly imitated life in the witch-hunt atmosphere of *People Will Talk*. Because of Elwell's obsessive quest to brand Praetorius as a heretic and have him dismissed from the medical school faculty, many historians have seen this film as a metaphor for the Congressional hearings into Communism in the film industry which were occurring at the time of the picture's release. But any correlation was purely coincidental, and not because of anything specifically done by Mankiewicz. He simply adapted the original trial scene from the Goetz play to his screenplay. A self-professed apolitical man, Mankiewicz was more concerned with expressing his discontent about the current practice of medicine than commenting on the HUAC hearings. However, the irony of a HUAC parallel pales in comparison to the even starker but still coincidental mirroring of an event that was occurring in Mankiewicz's own life.

Mankiewicz was derailed from his writing schedule on *People Will Talk* when Cecil B. DeMille launched a campaign to have him recalled as president of the Screen Directors Guild over a controversy concerning the mandatory signing of a loyalty oath. Mankiewicz found himself in a heated battle with the aging Hollywood icon who struggled to maintain a conservative stranglehold over Guild policy. But DeMille lost the battle as the majority of the Guild lined up behind Mankiewicz. Mankiewicz insisted, throughout the remainder of his life, that this was just another strange happenstance of fate. But it is difficult to believe that some of his feelings about the autocratic DeMille did not seep into his creation of the Elwell character. (Goetz named the antagonist "Spiter" in his play. Mankiewicz changed the name to Elwell which can easily be read as "ill-will" or "e-vil.") And just as the calculating Elwell detested Praetorius, and tried to have him fired from the school's faculty, so too did DeMille attempt to undermine Mankiewicz's position in the Guild because he represented the end-of-an-era for DeMille and his conservative cronies.

People Will Talk unfolds as a conventional narrative. The mystery of Shunderson and Praetorius' past is interwoven with the story of the transgressive woman, Deborah Higgins. The new style employed by

Mankiewicz, which began with *A Letter to Three Wives*, favored nonlinear narratives that employed flashbacks and voice-over narrations to help the viewer understand the motivation of the protagonist. In *People Will Talk*, however, Mankiewicz crafts a linear narration with no narrator that might prevent the characters from speaking for themselves.

He interweaves two plotlines: the Elwell vendetta against Praetorius; and the tale of young Deborah Higgins and her eventual romance with Praetorius. Deborah is another strong woman in the Mankiewicz *oeuvre*. However, unlike many of his films in which the woman's point of view is dominant, *People Will Talk* is not Deborah's story. Her issues are relevant only as they apply to the sympathetic male protagonist.

Besides the clever selection of the affable Cary Grant, Zanuck and Mankiewicz created a cast that was stellar (with the possible exception of Jeanne Crain as Deborah—an actress with whom Mankiewicz was not fond of working, even though he had agreed to her selection by Zanuck). Finlay Currie is mesmerizing as Shunderson, the ever-faithful shadow of Dr. Praetorius. Cronyn delivers a memorable performance as the jealous Elwell. And in the small supporting role of Deborah's father, Sidney Blackmer is sensitive without being weak. But the delight of the film is Walter Slezak as Praetorius' good friend, Professor Barker, a bass-playing physicist who provides some of the film's most lighthearted moments.

Well known for his films of high comedy, Mankiewicz could not let a movie with such gifted comedic talent go by without taking advantage of their skills. He created memorable scenes of lightness which serve to illustrate the depth (or shallowness) of character of the participants. The first is the most remarkable because he was able to add an element of humor to an exceedingly nasty scenario, thanks in large part to audience expectation.

As Elwell prepares to overthrow Praetorius, he meets with a collaborator who is willing to reveal the good doctor's past. This co-conspirator, a Miss Sarah Pickett, is the gruff former housekeeper of Dr. Praetorius. In an inspired casting choice, Zanuck and Mankiewicz chose none other than the Wicked Witch of the West—Margaret Hamilton—to play the prudish Miss Pickett. In an absurd sequence, the dowdy maid is more concerned about the propriety of keeping the door open to Elwell's office than she is about passing along fallacious information that could destroy a man's career. Through this device, Mankiewicz illustrates the pettiness of Elwell's quest by exposing the absurdity of the characters involved in his plot.

A "character" in *People Will Talk* that gets no special screen credit is a piece of music. Mankiewicz employs Brahms' "Academic Overture" (with an extended sequence featuring the traditional collegiate anthem, "Gaudeamus Igitur," whose title translates as "Therefore Let Us Rejoice") as a symbol of camaraderie, academic unity, and love of life. This is a decidedly highbrow element, but the choral tune is so well known that Mankiewicz must have suspected that it would bring an air of triumph that would foreshadow the film's finale. He also uses the music as an avenue for another light interlude as Praetorius conducts (enthusiastically, but not very skillfully) a university orchestra comprised of medical students and faculty members. In this scene, Mankiewicz illustrates that Praetorius' love of music is akin to the exuberance with which he practices medicine. This episode also allows Mankiewicz to illustrate the Praetorius view that laughter is the best remedy for an ailment—whether a musical calamity or an issue of physical illness.

The ease with which Mankiewicz moves from the comedic moment in the orchestra rehearsal to the intensely serious exchange between Barker and Praetorius which follows is masterful. As Barker warns his friend Praetorius to beware of incurring the wrath of Elwell, Mankiewicz briefly inserts a touching exchange between two strong male characters who openly express their affection for each other. It is rare for such a genuine expression of male friendship to be witnessed in the films of this era (unless in a war setting).

Perhaps the most poignant and yet oddest element in *People Will Talk* is the character Shunderson (also known as the "Bat" because of his stealth-like movements). A tall, hulking, slow-witted individual who rarely talks to anyone other than Praetorius, Shunderson may be the man of mystery who focuses Elwell's curiosity, but it is Shunderson's unfaltering allegiance to Praetorius that most provokes the loner Elwell.

In another HUAC-related framework, Shunderson can easily be misread as a symbol of "the Communist menace" that shadowed the leftist Hollywood inhabitants of the day. However, this character was actually a creation of Curt Goetz, and not a Mankiewicz statement on the times. In the context of this film, Shunderson is a metaphor for unconditional love. He is bound to Praetorius because the doctor brought him back to life. He appears to be a slow, plodding Frankenstein-like creature, but Shunderson is no monster. He is a gentle man with a profound capacity to understand the troubled soul. The most touching example of his intuitive instincts occurs when he calms a ferocious dog that frightens Praetorius. Not only does Shunderson stop the dog's barking, but also he recognizes that the dog is hated by his owner. He calms the beast; and it never leaves his side. Only Shunderson is capable of knowing that if the one is treated like a monster one often complies with the expectation.

By pitting Elwell against Praetorius, Mankiewicz metaphorically presents his belief that the medical profession was becoming more focused on its own issues than with treating the concerns of patients. The choice of the inclusion of the triumphal rendition of "Gaudeamus Igitur" in the final scene encapsulates the Praetorius approach to healing—that life is fleeting and we should cherish the time we have on this earth rather than preoccupy ourselves with petty concerns.

In *People Will Talk*, Mankiewicz created a film that advocates a respect for life and a compassion for all human beings. By portraying serious adult issues in a lighthearted manner, he succeeded in making an enjoyable piece of entertainment coupled with a strong message about the dehumanization of the medical profession. The viewer of this delightful film will eagerly swallow Mankiewicz's medicine when it is laced with such delightful candy coating.

The Barefoot Contessa

Perhaps no other Mankiewicz film debunks pretense and duplicity more than *The Barefoot Contessa*, his first film as an independent producer-writer-director. Like so many of his colleagues who delighted in scrutinizing their own industry, Mankiewicz took this opportunity to unmask some of Hollywood's most despicable denizens; yet he goes further in this film than to simply carp on the industry's failings. He cleverly combines his assault with a cynical variation of the Cinderella story in which he convolutes the ending, leaving the viewer with a bitter reminder that success does not always bring happiness—in Hollywood or real life.

After establishing himself as a master of high comedy, it is curious that Mankiewicz would make such a dark, tragic film as *The Barefoot Contessa* for his first independent project. Perhaps it was due to the years he spent as a producer at MGM, a job he despised because he believed he was not allowed to use his creative talents to the best of his ability. In *The Barefoot Contessa*, he unleashed his pent-up frustrations about an industry controlled by callous men with money to burn, but who lacked taste and imagination.

Unlike the biting wit he delivered in *All About Eve*, his first critique of the entertainment world, *The Barefoot Contessa*, is a gravely serious work that is devoid of the sense of humor that makes most of his films masterpieces. That is not to say that Mankiewicz does not explore humorous aspects of individual characters in *Contessa*, such as the smarminess of the ever-sweaty public relations agent, Oscar Muldoon. But for the most part, the tragic overtones of *Contessa* consume the viewer's attention.

The voice of wisdom in it is Harry Dawes (played by a particularly well-cast, world-weary Humphrey Bogart). Dawes is a longtime Hollywood writer-director and a recovering drunk, who, like Faust, thinks he has to sell his soul to the devil to live happily. Dawes tolerates the abuse he receives from his metaphorical demon, the producer Kirk Edwards, because he believes that filmmaking is his only outlet for creative expression. Unlike the Mankiewicz surrogate in *All About Eve* (Addison DeWitt), Dawes is not an effete snob who lords it over others to maintain his sacrosanct status. Rather, Dawes is a gentle man who simply uses his wits to keep afloat. He is an older, more downtrodden version of Mankiewicz (except for the alcohol), who knows that he has to work within a system permeated by insufferable lowbrows. That Mankiewicz would invent a Harry Dawes at this midpoint in his career illustrates how depleted he must have felt from working most of his life beholden to superiors whom he did not respect or trust. Yet this was his opportunity to express himself without studio constraints, and in the Dawes character, Mankiewicz reveals much about his working style.

The Barefoot Contessa is a seemingly simple story made complex by the depth of Mankiewicz's disdain for pretense. The film begins with the wealthy business tycoon-turned-independent producer, Kirk Edwards (a character seemingly based on Howard Hughes) scouting for a new face for his first film. Along with his unctuous publicist, Oscar Muldoon, and writer-director Harry Dawes, Edwards travels to Madrid to see the beautiful nightclub dancer Maria Vargas. Unimpressed by Edwards and Muldoon, Maria refuses their offer to make her a big Hollywood star. Only when Harry is told that his job depends on getting her to cooperate does he attempt to persuade Maria to leave Madrid for a screen test. She agrees because she is a film fan and admires Harry's work, but she has one stipulation—that Harry consent to help her become a good actress, not just a movie star. Harry becomes the Fairy Godfather to Maria's Cinderella in this cinematic fable as he takes her under his wing to help her navigate the treacherous waters of Hollywood stardom. He also helps her deal with Edwards' personal agenda—to acquire her as a sexual companion and then, perhaps, make her a star.

Because Harry's interest in Maria is not physical, she feels free to confide in him about her troubled past as a poverty-stricken child in the Spanish Civil War. To protect herself during the frequent bombings she hides wherever she can find shelter and calms herself by digging holes in the dirt with her bare feet. Cowering in the earth until the attacks stop, she distracts herself with visions of a future better life as a rich woman who can afford to buy exquisite shoes. As she grows older, Maria needs more than just the dirt to comfort her, and she turns to the arms of many different men. However, even after the war is over, whenever she feels afraid, she removes her shoes, digs in the dirt with her bare feet, and looks for a man to make her feel secure. Seeing her dependency as a sickness, she cannot tolerate this trait in herself or others. By leaving Madrid for a life in Hollywood, Maria believes that she can buy those expensive shoes she dreamed about, and control her sickness as well as those who tried to control her. Rather than making love to the wealthy man who directs her career, she continues to shed her shoes to fall into the arms of lower-class workers who remind her of home. Eventually, she discovers that impersonal sexual liaisons are not enough for her; she yearns for her Hollywood fairy tale life to begin another chapter. The Hollywood Cinderella wants a Prince Charming to sweep her away from the evils of her false existence. Until then, she seeks solace from any man who allows her to shed her star persona to be her true self.

Except in the case of Harry, with whom she has a trusting, platonic relationship, Maria despises the sterile falseness of the men in Hollywood, who, like Kirk Edwards, fawn over her beauty and use her as a trophy in order to perpetuate the myth of their virility. When she abruptly leaves Edwards and Hollywood to travel with the wealthy South American, Alberto Bravano, she falsely believes that Bravano will care for her as more than a possession. Unfortunately, she quickly learns that Bravano, who appears to be a man of honor, is no different than the controlling Edwards. Even though she has freed herself from the falsity of her Hollywood life, Maria is expected to comply with the demands that Bravano places on her. This shattering discovery plunges her into further despair. It is only after she steals money from him to give to one of her poor lovers that she is awakened from her enslavement and whisked away to safety by a knight in shining armor, the nobleman, Count Vincenzo Torlato-Favrini.

To Maria's utter amazement, Vincenzo does not know who she is. She is finally allowed to shed the mask she donned for stardom to return to her real self. She has found her prince. Unfortunately, the count has a hidden agenda. As the last in the Torlato-Favrini line, Vincenzo wants a beautiful countess to adorn the picture-laden walls of his villa. He may be Maria's Prince Charming—a man who loves her for herself, marries her, and offers her comfort and security—but he fails to tell her one important thing. He is impotent.

Maria is the most blatantly sexual creature in all of Mankiewicz's films, and quite something for 1954 when the Production Code Administration still demanded allegiance to its conservative dictates. In *The Barefoot Contessa*, Mankiewicz again created a transgressive, overreaching female protagonist who succumbed to the structural confines of a conservative patriarchal society. In Maria, Mankiewicz crafted a strong woman who uses her sex appeal to gain fame and fortune, all the while despising that she has to live a false life. Yet she constantly breaks free from this pretend existence to experience carnal pleasure in the arms of men who do not care that she is a star. These men want her for her body, which she gladly exchanges for a few moments of tenderness, although she yearns for the traditional satisfactions that a loving husband and children can provide.

The myth of Maria's duplicitous existence is that neither Maria D'Amata, the movie star, nor Maria Vargas, the sexual animal, are allowed to succeed on their own terms in a patriarchal culture. The reason is that Maria does not realize she is the prize in a male-driven contest that will not allow for her wishes to come true. She wants to be a free-loving, sexual woman *as well as* the wife of Prince Charming, *and* control her own destiny. The inevitable clash of desires does not bode well for such an overreacher.

The casting of sex goddess Ava Gardner as Maria was a curious one for the award-winning Mankiewicz, who was accustomed to working with stars who had considerable acting talent. Gardner was known for her beauty, but not for her skill before the camera, having given many one-dimensional performances as grasping femmes fatales in the films noirs she was regularly cast in during the forties. Mankiewicz and his independent production company, Figaro, Inc., searched for an "unknown" for the part of Maria but jumped at the chance to cast Gardner when she expressed an interest. No doubt, Mankiewicz was persuaded that Gardner's own life of poverty as a child in rural North Carolina, and her meteoric rise to success in Hollywood, would contribute to her understanding of the part of Maria.

The Barefoot Contessa is framed by images of death that portend the outcome of Maria's quest. The circular narrative opens with a shot of mourners at a cemetery in a pouring rain. The only image of Maria we see is carved in stone. A statue in glowing white marble portrays her as the object of the gaze—handsomely attired and yet, surprisingly, barefoot. Even in death, she is deified for her ice-cold beauty. Only through Mankiewicz's trademark devices of extended flashbacks and voice-over narration do we learn how the young Maria came to such a tragic end.

Mankiewicz tells the story of Maria from the perspective of three men—Harry Dawes, Maria's friend and confidant; Oscar Muldoon, the obsequious publicity agent who "creates" the star, Maria D'Amata; and Maria's Prince Charming, her husband, Count Vincenzo Torlato-Favrini, who steals her heart and soul and then uses them to perpetuate his own myth.

The first flashback is from Harry's perspective. It serves, as do all of Mankiewicz's similar devices, to introduce the characters and to establish the mythical underpinnings of the film. Harry tells Kirk Edwards the tale of Faust, which unmasks Harry's unfortunate opinion of himself and constructs a cynical framework for Maria's Cinderella-like tale. Harry is the Mankiewicz surrogate in *The Barefoot Contessa* as he opines on the failings of Hollywood and rationalizes why he tolerates them. He is drawn from Mankiewicz's own experiences, merged with qualities of his recently deceased brother, Herman (well known for an impressive intellect compromised by prodigious binges). An unlikely hero, perhaps, Harry is the only one with a sword of valor to defend the helpless maiden, Maria. It is hardly surprising that he can hardly succeed at the task assigned him.

Through the Dawes character, Mankiewicz hints at how he succeeded at garnering good performances from his actresses. Not only does Dawes treat women with respect but also he fashions himself as psychically attuned to their concerns. He is proud of his witch-like sixth sense; this, he believes, makes him a good writer-director since he sticks to his intuition about human behavior (a distinctly Mankiewiczian trait that he proudly prized).

Maria does not speak for herself in the film. It is only through the memories of Harry Dawes that we develop an understanding of the dilemma that the beautiful Maria faced as the object of male fantasy. Years before the first feminist scholar articulated the concept of woman as the object of the gaze, Mankiewicz portrayed this idea on film.

From the opening shot of the statue of Maria on a pedestal to the following nightclub scene, he positions the camera as the surrogate of the spectator, who worships an image simply because it is sexually alluring. The nightclub episode is the most visually powerful scene in *Contessa*, not only because it positions Maria to be viewed through the eyes of others, but because Mankiewicz propels the images with an acceleration which matches the ever-quickening clicks of Maria's castanets and the cheers of the excited spectators. The reaction shots cut quicker and quicker, the music moves faster, and the final cheer from the crowd produces a psychosexual climax. This masterful opening posits Maria, the performer, as the object of the fanciful eyes of the gazing spectators. Through the crowd's reaction we "see" Maria—even though Mankiewicz does not show her dancing. The first time we actually see her is when Harry notices her bare feet hiding behind a dressing room curtain when he unmasks her charade of "talking" to her "cousin." He confronts her—a fiery beauty who is as astute about human behavior as is he. It is only after Maria learns that Harry is not interested in her sexually that she and he enter into a mutually beneficial friendship.

Ava Gardner is strikingly beautiful in this first Mankiewicz film in Technicolor. She is most convincing in her acting when she shrugs off the beauty queen image to reveal a vulnerable side, as when she admits to Harry that her sexual cravings are a "sickness," and that she hates sick people. In this revulsion of her own acts, Maria extols the precepts of a patriarchal culture as actualized in the Production Code where a woman is not allowed to explore her sexual nature. Or if she does, she must be labeled as aberrant *and* punished for her transgression. That Maria is proud of the fact that she has never been "bought" by any man redeems her enough for the film to continue, but in the end, this overreaching woman cannot be allowed to survive lest her unorthodox behavior seem endorsed, albeit tacitly, by the Code administrators.

In the second flashback Mankiewicz shifts the perspective from the morally upright Harry Dawes, to the high-strung obsequious public relations agent, Oscar Muldoon (in an Academy Award–winning performance by Edmond O'Brien). Not only does Muldoon take over the narrative, but he shifts the perspective from Dawes' sympathetic understanding of Maria's plight to a scathing commentary on pretense, which demythologizes both Hollywood and the International Set.

As a Hollywood mythmaker, Oscar's job is to transform the barefooted Maria Vargas into a properly adorned (and shod) screen star, Maria D'Amata. His career depends on perpetuating Maria as the object of the gaze, and it is only when she shatters this illusion that Oscar is forced to examine the falseness of his trade.

When her long-suffering father murders her cruel mother, Maria does not wait for Oscar to cover up the horrible event that may ruin her career. She simply boards a plane for Madrid to defend her father without a thought that it may create a negative image in the press. Oscar is so confounded by the positive public reaction to Maria's support for her father that he begins to question his professional motives as well as those of his boss, Kirk Edwards, who controls Maria like a marionette.

Mankiewicz never fails to use his films as a forum for his firmly held opinions. In *The Barefoot Contessa,* he not only mocks the principles that govern his own industry, he also takes a stab at the pretentious

International Set—those roaming idles whose conspicuous consumption and inbred festivities he abhors. But his diatribe would be more effective if he had not lost his sense of humor. Instead of exploring the paradox of Oscar's invective against these swinging lovers of the good life as the ultimate irony—a professional mythmaker being stymied by wealthy professional pretenders who live life based on pretense just as he does— Mankiewicz seems content to have Oscar simply rant on about the superficiality of the international vagabonds.

Oscar is an interesting Mankiewicz character. He personifies the shrewd salesman-like falseness of a promoter and yet Mankiewicz endows him with an almost child-like naïveté when it comes to real life. On one hand, Oscar is simply a leech who looks for the plumpest vein to suck out an existence. Yet Mankiewicz also allows him to comment on the shallowness of his own profession by being confounded when someone acts with integrity and honesty.

In the Oscar flashback, Maria is no longer the object of the gaze; she is the beautiful toy of a wealthy playboy, the outward emblem, he thinks, of his superiority to like-minded peers. Maria leaves Kirk Edwards and Hollywood behind in the false belief that her departure from the film business will bring her happiness. But then she is confounded to learn that the suave Bravano is just like all the other men she has known; he too believes she can be bought with lavish environs and fancy gifts. Like his name suggests, Bravano gallantly saves her from embarrassment at the hands of the surly Kirk Edwards. Yet he is not the knight in shining armor she had hoped for when he proposed she leave Hollywood to travel the world on his yacht.

After demythologizing Hollywood and the glorious pretenders of the International Set, Mankiewicz returns to his fairy tale by introducing Prince Charming to Cinderella. But a happy ending is not in the cards for Maria. Her prince fails to tell his passionate Cinderella how his body has been devastated by war wounds that have rendered him incapable of fulfilling her desires.

In *The Barefoot Contessa*, Mankiewicz first espoused one of his primary philosophies of life. Dawes speaks for Mankiewicz when he reflects that reality may occasionally mimic a B-movie. But just when we begin to think that we are masters of our own fate, reality rears its ugly head, and we learn the hard way that "life louses up the script." Mankiewicz's fractious dealings with the Production Code Administration over the film's story and themes proved the truth of this philosophy.

He originally envisioned the Count as a homosexual whose secret life would be the unspoken reason that the Torlato-Favrini lineage was about to die out. But he knew that the Breen Office would never allow him to pursue this theme, so he changed the cause of Vincenzo's impotence to humiliating wounds suffered in a war. Mankiewicz firmly believed that this weakened the impact of the film, but he knew that the Code administrators would not otherwise approve it. Unfettered, he could have made an even more powerful statement about another "type" of man: one who uses a sexually alluring woman to perpetuate (or perhaps even create) the myth of his masculinity.

Maria's fairy tale existence crumbles when she realizes that, once again, she is a pawn in the mythmaking agenda of men. But believing that she is the true master of her own destiny, she tries to reshape her life into one that satisfies her needs.

Even though she is devastated by Vincenzo's admission of impotence, she still loves him, and wants to do what is best for him. In a convoluted rationalization that she is giving him what she thinks he wants most, Maria gets pregnant by another man so that Vincenzo's family line will not die with him. But "reel" life rears its ugly head and louses up Maria's carefully crafted script. Only Harry understands what Maria cannot—that the male code of honor will be destroyed once Vincenzo learns that Maria has been with another man. Believing she knows her husband better than Harry, Maria runs to tell him that she will give him an heir that will continue the Torlato-Favrini line. Harry tries to warn Maria but arrives too late to save her. The Count has shot his wife and her lover before Maria has an opportunity to deliver the news. Vincenzo will go to prison with his honor intact even though his lineage will now not survive him. As a testimony of his wealth and taste (and perhaps also of his foolishness), he leaves behind a sculpture of the beautiful countess.

In *The Barefoot Contessa*, Mankiewicz not only demythologizes Hollywood but also deconstructs the concept that a woman exists only to please a man. Here he gives life to another in his long line of strong female protagonists who fall victim to patriarchal strictures. Maria is the ultimate object of the gaze: a woman who is never allowed to merge her real self with the image that men perceive of her. She is a token of Kirk Edwards' success, an expensive good luck charm for the rich playboy, Bravano, and a beautiful museum piece for Torlato-Favrini. The irony of *The Barefoot Contessa* is that only one man appreciates her dilemma, understands her needs, and yet does not disturb the delicate balance between mythic goddess and sexual animal. And that man can never truly satisfy her because he is Maria's *platonic* companion and confidant, Harry Dawes (a.k.a. Joseph Mankiewicz).

The tragedy inherent in this film is not that the beautiful Maria dies in the end, but that she was never allowed to live. Plagued by a 1950s conservative patriarchal culture that demanded acquiescence to a man's ideal of female perfection, an outgoing, transgressive woman was a mockery of one of its cardinal rules. A woman may adorn and serve a man but not act like one, and she most certainly cannot express the sexual side of her personality and expect to live life on her own terms. In *The Barefoot Contessa*, Mankiewicz, unwittingly and yet profoundly, addressed the constraints of these rigid postwar dictates that Hollywood espoused as gospel through the Production Code. The ultimate tragedy of *The Barefoot Contessa* is that such an overreacher as Maria, a woman who longed to live a completely realized life as a person with goals, ambitions, and sexual needs, was already dead before the first shot was fired.

Cleopatra

> Due to enormity of material in this four-hour epic,
> this essay will concentrate on the Mankiewicz vision
> of Cleopatra as a strong woman protagonist.

It is no wonder that Joseph L. Mankiewicz was the first person Elizabeth Taylor recommended to replace Rouben Mamoulian after he quit as director of *Cleopatra*. Respected for his keen understanding of women, and for skillfully depicting the intricacies of the male-female relationship, Mankiewicz was a natural to take over the film that Fox was banking on to resurrect its failing studio. Besides, Taylor was most eager to work again with Mankiewicz following their recent collaboration on *Suddenly, Last Summer*.

Mankiewicz was on a working holiday in the Caribbean when he received a frantic call from 20th Century–Fox President Spyros Skouras, imploring him to save *Cleopatra*—a film that was already seriously behind schedule, and well overbudget. Skouras begged his friend to discontinue his work on the screenplay, *Justine*, just long enough to take over where Mamoulian left off.[3] The script was written, the sets were built, and the cast was ready to go. Surely, Skouras believed, it would not take more than a few months of Mankiewicz's time to wrap up the film, and then he could return to *Justine*.[4] But Mankiewicz was reluctant to abandon his work, especially at the thought of taking over another director's film.

Desperate to finish *Cleopatra* (to save his job as well as well as to produce a film that would buoy a studio drowning in debt), Skouras would not take "no" for an answer. He pleaded with Mankiewicz—calling it a matter of life and death. Skouras was prepared to offer him anything he wanted as incentive to take over the floundering film.

The desperation Skouras faced was characteristic of the anxiety felt by many of the heads of major studios in the late fifties and early sixties. They all had watched their profit margins decline because once faithful filmgoers were staying home in droves to watch the new medium of television.

Major studios that once took their audiences for granted were scrambling for film projects that would entice viewers out of the comfort of their living rooms and back into the movie theatres. Their job was to supply a product that would surpass what could be seen on the small screen. They relied on technical advances such as Technicolor, 3-D, and wide-screen cinematography to pique the viewer's interest. Only a large-scale spectacle, with a cast of thousands, opulent sets, and gorgeous stars would keep the audience coming back. Unfortunately for the studios, the cost of producing such blockbusters was staggering.

While film studios could sustain a loss on a small-budget project, it was the big-budget monstrosities that could make or break them. Even the major studios that were considered indestructible were at risk of collapsing under the financial strain. *Cleopatra* was just one of the blockbusters produced by 20th Century–Fox during this era, but it was the most expensive because it started production with the dubious distinction of being the first film for which the star was paid a one million dollar salary.

When Elizabeth Taylor signed on at then such an exorbitant sum, in 1959, the press and the public took notice. But this was just the beginning of the massive amount of attention this film would garner before it premiered four years later. Issues surrounding *Cleopatra* would stay on the front page of newspapers throughout the world during most of its production.

Skouras, producer Walter Wanger, and its megastar Elizabeth Taylor, all knew that the critically acclaimed Mankiewicz would be an asset to their floundering project. Even though it was against Mankiewicz's better judgment, Skouras persuaded him to take over the film by making him an offer that he simply could not refuse. Not only would Mankiewicz earn a tremendous salary, 20th Century–Fox bought out his production company, Figaro, Inc., and gave him a share of the film's profit.

Even though Mankiewicz had a successful working relationship with the film's star, Elizabeth Taylor, and was pleased at the idea of working with her again, he knew that he was not a "blockbuster" filmmaker. His best work was close, small ensemble projects in which dialogue was more important than the setting. With *Cleopatra* he would be stepping out of his element—not only working on a spectacle of immense proportions, but working with a cast that he had not chosen and a script with which he was unfamiliar. Not willing to risk his reputation with so many variables, he took over the production, but only after negotiating a contract that would enable him to write as well as direct the film. This turned out to be one of his wisest decisions—but also one of the most debilitating.[5]

Thoroughly displeased with his predecessor's conception of a Cecil B. DeMille–like *Cleopatra*, filled with feline symbolism, overblown sentimentality, and preposterous pomposity, Mankiewicz persuaded Skouras to scrap the 12 minutes that Mamoulian had put on film and allow him to write his own screenplay based on historically valid resources. Reluctantly, the Fox board of directors granted its permission, knowing that their action would further delay a project that was overdue and over-budget. But having faith in the skills previously demonstrated by Mankiewicz, they allowed him to proceed with the work as he saw fit. In February 1961, he recast the male leads and began writing his own screenplay.

Contrary to his predecessor's script which portrayed Cleopatra as a virginal young girl waiting to be deflowered by the god, Caesar, Mankiewicz stamped his mark on the project by depicting Cleopatra as a cunning and intelligent young queen who flowers into maturity as the world's most powerful and provocative woman. For Mankiewicz, only such a strong woman would be capable of conquering the hearts of two of the ancient world's most powerful men. Drawing on the historical works of Suetonius, Plutarch and Shakespeare, Mankiewicz contributed a psychological study on what motivated Cleopatra to achieve such dominance.

By letting the star, her elegant costumes, and lavish scenery provide the glamour and the glitz that a blockbuster required, Mankiewicz could concentrate his writing on what interested him most. For him, it was Cleopatra's mind that was as interesting as her body.

Joseph L. Mankiewicz envisioned *Cleopatra* as a film in two parts: "Caesar and Cleopatra," followed by "Antony and Cleopatra." In Part I, he introduces Cleopatra as a beautiful young woman who knows how to use her mind as well as her body to achieve what she wants most in the world—political power and authority.

Confident of her status as Queen, Cleopatra tolerates Caesar's incessant references to her as "young lady," but she draws the line at being treated as an inferior:

CLEOPATRA: Caesar, it is essential that we understand each other—
only through me can you hope to escape from the desperate
situation in which you find yourself.[6]

Mankiewicz develops an interesting metaphor as a means of displacing the gender inequity between Caesar and Cleopatra. Throughout Part I, the Roman Empire and Egypt become representations of Male and Female. Where Rome is instilled with masculine traits of strength and dominance, Egypt represents feminine maternalism.

Rome (Caesar) has the authority to intercede on behalf of Egypt (Cleopatra) to end its civil war, remove her inept brother from the throne, and establish her as the country's sole ruler. In exchange, Egypt will supply what Rome lacks to feed and support its army—grain. But even though Mankiewicz was an ardent admirer of strong women, he would not deign to rewrite history. And history has shown us that even the most powerful woman in the world could only attain greatness from the aid of a strong man:

CLEOPATRA (to Caesar): Shall we agree, you and I, upon what Rome
really wants—has always wanted of Egypt? It's the old story.
Roman greatness based upon Egyptian riches. You shall have
them all. And in peace. But there is only one way. My way.
Make me queen.

By transforming what could have become a battle of the sexes rivalry, Mankiewicz turns the relationship between Caesar and Cleopatra into a beneficial alliance—a type of hunter-gatherer relationship in which each country (and its ruler) needs the other to achieve success. By framing Caesar and Cleopatra foremost as representatives of their respective countries, Mankiewicz eliminates the obligatory patriarchal power struggle between male and female; he thus allows Caesar to see Cleopatra as a worthy head of state who must be returned to power if he is to achieve his goals.

Acutely aware of the difficulties a woman faces in a male-dominated political arena, Mankiewicz illustrates how Cleopatra is no different from any other women who rises to a position of authority in a patriarchal culture. She is ridiculed for displaying the same traits that men value in other men:

AGRIPPA (to Caesar and Rufio): Reputed to be extremely intelligent,
and sharp of wit, Queen Cleopatra is widely read, well versed
in the natural sciences and mathematics. She speaks seven

languages proficiently. Were she not a woman, one would consider her to be an intellectual.

To drown out what surely would have been groans from the women in the audience, Mankiewicz strongly counters these misogynistic comments. He directs Rex Harrison (a splendid Julius Caesar) to appear distracted and unconcerned by his men's insults. In so doing, Mankiewicz tacitly debunks the myth of woman's inferiority to man.

Part I of *Cleopatra* is most successful when Mankiewicz juxtaposes the traditional male-female characteristics of the two protagonists.

Cleopatra enters as an obsessed, would-be ruler who wants to reclaim her throne at any cost (including the death of her brother). However, Mankiewicz transforms these masculine-dominant traits into more traditional female-nurturing behaviors once she witnesses Caesar's epilepsy. But Mankiewicz does not stop the gender-bending with Cleopatra. His Caesar seems less a conqueror preoccupied with war and political domination and more an aging ruler who doubts his own strength.

By transposing each character's strength into vulnerability, Mankiewicz explains how Cleopatra and Caesar grew from competitors into lovers, with each strong ruler concerned with the welfare of the other. What begins as a male-driven political power struggle turns into a female-style support system.

Even though Part I is confined to the story of "Caesar and Cleopatra," it drives the entire film. Here Cleopatra is indelibly portrayed as a complex woman with an intense political ambition, as well as an utter devotion to Caesar.

The cinematic highlight of the film is Cleopatra's triumphant procession into Rome, in which Mankiewicz mounts a spectacle's spectacle—one that would have made Cecil B. DeMille proud. Not only is this scene successful for its audience appeal, but it serves as a tangible expression of Cleopatra's political savvy, demonstrating how knowledgeable she is, not to mention how capable she is of using her feminine beauty to captivate and conquer the enemy.

Cleopatra's acumen merges with her beautiful appearance in the entertainment she arranges to introduce herself (and Caesar's son) to the people of Rome, who have long been wary of the Egyptian queen's power over their beloved Caesar.

Preceded by examples of everything Egypt has to offer the Roman Empire—from noble trumpeters on horseback to rushing chariots; from belly dancers to Nubian warriors; from archers to doves of peace—Cleopatra enters Rome atop an enormous Sphinx drawn by hundreds of

Egyptian slaves moving in tandem to a mighty pendulum of metronomic precision.

This awe-inspiring scene captivates not only the diegetic world, but also those in the audience who have read countless accounts of the exorbitant costs of the film. On-screen, director Mankiewicz mingles shouts of joy with star-struck silence. Offscreen, Mankiewicz gives the filmgoers what they have been waiting for—an eye-popping, wide-screen extravaganza that is mesmerizing to behold.

Once the podium carrying the Egyptians is brought down from on top of the Sphinx, the Roman crowd watches in awe as Cleopatra and her son Caesarion move to greet Caesar. It is only when she bows to honor Caesar that the crowd erupts into shouts of joy. This scene juxtaposes the ruler with the subject—the dominant male with the subservient female. In this bow Mankiewicz mirrors a prior scene when the mighty Caesar kneels before Cleopatra once she is declared queen of Egypt. In the procession scene, however, once the crowd begins to shout its acceptance of Cleopatra, Mankiewicz offers a double entendre for Caesar and the theatre audience. As Cleopatra rises, she winks at Caesar. This bit of 1960s kitsch is better understood in light of the tremendous apprehension that surrounded the release of the film. With the Romans representing the film audience, Elizabeth Taylor's wink signifies that all the hype was worth the wait. But, more importantly, within the diegesis, Cleopatra's wink indicates to Caesar that they are equal and know what is best for each other.

It is a shame that the film did not stop with Part I. Mankiewicz was clearly at his best developing the female character. Once Caesar dies, Marc Antony takes his place—in Rome and in Cleopatra's bed, and the film's focus shifts from a political analysis of Cleopatra's motivation to a psychological one of Marc Antony's.

No doubt the second part of the film was exactly what audiences wanted to see—an on-screen representation of the love affair that filled the newspapers for months before the film's release. Art definitely imitates life in Part II of *Cleopatra*. In real life, Elizabeth Taylor and Richard Burton met, and began and carried on a torrid love affair while making the film. Newspapers and magazines overflowed with lurid details of their dalliance. Their romantic hijinks made for an interesting dynamic on film since Part II of the movie is the story of the love affair of Antony and Cleopatra.

Unlike Part I of the film, where the relationship between Caesar and Cleopatra evolves out of mutual respect for each other's political and intellectual skills, Part II offers a battle of the sexes as Antony and Cleopatra strive to conquer one another.

Mankiewicz explores the relationship between Antony and Cleopatra as an evolution from a sort of sibling rivalry to an obsessive love affair that clouds each protagonist's political savvy. But even though Part II is a more traditional love story in which the male seeks to dominate the female, Mankiewicz is not finished toying with gender reversals.

While Cleopatra retains the strength and determination she displayed in Part I, in her relationship with Antony she is no longer the young devotee that she was with Caesar. She now sees herself as the political equal of Antony, and the second half of the film emphasizes the discomfort Antony feels at being seen as any woman's equal.

Cleopatra begins her relationship with Antony well aware of his reputation as a womanizer. Initially clear in her resolve, she restates her opposition to his dominance:

> CLEOPATRA (to Antony's general, Rufio, who beseeches her to come to Rome to meet Antony): I do not intend to join that long list of queens who have quivered happily at being summoned by Lord Antony.

In Cleopatra's refusal to be considered a pawn of Antony, Mankiewicz foreshadows the necessity for Antony to modify his stance if he is to have a relationship with this powerful woman.

When Antony refuses to go to Egypt to ask for her help for Rome, an emissary is dispatched to ask Cleopatra to come to Antony. With Caesar dead, Cleopatra is keenly aware that her strength lies in Egypt, and if there is to be a meeting, then Antony can come to her just as the mighty Caesar once did. The only way around this stubbornness is for Cleopatra to devise a strategy that will enable them to meet in a way that will not diminish either of their sovereign images.

In another amazing spectacle, Cleopatra arrives in Tarsus on her golden barge, but to the chagrin of Antony, she refuses to leave the boat, claiming it as Egyptian "soil," no matter where it might dock. Antony must come to her if he is to seek the riches his country needs.

He comes aboard to be met by a radiant Cleopatra bedecked with a gold necklace made of coins imprinted with the image of Caesar—the man he seeks to replace in her mind and heart. After Antony is unsuccessful in his attempts to seduce Cleopatra, Mankiewicz creates an elaborate scene in which the Roman is mocked for his weaknesses—women and liquor. Round one in the battle of the sexes goes to Cleopatra.

It is only after he has been ridiculed that Antony reasserts his manhood. He thunders past Cleopatra's guards, enters her bedchamber, shreds the curtains that surround her bed with a sword and makes love to her—thus reclaiming his position of power. This blatant exhibition of male dominance is furthered by the phallic image of his sword, which Mankiewicz employs throughout the remainder of the film as a symbol of Antony's strength or weakness or both.

Once in the arms of Antony, Cleopatra transforms into a tender, loving woman who shifts her preoccupation with her political agenda to fulfilling his desires. She continues to rule Egypt with power and might, but now he is at her side. However, she becomes increasingly aware that he does not endorse the goal, shared by Caesar and her, of Rome and Egypt united, ruling together in peace.

Mankiewicz interjects another clever, gender-bending scene that symbolizes Antony's increasing weakness. After learning that he has refused to meet with his Roman generals to discuss the discord in Rome, Cleopatra seeks out her lover, only to find him enjoying a bath. By depicting him as naked and vulnerable, Mankiewicz makes her strength all the more evident. Antony's reluctance to leave the comforts he has found in Egypt to return to Rome only furthers his dependence on Cleopatra, who must make the decision for him—that he return to fight Octavian for power.

Part II begins with Antony's attempt to make Cleopatra subservient to his desires. That she mocks his weakness only furthers his need to dominate her, as when he rips the coins of Caesar off her neck and makes love to her. As the film proceeds, the deeper Antony falls in love with Cleopatra, and the more he becomes politically impotent. Even the needs of his compatriots are of no concern to him once he lives for her love alone.

It is this shift in focus from Cleopatra's strength to Antony's weakness that dulls the film. The dynamism of Part I, inherent in Cleopatra's political goals and her alliance with the mighty Caesar, becomes insipid in Part II as Antony's character falters and Cleopatra's political aspirations fade. The love story that drives the second half of the film pales in comparison to the fervor of Cleopatra's ambition in Part I.

Her strength of purpose invigorates Caesar, yet this same strength weakens Antony. In the second half of the film, she must establish herself in a more traditionally female subordinate position in order to empower Antony. Mankiewicz skillfully reveals that it is Cleopatra's strength, not her weakness, that allows her to sacrifice her position of dominance to buoy the sagging confidence of the man she loves.

Cleopatra realizes that Antony must leave her and return to Rome in order to forge a closer alliance between Octavian's Rome and her Egypt. And she is willing to sacrifice Antony for the good of her country. It is only when he marries Octavian's sister in an ill-conceived attempt to make an ally out of his most powerful rival that Cleopatra's jealousy erupts. She has not only lost her alliance with Rome; she has lost her lover to another woman's bed.

As Mankiewicz understands the character, Cleopatra experiences stereotypically female fears of abandonment; these fears are energized, however, by a masculine urge toward destruction. The director reintroduces the sword imagery that he used when Antony bedded Cleopatra for the first time, but reverses gender roles this time by putting the sword in the hands of the enraged woman. She slashes Antony's clothes and stabs at the bed the two lovers shared, more with the power of a mighty warrior than the passion of a lover scorned.

By continuing to fuse her male and female traits, Mankiewicz makes Cleopatra more interesting than the one-dimensional Antony. He remains hopelessly incapable of seeing what Cleopatra has to offer him. It is only when he returns to Egypt as a supplicant to solicit funds for Rome that he becomes aware of just how limited his understanding is:

> ANTONY: What has angered you? Jealousy or politics? Which?
> CLEOPATRA: Both. And damn you for not understanding either.
> ANTONY: It would not occur to me to look to you for instruction.

He is incapable of learning from a woman. His male pride prohibits him from developing into a complete person as Caesar did with Cleopatra.

Mankiewicz uses this argument as a turning point for Cleopatra. In what becomes a pivotal moment of gender reversal, she vows that love will never again be her master. With this statement, she returns to a dominant position relative to Antony and resets her political agenda as her primary concern. Now she demands a portion of the Roman Empire as well as marriage to Antony as a means of securing her own happiness. When Antony accepts Cleopatra's conditions, he subordinates himself to her authority. Eventually such subjugation not only diminishes his political strength but deprives him of his manhood. Now it is he who is mastered by love.

Cleopatra emerges as an emasculating woman in Part II of the film, not so much by her actions, but by Antony's servile acceptance of his subordinate role in her political agenda. The crowning blow to his manhood occurs when he abandons his comrades, in the middle of the battle of Actium, to run after Cleopatra's ship as it leaves him and the fighting behind.

By running from responsibility, Antony actually delivers the crowning blow to his own manhood. It is not something Cleopatra has forced upon him; rather, it is his choice. He has become subservient to his obsessive love for her—only in her can he find his reason to live. In this quest to reunite with her, he relinquishes his honor and his self-respect as he abandons his compatriots to chase after her.

In what follows, Mankiewicz replaces the Male (responsibility) as the dominant trait in Antony, with the Female (dependence). Instead of the juxtaposition being liberating and enriching, as it was for Caesar, it is devastating for Antony.

Once aboard Cleopatra's boat, Antony suffers a crushing symbolic blow of emasculation. Acting on Cleopatra's orders, Apollodorus demands that Antony turn over his sword for fear that he will kill himself once he realizes that he has abandoned his troops. Nothing Cleopatra can do to explain her actions can ameliorate Antony's sense of having committed the final blow to his manhood—a cowardly act:

> CLEOPATRA (groveling at Antony's feet): They told me you were dead.
> ANTONY: They were quite right. I am dead.

Only by returning to a subservient position can Cleopatra resurrect her beloved Antony. Even though she is aware that he will die in the process, she willingly sacrifices the man she loves to an honorable death rather than let him live in such a diminished capacity. She encourages him to battle Octavian's forces in the manner he sees best.

On the surface, her selfless act of sending her beloved Antony into battle reconstitutes the male-female balance. Going to war infuses him with life, and Mankiewicz again girds him with his sword. This act restores his position as an able warrior and renders Cleopatra subservient to his wishes. But, in fact, Mankiewicz is signifying that it is only because of her strength that she is able to make such a sacrifice.

Unsuccessful at dying an honorable death in battle, the dejected Antony returns to Cleopatra's palace only to be misinformed that she is dead. Dejectedly, he stabs himself with his sword, only to learn that she is not dead but waiting for him in her tomb. He dies a fallen warrior—in the strong arms of his beloved Cleopatra. The sword which was once a symbol of masculine power and dominance for Antony becomes the weapon of his own destruction.

Once Egypt is conquered by Octavian's forces, and Antony is dead, Cleopatra refuses to serve another master. In her last act of strength, as befitting a great ruler, she takes her own life rather than bow to another.

The weaknesses in this film are a result of outside forces that meddled with the vision Mankiewicz had for the project. His goal was to make a film about the strongest woman in world history—"a woman who almost made it" in a man's world.[7]

Much of the chaos that surrounded the final days of the production was the result of the tremendous costs the film incurred over its four year history. The most expensive movie ever made ($40 million) was bringing 20th Century–Fox to its knees.[8] Looking for a quick release of the picture to recoup their losses, the board of directors fired its president, Skouras, and hired Darryl F. Zanuck in the summer of 1962, with the thought that the energetic Zanuck, the studio's former head of production and its largest shareholder, could revitalize the faltering studio.[9]

Mankiewicz had been working on the *Cleopatra* project for nearly two years when Zanuck demanded to see the film. He prepared a rough cut and waited to hear from the new president. Zanuck never contacted Mankiewicz as he said he would. Instead, after a series of heated letters in which Mankiewicz pleaded with Zanuck to allow him to present his ideas on the film, including his concept of the film as two separate entities, Zanuck fired him. Calling a press conference to defend his actions on the lengthy project, Zanuck noted that Mankiewicz deserved a rest and vowed to take over the film and make the final editorial cuts.

Zanuck soon saw his error of publicly humiliating Mankiewicz, a highly regarded filmmaker with whom he had once enjoyed a fruitful working relationship. He quickly rehired him as the director for additional battle sequences, and consulted him during the editing process. But it was clearly Zanuck who edited the final version of the film.

Mankiewicz was circumspect about the chaos that surrounded this film that had engaged his energies for nearly 24 months. At a press conference he called following his firing, he conceded *Cleopatra* was "conceived in emergency, shot in hysteria and wound up in blind panic."[10] Unfortunately, his vision for the film was lost in the chaos.

Even though he collaborated on the film's final version, he was so debilitated by the project, and displeased with the way the film turned out, that he refused to talk about it in public for the remainder of his life.

What this film lacks is of less importance than what it communicates. In *Cleopatra*, Mankiewicz continued his quest of trying to understand and convey the power of strong women. For that, *Cleopatra* serves as an eloquent offering of the complexity of the issues that surround a woman who tries to rule in a man's world.

The Honey Pot

Following his demoralizing experience with *Cleopatra*, Mankiewicz took some time away from the big screen to rest and reflect on his future in the motion picture business. He was persuaded to return to directing in 1964 when he was presented with a Rod Serling teleplay entitled *Carol for Another Christmas*. This highly political adaptation of the Charles Dickens classic was a commercial-free television production in support of the United Nations. It aired only one time on December 28, 1964, but it was enough to preoccupy Mankiewicz temporarily. This came at a time when he was still reeling from the debilitating *Cleopatra* project that usurped over two years of his life and took a toll on his creative psyche for the remainder of his career.

When Mankiewicz chose to return to the big screen a year later, he selected a project that he molded to address his major concerns in life and filmmaking—time, greed, and "life lousing up the script." The end result, in 1967, was *The Honey Pot*, a film as dense and intelligent as any in the Mankiewicz *oeuvre*. This was the last time Mankiewicz directed one of his own screenplays, and he took full advantage of the forum to vent his frustration about the film business, albeit in the metaphoric guise of a murder mystery of high comedic proportions.

The movie is set in modern day Venice. In it, Mankiewicz pays homage to his high-culture upbringing through frequent references to the 17th century play *Volpone* by Ben Jonson that served as inspiration for his screenplay. Again, Mankiewicz turned to Rex Harrison to serve as his surrogate. This was the fourth project in which he had cast Harrison in the lead; their most recent collaboration being *Cleopatra* which had begun shooting nearly four years before *The Honey Pot*.

Harrison is the perfect Mankiewiczian male: highbrow, articulate, charming, handsome, astute, and clever. One can easily envision a love-hate relationship that must have existed between the director and the star since they were so similar in disposition. Both were exacting and demanding, and each believed he was in charge (especially later in Harrison's career, when he had distinguished himself as Caesar in *Cleopatra*, and won an Academy Award for his performance as Higgins in *My Fair Lady* the following year). It is a wonder that Mankiewicz ever cast Harrison again after their first project together, *The Ghost and Mrs. Muir*.[11] But no matter how temperamental the star, no matter how frustrating his imperious manner, Harrison delivered Mankiewicz's dialogue with such brilliant assurance that the writer-director could depend on his words being said just as he had created them.

The Honey Pot is a tale of greed on a grand life and death scale. The wealthy Cecil Fox (Harrison) has decided to play an elaborate practical joke (à la *Volpone*) on three of his former lovers who he believes all owe him an immense debt of gratitude. He sends each a letter in which he notes that he is deathly ill (he is not), and that before he dies he will name an heir to his estate. However, he has not decided who that will be, and therefore he suggests that each woman visit him in Venice before it is too late. To aid in his ruse, he hires a washed-up actor, William McFly (Cliff Robertson), to act as his stage manager, and to assist in persuading the women that he is indeed on his deathbed.

The women, all of whom live their days in comfort and luxury, eagerly flock to Venice, willing to do whatever it takes to be named the sole heir to the Fox fortune. Each comes bearing a gift of an elaborate timepiece for her former lover. Merle McGill (Edie Adams), a blonde Hollywood sexpot who owes her career to Fox, brings a modern, crystal clock that notes the time in different cities of the world. Princess Dominique (Capucine), an aristocrat whose connection to Fox is based on a long-ago sexual liaison, gives the "dying" man a family heirloom—an hourglass with grains of gold dust instead of sand to mark the passage of time. And Lone Star Sheridan (Susan Hayward), a fiery all–American woman with an insatiable sexual appetite that Fox likens to the combination of Venus and a giant squid, presents her former lover with an ornate porcelain piece in which dancing figures pirouette as the clock chimes the hour.

Unaware that Fox is taunting them with his "play," the paramours become unwitting participants in a charade that exposes the pettiness of each of their characters. Each woman seizes the opportunity to express her willingness to offer Fox any comfort that he might require in his time of need—including sexual satisfaction—in exchange for being named heir to his fortune. But what Fox wants (besides sex) is to see the depth to which the rich will grovel for even more money.

The script that Fox has crafted for his *Volpone* takes an abrupt turn when Mrs. Sheridan is discovered dead of an apparent overdose of sleeping pills. The comedy of manners suddenly shifts to a whodunit as Sheridan's nurse and traveling companion, Sarah Watkins (Maggie Smith), becomes preoccupied with solving the mystery of her patient's apparent suicide—because only she knows that Sheridan's sleeping pills were placebos.

The intricate web of deceit created by Cecil Fox ends up catching him. The script that he devised has been loused up by life—or rather, death. Mankiewicz goes on to resolve the mystery for the viewer but with alternative endings that pile atop each other. The result is pure entertainment on the visceral level. However, what makes this film so intellectually complex is that nearly every nuance of the picture refers to topics of which Mankiewicz was exceedingly fond—from the concepts of time and greed to the idiosyncratic nature of fate.

Following three intensely serious films—*The Quiet American* (1958), *Suddenly, Last Summer* (1959) and *Cleopatra* (1963)—Mankiewicz returned to the genre of high comedy in which he had found his earlier success. *The Honey Pot* is a film of manners and mores that underscores the human frailties of the exceedingly rich.[12] Just as Cecil Fox relished the 17th century masterpiece *Volpone*, Mankiewicz delighted in the theatre. Mankiewicz finally created his own theatre—within filmic theatre—in *The Honey Pot*. Following this play within a screenplay within a film and its many inside jokes and allusions demands the spectator's full attention. That Mankiewicz did not patronize his audience is most evident in this film's references to high-culture concerns such as classical theatre, music, dance, literature, history, and urbane wit. One can enjoy *The Honey Pot* without knowing about such minutiae as the title of the classical music to which Fox listens incessantly ("The Dance of the Hours"), or his ongoing references to Elizabethan England or 17th century Venice. But if the spectator is aware, Mankiewicz's humor and the myriad twists and turns of the plot are much more biting and delightful.

On a less highbrow level are the ever-present film references in *The Honey Pot*. The most obvious allusion is the name of the main character, Cecil *Fox*, the conniving scripter of deceit who creates mayhem for all concerned. Only the Mankiewiczian intellect could craft such a complex triple entendre as he does with this name. Not only is Cecil Fox a literal reference to a wily fox in a henhouse, Mankiewicz also uses this name to pay homage to the original play by Ben Jonson since "volpone" is Italian for "old fox." But Mankiewicz, himself a crafty *renard*, was perhaps more aptly suggesting a comparison between his title character and 20th Century–Fox or Darryl Zanuck, whose incessant meddling he had to endure throughout the filming of *Cleopatra*.

Mankiewicz also illustrated how films come into being in *The Honey Pot*. Fox's complex game-planning mirrored Mankiewicz's own creative process—from devising a "script" to hiring a "stage manager" (McFly), to casting his stars (Merle, Dominique, and Lone Star). But film-savvy spectators will find true delight if they envision Mankiewicz continuing his references to the debacles of *Cleopatra*, in Fox's "charade." These references further highlight Mankiewicz's personal belief that life will rear its head and louse up one's carefully planned script.

In *The Honey Pot*, Mankiewicz once again employs his trademark voice-over narration, but this time there are no flashback sequences as there were in many of his best works (they were cut by United Artists because the film ran long). These voice-overs help the spectator understand the intricacies of the plot and (in some cases) a character's motivation. The people who most communicate with the audience are the two Mankiewicz surrogates—Cecil Fox (as the writer-director of the "play"), and Sarah Watkins who metamorphoses from a quiet, repressed servant into a shrewd, conquering hero by film's end.

Once again Mankiewicz pays homage to women in this work. It is not a woman's film per se, but one in which a woman triumphs in a way that was never possible when Mankiewicz's career was under the watchful eye of the Production Code Administration. By the time *The Honey Pot* was made, the Production Code was a thing of the past. Sexual references could be quite blatant now. And instead of having to punish the transgressive woman in the end, Mankiewicz saluted her.

The women in *The Honey Pot* are not as completely drawn as one expects from Mankiewicz. No doubt the final editing process eliminated some of the motivation he had written into their characters. One element that he succeeds in conveying, however, is that women are as greedy and unscrupulous as men. Nothing stands in the way of their desire to outsmart the competition. Not only are Merle and Dominique willing to offer their bodies for a better chance at Fox's estate, they even consider murdering Lone Star once they discover that she is Fox's common law wife.

Cecil Fox justified his ruse by calling it "people-baiting"—an elaborate adaptation of Elizabethan bear-baiting. Fox, however, took delight in elevating this concept to one that would suit his own agenda. His game-playing turned into a murder and then suicide, once he was undone through his own reckless greed. In murdering Lone Star Sheridan, Fox intended to inherit her vast fortune to cover his debts, but he made a foolish mistake by stealing two rolls of quarters from her purse to use as betting capital in the poker games that he played with McFly. It is these missing quarters that led Nurse Watkins to investigate Sheridan's death as a murder rather than letting it rest as an accidental overdose of sleeping pills.

Mankiewicz reconfigured the ending of *Volpone* for his screenplay so that Fox and McFly do not go to jail for their little game (as do Volpone and Mosca in Jonson's play), but instead suffer a worse fate: They are outsmarted by a clever woman. Fox commits suicide because Nurse Watkins has unmasked his game (even though she misinterprets who is the true murderer of Mrs. Sheridan), and McFly is fooled into signing Sarah's name on Fox's will. In what appears to be the dramatic climax of the farce, the wily Sarah Watkins is honored for her cleverness in outfoxing Fox and McFly. Mankiewicz bestows his highest honor on this quiet, unassertive woman through the character of the police inspector, who congratulates the nurse on her ingenuity in getting what she wants (Fox's money and McFly as a husband). Maggie Smith, in her first major film role as Nurse Watkins, is the recipient of words that Mankiewicz never directly expressed in a film until *The Honey Pot*, "I salute the Anglo-Saxon woman."

By 1965 when production on *The Honey Pot* began, the social climate had changed sufficiently for Mankiewicz to create female protagonists clearly capable of triumphing over men. What pleasure he must have had in this experience. As an advocate and creator of some of film's strongest women characters for over 35 years, he was finally able to end a film the way he wanted—with a triumphant transgressive woman. But, in another filmic reference, and with tongue firmly in cheek, he created more than one ending to *The Honey Pot*. However, in none of them does Sarah Watkins succumb to the wishes of her male companion.

Mankiewicz added six convoluting endings to the film: (1) Fox's suicide and tacit admission of his murder of Lone Star; (2) the revelation that Fox's estate is worthless; (3) Sarah's duping of McFly; (4) a proclamation from the now dead Cecil Fox that there should be no happy ending to the film; (5) the also dead Lone Star quieting Fox by acknowledging that life goes on and that he should let the young people direct their own future; and, (6) Fox's last words: "You know what would be nice? If just once, the bloody script turned out the way we wrote it."

Fox's obsession with time (from his collection of clocks to the music he listens to ad nauseam) was shared by Mankiewicz, especially after the excessive time and energy he expended on *Cleopatra*. Weary from fighting lowbrow studio executives who were more concerned with quantity (picture length) than quality, he allows Cecil Fox to speak for him in the scene where Fox tells Nurse Watkins that perhaps his life of quality, albeit only 50 years, is superior to that of a long life of unfulfilling events. When Fox poisons himself with barbiturates which he has inserted into chocolate-filled candies with centers of pure gold, one wonders if Mankiewicz is not indicating that he soon will end his filmmaking career lest he encounter even more *Cleopatra*–like studio-generated shenanigans that are morally debilitating and physically draining.

Like Fox's practical joke in which he was dying from complications of a massive heart attack, Mankiewicz suffered from a broken spirit following *Cleopatra*. He would direct only two more films after *The Honey Pot*—*There Was a Crooked Man* (1970), and *Sleuth* (1972)—neither of which he wrote himself (although he contributed to the dialogue). Although he continued to work on projects for the remainder of his life, the film business was changing dramatically. No longer were studios interested in the high comedy films of manners and mores that were staples in the Mankiewicz *oeuvre*. Talk was out. Special affects were in. He took Lone Star Sheridan's advice and left the business to the young people.

Though Mankiewicz worked in the industry for nearly 50 years, with a total output of well over 70 projects, he was only credited with writing *and* directing 11 films.[13] Filmographies note that he left the business on a high note, having received an Oscar nomination as best director for his last film, *Sleuth*, in 1972. He never made another film because of his intense refusal to sacrifice literary quality to the changing standards of the industry for which he came to have little respect. When Cecil Fox speaks of preferring a life of quality rather than quantity, Mankiewicz is referring, with pride, to his own extraordinary, albeit shortened, career.

NOTES

1. Joseph L. Mankiewicz, "1958 Diary" in Mankiewicz private collection.
2. Joseph L. Mankiewicz, interview with Michel Ciment, *All About Mankiewicz*, Janus Film, France, 1983.
3. Mankiewicz was adapting Lawrence Durrell's *Alexandria Quartet* into a screenplay entitled, *Justine*, that was to be produced by *Cleopatra*'s producer, Walter Wanger, for 20th Century–Fox, once *Cleopatra* was completed. It was never made into a motion picture because of the ill-will Mankiewicz felt for Fox following *Cleopatra*.
4. Mankiewicz began his work on *Cleopatra* on January 20, 1961. The film did not premiere until late June, 1963. He never returned to *Justine*.
5. Because the film was so far behind schedule, scenes were often written the night before they were to be shot. Mankiewicz was the principal screenwriter on the project even though he shares onscreen credits with Ranald MacDougall and Sidney Buchman. MacDougall and Buchman used Mankiewicz's detailed Screen Outline (complete with dialogue) to expand his concepts.
6. All film quotes throughout this essay are taken from a videorecording of *Cleopatra*. Dir. Joseph L. Mankiewicz. Perf. Elizabeth Taylor, Rex Harrison, and Richard Burton. 20th Century–Fox, 1963.
7. Joseph L. Mankiewicz, "A Statement Concerning the Writing of Cleopatra." 6 Oct. 1962.
8. *Cleopatra*'s cost would be approximately $300 million by today's standards which exceeds the expense of *Titanic*.
9. Zanuck had recently completed filming another of Fox's blockbusters, the war film, *The Longest Day*.
10. *Hollywood Reporter*. "Mankiewicz Denies Charges by Zanuck, But Won't Fight." 31 Oct. 1962: 1+.
11. Harrison starred in four Mankiewicz films: The *Ghost and Mrs. Muir* (1947); *Escape* (1948); *Cleopatra* (1963); and *The Honey Pot* (1967).
12. Mankiewicz was not pleased with the title United Artists created for his film. He thought it crass. They thought it marketable. (His working titles varied from "Anyone for Venice?" to "It Comes Up Murder.")
13. Mankiewicz directed 22 films in all: 20 narrative films for the big screen; one for television; and one of minimal contribution for which he directed the linking sequences to a Martin Luther King, Jr., documentary.

Filmed Theatre

All About Eve

A Letter to Three Wives and *All About Eve*, Joseph Mankiewicz's two most highbrow and acclaimed directorial efforts, were made from scripts sparkling with wit penned by Mankiewicz himself. And yet the films derive ultimately from subliterary properties published in *Cosmopolitan*, one of the era's more sophisticated women's magazines. In a sense, this is profoundly ironic, especially since one of the targets of Mankiewicz's satiric wit in *Letter* is the very "culture industry" to which publications such as *Cosmopolitan* belong. To be sure, both the properties that he discovered in the pages of these magazines came to enjoy a public life beyond that bestowed upon them by the writer-director. This is likely an indication that they exceeded in some ways the artistic limits of their type.

The original published version of what, under Mankiewicz's direction, would become *A Letter to Three Wives* was expanded by its author, John Klempner, into a novel of modest success some three years before the film was made (even though Mankiewicz, by all accounts, ignored its existence). Similarly, "The Wisdom of Eve," written by the very undistinguished Mary Orr, became the source of a play of the same title (coauthored by Orr's husband Reginald) nearly 15 years after the film's release. Her story provided the material for yet another dramatization, the better known Broadway hit *Applause*, which is actually a conflation of the filmscript and story (but lacking Addison De Witt, Mankiewicz's most famous addition). There is no doubt, however, that *A Letter to Three Wives* and *All About Eve* are far superior to the original and other subsequent versions of the same properties. The usual cultural wisdom is that Hollywood treatment extracts rather than adds aesthetic value. With these two films, however, Mankiewicz joined a very small club of director-writers (Alfred Hitchcock is its most famous member) who found their greatest success adapting middlebrow rather than literary sources. Having won Academy Awards for writing and directing *Letter* and *Eve*, Mankiewicz, one might say, deserved another pair for resourcefulness as well.

All About Eve's origins and subsequent achievement, however, do more than confirm the writer-director's credentials as a leading practitioner of the sow's ear–silk purse theory of artistic creation. The film is undeniably a supreme example of that most literary of cinematic forms, "filmed theater." Paradoxically, though, some of its most telling effects are achieved by characteristically filmic devices, particularly voice-overs of various types and the flashback main structure typical of many forties Hollywood masterpieces. Yet, in addition to its artistic success, *All About Eve*, again much like *Letter*, remains true to the then popular film genre to which its title quite obviously connects: the woman's picture. Its *Cosmopolitan* story source, in other words, provided more than verbal dross to be converted by Mankiewicz's talent into cultural precious metal. The writer/director was deeply interested, as well, in exploiting and furthering its narrative and thematic conventions. Its essentially high cultural meditations on theatricality and the theater are original and noteworthy. Yet *All About Eve* is perhaps best remembered as a profound, if sometimes humorously misogynistic, commentary on the female sensibility as it was lived in postwar America. From this perspective, the film constitutes, along with *Letter*, an impressive diptych of contemporary mores and experiences.

As in *Letter*, Mankiewicz focuses primarily on women characters in *Eve*. The men, not as interesting or complex, are, shall we say, supporting players, except in one important instance. The different styles and values of the three female leads and two minor female characters create and energize the dramatic conflict. Yet, in a surprising ironic twist, the narrative's resolution has its terms fixed by Addison De Witt, the only man (albeit a somewhat androgynous one) who is able to out-viper the viperish Eve and thereby defeat the protagonist at her subtle and contrasting games of passive-aggressive self-assertion and blackmail.

From this point of view, perhaps the most profound similarity between the two films is not their subliterary origins, but the way in which each discovers *in extremis* a male character strong enough to foil the destructive plottings of a powerful woman. In each case, this character is bent on carrying out the most unforgivable of female treasons: the theft of a loving (if feckless) husband from one of her erstwhile friends. In the

The classic scene from *All About Eve* (1950) with (left to right) Anne Baxter, Bette Davis, Marilyn Monroe, and George Sanders, where Addison DeWitt (Sanders) introduces his companion, Miss Caswell (Monroe), as a graduate of the Copacabana School of Dramatic Arts, to Margo Channing (Davis) and Eve (Baxter).

earlier film, Porter's confession breaks the hold that the sophisticated and worldly Addie Ross, the film's would-be *dea ex machina*, has over both him and the wives held hostage to her predation, even as it exculpates Brad, whose suspicious behavior is never otherwise adequately explained. Thus rejected, Addie must depart the upper middle class community of which she can no longer be a member, but without one of these men in tow as a prize. Yet she remains a powerful presence because she is forever unseen and thus continues to exist in some sense omnipresently, occupying some strange existential interstice between the story world and its narration. Her gaily flip final comment ("heigh ho, goodnight, everybody!") implies that, if defeated, she may not have been dissuaded for all time from an unrestrained assertion of self.

In *Eve*, Addison's name, perhaps deliberately, recalls Addie's. There is no doubt, in any case, that he performs a similar function. In contrast, however, he is not only a controlling narrative consciousness, he is also solidly present throughout as a character. Like the other "supporting players," Addison is a sympathetic—if ultimately rebellious—spectator of Eve's performances, those both on and off the stage. Attracted by Eve and her talent, he abandons his role as critic for those of writer and director when, at the very peak of her success, Eve, thinking she has made the most of their connection, attempts to leave him behind.

Addison's crucial role is due to Mankiewicz's reworking of his source; we can conclude then that the writer-director wanted to emphasize this striking similarity to *Letter*. From this perspective, the change in gender from female to male is significant. *Letter* features an Olympian voice-over narration by a scheming woman, whose ambiguous and cruel letter has set the narrative into motion. Importantly, however, Addie's narration is synchronous with the present order of events; thus, like the pawns she attempts to manipulate, Addie does not know until the conclusion how her "story" will end. The three wives, under pressure from the current collective marital crisis, generate memories that constitute flashbacks they in a sense narrate, but Addie never attains such control of her story materials. Furthermore, though forever above the action (sometimes literally), Addie exists during the time of the story only as a text (the famous letter) for the other characters and only as an intermittently heard voice for the spectator. Addison, in contrast, is assigned a more powerful version of the same role. As a character, he manages to determine the outcome of the story (which Addie fails to do).

And as a narrator, he is also able to dictate the manner in which the story is represented (shaping the image and sound tracks for the spectator after the fact, that is, in an asynchronous fashion impossible for Addie, who remains trapped in unfolding story time). The film begins *in medias res* with Addison's narrative laid over images of the awards ceremony that confirms Eve's huge success. As master narrator, Addison "turns off" the sound so that we cannot hear the master of ceremonies (Addison summarizes the speech for us in any case) until he decides that he has come to the main point, which is handing over the acting award to Eve. As Eve is about to receive her plaque, Addison freezes the frame, and it remains frozen until after the flashback narratives, which he seems to both cue and oversee, have come to an end. In the separate flashbacks that follow, Karen and Margo have the power to comment on the images of their past. Only Addison, however, is able to control both the image and sound tracks so thoroughly and decisively

Thus, in Mankiewicz's two most effectively dramatic renderings of the battle between the sexes, the men not only have the last laugh (as does Diello in *Five Fingers*, for example), but in some sense the last word. Only in *Eve*, however, is male control fully and firmly established. Addison and Porter, otherwise so dissimilar, manage, if from different motives, to restore the bourgeois family. They save it from the threat of an immoral if fascinating assertion of feminine desire (though in Addison's case this socially conservative result is an accident of his looking out for his own advantage). Yet in *Letter*, Addie retains her freedom. Porter asserts himself by abjuring the possession of Addie he might have enjoyed and thus, perhaps ironically, saves her from the marriage bond. In *Eve*, the resisting male does not flee the dangerous woman, but, instead, deprives her of the power to act independently. In possession of the somewhat sordid truth about her (information that, if published, might adversely affect the career she has worked so diligently to construct), Addison takes charge of Eve's life on stage and off through blackmail. Thus, he prevents her marriage to the more easily manipulated playwright she has seduced, while he mandates, for reasons never explained, her move to Hollywood. In the first of the film's two ironic reversals, Eve, with Addison's help, is hoisted on her own petard.

Though this theme is anticipated in *Letter*, *Eve* is more centrally concerned with the kind of power that women can acquire in a man's world that usually offers them more limited opportunities for freedom and advancement. Addie's power comes from her beauty, charm, and sophistication, while Eve's results from the stage success she achieves with talent and ruthlessness. *Eve's* Broadway theater setting offers a working environment, cut off from traditional domestic responsibilities, in which women have a chance, perhaps even a roughly equal one, of achieving preeminence. Here their value is determined not simply by their desirability, but by their ability to fill theater seats, a skill that can be precisely measured in dollars earned.

Margo Channing (Bette Davis) is such a woman, a star actress whose presence in a play is vital to four men, all of whose professional careers in some sense depend on her success as a performer. They are: playwright Lloyd Richards (Hugh Marlowe), director Bill Sampson (Gary Merrill), producer Max Fabian (Gregory Ratoff), and critic Addison De Witt (George Sanders), who is the most symbiotic (or parasitic) of the foursome since, in his own words, he neither "reaps nor sows." Though the men resent their dependence on a temperamental talent (perhaps because she is a woman), they all grudgingly acknowledge that the right actress in a starring role can make a play, while the wrong one can doom an otherwise promising production. The men's common assumption seems to be that as a performance art, the theater succeeds or fails with acting talent (of which Margo has a superabundance), a fact beyond dispute since it can be measured by a production's economic bottom line.

Bette Davis' performance as nothing less than Bette Davis tellingly exemplifies the star appeal so vital to the theater. Like Bette, Margo has the knack for converting herself into an appealing spectacle, her imitative abilities deriving from a relentless self-assertion. Margo's need for constant display and the attention it can win for her, however, gives rise to potentially disabling discontents. She evinces an insatiable appetite for flattery and reassurance that is unappealingly childish, especially when it leads, as it frequently does, to jealous tantrums. Insecure, she is in addition hostage to a self-concern that is dangerous because it can blind her to how others exploit her. Finally, she suffers from a panicked obsession with the aging that will inevitably steal her looks and, afterward, her position because the best roles go to actresses who can at least appear young. In sum, though Margo has achieved professional success, she is haunted by its transitoriness. Moreover, she is disgusted by the fickle hunger of her fans, who not only create but consume her celebrity.

Enjoying her position of power, Margo ignores an obvious fact: that what we call the "theater" depends not only on the willingness of some to display themselves, but also the agreement of others to watch that display with forbearance and, perhaps, admiration. Without that unreliable audience, she would be nothing. Because of Mankiewicz's able rewriting, *All About Eve* deploys enough thoroughly recognizable stereotypes to limn a comfortably conventional representation of the Broadway stage. The egotistical director, fiercely intellectual, falls in love with his star, while the Jewish producer suffers constantly from dyspepsia caused by financial uncertainty. The talented but naïve playwright is easily flattered and seduced, first by a young student and, years later, by his star player, while the two featured actresses enjoy a brief friendship that soon degenerates into a vicious catfight over a choice role.

Mankiewicz's interest in the theater as a subject, however, goes deeper than this series of character sketches and relationships, of a type familiar to film audiences at the time from their recycling in productions so numerous they might be said to constitute a subgenre. *All About Eve* is, on its most profound level, about the psychological dynamic that enables theater to exist, a dynamic that affords some the power of display and others the power of the gaze. The film, in other words, offers an intriguing variation on a familiar Mankiewicz theme: the contesting interplay of the domineering and the dominated. This intellectual interest on

Mankiewicz's part explains why his stereotypical characters find themselves involved in such an implausible story.

The tale that *All About Eve* has to tell is extraordinary because it is set in motion by a disruption of the dialectic between performer and spectator. Such a theme is not common to the show business movie, whose conventional concern (also present to some degree in Mankiewicz's film) is the American success ethic and its discontents. Normally, the stage functions as an impassable barrier, though, of course, it is one constructed by a tacit agreement between actors and audience. In *All About Eve*, however, this willed separation is transgressed from the direction of the orchestra seats by a spectator determined to expand to its maximum her power to look and by so doing transfer the gaze to herself. Such looking, as Mankiewicz slyly suggests, can itself become a performance, especially when the spectator's most intense desire is to become the object of adoration. This theme is picked up in the only other show business movie to follow Mankiewicz's lead: Martin Scorsese's *The King of Comedy*, in which an unbalanced fan first importunes then blackmails the celebrity—whose every move he emulates—into giving him a "big break" on the air, during which he improbably succeeds in establishing his own talent.

Eve Harrington (Anne Baxter), who will eventually replace Margo as the theater's most acclaimed star, makes her initial appearance as an unglamorized stage door johnny dressed in masculine rain gear. Attending for some six weeks every performance of Margo's current hit play, Eve mounts a performance of her own each night after the theater shuts its doors. Self-abasingly, she waits in the shadows outside the dressing rooms, hoping for yet another glimpse of the actress who has become her idol. But the monotonous sameness of her nightly appearance (as if *en costume*, she is always attired the same) not only rivals Margo's; it is its mirror image, with one exception—Eve lacks an audience. Paradoxically, perhaps, Eve's ostensible attempts to deny herself any status as spectacle become most spectacularly effective. Her dogged acceptance of a subservient role (that of worshiper), her unappealing dress, and her place in the shadows (rather than on a spotlighted stage) actually gain her notice, for which she secretly wishes.

Eve's story proper, in fact, can begin only when her bizarre and ritualistic observance finally attracts an audience. Karen Richards, the wife of the playwright, reacts to Eve's presence just as her husband and his compatriots will soon do, that is, with pity and a self-flattering sense of superiority, the latter emotion encouraged by Eve's nearly unbearable humility. Karen invites Eve backstage, and the young woman, much like a petitioner at court, must wait in an anteroom while her eager sponsor seeks an audience for her from Margo, who, with postperformance gaiety, is talking to the others. Invited to join the group, they fish for compliments, which, like the proper fan, Eve enthusiastically provides. Asked to speak, however, Eve soon shifts roles. Her confessions of a miserable childhood, an early widowhood, and maniacal devotion to Margo (whom, she says, she followed from California to New York) leave no eyes dry among her listeners (except for Margo's cynical stage assistant), whose captivation is recorded by Mankiewicz's camera in telling reaction shots. Admitted into Margo's inner circle, Eve is informally signed on as a kind of personal manager. Eve, as perfect fan, completes the gallery of those dependent upon the star. Margo's insecurity and narcissism are nourished perfectly by Eve's constant attentiveness and apparently bottomless admiration.

The rather predictable remainder of the story unfolds in a number of dramatic set pieces, made memorable by Mankiewicz's wittily overblown dialogue, which is the perfect means of expression for the film's constantly posturing characters. The more Eve appears to do Margo's bidding—especially unbidden—the more she insinuates herself into Margo's life. After failing to seduce Bill Sampson, Margo's fiancé, Eve succeeds in getting hired as Margo's understudy (for who would know either the part or Margo any better?). But Margo, an inveterate trouper, never misses a performance. Thinking she is aiding a pathetic youngster in need of a break, Karen arranges for the play's star to be marooned in Connecticut one afternoon. Eve's performance is viewed and then favorably reviewed by a number of the city's critics (they were summoned by Addison, who, like Karen, has become a sponsor of sorts). Eve eventually parlays that opportunity into an audition for Lloyd's new play, an audition to which Margo, who thought she was certain to get the part, arrives late.

Recognizing that she cannot compete with this younger newcomer, Margo bows out graciously, seizing the opportunity to marry Bill Sampson and begin a long-postponed domestic life. With Addison's support, Eve has schemed to blackmail Karen, who is, against her better wishes, to suggest that Lloyd give her the part; though Karen is willing to go through with this plan, Margo's retirement intervenes. Eve, however, is not satisfied with simply having displaced her erstwhile idol; she wants to insure further success and decides that the love and affection of Broadway's most acclaimed playwright, Lloyd Richards, is the way to do so. She persuades Lloyd to leave Karen, but Addison blackmails the blackmailer, and Eve passes under his control.

Academy Awards (1950). The winners for *All About Eve*: (left to right) George Sanders, Best Supporting Actor; Darryl F. Zanuck, Producer of Best Picture (who also won the Irving Thalberg Award); Ralph Bunche (presenter); and Joseph L. Mankiewicz, holding his two Oscars for Best Screenplay and Best Director.

In the film's last sequence, this irony is compounded. Eve wins the coveted Sarah Siddons award for her performance in Lloyd's new play, but this hollow triumph, carefully surveilled by Addison, leaves Eve unsatisfied. She returns home to find a doppelgänger of her former self: a desperate young woman who has broken into her apartment in order to catch a glimpse of the star she idolizes. The intruder's desire to serve Eve the same way she served Margo is obvious, but Eve is too jaded to really care, even when the young woman's interest seems vaguely provocative, even seductive. Eve's moment of triumph thus signals the very process that will perhaps soon displace her from preeminence. The fan who replaces the star finds herself challenged in the end by a critic and by yet another fan, a rival summoned into existence by Eve's own success. Appropriately, in the film's last image Eve is displaced by her admirer, whose reflection, as she watches herself in a bank of opposing mirrors, is projected into infinity. This stunning image not only actualizes the young woman's narcissism, but, perhaps most important, metaphorizes the irresolvable dialectic between posing and gazing, between the different but connected desires of performer and spectator.

Like *Letter*, *Eve* ends by endorsing a conservative view of women's roles. In so doing, it remains true to its genre. The career woman winds up imprisoned by an aggressive, perhaps parasitic male desire that cannot offer the pleasures of romance or domestic happiness. Margo, in contrast, seems genuinely happy in the end with her choice of marriage over career; Bill's devoted love is adequate recompense for her loss of the spotlight and her audience's adulation. Though her marriage is shaky, Karen is still at Lloyd's side as the film ends, once again proof that this woman has made the correct choice; he appears repentant and attentive, certainly not regretful that Eve threw him over. At the awards banquet, the happy couples contrast sharply with Eve's joyless pairing with Addison. And the predatory, lesbian overtones of the film's final sequence offer a fitting coda to the condemnation of Eve's immoral and relentless pursuit of her own self-interest. It is poetically just that the story's two most selfish and unpleasant characters wind up in a relationship based on power and domination rather than love. As in Mankiewicz's other pessimistic productions (*Five Fingers*, *The Honey Pot*, *Sleuth*, and *The Quiet American* especially come to mind), the elaborate plottings of morally dubious characters either come to naught or, even worse, wind up trapping those who have set them into motion.

R. Barton Palmer

Guys and Dolls

Brando sings!

Producer Samuel Goldwyn's *Guys and Dolls* capitalized on this incongruity to sell his picture to an audience curious about how the street thug of *On the Waterfront* would perform when singing a ballad to the lovely Jean Simmons. To the film community, however, nothing seemed more inconceivable than the high-minded Mankiewicz directing a lighthearted musical. But Goldwyn wanted the best director in Hollywood, even if he had no experience writing musical comedy, and Mankiewicz was basking in the glow of having won Oscars for writing and directing in two consecutive years. Goldwyn knew that Mankiewicz would adapt the award-winning Broadway show into interesting film fare that would draw filmgoers away from their television sets.

Gone were the glory days of the lavish Hollywood musicals that generated huge box office appeal in the 1940s. By the fifties, if a film musical were to guarantee an audience, it had to be an adaptation of a successful Broadway production. The astute Goldwyn knew that to ensure himself a hit, not only would he need a top-notch vehicle, he would have to hire the best Hollywood had to offer to draw in the audience.

Goldwyn paid a record $1 million (plus 10 percent of worldwide box office gross) to get the screen rights to one of Broadway's hottest musicals. Not only did he hire Mankiewicz to direct and adapt the Abe Burrows–Jo Swerling book for the screen, he tapped Broadway choreographer Michael Kidd to reproduce his dance numbers on film. He also commissioned composer Frank Loesser to write three new songs for the movie that were not in the Broadway hit, and he cast a number of the actors from the stage production in his film. The crowning achievement of Goldwyn's spectacular project was casting superstars Marlon Brando, Jean Simmons, Frank Sinatra, and Broadway's Vivian Blaine as the leads. It was of little concern to Goldwyn as he prepared to mount a musical extravaganza that Brando and Simmons had never sung a note in public.

Marlon Brando was Goldwyn's number one pick to play the young, romantic lead, Sky Masterson, but Goldwyn had a difficult time getting Brando to consider a role that would require him to sing. Turning to Mankiewicz, who had recently directed the actor in *Julius Caesar,* Goldwyn pleaded with him to do what he could to get Brando to accept the role. Mankiewicz (also reluctant about the film because he was dabbling in a genre outside his ken) sent Brando the following telegram:

> Understand you don't want to do *Guys and Dolls* as you've never done a musical. You have nothing to worry about as I haven't done one either. Love, Joe.[1]

Brando accepted and made movie history when he sang one of the show's most well-known numbers, "Luck Be a Lady Tonight," as crooner Frank Sinatra looked over his shoulder.

Mankiewicz's previous film, *The Barefoot Contessa,* was his first independent project as writer, director, and producer. This taxing experience led him to look for a subsequent project that would allow him to step aside from the producing chores that he found so tedious to concentrate on what he did best—adapting an established work for the screen and directing the finished product.

As a lover of theater, Mankiewicz was not as outlandish a choice for directing this adaptation as some reviewers thought. While he had never done a Broadway musical, he had recently staged the first English language version of *La Bohème* for the Metropolitan Opera. Besides, the subject matter of the film was of primary interest to him—the relationship between men and women.

The film version of *Guys and Dolls* shows a decided Mankiewicz touch. Even though he knew he was writing a musical screenplay, he crafted the narrative so that it could stand on its own—without the music. While the screenplay remains faithful in scope to the Broadway show, Mankiewicz significantly expanded the love story between the nonsingers in the film (Brando and Simmons) to such a degree that the fact that they are the weakest singers in the ensemble is of little concern to the overall work. In fact, Brando's soft, sweet voice is almost beguiling in the love songs he croons to Simmons. His skill as an actor keeps the viewer focused on the specific text of each song he sings so that one realizes its importance in advancing the plot. This intense acting style also serves to distract the viewer from the nasal quality of Brando's small voice.

Sky Masterson's love interest, mission leader Sarah Brown, is played with great enthusiasm by Jean Simmons. Like Brando, she is a weak singer, but when her part calls for a song, she sings it with such gusto (especially "If I Were a Bell") that one does not mind her faulty intonation.

The true crooner in the film, Frank Sinatra, sings with his usual carefree style, but his acting is wooden and only serves to accentuate Brando's skill. Ironically, it is when Brando sings one of the most popular melodies from the show, "Luck Be a Lady," that one wishes it were Sinatra belting out the tune, rather than Brando who sings it like a schoolboy quietly praying for success on a big exam. The fact that Sinatra went on to record this song (and make it one of his signature pieces) only further underscores the notion that he realized he was miscast.

However, Frank Sinatra was not the star we think of today when Goldwyn made *Guys and Dolls* in 1955. His singing career began to falter in the late forties and was nearly at an end when he suffered a vocal chord hemorrhage in 1952. Soon after this illness, he was unceremoniously discarded by the talent agency that had been with him throughout his years

The sewer scene from *Guys and Dolls* (1955). Marlon Brando (center) sings "Luck Be a Lady" as Frank Sinatra looks on by his shoulder. Sheldon Leonard (crouching) and Stubby Kaye are on Brando's right.

as a big band singer. In the early 1950s, he turned to acting as a way to resurrect his ailing career. It was Sinatra who pleaded with Goldwyn to cast him as Nathan Detroit (the impresario of the "oldest established permanent floating crap game in New York") the year following his award-winning performance in *From Here to Eternity*.

Even though Mankiewicz believed Sinatra was miscast as Nathan Detroit because his singing talent was far superior to Brando's (who had to sing the show's most lovely ballads), Goldwyn's vision of the romantic lead, Sky Masterson, was more appropriate to the younger Brando. And no matter how miscast Sinatra may have been, according to Goldwyn biographer A. Scott Berg, it was Sinatra himself who wanted to play Detroit.[2]

Whatever the casting decisions, Mankiewicz was able to live with them because of Goldwyn's enthusiasm for the project. Turning his attention to writing the screenplay, Mankiewicz looked to the original Damon Runyon story, "The Idyll of Sarah Brown," for inspiration for his film adaptation.

Runyon created a world of lovable petty criminals who inhabit the underworld of New York's Times Square—card sharks, pickpockets, and "lovely ladies" for whom the process of scamming is as much a way of life as breathing. The guys and dolls in Runyonland are caricatures of what out-of-towners fear they will encounter when visiting New York for the first time.

Mankiewicz remains faithful to the humor of the Burrows-Swerling book that serves as the basis for the Broadway production. His screenplay barely alters a word of the play's text regarding the hapless Nathan Detroit, his long-suffering fiancée, Adelaide, and Detroit's gambling cohorts. But what Mankiewicz develops that is unique to the film is a psychological dimension to the Sky Masterson–Sarah Brown relationship which works nicely because neither one of them can hold the attention of the audience with their weak singing.

Interwoven with the gambling antics of Detroit (who needs $1000 to secure a place for his next crap game) is the humorous evolution of the 14-year engagement between Nathan and his beloved Adelaide. In parallel to this guy-doll scenario, is a love story of loftier dimensions involving the high-stakes gambler, Masterson and the missionary, Sister Sarah. These two stories intertwine because Masterson has what Detroit needs— money. In betting Masterson that he cannot persuade Sarah to accompany him to Havana, Detroit sets the plot in motion.

Even with the film's devotion to Runyonese banter and Abe Burrows humor, Mankiewicz made the movie more provocative than the play by exploring good and evil as portrayed in the romance of Sky and Sarah. By developing the dramatic elements of the romance between Sky Masterson and Sarah Brown, Mankiewicz taps his ongoing interest in the strong woman who meets her match in an equally strong man. And he strengthens the film's narrative to capitalize on the acting talents and charisma of Jean Simmons and Marlon Brando (while also compensating for their musical weaknesses).

Known primarily for his biting satirical dialogue, Mankiewicz adds another dimension to his skill as a director by creating a distinctly nonverbal gesture that speaks louder than any words. Jean Simmons as the prim and proper young mission leader, Sarah Brown, always seems to have forgotten to button one of the buttons on her jacket. She is constantly fiddling with this button whenever faced with temptation. As the film proceeds, the viewer realizes that Sarah Brown's opinion of herself is bound up in the buttons on her jacket. Whether she is unconsciously forgetful of the missed button because she is preoccupied with the business of keeping the mission running or faced with the quandary of rejecting the perfectionism she espouses, Sarah often must rely on others to remind her to secure her missed button. Mankiewicz heightens the paradox of the imperfect perfectionist when he illustrates that Sarah must often depend on the men in her life (Uncle Arvide and even Sky Masterson) to rebutton her jacket whenever she teeters on the verge of stepping outside the boundaries of propriety.

This is a quintessential Mankiewicz touch—adding a psychological dimension to his keen sense of humor. In Sarah's subtle nonverbal act, the spectator learns that her nervous habit is an outward manifestation of the ambivalence she feels about the prudish lifestyle she has chosen. But Mankiewicz cannot resist giving Sarah a chance to verbalize her quandary:

> SARAH (to Masterson): I'm nothing but a repressed neurotic girl— I've read two whole books on the subject—who is abnormally attracted to sin and therefore abnormally afraid of it.

Indeed, the buttons on Sarah's jacket represent her latent sexuality that she must continuously monitor lest she abandon herself to sinful desires— as when she dances, fights, and flirts with Masterson in Havana. It is only after Sky rebuttons her jacket that Sarah resurrects her composure.

That Mankiewicz is a master of psychological insight is without question. This learned man wanted to be a psychiatrist when he enrolled in Columbia University. And even though he moved on to writing and directing, his films are full of his attempts to understand human behavior.

While praised for his clever crafting of dialogue, Mankiewicz's films are often criticized as being too static. *Guys and Dolls* counters this view and illustrates the Mankiewicz love of varied camera angles. Capitalizing on the film's CinemaScope format, coupled with Michael Kidd's excellent choreography, Mankiewicz elevates the camera on a boom to heighten the visual drama of the ensemble's dance sequences, but then just as quickly, he drops down for a low-angle shot to give the viewer the feel of watching a game of craps. This effective execution of different angles works especially well during the musical numbers and intensifies the visual and narrative excitement that accompanies the terrific Frank Loesser score.

Another visual element that is completely unique in the Mankiewicz

oeuvre is the bold Technicolor look of *Guys and Dolls*. Goldwyn wanted
to produce the best musical ever filmed so it had to look good as well as
sound good. Mankiewicz accomplished this by adding a Runyonesque
look to the film's *mise en scène*. Bold colors accompany even bolder characters in *Guys and Dolls*. The sets look like hand-painted postcards of a
hustling and bustling Times Square. Indeed, this film looks like a comic
book with its abundance of vividly colored costumes that match the array
of vibrant Runyon caricatures of New Yorkers.

To accompany the colorful look of the film is the extraordinary musical score by Frank Loesser. Using 11 of the 16 original songs from the
Broadway version, Loesser wrote three new songs for the film—including one written especially to satisfy Frank Sinatra's bobby-soxers.[3] Even
though Sinatra croons "Adelaide" with his usual flair, it is Broadway star
Vivian Blaine who steals the show from him with her rendition of "Adelaide's Lament"—a crazy song about the psychosomatic illness she has
developed over her 14-year engagement to the commitment-wary Detroit.

While Mankiewicz was faithful to the principal narrative elements
of the stage version, his primary alteration comes at the conclusion of the
film. Instead of having Sky Masterson don a mission uniform to join his
beloved Sarah Brown as she saves the sinners of the world, Mankiewicz
maintains the Masterson high-roller persona even after he and Sarah are
married in a double wedding with Nathan and Adelaide. Mankiewicz
could not envision Masterson in mission garb so he elevated the status of
one of the gamblers to the role of missionary and quickly segued into the
big musical finale.

The musical extravaganza that Goldwyn sought to cap his years as
a film producer served as an entry for Mankiewicz into the genre of film
spectacle. It would be six years before Mankiewicz would encounter
another film of epic proportions—*Cleopatra*.

Cheryl Bray Lower

NOTES

1. David Shipman, "A Conversation with Joseph L. Mankiewicz," *Films
and Filming* Nov. 1982: 13.
2. Scott Berg, *Goldwyn*. (New York: Alfred A. Knopf, 1989) 471.
3. "Pet Me Papa," "A Woman in Love," and "Adelaide" written for Sinatra.

Literary Adaptations

by R. Barton Palmer

The Late George Apley

The postwar era witnessed the phenomenal Broadway success of three family generational dramas set during the late nineteenth or early twentieth century, each of which deals with the class-bound mores of early modern America. *I Remember Mama*, John Van Druten's adaptation of Kathryn Forbes' autobiographical account of immigrant life in San Francisco, is a nostalgia piece, an unabashedly melodramatic celebration of "greenhorn" success in the New World. In contrast, Howard Lindsay's *Life with Father* and John P. Marquand and George S. Kaufman's *The Late George Apley* both offer more of a social critique. Each features a self-important and upper-crust white patriarch—the somewhat comic mouthpiece of traditional values—whose determined resistance to change, urged by the women and children in his life, is not proven ineffective but is genially satirized.

Not surprisingly, Hollywood attempted in each case to turn these stage successes into profitable films. *Life with Father* was snapped up by Warners (Robert Bruckner producing) and turned into a literate filmscript by noted screenwriter Donald Ogden Stewart. Michael Curtiz directed a stellar cast of William Powell, Irene Dunne, ZaSu Pitts, and Elizabeth Taylor in what turned out to be a financial and critical blockbuster (even spawning, not long after, a long-running television series). This 1947 release garnered five Academy Award nominations. The curmudgeonly Powell is marvelous as a rigid paterfamilias who refuses to be baptized, but in the end relents. The following year, RKO tried to work the same magic with *I Remember Mama*. Producer Harriet Parsons and director George Stevens made an excellent film from De Witt Bodeen's script. This film also proved a hit with critics and the general public; it too received five Academy Award nominations. Once again, the cast was superior, including Irene Dunne, Barbara Bel Geddes, Oscar Homolka, and Edgar Bergen.

Like Warners and RKO, Fox hoped to make money from the current Broadway trend, paying, after a bidding war, an astounding $275,000 for the screen rights to *The Late George Apley*, which had achieved notoriety first as a fictional bestseller and then as a Broadway play. Marquand's novel is largely epistolary, consisting of Apley's correspondence, diary entries, and other papers—the whole assembled and presented by an anonymous "compiler" as the work of the now deceased writer. This narrative structure permits Apley to explain himself to the reader even though he is too much of a snob himself ever to feel the urge to communicate his views to "people." The letters—composed as private communications, but then somewhat mischievously made public by the compiler—offer the perfect formal structure for expressing the title character's unbending formality as well as his conformity to upper-class conventions. They also focus the unforeseen reader on the author's bravura verbal performances, his stylishly penned understandings of his world and those who inhabit it. A Pulitzer prize winner in 1937, the novel perceptively chronicles the changes that overtook America during the seven tumultuous decades from the beginnings of Reconstruction in 1866 to the end of Prohibition in 1933.

The stage version, of course, could not hope to paint such a huge canvas. The collaboration between Marquand and Broadway luminary George Kaufman wisely focuses on one year in Apley's life—1912. It is then as a middle-aged father and husband that he is forced to confront the different values of a younger generation and a newer age. Kaufman's influence is particularly noticeable in the play's altered conception of Apley. The novel's serious patrician, who finds his proper Bostonian upbringing both comforting and restricting, becomes in the play a more sympathetic if somewhat buffoonish fuddy duddy whose concerns for propriety are broadly ridiculed. Kaufman's Apley is the stereotypical Boston WASP, and he becomes a butt of class, ethnic, and regional humor. In the play, for example, Apley's most fervent aim is to be elected president of a local society of bird watchers, and this joke is played for more laughs when he is ultimately rejected by its members as far too prim even for them. Yet the Broadway version, like its novel source, does not downplay the stultifying effects of Apley's obedience to tradition. Just as he is himself unable to escape the class-defined restrictions into which he was born, so George makes sure his son rejects the woman he really loves (a middle-class girl from nearby Worcester, which, for those from Back Bay, might as well be Outer Mongolia!). In fact, Apley makes the reluctant boy contract an approved and loveless marriage to his cousin. This inbreeding is yet another family tradition because George is likewise married to a cousin, even as it is also a potent index of Boston society's stifling self-containment. Much like Lillian Hellman's earlier Broadway hit *The Little Foxes*, Kaufman's play is part romantic family comedy, part penetrating critique of core American values, especially the received wisdom that sons should obey their fathers.

Because the studio thought the play's literary values should be preserved and, if possible, enhanced, Fox engaged veteran screenwriter Philip Dunne to work with Mankiewicz on the adaptation. It was thought that the two former Ivy Leaguers (Mankiewicz from Columbia and Dunne from Harvard, Apley's alma mater) would not only understand Marquand's characters and milieu, but would be able to sharpen the humor that Kaufman had made the play's main focus. Dunne and Mankiewicz, as it turned out, went on to work on this and two additional projects in rapid succession: *The Ghost and Mrs. Muir* and *Escape* round out the trio of collaborations. Of these, only *Ghost* was both a critical and box office success. All three films, however, are interesting examples of what might be called "literary cinema": that is, filmmaking that enhances the appeal of admired literary models through the power of effective *mise en scène* and stylish scripting. *Escape* and *Ghost* both rely heavily on the expressivity of images, many of which, especially in the former film, are stitched together to create silent sequences.

In *The Late George Apley*, Dunne and Mankiewicz based the film's visual design more on a seamless series of dramatic encounters that are staged, photographed, and edited in a fluid style that focuses attention on performance. Compared to standard Hollywood films, including many by Mankiewicz himself, there is less shot breakdown (use of changes in scale to provide visual variety) and more building up of sequences around medium shots that emphasize the character's place within the setting. The result is somewhat similar to the style Jean Renoir perfects in *La Règle du Jeu*, a film which, with a similar mixture of humor and serious political comment, also chronicles the complex, shifting relations between characters in a shrewdly detailed environment. Mankiewicz recalls that

Dunne's providing the script freed him from his usual rewriting duties. As a result, he could concentrate on the more purely cinematic aspects of the project, continuing to teach himself the art of directing (this was, after all, only his third directorial assignment). The result was an eminently well-made film that undoubtedly struck most filmgoers as highbrow and stagy, which it is, though these qualities do not necessarily make for ineffectual cinema, as *A Letter to Three Wives*, among other and later Mankiewicz films, bears witness. The production had other serious faults, the most important of which is a palpable coldness which is also evident in *Dragonwyck* but is not to be found in later Mankiewicz productions. With its endless talk, its precious humor, which is neither broad nor easily understandable, and its somewhat unsympathetic characters, *The Late George Apley* lacks not only the bonhomie and life-affirming heartiness of *Life with Father*, but also the tear-jerking folksiness of *I Remember Mama*. Just to take a central and illuminating example, Dunne follows his sources in making Apley an ardent Emersonian. Early in the film, George finds himself discussing New England's most famous author with Eleanor's Harvard professor beau (who attended Lehigh, where he worked his way through, and not the institution where he now teaches). Roger Newcombe informs Apley that Emerson was considered one of the "Concord Radicals" as a young man and that he was for some time persona non grata in Boston Brahmin circles. Apley reacts with disbelief to Newcombe's views, which, he thinks, are explained by Roger's "questionable" educational background. The humor Dunne builds into this scene depends very much on the spectator knowing that Emerson was not only tolerant of human differences but welcomed them—the catholicity of his social attitudes is far removed from the narrow-minded provincialism of George Apley. Yet how many among the moviegoing public, then or now, would be sufficiently informed about American intellectual history to "get" the joke?

And yet Dunne's conception is even more complex and layered. For it is his failure to be elected president of the bird watching society—an event as poignant as it is humorous—that instructs George in the very Emersonianism he had previously been unable to embrace. Now understanding his "love of nature" as an emotional and intellectual longing that exceeds any social usefulness (i.e., as an excuse for yet another exclusive and snobbish society of sorts), George begins to see birds and himself in another light. The petty defeat and rejection initiate him into the transcendental. Without willing it in any sense, he thus becomes for the first time a true Emersonian (his previous attachment to the author, based on a fundamental misunderstanding of his philosophy, is revealed as superficial tribalism, the affection one might feel for the success of his close fellow). The benevolence with which George now regards his children is thus the index of an inner transformation (unfortunately, it is not effectively "acted out" in the film). He has acquired the respect for the difference and integrity of others that is at the core of Emerson's thinking. Once again, however, the subtlety of this change in character cannot help but be lost on a mass audience. Hollywood's paying customers were much better able to follow the softening of Leon Ames' patriarch in *Life with Father*. Here is a transformation effected in true Victorian fashion by the benevolent and loving nagging of his wife, who is finally able to persuade him to become a Christian gentleman. Such sexual politics require no special learning to understand and were easily converted into the "situation" of the immensely popular television comedy series based on this film.

Dunne believed that Kaufman had distorted Apley's character, transforming into a clownish caricature a character who is sympathetic because of his resistance, at times, to claustrophobic conventionality. In his adaptation, he attempted to divert some of the play's biting satire away from Apley and toward Horatio (played with mincing obnoxiousness by British character actor Richard Haydn). Horatio is a stock figure, an interfering and mean-spirited teller of tales, the purveyor of malicious gossip who can destroy reputations with ease in a closed society such as the one George Apley inhabits. Yet Horatio's claws are drawn in in Dunne's version. More silly than vicious, he proves unable to prevent the festive celebration of renewal toward which the narrative inexorably moves. For if in the play Apley prevents the marriage for love that should cement the emotional fortunes of the next generation, in the film the reportedly ugly duckling cousin the son must marry to please his father turns out to be incredibly beautiful—and also quite obviously his soul mate.

Thus Dunne constructs a wish fulfillment every bit as satisfying and improbable as that which transcends the contradictions of Chaucer's *Wife of Bath's Tale*, where the knight promises obedience to an ugly woman who is suddenly transformed into a beauty by his submission. As reviewers at the time, especially Bosley Crowther, observed, the film thus has a happy ending that blunts the irony of Marquand's conception of a father who resists in his youth the very compromises demanded by society that as a middle-aged father he forces his own son to accept. Moreover, in the play and novel Apley is finally defied by his daughter, who elopes to marry the man he urges her to abandon. The film version, however, softens his disapproval; George is the one who provides for her honeymoon travel. Like one of Shakespeare's festive comedies, the story ends with a double wedding that reaffirms tradition in the very act of displacing it.

With better casting, Dunne and Mankiewicz's shaping of the material might have proven effective. But here again the director had to endure the same kind of ill luck he experienced in the production of *Dragonwyck*. Hollywood tradition called for the casting of British actors (speaking a kind of "transatlantic" dialect) in the roles of upper-crust New Englanders. Fox sought out the services of Ronald Colman, for many years, mostly at MGM, one of Hollywood's most distinguished leading men, for the title role, and he agreed to do the film after finding out more about Mankiewicz, with whom he was at the time unfamiliar. The much less well known Peggy Cummins was signed to play the second lead, Apley's daughter Eleanor.

As Dunne later maintained, these two actors were hopelessly miscast. Cummins lacked the energy, vivacity, and tenacity to make Eleanor's loving but disputatious encounters with her father suitably dramatic. And Colman simply could not portray Apley's deeply conflictive self-restraint. His Apley is too benign, too bland, too untroubled by the changes taking place in his world. Colman was always best in roles that called for broader effects: the intense melodrama of two James Hilton adaptations, *Random Harvest* and *Lost Horizon*; the pervasive theatricality of *A Double Life*, a bizarre film noir about an actor who can't get out of character; the swashbuckling romanticism of *If I Were King*, where he hams it up as poet François Villon; the intense eroticism of the many dark romances with temptress Vilma Banky that made him one of Hollywood's most bankable attractions in the twenties. Although the ensemble of actors played admirably in *The Late George Apley* under Mankiewicz's expert direction, the film suffered because the main character never became sufficiently attractive or sympathetic. A director's best efforts cannot negate a fundamental error in casting, and for this failing in the project Mankiewicz shoulders no blame or responsibility.

In tone and theme, *The Late George Apley* bears little resemblance to the standard Hollywood film. Like the two others made by Dunne and Mankiewicz, it has a distinctly British aura. This is not just the result of the influence of the British stars involved (Rex Harrison plays the lead in the other two films and other Britishers, notably George Sanders and Edna Best, figure prominently) or the use of British sources (*Escape* is based on a Galsworthy play) and settings (*Ghost* appears to take place in England, and *Escape* was made on location in the United Kingdom). These three collaborations are also literary (that is, stagy and intellectual) in the fashion of the pre–New Wave British cinema, which was very influenced by West End theater. While such an approach to filmmaking was undoubtedly natural for the well-educated, highbrow Mankiewicz (a predilection certainly shared by Dunne), it probably would not have served him well in the American film industry, as the indifferent reception accorded *Escape* and *The Late George Apley* demonstrates. *The Late George Apley*, despite its inappropriate casting, is in many ways an excellent work. The movie as a whole, but in particular his devising a visual style appropriate to the story, further displays Mankiewicz's filmmaking virtuosity. It is to his credit that he took this project on when he was able to turn to making films that conformed more closely to the industry model.

Julius Caesar

The postwar era brought financial crisis for Hollywood that, in a somewhat strange consequence, precipitated a move—if only in part— away from entertainment to "serious" productions. The box office vitality of imported art films at a time of generally declining attendance revealed the existence of patrons who wanted more than stars, overworked generic conventions, and glitz. Beginning with Elia Kazan's *A Streetcar Named Desire* (1950)—a surprising success in spite of its innovative adult themes—audiences clearly showed their affection for well-made films based on esteemed literary sources. It is no shock, therefore, that the period witnessed a number of Shakespeare adaptations directed by such luminaries as Laurence Olivier and Orson Welles. One, a lucrative art film, was a daring version of *King Lear* directed by Akira Kurosawa, more famous for his samurai adventure films, and released under the sensational title of *Throne of Blood*.

Joseph Mankiewicz, the most renowned "literary" director of the time, not surprisingly became involved in the emerging series of Shakespeare films. The project in which he eventually took part, however, was not his own (his taste in Shakespeare ran to the romantic comedies such as *Twelfth Night* and *Measure for Measure*, plays he unfortunately never had a chance to adapt). The creative force behind MGM's decision to make a film version of *Julius Caesar* (certainly an unusual choice) was producer John Houseman. Since his collaboration with Welles on several Mercury Theatre Shakespeare productions, including *Julius Caesar*, during the thirties, Houseman had been interested in doing a film version of this rather unpoetic meditation on republican values and regicide. The Mercury Theatre group had mounted the play with a great deal of success in 1937, a time when its political themes had substantial resonance. It had, however, been much sharpened by Welles' modernizing treatment. Having persuaded MGM's Dore Schary that he should produce the

Mankiewicz directing on the set of *Julius Caesar* (1953).

studio's intended version, Houseman picked Mankiewicz to handle the directing. He was delighted with the challenge of creating a Shakespeare film designed to have popular appeal.

Despite the box office success (mostly in art houses) of Olivier's *Henry V* and *Hamlet*, the view in Hollywood had long been that Shakespeare was too arty for average theatergoers. This conclusion was based on the disastrous failure of both Max Reinhardt's expressionistic yet uninvolving *Midsummer Night's Dream* (1935) and George Cukor's tepid *Romeo and Juliet* (1936). There was no mainstream Hollywood Shakespeare film produced again until Houseman and Mankiewicz tried their luck. Their *Julius Caesar* received generally favorable reviews from journalists who lauded Hollywood's attempt therein to raise the cultural level of movies; ordinary patrons who saw the film were less enthusiastic, and it did only moderate box office. Houseman and Mankiewicz did not inaugurate a new series of Shakespeare films. Thus the conventional wisdom about literature's most renowned author being box office poison for mass audiences was only refuted decisively some 40 years later. In the nineties, a growing number of film adaptations, mostly British, have found success in a transformed American market, and the trend shows no signs of abating. Mankiewicz's *Julius Caesar*, however, has not found another life on video even though the Welles and Olivier adaptations have achieved a modicum of popularity in the new medium.

Mankiewicz had a personal reason for undertaking this project. He was determined to make a profitable prestige picture at the studio from which he had been summarily dismissed in 1943. He thus derived no little satisfaction from Houseman's invitation and studio mogul Dore Schary's tacit endorsement of his now eminent position among studio directors. Despite Houseman's avowed willingness to accept something more daring than a faithful mounting of the bard's text, Mankiewicz had no intentions of following Welles in a radical reinterpretation of *Julius Caesar*. Welles set his production in contemporary Italy, making an obvious and effective reference to the advent of Mussolini as dictator and fascism as political ideology. This reframing had the unfortunate consequence of giving the treason of the conspirators an unambiguously positive value that ran contrary to Shakespeare's more balanced presentation. Perhaps this is why Mankiewicz decided against a similar modernization.

In any event, though the Cold War had in recent years intensified with the invasion of Korea, Mankiewicz did not make his *Julius Caesar* an anti–Stalinist tract. He was determined to produce a traditional and effectively dramatic version of the play, perhaps fearful that any drastic changes would reflect badly on him and MGM's cultural bona fides. Unfortunately, Mankiewicz gave little thought to the overall design of his film, which is, in consequence, not as visually interesting as Welles' virtuoso *Othello* (the Cannes festival award winner in 1952). The choice of black and white film stock, rather than the increasingly standard color, did give the film a documentary feel not out of keeping with its political subject matter. Though the play offered other, perhaps even more obvious opportunities for effective stylization, Mankiewicz's *Julius Caesar* was not to prove particularly cinematic. This is surprising for a director who had demonstrated at this point in his career a flair for the use of images to tell a story or embellish a theme. Part of the blame for this failure must be laid at the door of Dore Schary, who allowed Houseman only a very low budget for the time (about $2 million). Apparently MGM had little confidence that the film would make any money, and one wonders why they were so eager to develop this particular project.

The limited budget certainly shows to bad effect on the screen. The

sets and art design are ineffectively stagy at best, laughably unconvincing
at times. The battle scenes in the second part of the film, inappropriately
filmed in a California valley though the text emphasizes the "plains of
Philippi," lend little verisimilitude to what could have been a quite
effective cinematic addition to the playtext: an affecting representation of
the larger public consequences of the assassination. Built into Shakespeare's text is a dramatic weakness. The assassination of Caesar and
Antony's subsequent rhetorical reversal of the revolutionary energy it
unleashes come at the play's midpoint; the final acts are sustained largely
by Brutus' crisis of conscience, a psychological development that is brought
to a head by the appearance of Caesar's ghost. A well-handled battle of
Philippi, one that emphasized the intensity and uncertainty of the struggle between Caesar's heirs and the assassins, would have done much to
remedy the imbalance of the two parts. Olivier's *Henry V* shows how
effective such "opening out" can be. Mankiewicz may be to blame in part
for the film's failure to provide suitable spectacle. He was temperamen-
tally unsuited to directing such sequences, which he regarded as pander-
ing to mass tastes for violence and visual titillation. This limitation, if
that is what it is, would prove to have more disastrous results when Mankiewicz revisited the Roman civil war (though relying more on Plutarch
and Shaw this time than on Shakespeare); the seemingly unending scenes
of public ceremony and battle in *Cleopatra* are without a doubt the most
problematic elements of the picture.

Similarly, *Julius Caesar* is in general weak in those aspects that might
be collectively termed spectacle. Caesar's ghost appears in an amateur-
ishly handled double exposure that would have seemed cheesy in a "B"
horror production; thunder and lightning effects are barely theatrical quality and are hardly worthy of a major studio, especially one that prided
itself on a tradition of prestige production. Just to add insult to injury,
MGM determined to blow the release print up to 55mm, perhaps convinced that the film would best be marketed as a classical epic; this repro-
cessing cut off the heads and feet of the actors in some sequences,
heightening the effect of low-budget and shoddy production values. To
Metro's financial controller, the aged Nicholas Schenk, Mankiewicz
protested vehemently about this misbegotten decision, which implicitly
reflected badly on his supervision of the cinematography. This occasioned
a battle royal, with the director, his advice unheeded, storming out of the
executive offices amidst a torrent of invective and threats. Mankiewicz's
only reason for satisfaction after the encounter was that Schenck and
Metro could not fire him since he had signed on with Houseman as an
independent for this film alone.

With only a limited budget, he and Houseman pinned their hopes for success on the dramatization of the play, the most important elements of which would be casting and the molding of performance, the latter being a Mankiewicz specialty. In fact, viewed as simply a production of the play and not as a film, their *Julius Caesar* works quite well. Houseman proved able to assemble a quite remarkable, star-studded cast (much like Reinhardt's ill-fated *A Midsummer Night's Dream* in fact); this was possible because the studio still had a number of leading and second-level performers on contract. Metro had originally offered a somewhat lackluster slate of players. Houseman, however, worked hard to improve on the original selections, working first with those on the studio lot. He persuaded both Louis Calhern (Caesar) and Edmond O'Brien (Casca) to appear; in addition to their successful film careers as supporting actors, each had substantial Shakespearean theatrical experience and performed admirably in the ensemble. Houseman also succeeded in signing on two of Metro's stable of female stars, Greer Garson and Deborah Kerr, who appear only briefly in the film as the wives, respectively, of Brutus and Caesar.

Houseman wanted James Mason for Brutus, and got him. Mankiewicz was pleased to work again with the star whose smooth yet amoral charm had been so successfully exploited in *Five Fingers*. This casting decision, however, was not an altogether happy one. Brutus is a man of principle caught between conflicting loyalties: his patriotic love of republican institutions and his admiration for Caesar, who had been the savior of the very state whose traditional politics he was now threatening. In a sense, Shakespeare's play focuses on the tragic consequences for the all too virtuous man trapped by this conflict and forced to do what horrifies and repels him; the civil war precipitated by his choice claims him as its most notable victim, killed by the very hand that put an end to Caesar. Mason was simply too much the attractive antihero (as his bravura performance as Diello proves) to provide the production with its emotional center, a hero who would arouse both pity and fear. In persuading John Gielgud to join the company, Houseman did find a better Cassius; the eminent stage actor expertly embodied Cassius' less than idealistic desire to destroy Caesar, his envy and viciousness effectively setting off Mason's clear expression of Brutus' higher, more conflicted motives.

Having chosen eminent British actors for two of the three principal speaking parts, Houseman and Mankiewicz made what seemed at first an odd choice for the third: the American Marlon Brando, who had hitherto achieved international fame as the brutish, mumbling yet sympathetic Stanley Kowalski in Tennessee Williams' *A Streetcar Named Desire*.

Paul Scofield (yet another Britisher with an impeccable stage reputation and much experience with Shakespeare) had first been considered for the role of Brutus but, when Mason was cast in that part, did a test for Mark Antony. Scofield's affecting portrait of the conscience stricken Sir Thomas More more than a decade later in *A Man for All Seasons* hints at the kind of success he would have found in either role. However, perhaps with an eye toward the box office, the film's producer and director preferred one of America's hottest actors for the role of Antony, and he was shocked by Mankiewicz's invitation. So were many in New York when Brando eventually accepted after putting himself through a crash course in Shakespearean acting and developing an interesting approach to Caesar's eulogizer, whom he portrayed as a canny, sophisticated seeker after revenge and advantage, a character perhaps not too far removed after all from Williams' Stanley.

Just as he had made Stella's nemesis an engaging brute, so he turned Antony into a sympathetic character, thereby undercutting Brutus' claim to be acting in the best interests of the state, an effect increased by Brando's not inconsiderable sex appeal and charisma, qualities in which he definitely outclassed Mason. Because of Brando's calculatingly appealing performance, the production becomes slightly unbalanced, which Mankiewicz seems to have recognized since one of the few scenes added to the original playscript features Antony playing with a bust of the now departed Caesar and sitting smugly in the former leader's chair—a clear image of his pleasure at this political transition that has so obviously benefited him. As often in classical or biblical epics of the period (the best example is *Spartacus*, where the oppressive Romans are played by English performers and the slaves by Americans), the mixture of accents has an unintended and unfortunate effect; Cassius and Brutus seem effete and cold-blooded, while Caesar, Mark Antony, and Casca are worldly-wise, sharply articulate, even charismatic and sympathetic. (Had Scofield been cast as Brutus, the contrast would have been muted and less disturbing.) This problem was carefully noted by Mankiewicz after filming had ended. He made sure that he would not repeat the error when he came to film *Cleopatra*. Caesar, Antony, and Brutus are all British (Rex Harrison, Richard Burton, and Kenneth Haigh); the contrast of their "Roman" English with Elizabeth Taylor's quite different accent is entirely appropriate and effective.

For all its faults, *Julius Caesar* deserved a better fate than it received. Even in its ludicrously blown-up version, the production very much succeeds at being "filmed theater," a specialized genre unfortunately appreciated more in Europe than in the United States. Unfortunately, Europeans were deprived of an important opportunity to judge the film and the agenda of more serious and artistically challenging productions from Hollywood that it exemplified. Though MGM lobbied strenuously, the Venice Film Festival refused *Julius Caesar* as an entry, choosing instead a Burt Lancaster western of no special merit as the American selection that year. In any event, Houseman and Mankiewicz succeeded in mounting an impressive and interesting production of one of Shakespeare's more challenging plays. That was no small achievement in the Hollywood of the early fifties.

Suddenly, Last Summer

With continuing problems limiting the operation of Figaro, his own production company, Mankiewicz was pleased in the late fifties to find work with producer Sam Spiegel, an old-time Hollywood professional. In the poststudio world of independent production, Mankiewicz was indisputably the most talented writer-director of the period. He did not have to wait long for the phone to ring. The opportunity was a good one since it allowed him to participate in the decade's most notable series of literary adaptations. Spiegel had just acquired the rights to one of the year's hottest properties: Tennessee Williams' one-act play *Suddenly, Last Summer*. Paired with another one-acter, *Something Unspoken*, and collectively produced as *Garden District*, this play had just finished a very successful New York run in the 1957–8 season. Spiegel felt, and rightly so as it turned out, that the erudite and literate Mankiewicz would make the ideal director for the screen adaptation.

In the forties, Spiegel had specialized in making first-class versions of standard genre films. A useful example is *The Stranger* (1946), an Orson Welles thriller that made the most of excellent writing, bankable stars (Welles, Edward G. Robinson, and Loretta Young), and limited but judicious spending on location shooting and set design. In the fifties, Spiegel adapted well to the sweeping changes within the industry. He enjoyed a great deal of success with the current fashion for socially conscious, adult films by making *On the Waterfront* and *The Bridge over the River Kwai*. These two films, the first a noirish exposé of union racketeering and the second an offbeat war story, were among the most critically acclaimed and profitable productions of the period.

Because he was on the lookout for similar material, it was natural that Spiegel would find the latest hot theatrical property from Tennessee Williams interesting. With the exception of *Camino Real* (an archly modernist allegory that flopped on Broadway), all of Williams' plays from the forties and fifties were adapted for the screen. None of these films bombed. Elia Kazan's version of *A Streetcar Named Desire*, and Richard Brooks' *Cat on a Hot Tin Roof* and *Sweet Bird of Youth*, became box office smashes in a decade when the studios were desperate to lure patrons back to theaters. The adult themes that, in part, had made Williams' plays a success in New York were found to be attractive, even in a necessarily diluted form, to the moviegoing public as well. Spiegel had hopes that a screen version of *Suddenly, Last Summer* would do well too, even though the adaptation process would not prove easy. For the play, with its mythological cadre (a dark restaging of the Orpheus myth), expressionist setting, limited dramatic action, and unusual sexual themes, was a far cry from the more realist Williams efforts that had earned the playwright his widespread popularity. Hollywood versions of Williams' other modernist plays (most particularly Sidney Lumet's *The Fugitive Kind*, an adaptation of *Orpheus Descending* (starring Marlon Brando) had done or would do only moderate business at the box office. It was hardly insignificant that the Williams double bill of which *Suddenly, Last Summer* was part had opened at an Off Broadway theater, not at the midtown venues where *Cat* and *Streetcar* had earlier in the decade enjoyed such profitable runs. Spiegel was too canny a producer not to heed this obvious warning sign.

Spiegel needed no convincing that *Suddenly, Last Summer* would require a great deal of modification if it were to be turned into a filmable story. Like many of Williams' plays, it is heavy on talk but light on drama. In fact, the play consists entirely of two contrasting, conflicting dialogues. It opens with a conversation between Dr. Cukrowicz, a psychiatrist, and Violet Venable, a rich widow from New Orleans' Garden District. And it ends with the doctor's interview of her niece Catherine Holly at Violet's insistence. Surprisingly, perhaps, these limited dramatic encounters provide a compelling theme suitable for a feature-length film. Each is equally eager to convince the psychiatrist she is right about the meaning of the life and death of Violet's son Sebastian, a poet manqué who, it is only gradually revealed, used his mother and then Catherine to attract young men to satisfy his unnameable, yet unmistakably homosexual desires. Violet refuses to see the perverse, destructive elements in her son's behavior; she thus wants to silence Catherine, who is intent on speaking the truth about him. Violet prefers to idealize Sebastian as a Nietzschean antihero eager to discover the central truth of existence. His experiences with nature and his fellow man convince him of what he already believes: that the cruel, destructive pursuit of self-interest is what underlies all experience, human and animal alike. Violet has deluded herself that

Sebastian is virginal and physically pure, untouched by the evil he sees around him.

Williams gives Sebastian's vision of red tooth and claw an unforgettable stage presence in the primeval garden (dominated by rare insectivorous plants) that the son designed to border the family's genteel home. Sebastian's desire to live as a human version of the Venus Flytraps he raises has destroyed Catherine's innocence. Pressed into service as her cousin's companion during his annual summer trip abroad, she suffers a mental breakdown after his restless journey in search of exploitative pleasure ends disastrously. In the course of her therapeutic dialogue with Dr. Cukrowicz, Catherine recalls witnessing the Nietzschean primal scene that drove her into insanity. Sebastian is pursued and then eaten alive by the impoverished young male prostitutes he had used but now scorns. Desperate to prevent what she sees as an attack on her brilliant son's reputation, Violet wants Catherine silenced forever. Dr. Cukrowicz has been lured to the rich lady's home by the hope of obtaining a donation to fund much needed improvements for his hospital; he soon learns that Mrs. Venable's generosity is contingent on his agreement to perform a prefrontal lobotomy on Catherine. He agrees to speak to the young woman. Catherine must convince Dr. Cukrowicz that her version of the events leading to her breakdown is the truth, not a self-destructive delusion that, if literally cut out by brain surgery, would bring her peace again.

Undeniably, Williams' play is powerfully dramatic. Yet it is completely dependent on outstanding acting from the two female leads, who each must deliver what are in effect very long monologues. The boyishly good-looking Dr. Cukrowicz functions less as a full-fledged character and more as an onstage narratee. He is also a visible reminder of Sebastian, whom he is meant to resemble. A successful film version would have to find effective ways of "cinematizing" the monologues and giving the psychiatrist a more central role; it would also have to invent some kind of dramatic framework into which the play's endless, highly poetic talk could be set. Also in need of careful handling would be Williams' offcenter sexual theme: a homosexual predation connected intimately to an unacknowledged but hardly subliminal Oedipal romance. Mankiewicz handled all these problems ably.

His producer assembled a first-rate team to make the film. To help Mankiewicz with the writing, Spiegel wisely engaged novelist Gore Vidal, a New York intellectual familiar with Williams' work and no stranger to homosexual themes. As he sometimes did with the films made from his plays, the playwright himself took some part in preparing the screenplay, though this was only at an early stage in the project. Apparently lacking confidence in the possibility of an adaptation faithful to his original vision, Williams soon left Vidal and Mankiewicz to their own devices. He did think the finished film laughable, concluding that his lyrical, morality play had in their hands become little more than a sensational bit of Southern Gothic. The evaluation is understandable but hardly fair. With Vidal's help, Mankiewicz was able to construct a suspenseful and affecting drama from Williams' frightening fable, even if some concessions had to be made to Hollywood conventions (most notably, adding a romantic connection between the psychiatrist and Catherine, as well as hinting strongly at a happier ever after finale).

Spiegel also provided the acting talent and star appeal necessary to the film's success, assembling a superior cast. Montgomery Clift and Elizabeth Taylor had earlier in the decade played one of the era's most celebrated screen romantic duos in George Stevens' *A Place in the Sun*. Taylor, in addition, had earlier been a great success in a similar Tennessee Williams role: as Maggie the Cat in the film version of *Cat on a Hot Tin Roof*. Spiegel engaged them to play Dr. Cukrowicz and Catherine, a risky move since Clift's drug and alcohol addiction was making it increasingly difficult for him to work. Somehow Mankiewicz proved able to extract a nuanced performance from the failing star. A problem of another kind came with the engagement of Katharine Hepburn to play Mrs. Venable, a part eminently suited to her imperious charm and still attractive middle-aged appearance. Hepburn quickly resented Mankiewicz's gentle attempts to mold her interpretation of Violet. By the end of production, the two were no longer on speaking terms. She refused to view the completed film, even though it offers one of her finest, most subtle acting efforts. Mankiewicz also had to deal with Elizabeth Taylor's most obvious limitation as an actress: her voice, which tends to be monotone and even shrill, qualities that would likely be quite noticeable since Catherine has a very large speaking part. It is a testimony to Mankiewicz's talent and tact that both actresses delivered superior performances and were nominated for Academy Awards that year.

Like many stage adaptations, *Suddenly, Last Summer* takes advantage of the film medium's capacity to "open out" beyond a limited set. The screenplay offers an effective counterpoint to the Venable house, whose powerful guardian, unable to accept the truth, eventually escapes into madness. It is the state mental hospital, where Dr. Cukrowicz is on staff and Catherine a newly arrived patient and surgical candidate because her family, bribed by Violet, has agreed to the lobotomy. Much of the film is set there, including some of Williams' original dialogue between the psychiatrist and the young woman. These sequences are effectively cinematic in their lack of dependence on dialogue. In the most notable of them, Catherine wanders off in confusion and finds herself walking on a ramp above the ward where the most violent men are housed. The beautiful woman's sexual appeal, hardly disguised by institutional garb, moves the inmates to an assault from which she barely escapes. The sequence appropriately connects to Williams' themes in a number of intricate ways. Catherine's successful if inadvertent "display" recalls Sebastian's deliberate use of her attractiveness to lure men to his side. Their wordless, bestial attack also echoes Violet's frightening tale of the baby turtles she and Sebastian saw devoured by savage birds in the Encantadas. An innocent who believes in human virtue and not in Sebastian's Darwinian vision, Catherine escapes from her attackers, while Sebastian, condemned in a sense by his own amorality, is devoured by his; the sequence thus interestingly rhymes with the film's climactic reenactment of Sebastian's murder. Finally, Catherine's escape, and subsequent comforting by Dr. Cukrowicz, presage her eventual flight to sanity and safety when, aided by the psychiatrist's careful administration of sodium pentathol, she is able to recall completely the horror of Sebastian's death and thus release herself from the guilt she wrongly feels.

This last sequence is the dramatic center of the film and is handled with absolute brilliance by Mankiewicz, who again uses images, this time to underscore the power of Catherine's involuntary narrative. Onstage, the stories both women tell about their experiences with Sebastian remain just that: narratives that illuminate the present concerns of their narrators as much as they evoke a series of past and unrecoverable moments. Sebastian never appears on stage because the dramatic action remains completely in the present. In film, such reminiscences are usually handled more dramatically: through flashback, with the teller's narration gradually transformed into an objective, enacted representation of the past. The stage method inevitably emphasizes the teller more than the tale, while the cinematic flashback, even when accompanied by sporadic voice-over narration (another hackneyed Hollywood convention), literally makes the teller largely invisible. Mankiewicz and Vidal correctly thought that Mrs. Venable's unrelieved narration of the past was all the film could bear, since it was already pretty much a talkathon with nearly all of Williams' dialogue retained in the screenplay.

But Catherine's recollections, aided by sodium pentathol, are not only "true" (for it is his mother's version of Sebastian that is delusional), but dramatically indispensable (for they establish Catherine's sanity by grounding her fears in true horror). This part of the story could not be all talk. To actualize Catherine's monologue, Vidal and Mankiewicz designed a unique combination of stage and film methods, utilizing strikingly composed and photographed double images. Catherine tells her story from beginning to end, but the images and sounds of her telling are combined in the same frame with silent, fragmentary enactments of the story she relates. These images are intercut effectively with reaction shots of the psychiatrist and Mrs. Venable, thus reminding the spectator that Catherine's story is both exculpatory (she is sane and requires no lobotomy from Dr. Sugar) and condemnatory (the mother's image of an asexual child is revealed as a destructive self-deception). Mrs. Venable must listen to a horror about Sebastian she cannot deny (especially since her son's death reenacts Sebastian's Darwinian understanding of life, which he gained while visiting the Encantadas with her). As her niece proves irrefutably that she is not delusional, the stricken woman gradually lapses into insanity. Mankiewicz wisely aids this transition by shooting the final reaction shots without the normal glamorizing techniques employed earlier. The result is that Katharine Hepburn literally ages before our eyes as she must face the truth about her son and herself.

The film's success at the box office was substantially aided by posters and a trailer which featured Elizabeth Taylor posing seductively on a beach dressed in a wet bathing suit that was almost transparent. (In the story, the costume was purchased for Catherine by Sebastian.) The pictures, though on one level a cynical attempt to boost business, reflect the film's expression of the changed sexual politics. Mankiewicz does not deny the story its most compelling element (Sebastian's homosexual predation and its horrifying consequences). But he makes the film's erotic center the beautiful Catherine. The pairing of Taylor and Clift decisively claims the film for heterosexuality. In fact, the film makes this coupling a normal and sanctioned response to the perverse, manipulative relationships between Catherine and her cousin, on the one hand, and Sebastian and Violet on the other.

Mankiewicz and Vidal, thereby, not only suggest the objectionable selfishness of Sebastian's brand of homosexual promiscuity (an undeniable theme in the original play); they also dramatize a process of psychic healing that ends in Catherine establishing a quite different kind of sexual connection. The film even hints that homosexuality can be overcome with the love of the right woman since the doctor is a stand-in for Sebastian. Montgomery Clift's feminized brand of masculinity suits well this aspect of the film. This was not Williams' intention at all. However unfaithful such a transformation was, it made the playwright's themes and material more palatable to mainstream audiences. Mankiewicz was not going to fail at such an important project, and in fact did not. *Suddenly,*

Last Summer remains today the only Williams film adaptation of the decade that largely preserves the play's original dialogue and ideas, yet also develops these effectively through the canny deployment of the cinema's quite different resources.

The Quiet American

In 1957, a number of Mankiewicz projects announced in the press— including an adaptation of *Twelfth Night* starring Danny Kaye and Audrey Hepburn that might well have become a classic—embarrassingly came to nothing. Then Figaro and the director turned their creative and corporate attention to more current source material: British novelist Graham Greene's recent bestseller, *The Quiet American* (1956). Set in Vietnam during the final stages of the failed French attempt to recolonize the country after the expulsion of the Japanese, Greene's novel is a political allegory. Old Europe is represented by two middle-aged men, the British journalist Fowler, a jaded intellectual, and the French political functionary Vigot, a man who impotently recognizes the hopeless mission his country's shortsighted policies have committed him to serving. The representative of the New World, and the new world order enforced by American military might, is a nameless and hence generic American—fresh-faced, Princeton-educated, and eager to save Vietnam from both the corrupt establishment and the communists by locating and strengthening a "third force." In Greene's orientalist perspective, which metaphorizes colonialism as a seduction of the feminine East by a masculine West, Vietnam is a young woman, the beautiful Phuong (her name means "phoenix," a reference to the country's rise from destruction at the end of the Japanese occupation in 1945). Fowler and the American vie directly and bitterly for Phuong's affection in what is the novel's main plot.

In the end, Fowler betrays his rival, a hopeless naïf with no understanding of *Weltpolitik* who stupidly trusts the Englishman, believing that his own commitment to fair play will be reciprocated. The communist assassins eager to rid the country of yet another meddling American easily gain Fowler's cooperation. They simply implicate the young man in a plot, which, they tell Fowler, was hatched by a general friendly to the emerging "third force." Fowler convinces himself that the American's murder is justified because of the man's participation in a plan to overthrow the government by a campaign of terror bombing.

Investigating the murder, Vigot quickly discovers that the communists have simply exploited Fowler's jealousy and insecurity. They have fooled him with a fabrication that any experienced journalist should never have credited. In the end, then, the American is as much a victim of European perfidy as of the Vietnamese desire to be rid of interfering westerners. Yet his death does call into question the efficacy of an American problem-solving approach to Vietnamese political instability. It also challenges the moral fitness of Old Europe to offer some viable alternative. Like the beautiful pawn Phuong (in the film Fowler says she is too busy staying alive to think about politics), the Vietnamese are a shadowy presence in their own country. They are the exotic and ultimately unknowable means through which the western powers work through their own obsessions, differences in national characters, and inadequacies.

Like all Greene's novels and "entertainments," *The Quiet American* features complex characters involved in an engaging, suspenseful plot. The book's major themes—ones that Mankiewicz would appreciate— are friendship, betrayal, crime, and retribution. *The Quiet American* is in fact strongly reminiscent of the writer's most famous thriller, *The Third Man*, realized for the screen by director Carol Reed. *The Third Man* was based on a Greene script that despite its political tendentiousness (also vaguely anti–status quo in its indictment of postwar profiteering) made for an exciting film. Several years before agreeing to film *The Quiet American*, Mankiewicz had altered L. C. Moyzisch's *Operation Cicero* to give that war memoir qualities not unlike those of the typical Greene novel. *Five Fingers'* jaded loners—Diello, the countess Staviska, and the German ambassador chief among them—find themselves trapped within a larger political struggle to which they cannot, will not commit. Yet their restless pursuit of self-interest leads nowhere. In fact, the only Greenian touch missing from *Five Fingers* is a transcendent framework of religious values that would force the amoral and guilty to confront their sins in the light of possible redemption. Diello's existential crisis, precipitated by his discovery that all he has worked for is worthless, leads only to his derisive laughter at the ironies of destiny. By way of contrast, in *The Quiet American* the novelist, in his typical fashion, moves the reluctant hero toward a moment of self-recognition and moral choice, which Fowler does not embrace but refuses, largely because he keeps Phuong in the end. Predictably, Mankiewicz ignored Greene's Catholic ideas, if not their ethical implications, as he shaped the script. His Fowler is forced by Vigot not God to face the crime he has committed, and Phuong, learning of his betrayal, will have nothing to do with him even though, ironically, his wife will now divorce him, allowing the marriage that Phuong had always wanted but now is revolted by. Except for its religious themes, the book offered Mankiewicz the complex characters, moral ideas, and suspenseful thriller plot he had found so congenial when making *Five Fingers*.

Yet in large part, the novel seems today a strange choice for Mankiewicz; it must have seemed so to many at the time as well. Finding his way through an emerging post-studio world of semi-independent production through his association with Figaro, he aimed above all else to maintain his career in a Hollywood where, during the fifties, ideological correctness was deemed important. The publication of *The Quiet American* confirmed the suspicions of official America that Greene was soft on communism, perhaps even a fellow traveler; the novelist became persona non grata in this country and remained so for many years. His novels are always set in non–Western countries experiencing political upheaval; these fictional realms contain few flattering portraits of Americans, and *The Quiet American* is perhaps the worst offender. In the late fifties, the Eisenhower administration prepared to take up the burden, now abandoned by the French, of containing communist "expansion" in Southeast Asia. Greene's indictment of feckless if idealistic American opportunism probed closely the goals and tactics of current official involvement, in a manner much closer to political reality than most Hollywood filmmakers would have found comfortable or deemed profitable in the wake of the Red Scare and the divisive inconclusiveness of the Korean War. Earlier in the decade, Mankiewicz himself had suffered during the witchhunt for communists and fellow travelers in the film industry; yet here was a project that could be interpreted as sympathy for the Cold War enemy at a time when the blacklist was still in force, if unofficially. The project was daring, to say the least, and it certainly tempted fate, especially since Mankiewicz added to his source materials an even more specific, undoubtedly controversial reference to current Southeast Asian policy, as we shall see below.

In part, the novel's attack on American policy and character could be blunted, and in his rewriting Mankiewicz indeed took this approach, though not, he declared, out of any political motive. In order to portray more accurately, he said, the young people then running various "aid" agencies, he made the American's idealism less noxious, more wholesome. At the same time, Fowler's betrayal became more villainous and self-servingly stupid—even as, almost paradoxically, Mankiewicz increased the sympathy for the older man made a fool in love by his younger and more righteous competitor. In Mankiewicz's version, Fowler is more obviously the main character and functions as the narrator of the story, told in flashback after the American's murder, for which Fowler is initially suspected by Vigot (the Frenchman's interrogation prompts Fowler's flow of memories). Though in the novel, Fowler not only gets away with but is rewarded for his complicity in the American's murder, the film condemns him to a life of guilt-ravaged isolation. In the final scene, Fowler, abandoned by both Vigot and Phuong, makes his way alone through a crowd of Vietnamese celebrating by the riverside the Tet holidays; the image suggests his severance from Western society even as it represents his separation from Eastern culture. In a fitting parallel, the sequence rhymes with the opening scene where celebrations of the Chinese New Year by the same river are interrupted by the startling discovery of the American's body lying face down in the water. In this way, Mankiewicz gives the story a very Karamazovian sense of crime and punishment.

Even rewritten, however, *The Quiet American* hardly presents American involvement in a positive light. Mankiewicz retains Greene's dismissive handling of the American's search for a "third force" and sharpens its reference to what was at the time happening in Vietnam. The American attempt to find a viable alternative to colonial or communist domination of the country was much in the news during the film's production and release. In fact, it dominated Washington's policy during the period. The official search for a third force resulted in Ngo Dinh Diem being discovered by John Foster Dulles at Princeton (precisely the university where the American is said to have received his political training). Diem was subsequently installed as a political strong man by the CIA and later eliminated in an agency-organized coup when he proved a liability. Mankiewicz has the American mention the discovery of a Vietnamese in exile at Princeton who would make an ideal leader for the country if the communists and corrupt military could be held at bay. Yet the film script also portrays the American as a political innocent, an idealistic do-gooder working for an independent aid agency, not the government. If he is to be truly "quiet," the opposite of the stereotypically brash operatives, the military advisors that Greene thoroughly exposes to ridicule, then the American can hardly be at the center of this maneuvering at the highest levels. We must conclude that the politics of novel and film alike are somewhat confusingly worked out. And yet both forms of *The Quiet American* are tendentious in ways that many at the time must have felt to be at turns disquieting yet insightful.

Greene's story, in any event, had excellent dramatic qualities, and it was to these that Mankiewicz was undoubtedly attracted the most. Casting was difficult and controversial, but in the end quite effective. Originally, Laurence Olivier agreed to play Fowler, but only on the condition that Montgomery Clift, who was much enamored of the script, would appear as the American. Unfortunately for Figaro and Mankiewicz, however, Clift was having personal troubles, the legacy of his mental breakdown and an auto accident that had left him in need of extensive plastic surgery. Though he would later work, and quite effectively, for Mankiewicz on *Suddenly, Last Summer*, Clift passed on this project. Olivier reneged as well when he learned that the American would be played by Audie Murphy, then enjoying his greatest popularity. Not a professional actor, Murphy's road to Hollywood stardom was unique. Soft spoken, always smiling, and short of stature, he was America's most decorated soldier in World War Two. After starring successfully in his own screen biography, he was able to sustain a quite consistent Hollywood career, mostly in westerns, but most effectively perhaps as the main character in John Huston's version of *The Red Badge of Courage*.

Murphy was as American as apple pie, but his pleasantness did not mask an irrepressible self-confidence that bordered almost on arrogance. In fact, these were precisely the contradictory qualities that made Greene's character so attractively "quiet" and yet so threatening. These are the qualities, the novelist suggests, of a postwar America, a country which had abandoned in a few short years its self-satisfied isolationism to embrace a quite different role as the world's policeman. The American wants to control the future of Vietnam and rescue Phuong by marrying her (after a career as a "dance hostess" that shocks him) and taking her back to the States. And yet the American acts, he thinks, from the best of motives, justifying his pursuit of Fowler's woman by the forthrightness of his announcement to the bewildered man that he intends to woo Phuong away. The American is innocent enough to drive through a mortar barrage without realizing he is being shot at, but sufficiently self-possessed to challenge directly and forcefully another man's possession of a woman, which is his reason for journeying to the war zone where Fowler is plying his trade as a journalist. Only such a man as this "quiet" American could be genuinely shocked when Fowler, faced with the loss of the woman he loves, lies to him about the future he can promise Phuong. The American believes in the rules that govern the "fair fight," and it is precisely his continuing trust in Fowler that blinds him to his rival's plot against him. Fowler audaciously signals his betrayal by reading to the American at the crucial moment a passage from *Othello* that recounts Iago's treacherous jealousy. Fowler waits to be discovered and then dissuaded from his villainy, but, ironically, the American, who recognizes the passage, believes too strongly in the older man's basic goodness to see what is plainly in front of him. It is not his being "quiet" that kills him: it is, instead, his failure to perceive that the world and its people live by their own standards and behave in ways that he cannot understand, given his limited vision of human possibility.

The Montgomery Clift of *A Place in the Sun* would have been perfect in this role, but by 1957 Clift no longer had the necessary youthful self-confidence. His nervous instability, so effectively put to use in *Suddenly, Last Summer*, would not have suited this quite different project. Despite doubts at the time about Murphy's suitability (he does not, for example, really pass muster as a Princetonian), he is ideal as the American and functions magnificently as the film's ideological center. Interestingly, Olivier's replacement also turns in a better performance than the more famous actor could perhaps have given. The still handsome Olivier, a man of irrepressible energy whose presence is always forceful, might have been too strong as Fowler. Michael Redgrave, successful at "weaker" roles, was in many ways a better choice. In *The Entertainer*, Olivier plays a vaudevillian who has failed to sustain either career or his family life; his ultimate stage catastrophe, however, never suggests he is simply a pathetic has-been.

In *The Browning Version*, by way of contrast, Michael Redgrave turns in a brilliant performance as a middle-aged schoolmaster at a public school, who is despised by the students he tyrannizes and hated by the wife he has failed as a man. Yet Redgrave's playing is sympathetic enough to make poignantly affecting the master's eleventh hour apologies to all he has harmed. Similarly, Fowler is a man destroyed by his own bad character and ill luck; he too is redeemed only by his capacity to embrace and understand his own failure. In retrospect, it is easy to see that Olivier might well have been too strong in the part. He is much better used at the end of Mankiewicz's career in *Sleuth*, where he plays a beaten man who cannot accept defeat and must resort to violence in order to restore his sense of self.

As in the case of *Five Fingers*, Mankiewicz saw that *The Quiet American*'s topicality and timeliness would be enhanced by location shooting. The director and principal members of the cast traveled to Saigon where, in the disintegrating and dangerous political environment, many of the film's exteriors were shot. Mankiewicz was especially concerned to get footage of both the Chinese New Year celebration and ceremonies involving the followers of the Cao Dai religion. Though the climate proved difficult for the director and his cinematographer (Robert Krasker, who had worked wonders photographing postwar Vienna for Reed's *The Third Man*), the resulting footage proved indispensable in creating the proper atmosphere for what would otherwise have been a very stagy drama. Interiors were filmed at the Cinecittà studios in Rome.

As a thriller, *The Quiet American* is undoubtedly less affective than either *Five Fingers* or *The Third Man*, both of which offer exciting and suspenseful action sequences that advance the narrative and enrich its themes. In contrast, *The Quiet American* is heavy on talk not action, finding no equivalents for, by way of example, the silent sequences detailing Diello's theft of secret documents or, indeed, the underground chase that so successfully—and in a metaphorically appropriate fashion—energizes the final reel of *The Third Man*. The last 20 minutes of *The Quiet American* are devoted to the dramatically necessary encounter between Vigot and Fowler; unfortunately, the sequence plays out very much like canned theater. Unlike more "dramatic" Mankiewicz adaptations, *The Quiet American* depends too much upon the spoken word. The script is very effective, as one might imagine since it is a joint product of Hollywood's most successful writer-director and one of the century's most noted British novelists. Because it does not rely enough on effective images, however, the film in the end fails to live up to the high standards of *The Third Man*, its most obvious model. At the same time, *The Quiet American* is an intellectually satisfying and uncompromising version of an acerbic, perceptive novel about twentieth century politics. This is no inconsiderable achievement, for which Mankiewicz deserves most of the credit.

Sleuth

By the 1970s, the prospect of adapting the most popular of recent Broadway hits, Anthony Shaffer's *Sleuth*, must have seemed a natural to Mankiewicz. During his substantial directorial career, he had gained a great deal of experience in turning stage successes into cinematic ones. In fact, the most acclaimed project he had directed in recent years had been a Tennessee Williams adaptation.

In filming *Suddenly, Last Summer*, Mankiewicz had enjoyed a number of advantages in his well-conceived effort to make this theatrical material attractive to filmgoers. Only one act in length with just a bare minimum of business, the property could easily handle expansion. To suit Hollywood requirements, the romantic connection between Dr. Sugar and Catherine (merely hinted at by the playwright) could be developed in greater depth. And Mankiewicz could add silent sequences detailing the dangers posed to Catherine by the hospital (dangers analogous to those she endured while Sebastian's companion). Furthermore, because the plot involved a backstory that could be dramatized, Mankiewicz could effectively alleviate any overdependence on spoken dialogue by using split-screen framings that made room for images of both Sebastian's last summer expedition and Catherine's near hysterical narration. The result of these alterations was a film that neatly balanced spoken poetry with engaging or shocking images, even as it escaped the confinement of its original stage setting to find another location in the mental hospital that, at one and the same time, functioned as a provocative metaphor and useful playing space.

The screen version of *Suddenly, Last Summer* demonstrates clearly that, by this stage of his career at least, Mankiewicz was not a "literary" director who routinely emphasized words over images. Even when the words were those of the decade's most prominent playwright as revised and augmented by a skilled screenwriter, himself a playwright and novelist of some note, Mankiewicz thought beyond them, creating a visual experience that enhanced their power and value. We might usefully compare his Williams adaptation with the noted versions of *Cat on a Hot Tin Roof* and *Sweet Bird of Youth* mounted by Richard Brooks. During the fifties and early sixties, Brooks was Hollywood's most noted adapter of prestige classics, with films based on Sinclair Lewis, Williams, Dostoevsky, and Joseph Conrad to his credit. In the case of the two Williams plays, his approach was almost solely to rewrite and reconfigure the Broadway versions, concentrating on photographing effectively what remained largely stage-bound dramas. With rare exceptions, Brooks designed no visuals or silent sequences to supplement the playtext. In contrast, Mankiewicz showed himself able to make a moving and intellectually satisfying film from a play, not just a competent and appropriate film of it. *Suddenly, Last Summer* is without doubt the finest cinematic adaptation of the postwar era's most filmed playwright. It is an eminently well-conceived transposition of material from one medium to another.

Adapting *Sleuth* proved more of a challenge to Mankiewicz. Probably Broadway's most successful thriller ever, *Sleuth* posed difficult, perhaps intractable problems for any director eager to make a truly cinematic screen version. In accordance with Broadway trends of the late sixties, Shaffer's play is a two-hander involving minimal action that unfolds on a single set. Its drama is largely conversational and mental, a battle of words between two intelligent, witty, and inventive characters from different social backgrounds, whose contrasting experiences and views must largely emerge from how they speak and what they say. Any faithful adaptation, therefore, would have to consist largely in the play's being simply restaged to suit the requirements of the camera. Little "opening out" would be possible since adding other characters or transferring some of the action to different locales would dilute the carefully modulated tension that develops between the two principals and leads only twice to moments of suspenseful action. Substantial rewriting or cutting would likely vitiate the many virtues of Shaffer's well-crafted dialogue. Wisely, the playwright was engaged to fashion the screenplay, with the natural result that the film version closely follows the playscript.

Suddenly, Last Summer depends upon opposed interpretations of a terrifying past that can be dramatized to good effect, as Mankiewicz proved. *Sleuth*'s conflict, in contrast, is rooted firmly in the present, and in this case any additional "pictures" Mankiewicz could devise would definitely not be worth a thousand words. How then to keep the rapid-fire flow of dialogue interesting? Luckily, the director could depend heavily upon two superb actors, whom he rehearsed extensively to develop the requisite chemistry and timing. Much would depend also on carefully designed editing, which could lend the appearance of motion to what, on the physical level at least, is a quite static, if undeniably dramatic encounter.

Andrew Wyke (Laurence Olivier) is an upper-crust, has-been writer of traditional detective fiction who inhabits a huge country estate, Cloak Manor, which he has fitted out to satisfy his enthusiasm for games of all kinds. He has invited his new neighbor Milo Tindle (Michael Caine) to join him for a cocktail. The guest is a young, handsome East London hairdresser whose appeal to the rich women he serves has enabled him to open two salons. Milo has hopes of even greater success as he moves, literally and figuratively, into Andrew's exclusive neighborhood. The play's social symbolism is writ large. Andrew is a self-isolated and somewhat pathetic representative of an increasingly irrelevant former ruling class. He is the reduction, to adolescent absurdity, of the gentlemanly types "formed" on the playing fields of Eton. In contrast, Milo is an aspiring member of the glitzy urban set who have moved from across the river to seize control of swinging London. He has no traditions to uphold or defend since he is an Italian immigrant's son whose father struggled to "make" his children English, as Milo unabashedly reveals. This confession his chauvinist host finds appalling. For no immigrant could aspire to be what can only be a birthright—*his* birthright, as he sees it. Only a shameless social climber would be matter of fact about coming from nothing.

This rivalry between the old "England" and new "United Kingdom" is not just a matter of class and ethnic affiliation. It engages the most elemental of male feelings: the desire to possess a beautiful and refined woman. As soon becomes clear, both men consider such possession the ultimate index of self-worth. And it is not simply a question of winning her, but taking her away. Milo has seduced Andrew's disaffected wife (who is tired of tolerating her husband's mistress and self-absorption). Eager to enjoy the good life that she symbolizes in trophy fashion, Milo now

On the set of *Sleuth* (1972)—Mankiewicz (left) directing Michael Caine (in clown costume) and Laurence Olivier.

thinks to marry her himself, a truth with which Andrew confronts the nonplussed Milo soon after his arrival. Thus Milo seeks not only to rival his host's position and accomplishments, he hopes to replace him as well.

Andrew tries to play the wronged husband, but his guest will not be rattled by this ploy. Andrew's wife has gathered evidence of his indiscretion, Milo declares, and the would-be couple have expectations of obtaining an easy divorce, even if Andrew proves intransigent. When the question of who has the power is broached, the encounter quickly degenerates into an escalating exchange of threats. Sensing no common ground with Andrew, who is not being "sensible," Milo gets up to leave. He is suddenly halted, however, when Andrew hits a nerve. How, the older man asks, does Milo intend to support his new wife in the style to which, enjoying Andrew's considerable fortune, she has become quite accustomed? His insecurity now showing, Milo contends that he is on his way up; at the moment, however, he is cash poor. Andrew quickly proposes a scheme that Milo, if he thought better of it, would likely dismiss out of hand since it involves trusting someone who has every reason to see him ill-served. If Milo will steal the family jewels (which are suitably insured, Andrew avers), then he'll be able to pay for his newly won purchase. The erstwhile rivals quickly become partners in crime, or so Milo believes. Surprisingly, the younger man becomes the easy victim of Andrew's charming seduction, which even has its pronounced homosexual implications (especially when the two play dress up to help Milo get into character for his heist, which is intended to solve the problem that possessing the beautiful woman poses).

At one point, Andrew's now eager dupe even dons women's clothes and swishes about a little for his host's amusement. The point Shaffer and Mankiewicz make here is gently misogynistic; for the woman, with her voracious and hardly satisfiable appetite for what her man should provide, is a burden difficult for any man to bear, causing the two to find apparently common ground. Interestingly, this burden is symbolized by the jewelry, which, because it belongs to her, is also a metaphor for the woman herself. Andrew gave her these beautiful and eminently convertible items as a token of his love; they can, he declares, be readily transformed into money for him (from the insurance claim) and money for Milo (who will fence them for a small fortune). As a sign that the theft is but a game, Milo eventually chooses a clown's costume for his disguise, which he then carefully dons, including a pair of outsize shoes. Under Andrew's careful direction, Milo climbs a ladder so that he can break into an upper story window. Now inside Andrew's room (for her valuables are naturally stored there), the pair make a game out of Milo discovering the location of the safe, which he does with wit and dispatch. Milo then blows it open (another of Andrew's overdramatizations that seem part of the fun) and removes the jewels. Milo appears to have successfully completed the task set for him, a kind of game with its own distinct challenges, but then the tone of the scene suddenly changes.

No longer Milo's willing co-conspirator (at least apparently), Andrew suddenly pulls a gun from his pocket and tells Milo that the theft, which was real yet a game for the two conspirators, is actually a ruse. In other words, it is neither real nor a game, but instead a pretext for getting Milo to leave clues around the house. When he phones the police after the shooting, these clues will provide Andrew with a plausible alibi for gunning down Milo as a thief caught in the act. Andrew convinces Milo that his life is just about to end, and his façade of self-possession and cockiness dissolves into tearful and helpless pleading. The first part of the film ends exactly like act one of the play. Andrew presses the gun to Milo's head (ironically still covered by the clown mask) and pulls the trigger. Mankiewicz does not show the result of the apparently fatal shot.

The action resumes at what seems a later point, though for some time we are not informed how much later. Andrew is alone in Cloak Manor, preparing a suitably aristocratic repast of champagne and caviar when suddenly the bell rings and, with symbolic appropriateness as it transpires, ruins his supper. At the door is a man who calls himself Inspector Doppler, a member of the local constabulary. Pushing 40, paunchy, of a shaky gait, and with a pronounced West Country accent, Doppler does seem at first quite what his name suggests—a double for the late departed Milo. Here is yet another member of the lower orders arriving at Cloak Manor, but this time uninvited. Unlike Milo, Inspector Doppler immediately takes charge of this evening's game, which is the interrogation of his host, whom he accuses of having murdered Milo. Andrew declares that Milo's visit ended happily two days before. The revolver held only a blank cartridge, and the pair parted friends after a few more drinks. But then Doppler discovers blood on the carpet, a bullet hole in the wall, and what might be a freshly dug grave in the garden, among other "clues." Andrew is reduced to helpless panic, but then Doppler begins removing what now is revealed as a disguise (a triumph of make-up replete with colored contact lenses). Inspector Doppler is none other than Milo, come back—with the aid of some theatrical friends who have transformed his appearance— for his revenge. Appropriately, he is investigating his own "death," which only he knows about.

For Andrew the initial game was just that because he was not humiliated and could enjoy his moments of domination over the younger, more virile and handsome Milo, who had stolen his wife's affections. The first part of the film plays out like a game version of the unwritten law, with Andrew "shooting" Milo after catching him in the act of violation (and the woman represented metaphorically by her purloined jewels). The second game "plays" out what might truly have happened to Andrew if, like all the villains in his country house detective novels, he had actually murdered his rival. Such a murder would be the precise kind of material that would suit the genre, particularly with a wily malefactor eager to stage the perfect crime who is then undone by the clues he mistakenly leaves behind.

The "plot" does embody, however, an intriguingly ironic reversal. For Andrew's detective is an amateur sleuth of aristocratic birth, a figure of immense wish fulfillment for his creator. Milo's detective is working class, unfamiliar with the lives of the nobility, but with a Low Church dedication to conventional morality—an interesting alter ego for Milo, who becomes thoroughly subsumed by Doppler and his homely Englishness (despite the twist that his name is German; perhaps in its "foreignness" another link to Milo). The acting job, for Milo, represents an ironic fulfillment of his father's dream that the son "become English." At this point in the film, the two games balance one another, with both Andrew and Milo suffering the agony of thinking that their deeds (Milo's adultery and theft; Andrew's calculating "murder") have actually called down retribution. Ordinarily, games are human constructs in which all participants abide by the rules and principles which set the activities apart from "real life." But the games that these two characters play are different. In each case, only the perpetrator or controller of the games knows that that is what they are. The other participant is made to feel precisely that there are no games at hand; that the activities are "real" and involve "real" consequences of the worst kind. These are the games of a sado-masochist, eminently suitable for an author used to pulling his characters' puppet strings.

Not satisfied with the revenge gained against Andrew so far, Milo announces a new trial for his unwelcoming host, who does not admit defeat (a move that might have saved him further difficulty). This trial, cast in the form of a game (and now both parties acknowledge they are "playing" it), is a variant of the one that has just transpired. It involves, yet again, a Hitchcockian transfer of guilt, and it seems rather to have been inspired by the old master's *Strangers on a Train*. Milo now convinces Andrew that he has murdered his tormentor's mistress at Cloak Manor, though this is not true, only part of the plot against Andrew. To make the deception work, he has enlisted the girl's roommate, who blurts out hysterically when Andrew calls her at Milo's suggestion that her friend has suddenly and unexpectedly disappeared.

Clues to the murder, clues that the police will surely find, are hidden around Cloak Manor and Andrew must retrieve them in time to exculpate himself; these are the conditions Milo imposes. Not only has Milo apparently murdered the woman Andrew loves, but—a much worse humiliation—he learned before her death that Andrew is now impotent. And Milo satisfied her sexual hunger before he strangled her. This game has a time limit—as the police are summoned and will arrive in but a few minutes. Working feverishly and enthusiastically from Milo's riddling hints, Andrew manages to locate all four clues.

Triumphant but distraught, he then learns that the murder never happened, that this was a humiliating game planned by Milo and his mistress to get revenge against the arch manipulator. Truly and thoroughly beaten this time, Andrew cannot let Milo live with the knowledge that he is no longer a functioning man. As police sirens sound in the distance, Andrew shoots Milo. At the very end, the games have ended, and what was only playacting has finally become real.

In Eisensteinian fashion, Mankiewicz carefully controls audience response through judicious shot design and editing. There are few long takes—the basic visual figure of the film is shot-reverse angle or shot-reaction shot. Particularly noteworthy is the way in which Mankiewicz makes use of the automata (clocks, toys, dummies) that fill Cloak Manor—these are often featured effectively in reaction shots. The resulting film is not a filmed play. The "integrity" of performance is much more respected, for example, in the Brooks adaptations of Tennessee Williams. Mankiewicz's film is a carefully controlled version of the play that heightens but does not alter the effects of the stage original. His last major production, it provides a fitting end to his career as a "literary" director who learned much about the specifics of good filmmaking during the course of an outstanding and highly regarded three decades in the industry.

PART III

Guide to Resources

Notes on
the Resources

by Cheryl Bray Lower

This project began because I was confounded by the redundancy of the same few bibliographic references repeated over and over in biographical material on Mankiewicz. How could so few articles exist on a man considered one of the wittiest and most literate of all American writer-directors?

I initiated a search for new material in the hope of tracking down as many interviews and articles as I could find, not only to aid in my own understanding of the man, but to assist other scholars and generate further interest in Mankiewicz's work. What resulted was a wealth of information previously untapped by film scholars.

I approached the Mankiewicz family to learn the location of Mr. Mankiewicz's papers. I was told that, unfortunately, they had not been donated to a film library. I did, however, receive an invitation to visit and discuss my project with the filmmaker's widow, Rosemary Mankiewicz.

Thanks to the trust and enthusiasm of Mrs. Mankiewicz, I have the distinct honor of being the only scholar to have had access to the private files of Joseph L. Mankiewicz. Over the course of my research I have accumulated hundreds of articles from the United States and abroad. I have also discovered numerous inconsistencies in previously published filmographies on Mankiewicz. By using his personal files and film studio records, I have compiled a more complete filmography than has heretofore been available, and every attempt has been made to correct the errors previously published.

The papers of Joseph L. Mankiewicz, with their wealth of material, will eventually be donated to a research library, but for now they remain in private hands. Until they are made available, those interested in learning more about the man who considered himself a film-author long before the term entered the vernacular can discover a bit of his magic and foresight by examining this guide to resources.

My deepest thanks go to Rosemary Mankiewicz who opened up her home and these files to me. This project could not have been undertaken without her trust and enthusiasm. I will always appreciate her friendship, and guidance.

I also wish to thank Professor Bradford York Fletcher of Georgia State University, whose enthusiasm for bibliographic research inspired the literary detective in me.

Film scholars would be severely limited if it were not for the able assistance of Charles Silver of the Museum of Modern Art, the research librarians of the Margaret Herrick Library at the Academy of Arts and Sciences, and Ned Comstock of the Doheny Library at the University of Southern California. I am indebted to these gentlefolk for their time and assistance. My thanks also go to the New York Center for Visual History for allowing me to view an interview they filmed with Mankiewicz a few years before his death.

A few words about the content and format of the annotated bibliography are in order. First, in the matter of reviews, please note that only reviews of individual films that directly quote Mankiewicz or refer at length to his style are included in this bibliography.

Second, the reader will notice that not all entries include page numbers. Every attempt was made to secure the page numbers of bibliographic references. However, after working from clippings files at the Mankiewicz home as well as at MOMA, USC, AMPAS, and UCLA, I am sorry to say that very few newspaper articles had page numbers. Clipping services provided materials for Mr. Mankiewicz, but most did not retain the page number or the edition of the newspaper or magazine. Whenever possible, every attempt was made to locate the microfilm or microfiche of the original document. In numerous cases, I was able to do so and ascertain page and section numbers. In other cases, however, I did not succeed, because so many of the sources cited are no longer available in reference libraries. The abbreviation "n. pag." signifies that no page number was available.

Other abbreviations are as follows:

AFI	American Film Institute [Los Angeles]
AMPAS	Academy of Motion Picture Arts and Sciences [Los Angeles]
AP	Associated Press
BO	Box Office
CVH	Center for Visual History [New York]
DFZ	Darryl F. Zanuck
DGA	Directors Guild of America
GSU	Georgia State University
JLM	Joseph L. Mankiewicz
MGM	Metro-Goldwyn-Mayer
MOMA	Museum of Modern Art [New York]
Q&A	Questions and Answers
RMM	Rosemary Matthews Mankiewicz (Mrs. Joseph L.)
SC	Screenplay
SDG	Screen Directors Guild
SR	Saturday Review
UA	United Artists
UCLA	University of California at Los Angeles
UFA	Universum Film Aktien Gesellschaft
UGA	University of Georgia
USC	University of Southern California
W7	Warner–7 Arts

Annotated
Bibliography

Writings by Joseph L. Mankiewicz

1923

1 Mankicwicz, Joseph L. "An Interview with Comedian W. C. Fields." *Caliper* Nov. 1923: 12. High school student Mankiewicz (age 14) writes an account of his interview with Fields for his school paper. (Ironically, it would later be Mankiewicz who would write Fields' most famous quip, "My little chick-a-dee.")

1925

2 Mason, Joe [Mankiewicz pseudonym]. "My Wife Is an Interior Decorator." *Life Humor Magazine* 31 Dec. 1925: n. pag. College student Mankiewicz, writing as Joe Mason, wanted to see if he could get anything published. He succeeded and was paid $7.00 for his effort.

1928

3 Mankiewicz, Joseph L. "Books." *Columbia Spectator* 19 Jan. 1928: n. pag. JLM writes book review of E. Petit's novel, *Move Over*, for college newspaper.

4 _____. "Hauptman's One-Acter." *Variety* 5 Sept. 1928: n. pag. Unsigned Mankiewicz article about plans for new Hauptman play.

5 _____. "Chatter in Berlin." *Variety* 5 Sept. 1928: n. pag. Miscellaneous notes of works in progress in this unsigned article.

6 _____. "Chatter in Berlin." *Variety* 17 Oct. 1928: n. pag. Unsigned article of entertainment happenings in Berlin.

7 _____. "Ufa's New Houses." *Variety* 17 Oct. 1928: n. pag. Brief notices about Ufa's expansion of movie theatres in Berlin.

1943

8 _____. "The Pirate." Unpublished original screenplay, 1943. Mankiewicz private collection.

1945

9 _____. "Captain from Castile." Unpublished screenplay treatment, 1945. Mankiewicz private collection.

1946

10 _____. "Berkeley Square." Unpublished screenplay, 1946. Mankiewicz private collection.

11 _____. "The Gentle Readers." *Hollywood Review* 4 June 1946: 6. JLM's wit surfaces as he responds to a glowing review of *Somewhere in the Night* by writing a letter to the editor, Reed Porter. "I think you should know that some of my colleagues, in whom I have never before detected pique, suggest that I am your mistress. Others maintain that I am you. Still others deny having read your paper, although I personally set their copies, properly marked, beside their beds...."

1947

12 _____. "The Bright Promise." Unpublished screenplay, 1947. Mankiewicz private collection.

13 _____. "Film Author! Film Author!" *Screen Writer* 2.12 (May 1947): 23–28. Begins with a critical book review of Jean Benoit-Lévy's *The Art of the Motion Picture* and quickly proceeds to explain JLM's own concept of film authorship. Encourages screenwriters to improve their product even with the confines of US censorship and suggests that they consider directing what they have written since a good screenplay is half-directed in the first place.

1949

14 _____. "Joseph Mankiewicz Answers." *Motion Picture Herald* 6 Aug. 1949: 8–9. More letters to the editor over JLM's comments about exhibitors as "real estate operators" (see *84*). Includes a letter from Mankiewicz himself, who responds to the mail he has generated over his comment describing a film exhibitor as "a real estate operator whose chief concern should be taking gum off carpets and checking adolescent love-making in the balcony."

1950

15 _____. Untitled Advertisement. *Hollywood Reporter* 16 Oct. 1950: 6. JLM defends himself against verbal assaults labeling him a Communist by some members of the Screen Directors Guild. As president of the SDG, Mankiewicz explains his actions regarding the loyalty oath controversy. (*Note:* this paid advertisement is followed by a notice to SDG members to spurn the recall movement and retain JLM as president. It is signed by 36 directors.)

16 _____. Untitled Advertisement. *Variety* 16 Oct. 1950: 4. Duplication of Hollywood Reporter editorial by Mankiewicz.

1951

17 _____. *All About Eve.* New York: Random House, 1951. Published screenplay.

1953

18 _____. "Jefferson Selleck." Unpublished final shooting script, 1953. Mankiewicz private collection.

1957

19 _____. "'Shoot It in Tanganyika.'" *Saturday Review* 21 Dec. 1957: 14–15. Brief article (with many pictures), on the change in filmmaking practice wherein films are shot on location rather than in the backlot of a studio. Includes reference to *The Quiet American*, shot in Vietnam with the complete cooperation of the government.

1958

10 _____. "All the Livelong Day." Unpublished play, 1958. Mankiewicz private collection.

1960

21 _____. "John Brown's Body." Unpublished screenplay outline, 1960. Mankiewicz private collection.

22 _____. "Justine." Unpublished screenplay, 1960. Mankiewicz private collection.

1961

23 _____. "La Cleopatra di Liz Taylor rispettera la storia." *Epoca* 6 Aug. 1961: n. pag. Mankiewicz proclaims that his *Cleopatra* will rely on historical material with a special emphasis on the writing of Plutarch. In Italian.

1962

24 _____. "A Statement Concerning the Writing of *Cleopatra*." 6 Oct. 1961. Mankiewicz details his involvement in the writing of the film, for his attorney and the Writers' Guild Arbitration Committee. This outstanding work charts his involvement in the project (as of October 1961) and is one of the rare times Mankiewicz explains his concept of the characters and the theme of the film.

1963

25 _____. "American Report." *Cahiers du Cinéma* Dec. 1963—Jan. 1964: 57–58. Mankiewicz responds to questions posed by 30 American film directors in this special edition on American film. In French.

26 _____. "Great Ideas That Never Got Filmed: *Show* Poll #4." *Show* Aug. 1963: 59. Mankiewicz notes his great achievements but fears he will go down in history as the man associated with *Cleopatra*. His contribution to screenwriter poll (via telegram). "Propose your survey as you stated would seem to imply many if not most great ideas have already been filmed [STOP] Cannot agree but think it very brave and forward looking cause for you to champion and count me on your side [STOP] Unfortunately great ideas cannot be adlib [sic] by either nouveaux precieux with shaky hand cameras or actors with deep feelings and limited vocabularies [STOP] For better or worse film is irrevocably committed to talk and only when spoken word achieves equal critical and cult status with dropping cigarette and optically enlarged eye ball can great ideas be hopefully attempted [STOP] Let's start with Plato's Republic and you can take care of the financing."

27 _____. "The Movie Mailbag." *New York Times* 16 June 1963, sec. X: 9. JLM writes a letter to the screen editor correcting misstatements in a previously published article on *Cleopatra*. Sets the record straight on Buchman and MacDougall's contribution to the screenplay, and clarifies his reservations about the Battle of Actium scene.

1966

28 _____. "Mike Nichols." McDowall, Roddy. *Double Exposure*. New York: Delacorte Press, 1966. 196. An outstanding example of Mankiewicz's cleverness. What could have been a simple biographical sketch of fellow director, Mike Nichols, for McDowall's book of photographs of film greats becomes a classic illustration of the erudite mind of Joseph L. Mankiewicz.

1967

29 _____. "The Last One Left." Unpublished screenplay treatment, 1967. Mankiewicz private collection.

30 _____. "The Meteor." Unpublished play, 1967. Mankiewicz private collection.

1968

31 _____. "Couples." Unpublished screenplay, 1968. Mankiewicz private collection.

1971

32 _____. "What Directors Are Saying!" *Action* Jan.–Feb. 1971: 30. JLM, as originally quoted in Gow's article "Cocking a Snook" (*330*), on our voyeuristic society and film's recent technological innovations.

1972

33 _____. "All About the Women in *All About Eve*." *New York* 16 Oct. 1972: 37–42. Pending the rerelease of the published screenplay of *All About Eve*, this publication is an abbreviated version of the introduction to *More About All About Eve*.

34 Mankiewicz, Joseph L. and Gary Carey. *More About All About Eve*. New York: Random House, 1972. Introduction is a lengthy colloquy with Mankiewicz describing his preference for writing about women; the aging actress and the theater community as themes; and the once mythical Sarah Siddons Society which now exists as a result of the film. Followed by the complete screenplay.

1973

35 Mankiewicz, Joseph L. "Auteur de films! Auteur de films!" *Positif* Sept. 1973: 1–5. Reprint of JLM's "Screen Author!" article first published in U.S. in 1947. In French.

1975

36 _____. "Jane." Unpublished screenplay, 1975. Mankiewicz private collection.

1980

37 _____. "Madonna Red." Unpublished screenplay, 1980. Mankiewicz private collection.

1985

38 _____. "All Were Big and Some Were Bright." *New York Times Book Review* 8 Dec. 1985: 17. JLM reviews of books on Hollywood: *In Person* by Martin Gottfried, *Great Movie Actresses* by Phillip Strick, and *Astaire Dancing* by John Mueller.

1986

39 _____. "Joseph L. Mankiewicz: A Chronological Career Précis." Unpublished biographical sketch, 1986. Mankiewicz private collection.

1992

40 _____. "Joseph L. Mankiewicz—Profile." Unpublished biographical sketch, Nov. 1992. Mankiewicz private collection.

1997

41 Carey, Gary and Joseph L. Mankiewicz. "Mankiewicz on 'Eve.'" *Scenario* Fall 1997: 105+. Excerpts from *More About All About Eve* to accompany journal's reprint of *All About Eve* screenplay.
42 Mankiewicz, Joseph L. *All About Eve*. *Scenario* Fall 1997: 54–103. Reprint of JLM's original screenplay with illustrations by Gary Kelley.

Writings about Joseph L. Mankiewicz

1929

43 "Title Writer Holds Record." *Los Angeles Times* 7 July 1929, sec. III: 10. At 21, the youngest writer on the Paramount staff, JLM gets long-term contract after setting record for titling six films in eight weeks (*The Dummy, Close Harmony, The Studio Murder Mystery, Thunderbolt, The Man I Love, The Mysterious Dr. Fu Manchu*). Note reference to his recent work, titling Clara Bow's *Dangerous Curves*.

1930

44 "Film Dialogue Held Different from Captions." *Los Angeles Times* 26 Jan. 1930, sec. III: 26. Brief quote from 21-year-old JLM about writing film dialogue. "I try to figure out what I would say in the various situations which confront the characters. That helps to judge the naturalness of the words. I always speak the lines, also, to get the ear's reaction."

1932

45 Delehanty, Thornton. "*Million Dollar Legs*, a Travesty on a Variety of Things, Comes to the Paramount." *New York Post* 11 July 1932: 17. High praise for the story. Film seen in light of a René Clair's satire.
46 "Midsummer Madness." Rev. of *Million Dollar Legs*. *New York Times* 17 July 1932: 3. Film seen as light summer fare. Reference to JLM contribution. "Indications throughout the story suggest that its author, Joseph L. Man-

kiewicz, took himself to some quiet spot and then proceeded to write down a series of mad thoughts in the order in which they came to him. The result is a surprisingly insane sort of work. The cast and the director, Edward Cline, presumably used it only as a base on which to erect structure of their own."

1936

47 *"Gorgeous Hussy* a Hit; Crawford at Her Best." *Hollywood Reporter* 28 Aug. 1936: 3. On his first "big picture" for MGM, JLM credited with much more than production, but no specifics. Glowing review for film and Crawford.

48 Rev. of *Fury. Los Angeles Times* 30 Aug. 1936: n. pag. JLM is quoted at length in this column with a slight reference to his latest film, *Fury.* Article notes that he hopes to continue making films "with a viewpoint." But the article notes that he is "opposed to Communism"—a subject that will rear its head again in the 1950 loyalty oath controversy.

49 Scheuer, Philip K. "A Town Called Hollywood." *Los Angeles Times* 30 Aug. 1936, sec. III: 3. JLM learns the hard way how to be a producer by working with temperamental Fritz Lang on *Fury.* "You ruined my picture," Lang told JLM after the premiere. Although the film was critically acclaimed, Lang never returned to Metro. Mankiewicz quoted as wanting to do "pictures with a viewpoint." Also notes JLM's anti–Communism sentiments.

50 Wilkerson, W. R. "TradeViews." *Hollywood Reporter* 20 May 1936: 1–2. JLM's first picture as producer, *Fury,* garners high praise for his work. Background on how Sam Katz chose Mankiewicz to be a producer at MGM, thinking he would make a better producer than a writer.

1938

51 "Anti-Nazi Censorship." *Variety* [Daily] 8 June 1938: n. pag. Producer Mankiewicz corrects a *Time* magazine article on anti–Nazi censorship in *Three Comrades.* [See *Time* 6 June 1938].

52 Creelman, Eileen. "Joseph L. Mankiewicz Talks of Producing Dickens's *A Christmas Carol." New York Sun* 17 Dec. 1938: n. pag. Biographical data on young producer, JLM. Includes information on casting choices for the film that Mankiewicz called the happiest production he had worked on so far in his brief career. Note also that he cites a previous production, *Fury,* as a flop.

53 "Eligibles." *Philadelphia Bulletin* 25 Jan. 1938: n. pag. Hollywood's eligible bachelors' salaries. JLM's is given as $5,000 a week. He was aged 28.

54 "The Hollywood Roundup." *St. Mary's Press* [Pa.] 10 Feb. 1938: n. pag. JLM bought the song "Always and Always" from songwriter Edward Ward for a $2.00 horse racing ticket. Ward, "discouraged" about the song he composed for *Mannequin,* thought the race ticket a better deal, but JLM came out the winner as 50,000 copies have sold of the sheet music since the swap.

55 Holt, Paul. "Hollywood Is on the Brink of Civil War." *Daily Express* [London] 25 June 1938: n. pag. Analysis from Hollywood bigwigs (Capra, Schenck, Van Dyke, Warner, Goldwyn, Mankiewicz) about what's wrong with Hollywood. Answers vary from trade unions to Communism. Producer

Mankiewicz (aged 29), cited as the next Thalberg at MGM, predicts films will get worse before they get better because old men with old ideas are running the business and refuse to acknowledge that the filmgoing audience is maturing and wants new stories.

56 "Hot from Hollywood." *Bridgeport Herald* [Conn.] 6 Mar. 1938: n. pag. Gossip from Hollywood includes reference to JLM and Joe Breen of Hays Office. Breen wanted Mankiewicz to change all of the Nazi characters to Communists in *Three Comrades* lest it "antagonize" Germany into banning the film.

57 "Shades of Marley's Ghost." *New York Times* 18 Dec. 1938, sec. X: 7. Scurrying to get *A Christmas Carol* into theatres for the holiday, MGM made the film in 26 days. Young producer, Mankiewicz, delights in Dickens' social commentary and writing style: "He almost included 'dissolves' and 'fade-ins'.... His sequence of scenes and his continuity are ideally adaptable to the camera. And some of the lines and speeches he put into the mouths of his characters ninety-five years ago are as full of social significance today as if they had been written this morning."

58 Skolsky, Sidney. "The Gossipel [sic] Truth." Editorial. *Hollywood Citizen-News* 29 Aug. 1938: n. pag. JLM definition of assistant producer: "A mouse who is studying to be a rat."

1939

59 Erskine, John. "Why Films Have So Many Authors." *Liberty* [NY] 18 Nov. 1939: 13+. Roughly 10 years after the advent of motion picture sound, this article explores the complexity of writing for the screen. Cites 30-year-old Mankiewicz, "one of the most alert of the younger directors," as being in charge of an MGM project to develop promising young writers for films.

1940

60 "Producer Looks Over Orleans for Film Story Background." *New Orleans Item-Tribune* [La.] 18 Feb. 1940: n. pag. JLM considered a "top-flight" producer. Includes reference to *Strange Cargo, The Philadelphia Story*, as well as JLM comment that Spencer Tracy and Clark Gable are the "best guys" in Hollywood.

61 Skolsky, Sidney. "Dies Is Trying to See Red in His Hollywood Article." *New York Post* 10 Feb. 1940: n. pag. Skolsky denounces Martin Dies' article, "The Reds of Hollywood" (published in *Liberty*) as full of "half baked data." But the coming Communist witch hunt in Hollywood is foreshadowed in this brief article wherein Mankiewicz's chairmanship of the Finnish Relief Fund is noted, as well as his role as producer of *Fury*, a film which Dies sees as full of Communist propaganda.

1941

62 "New Pictures." *Time* 20 Jan. 1941: 77–78. Film review of *The Philadelphia Story* delivers background on how the show moved from stage to screen.

Notes JLM's putting together "a trial script" for backer (and one-time "suitor" to Katharine Hepburn) Howard Hughes.

1942

63 *"Woman of Year* Sure Hit..." *Hollywood Reporter* 14 Jan. 1942: 3. Praise for the highbrow-lowbrow farce. Mankiewicz seen as upholding MGM standards of excellence.

1944

64 Stanley, Fred. "Hollywood Spreads Itself." *New York Times* 13 Feb. 1944, sec. II: 3. Authenticates the fact that Mankiewicz rewrote the script once he took over as producer on *The Keys of the Kingdom*. Article cites Mankiewicz as saying that "few liberties are being taken with the Cronin novel." (*Note:* JLM shares credit with Nunnally Johnson for screenwriting.)

1945

65 Marsh, W. Ward. "Director Sees Fans Favoring Escape Films and Mysticism." *Cleveland Plain Dealer* 2 June 1945: 18D. Fascinating prediction of the changing film industry by JLM as he embarks on his first directorial project in which he foreshadows the demise of the studio system, and the change in filmic subject matter from realism to nostalgia. Chastises Hollywood for portraying psychological issues in a sensational manner. Sees mysticism (not religion) as the next wave in Hollywood films.

66 Sykes, Velma West. "National Screen Council Comment." *Boxoffice.* 17 Mar. 1945: n. pag. Detailed film credits and award citation included in review which pits *Keys* with current boxoffice competitor *Meet Me in St. Louis* (MGM). Interesting account of exhibitors around the country who vote for the Blue Ribbon Award and comment on film.

67 Wright, Virginia. Editorial. *Daily News* [Los Angeles]. 17 Jan. 1945: 21. Analysis of *The Keys of the Kingdom* credits JLM for keeping film in line with controversial best seller. Cites producer Mankiewicz as "an expert on women's pictures." JLM discusses his plans to leave MGM for 20th Century–Fox to direct—seeing directing as "the last half of a screenwriter's task," and more suitable to his skills.

1946

68 Creelman, Eileen. "Picture Plays and Players: Joseph L. Mankiewicz Talks of His Latest Production, *The Late George Apley*." *New York Sun* 28 Sept. 1946: 5. Youthful, exuberant JLM interviewed while making *Apley*. Brief biography with comments about Zanuck and JLM's concept of writer-director and producer.

69 Crowther, Bosley. *"Somewhere in the Night,* a Fox Melodrama Introducing Nancy Guild Opposite John Hodiak, Is New Attraction at the Roxy." *New*

York Times 13 June 1946: 24. Likens JLM's style of melodrama to that of Hitchcock. Too confusing a plot for the reviewer. Misstates that this is JLM's directing debut. (*Dragonwyck* was first film as director.)

70 "Film Review: *Somewhere in the Night.*" *Variety* [Daily] 3 May 1946: n. pag. Credits JLM with achieving a new angle on the "amnesia" plot.

71 Grant, Jack D. "*Somewhere* Smart Movie... ." *Hollywood Daily Reporter* 3 May 1946: n. pag. Favorable review cites Mankiewicz's contribution to screenplay (he was also the director) as reason for film's success.

72 Guernsey, Otis L., Jr. "The Playbill: Film Writer's Constructive Hint to Stage." *New York Tribune* 29 Dec. 1946, sec. V: 1. Foreshadows JLM's desire to move from film to Broadway. Discussion of the screenwriter and what his purpose is when he writes (he attempts to achieve audience self-identification with the character).

73 "*Somewhere in the Night* Spellbinding; Mankiewicz Gives Lawler Smash Pic." *Hollywood Review* 7 May 1946: 1+. Lengthy, glowing review of film, and especially complimentary to Mankiewicz. Film seen as one of the best of the year (along with *The Spiral Staircase* and *The Strange Love of Martha Ivers*). "Let the Screen Directors Guild meet some evening to see if any man among them could better the least of Mankiewicz's scenes. It is that rare and happy kind of picture in which every second means something, in which every word from a character's lips and every expression from a face is vital to mood and story."

1947

74 Creelman, Eileen. "Picture Plays and Players: Joseph L. Mankiewicz Talks of *The Ghost and Mrs. Muir* and of Plans for *Escape.*" *New York Sun* 2, June 1947: 15. Eager to learn about his new job as writer-director-producer at 20th Century–Fox, JLM travels to England to study the British film industry in hopes of shooting his next film there. He acknowledges his reverence for the theatre in this interview, while also expressing envy for British directors because they live and work in a theatre-rich city where they have London stage-trained actors at their disposal. He bemoans the current state of the Hollywood actor who seemingly stops developing when he gives up Broadway for a Hollywood film contract.

75 *Ghost and Mrs. Muir. Variety* 16 May 1947: 3+. Praise for JLM's direction of ghost story. Citing he "handled subject with sympathy and good taste...."

76 "*Ghost and Mrs. Muir* Fine...." *Hollywood Reporter* 16 May. 1947: 3–4. Complimentary review of film and praise for JLM's direction. "In guiding his stars' work together, Mankiewicz hits the peak of his superb direction."

1948

77 "Film Review: *A Letter to Three Wives.*" *Variety* 3 Dec. 1948: 3. *Letter* viewed as highlight of the season. "Mankiewicz moves his characters like pawns, entirely at his will, and they all come out kings and queens."

78 *A Letter to Three Wives. Hollywood Reporter* 3 Dec. 1948: 3+. "*A Letter to Three Wives* belongs in that rarefied theatrical climate of comedies which, more

than being hysterically funny, can also boast stories as real and human and exciting as every day life." Praises Mankiewicz for his brilliance in bringing it to the screen.

79 "State Control for Britain in 12 Months." *Cinema* [London] 28 Jan. 1948: n. pag. JLM discusses nationalization of British film industry after working for six months in England on *Escape*. "Unless America shows more imagination and trust in Britain, its Government will be forced to nationalize part of the industry to prevent further economic setbacks." JLM believes *Escape* was made for 40 percent less in England than it would have been made in Hollywood.

1949

80 Barnes, Howard. "On The Screen: *A Letter to Three Wives*." *New York Herald Tribune* 21 Jan. 1949: n. pag. Praise for JLM and his use of the flashback: "rarely (has it) been employed with more imagination and effect... ."

81 ____. "With a Bow to *A Letter to Three Wives*." *New York Herald Tribune* 30 Jan. 1949, sec. V:1. High praise for JLM's combined talent as director and screenwriter. "The importance of a unified command in the strategy of motion-picture making has rarely been more brilliantly illustrated than it is in the new offering at the Music Hall. *A Letter to Three Wives* combines sardonic humor with brilliant pictorial imagination... . Being director as well as the writer of the show, he has projected his fine script with impeccable authority."

82 Cook, Alton. "*Letter to Three Wives* Is Good Film News." *New York World Telegram* 20 Jan. 1949: n. pag. Seen as a "sprightly and diverting little comedy of a story that has aspects approaching tragedy, or at least very somber drama." Mankiewicz praised for merging writing and directing.

83 Crowther, Bosley. "Advice to Ladies." *New York Times* 30 Jan. 1949, sec. 2: 1. Praise for JLM (from a male critic), for setting the record straight in the battle of the sexes. Citing the "wisdom and candor" in *A Letter to Three Wives*, Crowther believes Mankiewicz "has turned out a picture about women in which that popular sex is regarded with ample affection but with full recognition of some of its faults. He has made a film in which women are acknowledged to be fallible and in which, at the final showdown, the pants are worn by the men."

84 Hodgins, Eric. "A Round Table on the Movies." *Life* 27 June 1949: 90–110. With box-office revenues dropping in the postwar television era, filmmakers, actors, critics, journalists, and a scholar discuss the current state of filmmaking in Hollywood. JLM is outspoken about his disdain for exhibitors. Citing them as real-estate operators who only think of films as "product" for their theatres and care little for creative talent.

85 "In Reply to Mr. Mankiewicz." *Motion Picture Herald* 23 July 1949: 8–9. Inflamed motion picture exhibitors respond with letters to the editor over JLM's comment in *Life* magazine's roundtable on the movies.

86 "Joseph Mankiewicz Answers." *Motion Picture Herald* 6 Aug. 1949: 8–9. More letters to the editor over JLM's comments about exhibitors as "real estate operators." Includes a letter from Mankiewicz himself, who responds to the

mail he has generated over his comment describing a film exhibitor as "a real estate operator whose chief concern should be taking gum off carpets and checking adolescent love-making in the balcony."

87 *A Letter to Three Wives. Look* 1 Feb. 1949: 80–82. Picture story on film with compliments to JLM for skillful use of the flashback.

88 *A Letter to Three Wives. Today's Cinema* 25 Feb. 1949: n. pag. High praise for JLM's "adroit adaptation" of Klempner's story. "Director Mankiewicz, who is also responsible for the scenario, has made from some aspects, a flawless film, for it is a long time since we have seen such clever, realistic and moving treatment of a familiar but always intriguing subject. He has a light touch, knows just when to be frank, when to be subtle, when to introduce a laugh and when to introduce sentiment. But even more than these, he knows how to re-create the domestic scene to make it seem part of an onlooker's experience."

89 "Mankiewicz, Joseph (Leo)." *Current Biography 1949*. Ed. Anna Rothe. New York: H. W. Wilson Co., 1949. 396–398. Fine biographical entry for the time, complete with citations to film reviews.

90 "Mankiewicz on Marriage." *New Yorker* 29 Jan. 1949: 53. Through his film, *A Letter to Three Wives*, "Mr. Mankiewicz proves that love knows no class distinctions...."

91 Scheuer, Philip. "Mankiewicz Sees New Film Targets After Dissecting Home and Marriage." *Los Angeles Times* 13 Feb. 1949, sec. IV: 1. Interview with JLM regarding his "pet peeves" which he allowed to come through in *A Letter to Three Wives*. "The movies," he says, "never defend themselves and seldom attack anything. It's about time they did." Explains that his motivation for the schoolteacher (Kirk Douglas character) came from growing up in a household with a father who was a professor.

92 Smith, Darr. Column. *Los Angeles Daily News* 2 Aug. 1949: n. pag. With movie exhibitors angry at JLM for his comments about what is wrong with today's film, this column tries to explain the Mankiewicz philosophy of production and exhibition.

1950

93 "25 Aid Mankiewicz in Loyalty Dispute." *New York Times* 16 Oct. 1950: 30. Screen Directors Guild controversy over signing of a loyalty oath draws support for Guild president Mankiewicz. His opposition to the compulsory signing of the oath has prompted a call by Cecil B. DeMille and others to have him stripped of his presidency and to blacklist those who refuse to sign the oath.

94 Allen, Marilyn R. *No Way Out. American Klansman* Oct. 1950: 3. Noting the source, this reviewer sees film as prejudicial to whites and, "a planned campaign to DEBASE THE WHITE CHRISTIAN people...." Sees Hollywood as anti–American communists trying to subvert society. Outrageous but worthy of attention since the film has engendered such emotion.

95 Alpert, Hollis. "The Case of Joseph L. Mankiewicz." *Saturday Review* 21 Oct. 1950: 31–32. JLM as "author." The Mankiewicz style is analyzed in this review of *All About Eve*.

96 Behlmer, Rudy. "Waves of Love Over the Footlights: *All About Eve* (1950)." *America's Favorite Movies: Behind the Scenes.* New York: Ungar, 1982. 200–214. Few JLM quotes. General discussion of events leading up to filming of *Eve*. Noteworthy for understanding of Zanuck's role of producer to JLM's double role as writer-director. Clarifies viewer's misconception that Tallulah Bankhead was the basis for the character, Margo Channing. JLM used 18th century London actress, Peg Woffington, as his model while short-story writer, Mary Orr's conception is based on Elisabeth [*sic*] Bergner.

97 Brady, Thomas. "Hollywood Divided by Loyalty Pledge Issue." *New York Times* 22 Oct. 1950, sec. II: 5. An excellent, lengthy discussion of the thorny SDG loyalty oath issue.

98 ____. "Hollywood Turmoil." *New York Times* 29 Oct. 1950, sec. II: 5. Outcome of loyalty oath controversy seen in the light of a "resounding victory" for Mankiewicz.

99 ____. "Mankiewicz Asks Signing of Oaths." *New York Times* 27 Oct. 1950: 25. One week after the Screen Directors Guild votes to support JLM's opposition to the mandatory signing of a non–Communist loyalty oath (lest those who refuse be blacklisted), Mankiewicz urges members to voluntarily sign the oath "in affirmation of confidence in your guild."

100 *Chaines conjugales.* [*A Letter to Three Wives.*] *Mon Film* [Paris] 28 June 1950: n. pag. Issue includes extended segments of *A Letter to Three Wives* screenplay. In French.

101 Cook, Alton. "Two New Films Bring Laughter." *New York World and Telegram* 2 Sept. 1950: 4. JLM discusses *No Way Out* (hardly a film to evoke laughter) and *All About Eve*. Includes references to American films for European distribution. Minor article, but with direct quotes.

102 Crowther, Bosley. "Thespis on the Ropes." *New York Times* 22 Oct. 1950, sec. 2: 1. High praise for Mankiewicz and *All About Eve* as a successful Hollywood assault on "the Theat-uh."

103 "Film Directors Guild Split by Recall Move." *Los Angeles Times* 15 Oct. 1950: 1+. Details about SDG loyalty oath feud. Lists names of those directors pro and con on the Mankiewicz recall petition.

104 Gilmour, Clyde. "More About Mr. M.—And *All About Eve*." *Vancouver Sun* 21 Nov. 1950: 17. Mini-bio on JLM and his early films pays homage to his talent as "one of the most resourceful, mature and adroit craftsmen creating commercial motion pictures anywhere in the world."

105 Goodman, Ezra. Untitled Interview. *Los Angeles Daily News* 13 June 1950: 24. Good interview expressing the Mankiewicz philosophy of filmmaking. JLM continues his assault on theatre exhibitors, calling them "real estate men not creative artists" who thwart the creative process by demanding quantity rather than quality. "Moviemakers should make the pictures they want to make just as writers should write books they want to write. You can only please yourself. To approach the job of making a movie with the attitude of what someone wants to buy is silly. Film is not a can of tomatoes or a Cadillac. Film is the creative work of two or three people—and it is up to us to keep movies from being a commodity."

106 Griffith, Ann. "Film Reviews: *All About Eve*." *Films in Review* Dec. 1950: 37–38. Success of film is due to JLM's witty dialogue. "It is brittle, polished,

fast, wonderfully slick. One is grateful that he doesn't spell everything out, one is enlivened by his subtlety and innuendo."

107 Guernsey, Otis L., Jr. "A Bonanza Week." *New York Herald Tribune* 22 Oct. 1950: 1+. Rave review for Mankiewicz, as much as for his film. "*All About Eve* demonstrates more powerfully and convincingly than any argument the greatness of the motion picture medium under the proper management.... One may continue to smile at some of Hollywood's film product; but only because there aren't enough Mankiewiczes to go around—and there aren't enough in the theater, either."

108 Lapin, Adam. "*No Way Out* Offers Distorted View of Anti-Negro Violence." *Daily People's World* [San Francisco] 26 Sept. 1950: 50. More social commentary than film review. This politically oriented newspaper sees the film as more melodramatic than credible, and woefully lacking in any real contribution to ending prejudice. Faults lie predominantly in the Widmark, race-baiter character, for being moronic, and one with whom no one in the audience could identify. The only praise for this, the latest of Hollywood's films dealing with "the Negro question," comes for its strong portrayal of the black family.

109 "Mag Names Mankiewicz Man-of-Yr." *Variety* [Daily] 8 Dec. 1950: n. pag. *Holiday* magazine honors JLM for directing *No Way Out* and *All About Eve. Eve* acknowledged as "the big-budget film of '50 that best typifies American life."

110 "Mankiewicz Asks Court Order to Restrain Recall Petition." *Hollywood Reporter* 16 Oct. 1950: 1+. Loyalty oath controversy escalates.

111 "Mankiewicz Asks Unity on SDG Oath." *Variety* 27 Oct. 1950: 1+. Lengthy quotes from a letter Mankiewicz sent to the guild members following the failed recall effort spearheaded by DeMille. Mankiewicz notes the rift within the SDG had "nothing whatsoever to do with the pro or con of a loyalty oath," but rather that he, and the guild itself, were the targets of the vitriolic attack.. He strongly urges the members of the SDG to join him in voluntarily signing the loyalty oath.

112 "Mankiewicz Hurls Gauntlet at TOA on Theatre Tele." *Hollywood Reporter.* 13 June 1950: 1+. Because TOA (Theater Owners of America) announced that they will show not only movies in their theatres but maybe even TV, JLM suggests that those working in film will and should apply their creative talents to the television industry as well.

113 "Mankiewicz in Plea for Action on Oath." *Hollywood Reporter* 27 Oct. 1950: 1+. Extensive quotes from JLM letter to Screen Directors Guild members on loyalty oath.

114 "Mankiewicz Loyalty Tilt Still Seethes." *Los Angeles Daily News* 16 Oct. 1950: n. pag. Loyalty oath controversy explained.

115 "Mankiewicz on the 'New Minority.'" *Variety* [Weekly] 20 Sept. 1950: 22. Speaking out against blacklisting and Communist witchhunts wins Mankiewicz the B'nai B'rith award as the person in arts and literature who most furthers the American democratic tradition. In his acceptance speech, JLM declares, "The American liberal—the new minority—is being hounded, persecuted and annihilated today—deliberately destroyed by an organized enemy as evil in practice and purpose—and indistinguishable from—the Communist menace that fosters and encourages that destruction... ."

Remember, that it is the hope of this new minority, too, that this world will some day become a world of human beings and for human beings who live together in decency and dignity. Let this new minority be destroyed—and this hope will die with it."

116 "Mankiewicz Pleads the Cause of the Liberal in U.S." *Variety* [Daily] 15 Sept. 1950: 6. JLM speech (upon receipt of the B'nai B'rith's annual award) cites need to respect the "new minority"—the American liberal.

117 "Mankiewicz Recall to Fail." *Variety* 16 Oct. 1950: 1+. Extensive details of how the drive to recall Mankiewicz as president of the Screen Directors Guild failed. Article includes text of the telegram sent by anti–Mankiewicz members (led by DeMille).

118 "Mankiewicz Sees Plot in Ouster Move." *Los Angeles Times* 14 Oct. 1950, sec. II: 5. Background on JLM's position on SDG loyalty oath.

119 "Mankiewicz Seen Retaining SDG Post vs. Opposition in Loyalty Oath Row." *Variety* [Weekly] 18 Oct. 1950: 3+. Excellent details behind the SDG loyalty oath issue, seen from Mankiewicz supporters' perspective.

120 "Mankiewicz Wins; SDG Bd. Out." *Variety* [Daily] 24 Oct. 1950: 1+. Coverage of the infamous meeting in which DeMille and his cohorts are not only chastised for their attempt to oust Mankiewicz as SDG president, but ordered to resign as members of the Board.

121 Moore, Louis, Donald Tait, and Julian Johnson. "The Truth About *All About Eve*." *Action* Dec. 1950: 4+. Lengthy, detailed account on the making of *All About Eve*, from its inception to the final editing and musical scoring. Fascinating account of filmmaking during the studio era.

122 "Movie of the Week: *No Way Out*." *Life* 4 Sept. 1950: 44–46. Film is banned in Chicago and no plans to exhibit it in the South. Picture story also includes comments from JLM and an exhibitor over the theory of what the public wants to see on the screen.

123 "*No Way Out*: Story of Negro Doctor Is Strongest of Race-Theme Movies." *Ebony* Mar. 1950: 31–34. Kudos to Mankiewicz and Zanuck for a film seen as the "first out-and-out blast against racial discrimination in everyday American life." Background on Lesser Samuels' story-concept based on real-life observations of hospital with one black doctor.

124 "Producers Guild vs. MPIC Oath." *Hollywood Reporter*. 13 Oct. 1950: 1+. Loyalty oath controversy in great detail.

125 Pryor, Thomas M. "Joseph Mankiewicz Scales Hollywood Peak." *New York Times* 24 Sept. 1950, sec. II: 5. Mankiewicz viewed as a hot property following *A Letter to Three Wives*. Biographical sketch addresses his outspokenness concerning theater owners, his new films (*No Way Out* and *All About Eve*), and a new project about "moms."

126 "A Quick Look at *No Way Out*." *Quick* 14 Aug. 1950: 1+. Publicity campaign for controversial picture unveiled.

127 "Recall Ban Sought for Mankiewicz." *Hollywood Citizen-News* 14 Oct. 1950: 1. Lists names of SDG members who signed injunction petition preventing the recall of JLM as guild president (Huston, Wilder, Wyler, Seaton, Robson, Brooks, Wise, Zinneman, Losey, Negulesco, Ray, Vidor, Farrow, and Hartman).

128 Rosten, Leo. "Film Review: *No Way Out*." *Reporter* 24 Oct. 1950: 40. Film is proclaimed courageous for shunning euphemisms, and praised for cross-

ing racial barriers. "It is worth noticing how successful the film is in getting the whites in the audience to identify themselves with Negroes beating up whites."

129 Rosten, Leo. "Mostly About Mankiewicz." *Reporter* 12 Dec. 1950: 40. Review
     of *All About Eve* is more of an appreciation for Mankiewicz, who is seen as
     a satirist and social commentator.

130 "Screen Guild Backing Given Mankiewicz." *Los Angeles Times* 24 Oct. 1950:
     13. Details of the SDG meeting in which Mankiewicz supporters overturn
     the recall petition to oust JLM as president and demand the resignation of
     those responsible for starting the recall. Lists those who will be asked to
     resign from the board as DeMille, Rogell, Butler, Lang, Garnett, Ford,
     Brown, Robson, Binyon, Borzage, Cooper, McDonald, Seiter, Wallace,
     Waters.

131 "SDG Members to Meet Sunday on Mankiewicz Issue; Ct. Halts Recall."
     Variety [Daily] 17 Oct. 1950: 1+. Good overview of loyalty oath issue and
     Mankiewicz recall.

132 "SDG Non-Red Oath Is Aimed at Infiltration From East." *Hollywood
     Reporter* 28 Aug. 1950. The real reason behind the loyalty oath controversy—
     fear of Eastern writers, ties to Communism.

133 "SDG Schism on 'Blacklist.'" *Variety* 11 Oct. 1950: 1+. Under the bold sub-
     heading, "Mankiewicz Will Not Sign Oath," *Daily Variety* details the heated
     debate among the Board of Directors of the Screen Directors Guild con-
     cerning the signing of a loyalty oath which contains a provision wherein
     those who refuse to sign will be blacklisted. Specifics of this controversial
     provision, as well as Mankiewicz's staunch stand on the subject, are detailed.

134 Taylor, Harvey. "*No Way Out* Is Hailed as Impressive Picture." *Detroit Times*
     30 Sept. 1950: n. pag. Review applauds reality of film. Black perspective
     appreciated and endorsed. Compliments the inclusion of scenes of blacks'
     home life: "a rarity on the screen."

135 Wolfenstein, Martha and Nathan Leites. "The Study of Man: Two Social
     Scientists View *No Way Out*." *Commentary* Oct. 1950: 388–391. While there
     is no specific mention of Mankiewicz in this article dissecting the social
     implications of the movie, "the makers of the film [read, Mankiewicz]," are
     addressed in this fascinating study of racial bias (bias that still exists today)
     and how it is approached generally in motion pictures.

1951

136 Brock, Ray. "World War II 'Operation Cicero' Crowds in Real-Life Spy
     Intrigue." *Variety* 12 July 1951: 2. On location with JLM during filming of
     Five Fingers; discussion of crowd problems and British Embassy's lack of
     cooperation.

137 Buchwald, Art and Robert Yoakum. "Mostly About People: Operation
     Cicero." *New York Herald Tribune* 24 July 1951: 5. JLM discusses meeting
     "Cicero," the real-life spy of *Five Fingers*, while filming in Turkey. Turkish
     government intervention in the filming included phone taps, censoring
     telegrams, and the suggestion that Mankiewicz not meet with "Cicero"
     because he was "persona non grata." Eventually they met (in secret) in Istan-

bul, where "Cicero" pleaded for money and a trip to the United States. According to JLM, "He wouldn't talk unless he got paid for it. He told me he had been standing in the crowds watching us shoot the exteriors every day since we arrived."

138 Catling, Patrick Skene. "Calling Mr. Mankiewicz." *Baltimore Sun* 1 Sept. 1951: n. pag. Q&A about *People Will Talk*'s theme of healing the mind as well as the body; JLM's favorite writers (those who look to the inner workings of those outside themselves rather than introspective writers); and his decision to move away from Hollywood, and future projects.

139 Chauvet, Louis. "Les Films nouveaux: *All About Eve.*" *Figaro* [France] 28–29 Apr. 1951: n. pag. High praise for Mankiewicz as the author of this critically praised film. In French.

140 Coughlan, Robert. "15 Authors in Search of a Character Named Joseph L. Mankiewicz." *Life* 12 Mar. 1951: 158–173. Fascinating article, on the eve of his winning two Oscars for *All About Eve*. Includes lengthy quotes from Mankiewicz, friends, producers, and family members. One of the best articles of its kind in a popular magazine.

141 Crowther, Bosley. "The Horn of Plenty." *New York Times* 30 Aug. 1951: 20. Positive review of *People Will Talk* and its theme of tolerance of human foibles. "All we can say is that a picture so mature and refreshingly frank as to hold that an erring young woman might be rewarded with a wise and loving mate is certainly a significant milestone in the moral emancipation of American films...."

142 Doniol-Valcroze, Jacques. "All About Mankiewicz." *Cahiers du Cinéma* May 1951: 21–30. Analysis of Mankiewicz and his films. In French.

143 Gilmour, Clyde. "Mankiewicz Film Looks Like 'Tops.'" *Vancouver Sun.* 26 April 1951: n. pag. Insight into JLM's behind the camera technique as Gilmour recounts a day on the set on "Dr. Praetorius" (*People Will Talk*).

144 Goodman, Ezra. "Long Shots and Closeups." *Los Angeles Daily News* 17 May 1951: 28. JLM negotiates new contract with 20th Century–Fox in which he will make one movie a year. Mankiewicz wants to move from Hollywood to New York to concentrate on writing for the theatre; columnist sees this as a boon for Broadway, as JLM's "penchant for rich, beautiful prose" can be utilized without cinema's "technical distractions."

145 Hoffman, Irving. "Tales of Hoffman." *Hollywood Reporter* 20 Mar. 1951: 3. Humorous quip about the Stork Club refusing JLM entrance because they did not recognize him—and his response to the rebuff.

146 "Mankiewicz, 20th Sever Contract." *Variety* [Daily] 27 Sept. 1951: n. pag. JLM ends association with Fox to become independent. Article notes Mankiewicz and Zanuck strike a seven-year deal to make one picture a year for Fox.

147 "Mankiewicz Reaps New Honors for Latest Pictures." *Deltan* [Phi Sigma Delta Quarterly] Spring 1951: 10-11. Fraternity publication cites "Frater" Mankiewicz's speech on the American liberal in light of *No Way Out*.

148 "New Films: *People Will Talk.*" *Newsweek* 27 Aug. 1951: 82. Called "Hollywood's ranking 'genius.'" Mankiewicz's latest film is discussed in this mini-bio which announces JLM's reasons for moving from Hollywood to New York.

149 Nugent, Frank. "All About Joe." *Colliers* 24 Mar. 1951: 24+. Interesting bio-

graphical sketch of JLM at the beginning of his glory days; seen as the "most brilliant commentator on the American scene." Includes rare references to second wife, Rosa Stradner, his hobbies (baseball and sailing), and his impending move from the "Ivory Ghetto" of Hollywood to New York.

150 Parsons, Louella O. "Cary Grant and Anne Baxter Get Leads in *Doctor's Diary.*" *Los Angeles Examiner* 23 Feb. 1951: 7. Reference to early title for *People Will Talk*; cites JLM's complete reworking of the German play, *Dr. Praetorius.*

151 *People Will Talk. Time* 17 Sept. 1951: 106. Seen as the third installment in JLM's critique of American manners and mores. *People* tackles the medical profession. Reference to Hollywood taboo subjects such as illegitimacy, medical ethics, and witchhunts.

152 Redelings, Lowell E. "The Hollywood Scene." *Hollywood Citizen News* 16 Mar. 1951: n. pag. Extensive quotes from JLM on the decline in the quality of Hollywood film.

153 Watts, Richard. "Dr. Cary Grant Practices at Roxy." *New York Post* 30 Aug. 1951: n. pag. Praise for *People Will Talk* includes a warning to JLM not to take himself too seriously. "Despite its humor and its scorn of stuffiness, *People Will Talk* has a way of growing oddly pompous. Its talk is not only intelligent and independent, which is fine, but also pretentious which is less commendable." Complaints of scenes and speeches being dragged out.

154 Weiler, A. H. "Random Observations on the Screen Scene." *New York Times* 29 July 1951, sec. X: 3. JLM discusses difficulties of filming *Five Fingers* on location in Ankara.

1952

155 Alpert, Hollis. "The Golden Touch of Mr. Mankiewicz." *Saturday Review* 8 Mar. 1952: 32–33. Review of *Five Fingers* groups Mankiewicz with Hitchcock and Carol Reed as masters of intrigue.

156 Crowther, Bosley. "The Screen in Review: *Five Fingers*, a Spy Thriller Starring James Mason, New Feature at Roxy Theatre." *New York Times* 23 Feb. 1952, sec. 7: 5. Praise for an intelligent spy thriller and JLM's contribution to the dialogue. "His sharp scenes—his scenes of greatest tension and most deliciously clever surprise—are developed through the manners of his actors and their handling of the excellent dialogue without the usual reliance of the director of melodrama on visual tricks."

157 "Film Preview: *Five Fingers.*" *Variety* 13 Feb. 1952: 6. Calling it a "melodrama," this review notes the film as long but good. "From a slow, methodical start that drags out the footage, Joseph L. Mankiewicz's direction gains pace near the midway mark and wallops over a stock bit of suspense drama, filled with thrills and tension."

158 "*Five Fingers* Fascinating." *Hollywood Reporter* 13 Feb. 1952: n. pag. Praise for this true story. "With Joseph L. Mankiewicz at the directorial helm, one's expectations of an interesting, compelling film are cleverly fulfilled."

159 Majdalany, Fred. "The Old School Spy." *Daily Mail* [London] 4 Apr. 1952: n. pag. Regarding *Five Fingers*, "On this core of irony the author, Michael Wilson, and the director, Joseph L. Mankiewicz (an old hand at the urbane

leg-pull), have constructed a light comedy which in its cynical zest reminds one of the vintage Lubitsch pictures during the thirties."

160 Mankiewicz, Don M. "Joe Mankiewicz: His Movies Make Women Mad, Turnstile Click." *Today's Woman* July 1952: 4+. Nephew Don (Herman's son) writes fondly about his Uncle Joe's style of filmmaking.

161 "Miseries of a Master Spy." *Life* 7 Apr. 1952: 139–142. Picture of JLM and real-life spy "Cicero" who came to Mankiewicz seeking money while filming in Ankara. Behind-the-scenes photos of filming of *Five Fingers* as well as information on what had become of "Cicero" since his spy days.

162 Pryor, Thomas M. "Greer Garson Set for 'Caesar' Film. *New York Times* 13 June 1952: 20. An unusual event in filmmaking—JLM plans three weeks of rehearsals before shooting begins on *Julius Caesar*.

163 _____. "Hollywood Report." *New York Times* 11 May 1952, sec. X: 5. JLM seen as entering his "classical phase" as he begins *Caesar* and a three-picture deal with MGM—especially in light of having just completed his Metropolitan Opera production of *La Bohème*.

164 _____. "West Coast Bid for Shakespearean Supremacy." *New York Times* 21 Sept. 1952, sec. II: 5. A look at the planning behind *Julius Caesar*; includes reference to Mankiewicz's confidence in Brando's ability to deliver Shakespearean English.

165 "Talk of the Day: Gielgud for Hollywood." *Evening News* [London] 16 June 1952: 4. Erroneous information that *Julius Caesar* is a film based on the "Carl Jonas novel, *Julius Caesar*."

166 Taubman, Howard. "A New 'Bohème.'" *New York Times* 21 Dec. 1952, sec. X: 9. JLM discusses his approach to staging *La Bohème* for the Met.

167 "Tele Followup Comment." *Variety* 17 Dec. 1952: 27. Overview of JLM's 15 minute appearance on "The Hot Seat." Topics range from the cinema box office slump to the loyalty oath. Regarding the decline in box office revenues, Mankiewicz notes that the film industry is "over-inflated" because during the war box office receipts increased, but now there are "too many pictures and too many theatres." Regarding his objection to the loyalty oath when he was SDG president, it was because the guild was a private labor union. JLM notes "the tremendous difference between a loyalty oath demanded by the state and one demanded by private persons."

168 Thompson, Howard. "Gielgud on Cassius." *New York Times* 16 Nov. 1952, sec. II: 4. Gielgud makes his Hollywood debut in *Julius Caesar*. Here, he reflects on acting in film and working with Mankiewicz and a cadre of Hollywood talent including Marlon Brando, James Mason, and Greer Garson: "Actually, it was Mankiewicz' consummate tact that kept us together as a working unit."

1953

169 Alpert, Hollis. "The Abuse of Greatness." *Saturday Review*. 6 June 1953: 26–28. Cover story on *Julius Caesar*. Film seen as "in the front rank of the great motion pictures."

170 Berg, Louis. "Friends, Romans, Brando." *This Week* 1 Mar. 1953: 24–25. JLM makes *Caesar* a closed set. Brando nervous. Long takes. Brando does eight

takes on the "Friends, Romans, Countrymen" speech. Asks for retakes on all his scenes.

171 Burnup, Peter. "Films." *News of the World* [London] 8 Nov. 1953: n. pag. Rave review for Mankiewicz, who is seen as a "courageous, disturbing man" for defying Hollywood conventions by directing *Julius Caesar* in a subtle way, allowing Shakespeare to speak for himself. "This 'Caesar' has the pace of a newsreel, the thrill and terror of melodrama, the timelessness of tragedy."

172 Crowther, Bosley. Rev. of *Julius Caesar*. *New York Times* 14 June 1953, sec. 2: 1. Cites JLM's directorial style of using close-ups to bring the spectators "so close to them [the actors] that the very warmth of their body heat and the intensity of their passions in thoughtful or violent moods seem to come right out of the picture and create the dynamic of the film."

173 "Film Review: *Julius Caesar*." *Variety* 3 June 1953: 3. Praise for JLM's adaptation and direction. "Even the purists who want every comma in its proper place will be unable to carp with the production, though possibly shaking up a healthy controversy with how some of the players bring the characters to life." Notes that JLM's changes, such as the omission of repetitious dialogue, are in the "interest of a better motion picture."

174 Frank, Elizabeth. "The Noblest Romans of Them All." *News Chronicle* [England]. 4 Nov. 1953: n. pag. "It is maddening to be forced to admit it—but it has been left to Hollywood to make the finest film version of Shakespeare yet to be seen on our screens." Praises Mankiewicz as the reason for the film's success, "tackling Shakespeare for the first time, [he] has obviously realized that the dramatist knew his onions and that it was quite unnecessary to indulge in any tricks."

175 Gielgud, John. "'Cassius' Places Laurel on *Julius Caesar*." *New York Times* 7 June 1953, sec. II: 5. Gielgud discusses his first film role in Mankiewicz's *Caesar*. Praise for the scenario's faithfulness to the text of the play.

176 Guernsey, Otis, Jr. "Ave Caesar!" *New York Herald Tribune* 5 June 1953: 14. Complete cast credits in review that hails *Caesar* as being in the hands of master director of dialogue, JLM. "Mankiewicz's *Julius Caesar* is a heroic figure of human geometry, chiseled in poetry and exalted on the huge pedestal of the screen."

177 _____. "*Julius Caesar* Film: A Character Study." *New York Herald Tribune* 14 June 1953: 1+. *Caesar* becomes a "study of character" in JLM's hands. "Mankiewicz's fascinating, ever-changing visual compositions are not of the show-stealing type; they are graceful compliments to the basic material of the play."

178 _____. "Movie Mystery: Which Version Did You See?" *New York Herald Tribune* 8 Nov. 1953: n. pag. The premiere of *Julius Caesar* occurred at the Booth (a theatrical stage equipped with a screen) but was soon transferred to the Plaza. Review reflects the difference in the drama when transferred from small screen to large.

179 Hale, Wanda. "*Caesar* Heads the Six Best." *Sunday News* [NY] 28 June 1953: 2. Credits Mankiewicz for helping Brando deliver his lines "better than cynics expected and sufficiently clear and forceful for his worshipers to keep saying that he is the best young actor of the time."

180 Houseman, John. "*Julius Caesar* on Film." *New York Herald Tribune* 29 Mar. 1953: n. pag. Producer Houseman's pompous interpretation of Shakespeare

for the uninitiated masses; explains the casting of the film, with minimal reference to the work of the director, Mankiewicz.

181 "*Julius Caesar* Has World Premiere Here." *Sydney Morning Herald* [Australia]. 9 May 1953: n. pag. World premiere (in Sydney), has audience applauding after each showing as though it were a stage production. Film executives were stunned since this was the first time they had ever seen this kind of reaction to a film in Sydney.

182 Majdalany, Fred. "True to the Bard—and a Fine Film." *Daily Mail* [London] 4 Nov. 1953: 6. High praise for JLM's camera set-ups as intelligent eavesdropping on the conversation of conspirators.

183 "Mankiewicz' Indie Link with UA to Rope Logan, Kazan, Hypo N.Y. Prod'n." *Variety* [Weekly] 13 May 1953: 3+. Mankiewicz begins life as an independent by forming his own production company (Figaro, Inc.) in New York. Establishes contract with United Artists and hopes that Joshua Logan and Elia Kazan will consider joining the organization in the future. JLM complains that New York, "which otherwise is the centre of the arts, already has lost out as the site for vidpix production just as it missed the boat years before on standard films."

184 "New Films: *Julius Caesar*." *Newsweek* 8 June 1953: 101. JLM praised for avoiding the temptation to make the film a color spectacle and staying with black and white to achieve a stark quality.

185 "New Picture: *Julius Caesar*." *Time* 1 June 1953: 94+. Gives comparisons to other Shakespearean productions on film. Receives praise for its faithfulness to the play.

186 Quinn, Frank. "'Julius Caesar' Lives Again in Brilliantly Acted Picture." *Daily Mirror* [New York] 5 June 1953: 40. Seen as one of the "finest examples of classic translation we've seen." Critic praises JLM for introducing "a new dignity and prestige" to the film screen.

187 Swope, John. *Julius Caesar. Life* 20 Apr. 1953: 135-9. Extensive photo essay of making of the film.

188 Tyler, Parker. "Et tu, Mankiewicz." *Theatre Arts* June 1953: 84+. *Caesar* reviewed as mediocre. Fault lies in JLM for poor casting and lackluster style.

1954

189 "*The Barefoot Contessa* Has Strong B.O. Qualities." *Hollywood Reporter* 27 Sept. 1954: 3. Mankiewicz's first independent production garners praise for his dialogue which "sparkles and bursts like vintage Burgundy." Reviewer suggests Howard Hughes is the inspiration for Mankiewicz's mythical producer Kirk Edwards.

190 Burnup, Peter. "Bing Sings It Again." *News of the World* [London] 7 Nov. 1954: 8. Reviewer of *Contessa* calls JLM, "one of the world's greatest moviemakers ranking with men like Hitchcock and John Huston."

191 Cook, Alton. "An Idealist in Pictures." *New York World Telegram* 25 Sept. 1954: 8. On the eve of the release of his first independent film (*The Barefoot Contessa*), JLM discusses themes that interest him. "I always have an argument on my hands because I believe there is room for pictures that will

bring in a profit and also have some comment on various phases of American life."

192 "Film Review: *The Barefoot Contessa*." *Variety* [Daily] 27 Sept. 1954: 3+. High praise for JLM's look at Hollywood in his first film as an independent.

193 Houseman, John. "*Julius Caesar*: Mr. Mankiewicz' Shooting Script." *Quarterly of Film Radio and Television* VIII (1953–1954): 109–124. *Caesar* producer, Houseman, praises JLM's "plain, functional shooting script" by editing two excerpts for publication to demonstrate how to adapt a classic stage play for film.

194 Jacchia, Paolo. "I malintesi di Joseph L. Mankiewicz." *Eco Del Cinema* 31 Mar. 1954: 15+. In-depth analysis of *All About Eve, Julius Caesar*, and *No Way Out*. In Italian.

195 Majdalany, Fred. "Films." *Time and Tide* [London] 13 Nov. 1954: n. pag. Review of *Contessa* claims dialogue is "ferocious as well as witty." JLM's allegory of Hollywood and human behavior is well received.

196 Rauch, Robert. "Con Mankiewicz mentre si gira *La Contessa Scalza*." *Cinema* 15 Feb. 1954: 68+. Behind-the-scenes of the filming of *The Barefoot Contessa*. Emphasis on JLM's directing style. In Italian.

197 Rogow, Lee. "The Hollywood Oasis." *Saturday Review* 16 Oct. 1954: 31. Calling Mankiewicz a "screenplaywright and craftsman of fresh-springing wit and welcome intelligence," this reviewer sees *The Barefoot Contessa* as a biographical film with easily recognizable characters.

198 Schallert, Edwin. "Director Lauds Ava for Work in 'Contessa.'" *Los Angeles Times* 24 Oct. 1954: 1+. Discussing his first project as an independent, JLM addresses the need for motion pictures to be international in scope, "Movies with limited horizons are bound to play only to a limited audience and restricted returns." Also muses about how audiences misinterpret his fictional characters to be based on real people (e.g. Warren Stephens' tycoon character in *Contessa* presumed to be Howard Hughes, even by Hughes himself).

1955

199 Alpert, Hollis. "SR goes to the Movies." *Saturday Review* 12 Nov. 1955: 25. Accolades for Mankiewicz and Goldwyn collaboration in *Guys and Dolls*. Calls JLM "pyrotechnical" for turning out an eclectic set of films. Cites JLM's improvements in screenplay that flesh out the characters of Sky Masterson and Sarah.

200 "Crosby Cancels Showing After Church Protest." *Los Angeles Herald Express* 25 Nov. 1955: 1. Catholics of the Legion of Decency protest showing *Guys and Dolls* for Notre Dame football team (while they are in California to play against USC). Citing concern for "moral laxity in films," Catholic bishops recently protested in Washington.

201 Downing, Robert. "Film Review." *Films in Review* Dec. 1955: 525. Claims *Guys and Dolls* is "amateur night and the cash customers shouldn't sit still for it!" (Note: *Motion Picture Daily* indicates the film grossed $4,200,000 in under 60 days.)

202 *Guys and Dolls*. *Time* 14 Nov. 1955: 116+. Cites Goldwyn's paying $1 million for rights to play. Cost of film $5 million.

203 Lyons, Leonard. "The Lyons Den." *New York Post* 17 Nov. 1955: n. pag. Gossip column social note sums up JLM during *Guys and Dolls* time frame: "Joe Mankiewicz, who directed and wrote the screen play for *Guys and Dolls* naturally likes to discuss his works. Yesterday Sam Spiegel, the film producer, had an after-dinner date at Mankiewicz' house. He invited Otto Preminger and Anatole Litvak to accompany him. 'No,' said Preminger. 'There'd be nothing for us to talk about at Joe's, because (1) he's an intellectual, and (2) he doesn't play gin rummy and (3) we haven't seen *Guys and Dolls*.'"

204 Mili, Gjon. "'Guys' Dolled Up." *Life* 19 Sept. 1955: 10+. Photo illustration by photojournalist Mili on the big musical hit.

205 "NBC Mankiewicz Pix Partner." *Variety* [Daily] 9 Nov. 1955: 1. Brief notice of NBC's acquisition of 50 percent of JLM's production company, Figaro, Inc.

206 Pryor, Thomas M. "Mankiewicz Sued for Plagiarism." *New York Times* 31 Aug. 1955: 16. JLM sued for $50,000. Charles Geary (Guttman) claims JLM's *The Barefoot Contessa* is a copy of his screenplay, "The Story of Gaby Deslys," which he wrote in the 1940s while working for MGM, when JLM was employed there as well.

207 "Runyonland Revisited." *Cue* [New York] 22 Oct. 1955: 15+. Interviewer misspells name as "Manckiewicz" throughout article. JLM clarifies his journalism work in Berlin after college. "I was a part-time *Variety* mugg [sic] and a copy boy in the *Chicago Tribune*'s Berlin office. I filled inkwells, changed typewriter ribbons, swept up the floor. (This translates, in the publicity handbook, as, a term of duty as 'a foreign correspondent in Berlin.') That's how I learned to write. And, believe me, there are worse ways."

208 Scheuer, Philip K. "Goldwyn Bets Big Bankroll on His *Guys and Dolls*." *Los Angeles Times* 13 Nov. 1955, sec. IV: 1+. Good background information on how film was adapted from stage.

209 Sondheim, Steve. Rev. of *Guys and Dolls*. *Films in Review* Dec. 1955: 523–525. Pans just about everything in the film from Michael Kidd's choreography to JLM's "heavy handling of Runyonese." While he finds some strengths in the film, this is more of a musical review—and the young Mr. Sondheim (then aged 25) is not thrilled.

210 Spear, Ivan. "Goldwyn's *Guys and Dolls* Magnificent Entertainment." *Boxoffice* 5 Nov. 1955: 22. Praise for JLM's directing and screenplay. Offers something for everybody from witty dialogue and glorious music, to flashy dance numbers in CinemaScope and Eastman Color.

211 Sullivan, Ed. "Little Old New York: The Passing Show." *Daily News* [New York] 16 Mar. 1955: 72. Sullivan details Mankiewicz career accomplishments as well as some anecdotes from growing up in New York. Notes the unparalleled accomplishment of winning double Oscars for writing and directing two years in a row.

212 Thompson, Howard. "Mankiewicz Blueprint." *New York Times* 23 Oct. 1955, sec. II: 5. Now an independent producer-director-writer in New York, JLM questions the wisdom of keeping filmmaking in California when the talent, advertisers, and corporate folks are in New York. Wishes there were independent studios on East Coast to tap theatrical talent such as is done in London.

1956

213 "$250,000 Suit Over 'Contessa.'" *Hollywood Reporter* 25 Sept. 1956: 9. Mildred Cantor sues for $250,000 for plagiarism of "Dancing Cannibali," claiming it is the basis for *The Barefoot Contessa*. Cantor claims she submitted the script to William Morris Agency and that Mankiewicz (also a Morris client), must have had access to it there.

214 "*Guys and Dolls* Gross $4,200,000 in Under 60 Days; Tops 'Best Years.'" *Motion Picture Daily* 5 Jan. 1956: 1+. Film sets records.

215 Pryor, Thomas M. "Mankiewicz Wins a Plagiarism Suit." *New York Times* 17 Mar. 1956: 12. Judge dismisses Geary suit against JLM.

1957

216 Breit, Harvey. "In and Out of Books." *New York Times Book Review.* 6 January 1957: 8. Mankiewicz clears up a rumor circulating during the filming of *The Quiet American* that he was going to change the title of Graham Greene's novel to "The Violent American." Because a certain actor was being considered for the lead, someone had quipped that perhaps he should be called, "The Violent American," but it was merely a joke and never under consideration.

217 "The Disquieted Americans." *Time.* 25 February 1957: 34-35. Describes Mankiewicz' crew's dilemma of trying to photograph a real-life Vietnamese religious festival for insertion into *The Quiet American*.

218 "The Film of the Book: Case of *The Quiet American*." *London Times* 29 Jan. 1957: 9E. Letters to the editor from the only British member of the cast (actor Michael Redgrave), in support of the filmic version of Greene's novel assures the British public that their integrity remains intact even though the film addresses the downfall of imperialism in Vietnam. More important is a letter from author, Graham Greene, who admits that what Hollywood does with his novel is out of his hands, but that the changes described by the correspondent (see *London Times* 8 Jan. 1957) only make "more obvious the discrepancy between what the State Department would like the world to believe and what in fact happened in Vietnam."

219 Mindlin, Michael, Jr. "No Rest for *The Quiet American*." *New York Times* 28 Apr. 1957, sec. II: 5. Behind-the-scenes anxiety in Vietnam during the shooting of film.

220 "*The Quiet American*: Film Travesty of the Novel." *London Times* 9 Jan. 1957: 3A. In Saigon during the scouting of locations for film, this editorializing correspondent says that Mankiewicz's version of the book is a safe one. The controversial novel, banned in Vietnam because of its "somewhat cavalier treatment of Vietnamese nationalists," is considered "anti–American," according to this report. The report spurs letters to the editor from actor Michael Redgrave and the author Graham Greene. (See *218*.)

1958

221 Carmody, Jay. "'The Quiet American' Is Tempestuous Film." *Evening Star* [Washington, D.C.]. 23 Jan. 1958: A30. Film review that highlights specific differences between Mankiewicz screenplay and the original Graham Greene novel. Reviewer notes that changes make the movie much stronger than its novel counterpart.

222 _____. "Will Movies Become Art After Being Industry?" *Sunday Star* [Washington, D.C.] 12 Jan. 1958: E1. Mankiewicz discusses everything from why he left Hollywood to his adaptation of Graham Greene's *The Quiet American.*

223 Coe, Richard L. "Independent's Word for Joe." *Washington Post and Times Herald* 8 Jan. 1958: B8. Lengthy quotes from JLM about using Graham Greene's novel as the basis for his own version of *The Quiet American.* "I do insist that films based on books should be viewed as films, not as adaptations, for I think it's perfectly valid to use a book as a stepping-off point for films. Classics in the novel form are different, I suppose, but Green's [sic] story, a best-seller, hit me not because of the innocent American but because of the wise Britisher, who was not so wise as he'd thought."

224 Godard, Jean-Luc. "Americain Bien Tranquille." Arts 16 July 1958: n. pag. High praise for Mankiewicz as a writer, but Godard believes he should have paid as much attention to the shooting of the film as he did to rewriting Graham Greene's novel. In French.

225 Knight, Arthur. "One Man's Movie." *Saturday Review* 25 Jan. 1958: 27. Fearing a box office trouncing of his latest film, Mankiewicz reflects his concern that his type of work is no longer a hit with the audience. "I like to do pictures that deal with some intriguing problem or some unusual, not quite normal character. But what is intriguing to me isn't necessarily intriguing to millions of potential moviegoers. I can't produce blockbusters, I don't want to make safe, ordinary little pictures, and I'm worried as hell about how the public is going to take my *Quiet American.*"

226 "Mrs. Mankiewicz Is Found Dead." *New York Times* 28 Sept. 1958: 87. Brief account of the discovery of the body of actress Rosa Stradner, JLM's second wife, who had died the previous day [later ruled a suicide].

227 O'Neill, James, Jr. "A Director's View." *Washington Daily News* 8 Jan. 1958: 14. Mankiewicz on why he retooled Greene's novel. The novel portrayed the American character as "a cardboard, stupid, weak-kneed idiot. In fact, Green's [sic] book made me so mad I was determined to make a picture out of it. The book was insulting to America and Americans."

228 "Personality of the Month. Joseph Mankiewicz: Quiet American." *Films and Filming* May 1958: 5. Kudos to the 49-year old Mankiewicz for offering brilliant, social satire that sells. Includes biographical sketch.

229 Robb, Inez. "Americans Abroad 'Live in Red, White and Blue Ghettoes.'" *World-Telegram and Sun* [New York] 20 Jan. 1958: 2. A rarely seen (in print) political diatribe from Mankiewicz who is quoted at great length about what he saw of Americans in Vietnam while he was there filming *The Quiet American.*

230 Rohmer, Eric. "Politique contre Destin." *Cahiers du Cinéma* Aug. 1958: 46–51. Rohmer continues his years of praise for Mankiewicz in this review of *The Quiet American.* In French.

231 Wald, Richard C. "Mankiewicz Film of 'Quiet American.'" *New York Herald Tribune* 2 Feb. 1958, sec. 4: 3. Interview with JLM about reworking Greene's novel gives insight into how Mankiewicz writes his films. "It's a

film written by me based upon a book by Graham Greene. My film has an entirely different emphasis than Mr. Greene's novel.... All the threads were in the book. I just pulled them together and it came out a different pattern."

232 "Wife of Film Producer Mankiewicz Found Dead." *Los Angeles Times* 29 Sept. 1958, sec. I: 8. Photo of Stradner accompanies article about her death.

1959

233 Beckley, Paul V. "*Suddenly, Last Summer.*" *New York Herald Tribune* 23 Dec. 1959: n. pag. Admires the "rock-hard direction of Mankiewicz" in this shocking film.

234 Cameron, Kate. "*Suddenly, Last Summer* Film Debut." *Sunday News* [New York] 13 Dec. 1959, sec. 2: 1. Anxious to get back to work after a year's hiatus following the death of his wife, Mankiewicz takes on the job of directing someone else's work.

235 Crowther, Bosley. "The Screen: *Suddenly, Last Summer.*" *New York Times* 23 Dec. 1959: 22. Pans film; faults actors, story. Sees direction as "strained and sluggish, as is, indeed, the whole conceit of the drama."

236 Watts, Stephen. "Americans in Action on Britain's Film Front." *New York Times* 19 July 1959, sec. II: 5. In London for shooting of *Suddenly, Last Summer*, JLM recalls producer, Sam Spiegel, tried to get him to write the screenplay but he could not envision the play as a film until Gore Vidal wrote the screenplay. Mankiewicz cites the public's interest in psychiatric concerns as the reason why this shocking play could be made into a film.

237 Winsten, Archer. "Rages and Outrages." *New York Post* 28 Dec. 1959: 48. Mankiewicz explains what drew him to direct *Suddenly, Last Summer*. "What excited me, in terms of imagery on a very deep level, was the recovery of pieces of the past, as it comes and goes. It was the first chance, on the screen, to present a torturous memory as it would be remembered, almost to the point of madness."

1960

238 Catling, Patrick Skene. "King of the Flash-backs." *Punch* [England] 27 July, 1960: 117+. Homage paid to JLM's intelligent cinema as National Film Theatre begins a JLM tribute.

239 Conrad, Derek. "Joseph Mankiewicz—Putting on the Style." *Films and Filming* Jan. 1960: 9+. An introspective JLM refers to his second wife's death and his "tragic phase," an era of filmmaking that moved from high comedy to bitter ridicule (*The Barefoot Contessa, The Quiet American*). "I think I started using a club where I previously used a very sharp knife on things that upset me. I got angry at them rather than exposing and ridiculing."

240 Hart, Henry. "Rev. of *Suddenly, Last Summer.*" *Films in Review.* Jan. 1960:39–41. Praises Mankiewicz for being on top of a difficult cast—claims no one could do anything with Clift; Hepburn's idiosyncratic behavior was difficult; but Taylor stayed on course.

241 Nathan, Paul. "Rights and Permissions." *Publishers Weekly* 9 May 1960: 41. Excitement in the theatre world surrounds the announcement that Mankie-

wicz holds a one year option on Peter S. Beagle's novel, *A Fine and Private Place*. (The project was never realized.)

242 Scheuer, Philip K. "Mankiewicz to Be Honored in London." *Los Angeles Times* 4 July 1960, sec. IV: 7. Reference to unrealized projects ("John Brown's Body" and "Justine") in article detailing the month-long festival of Mankiewicz films at National Film Theatre.

243 Taylor, John Russell. *Joseph L. Mankiewicz: An Index to His Work.* London: British Film Institute, July-Aug. 1960. Compiled for The National Film Theatre celebration of a season of Mankiewicz films. This index to JLM's films includes a brief introduction, with few quotes, followed by filmography that is incomplete regarding early films.

244 "Thoughtful Optimist." *Guardian* [England] 4 Aug. 1960: 4. Mankiewicz seen as "not so much a revolutionary as an intelligent eccentric who has managed to work on the fringe of the convention." Background on JLM interspersed with a few quotes, including Mankiewicz's description of his work as "filmed theatre."

1961

245 "20th Re-Launching *Cleopatra* with 'All New Concept.'" *Variety* 23 Feb. 1961: 1+. Mankiewicz holds press conference once he is named replacement for Rouben Mamoulian as director of film. Indicates he will scrap the previously shot 12 minutes to initiate a new concept. Bringing in Lawrence Durrell and Sidney Buchman who will work on script. Plans for on-location shooting in Egypt but notes that no new budget has been set even though Spyros Skouras, president of 20th Century-Fox, has assured him that "nothing will be spared" in allowing *Cleopatra* "to realize its potentialities as the most important picture in Fox history."

246 Costantini, Costanzo. "Ha letto anche Plutarco per girare il film su *Cleopatra.*" *Il Messaggero* [Rome] 19 Sept. 1961: n. pag. Lengthy Q&A with JLM about *Cleopatra*. In Italian.

247 "Fresh Start on £3m Film, *Cleopatra.*" *Daily Telegraph* [London]. 23 Feb. 1961: 1. As he takes over for Mamoulian, JLM notes he plans to begin shooting in early March. (He began Sept. 25, 1961.) "I see *Cleopatra* as economically as possible. My job as a film maker is to use as much of the existing set as I can. But some of what has been spent already is 'smoke ring' money that has gone."

248 "Long Schedule for 'Cleo' in Hollywood." *Hollywood Reporter* 24 April 1961: n. pag. Mankiewicz moves the production of the "ill-starred film" to Hollywood for interior shots. Notes he is the one who is now writing the screenplay.

249 "New Script—And Then *Cleopatra* Starts!" *Daily Cinema* [England] 24 Feb. 1961: 1+. Mankiewicz takes over as director from Rouben Mamoulian, hires Lawrence Durrell to write a new script, and scraps 12 minutes of screen time previously shot. Article notes that Mamoulian, a friend of JLM's, confided in him the difficulties of the project before Mankiewicz took over.

250 Norman, Barry. "Durrell Rewrites 'Cleo.'" *Daily Mail* [London] 23 Feb. 1961: n. pag. Excellent Mankiewicz quotes from brief interview following

press conference. On his new concept for the film: "I see Cleopatra as a remarkable woman who never quite made it—not as a pure, virginal girl." Regarding why he was selected to replace Mamoulian: "Why did they call me in? I don't know. When someone is drowning you don't ask how he got in the water."

251 "Plan to Make 'Cleo' in England 'Idiotic' Says Mankiewicz." *Variety* 24 April 1961: 1+. Mankiewicz returning to Los Angeles after scouting locations in Europe for *Cleopatra*, notes that the film will be shot where the story naturally occurs—abroad. "In this day and age of quick transportation we can take advantage of this. The public no longer will tolerate what we used to give them."

252 Schumach, Murray. "*Cleopatra* Given Hollywood Touch." *New York Times* 5 May 1961: n. pg. Extensive quotes from Mankiewicz about his vision for the film. In describing his concept of *Cleopatra*, Mankiewicz notes that he is veering away from the Shakespearean or Shavian image of Cleopatra to one more based on Plutarch which sees her as "the last of a long line of degenerate Ptolemies who looked upon herself as a woman of destiny.... The trouble with Shaw was that his Cleopatra did not have much sex. Shaw's idea of Caesar was what Shaw would have done if he had found Cleopatra. She won't be so kittenish." Mankiewicz favors moving the production from London (where it was located when Mamoulian was the director) to Egypt. His conception of the film varies so much from Mamoulian's that the picture will go from grand spectacle to a more typical Mankiewicz-style film of character analysis. "We are not making a movie about people eating grapes in reclining positions. This must be a picture that can be listened to as well as seen."

253 Skolsky, Sidney. "Talent Class Interesting." *Hollywood Citizen-News* 30 June 1961: 11. Mankiewicz talks with acting class about how to approach a part. Includes rare reference to Elia Kazan's interest in having Mankiewicz teach at the Actors Studio.

254 Thomas, James. "Brahms, Vodka and Bristles." *Daily Express* [England] 1 Mar. 1961: n. pag. Early in the making of *Cleopatra* and already functioning on just five hours of sleep a night, Mankiewicz discusses why he took over the film and how he wants it to be a sophisticated epic, and not one that panders to the masses. Envisioning the character of Cleopatra: "I see a girl of 19 who suddenly appeared in those decadent, drunken times, a girl who spoke seven languages, fostered the arts, who had such a big political grasp that both Caesar and Antony proved too small for her ambitions." Regarding his intellectualism in filmmaking: "No honest person can afford to write down, or direct down, to a taste lower than his own. People who make pieces for the crowd are the people whose talents coincide with the talents of the crowd. DeMille was like that."

255 "Wanger: 'It's Easier to Make a Picture Here'—But 'Cleo' Must Be Made Abroad." *Variety* 26 April 1961: 3. *Cleopatra* producer, Walter Wanger, raves about the choice of Mankiewicz to replace Mamoulian on his film: "*Cleopatra* is going to be a tremendous attraction and it couldn't be in better hands. Mankiewicz is enlightened, alert and one of the most sensitive showmen in the world. I have enormous confidence in him. I feel he is going to deliver an unusual picture."

1962

256 Alden, Robert. "Zanuck Dismisses *Cleopatra* Chief." *New York Times* 24 Oct. 1962: 46. Mankiewicz loyalists comment on his firing. Notes the caustic rivalry between the two men over Fox's most expensive films—Zanuck's *The Longest Day* and Mankiewicz's *Cleopatra*. Mankiewicz cites his intention to "regain the usurped right to finish my work, and hopefully, to prevent 'Cleopatra' from becoming 'The Longest Night.'"

257 Alpert, Hollis. *The Dreams and The Dreamers*. New York: Macmillan Co., 1962. 150–157. Minor assessment of JLM's career up to *Cleopatra*. Viewed as being "probably the most intelligent of our directors."

258 ____. "Joseph and Cleopatra." *Saturday Review* 18, Aug. 1962: 20+. Brief interview on set of *Cleopatra* wherein JLM discusses his burdens with budgets and rewrites.

259 Archer, Eugene. "Director to Shun Rift with Zanuck." *New York Times* 31 Oct. 1962: 34. JLM quoted on his dismissal from *Cleopatra*. "In view of what has happened, I don't think any self-respecting filmmaker will want to work for Mr. Zanuck again."

260 ____. "Zanuck Adamant on Aide's Ouster." *New York Times* 27 Oct. 1962: L14. More of the feud as Zanuck intends to edit *Cleopatra* and take away Mankiewicz's creative control of the finished product.

261 "As *Cleopatra* Story Appears to Mankiewicz." *New York Herald Tribune* 31 Oct. 1962: n. pag. JLM versus DFZ on the *Cleopatra* firing.

262 Brodsky, Jack. "*Cleopatra*: A Picture with Problems and an Unworried Mankiewicz." *Motion Picture Herald* 28 Feb. 1962: 7–8. Bitter irony in this article written near the beginning of the filming (pre–Taylor and Burton affair, budget crises, cast firings). Citing everything as going very well and hoping to finish ahead of schedule, Mankiewicz seen as the calming influence on what was billed as largest production in filmmaking history.

263 Canby, Vincent. "Zanuck Charges Mankiewicz's Method of Scripting 'Cleo' Added $7,500,000 to Prod'n Costs." *Variety* [Daily] 29 Oct. 1962: 1+. Zanuck's lengthy rationale for taking over *Cleopatra*.

264 Douglas-Home, Robin. "Enter Caesar in a Sweater." *Queen* 23 Oct. 1962: 47–48. Article about Rex Harrison includes his high regard for Mankiewicz, and sheds light on how JLM prepared for *Cleopatra*. Says Harrison, "People might think that because it cost all that money and got so much publicity it must be a super-colossal joke. But it's not, you know. It's a very serious attempt at throwing a new light on one of the greatest stories in history. Joe Mankiewicz, the writer-producer [*sic*], read every book on the subject from Plutarch to Shakespeare and Shaw. You can't fault him on the smallest detail. I took the part purely because Joe was doing the film: I never saw a script beforehand or anything. I'd worked with Joe before and knew his tremendous talent and almost brutal refusal to be sidetracked from what he wants to achieve."

265 Hawkins, Robert F. "*Cleopatra* Never Had It So Good." *New York Times* 7 Jan. 1962, sec. II: 9. JLM discusses his approach to writing *Cleopatra*, and how he based it on *Plutarch's Lives* (among other sources).

266 Hyams, Joe. "To Zanuck, a 'Dear Darryl' Swipe by Billy Wilder." *New York Herald Tribune* 26 Oct. 1962: n. pag. Backlash from JLM's firing from

Cleopatra. Wilder telegrams Zanuck in support of Mankiewicz, "No self-respecting picture-maker would ever want to work for your company. The sooner the bulldozers raze your studio, the better it will be for the industry." Article also alludes to the fact that Zanuck's pet project, *The Longest Day*, was not doing well and that perhaps that was why Zanuck sacked Mankiewicz and decided to take over the project himself.

267 "Last Time I Saw *Cleopatra*." *Variety* 31 Oct. 1962: 5+. Entire page devoted to Zanuck-Mankiewicz feud over *Cleopatra*. Zanuck attacks director's autonomy while director speaks of creative control.

268 "Love Is a Sometime Thing." *Time* 2 Nov. 1962: 47–48. Likening Zanuck to a general in a war to recapture his power at 20th Century–Fox, this article cites DFZ's rationale for firing JLM and discusses the backlash that ensued.

269 "Mankiewicz 'Cuts' Back at Zanuck." *Variety* [Daily] 31 Oct. 1962: 1+. The *Cleopatra* controversy continues with JLM's response to Zanuck's criticism of him "I've been a cotton picker too long (in the Hollywood fields) not to know Ole Marse can do with the cotton exactly what he wants." Notes that Mankiewicz's "Justine" project is now out of the question since he was fired from Fox.

270 "Mankiewicz Denies Charges by Zanuck, But Won't Fight." *Hollywood Reporter* 31 Oct. 1962: 1+. JLM discusses his decision not to fight Fox for control of the *Cleopatra* editing process.

271 "Mankiewicz Says Fox Mishandled Shooting of Movie *Cleopatra*." *Wall Street Journal* 31 Oct. 1962: 8. JLM's rebuttal to DFZ's press conference. Says that the film (the most expensive movie made to date), should have cost only half as much as it did. Forced to begin shooting without a shooting script (because Taylor was on salary), JLM explains that the film was, "conceived in emergency, shot in hysteria and wound up in blind panic."

272 Packard, Reynolds. "L'Amour Liz: New Leading Man." *Daily News* [New York] 6 Apr. 1962: 3. Gossip surrounds every aspect of *Cleopatra*, but most especially the Taylor-Burton romance. An Italian newspaper reported that Taylor was really having an affair with Mankiewicz, to which JLM wise-cracked, "The real truth is that I am in love with Burton and Miss Taylor is the coverup for us."

273 "Playing Footage with 'Cleo.'" *Variety* 21 Nov. 1962: 5+. Zanuck notes that additional shooting is necessary on *Cleopatra* for continuity purposes. Article also notes that the Directors Guild summoned Mankiewicz to discuss his being fired from *Cleopatra* before cutting the film.

274 Scheuer, Philip K. "Life, Hard Times of *Cleopatra*." *LA Times* 19 Aug. 1962: Calendar 7. Producer Walter Wanger reflects on the film from concept through final shooting. Little about Mankiewicz but very useful for overview of film's difficulties.

275 Schumach, Murray. "*Cleopatra* Rift a Film Symptom." *New York Times* 25 Oct. 1962: 48. Highlights what is at stake for major studios and independent writer-directors with Zanuck's demand to take over editing of *Cleopatra*. Acknowledges JLM as "fiercely independent and possessed of a devastating wit that can be humiliating for Zanuck."

276 Swainson, L. R. "*Cleopatra*'s Long Road." *Blade Sunday Magazine* [Ohio] 25 Feb. 1962: 6–8. One year after production began on film, article notes the

machinations the production has gone through, including the fact that JLM is writing the script as the production goes along. "I keep just a little ahead of the action. But at least I know where I'm going to end."

277 Thomas, Bob. "Director Foresees Film Release Next February." *LA Times.* 20 Aug. 1962: n. pag. Mankiewicz interview during the waning days of *Cleopatra*'s filming when he was still upbeat at the prospect of the final version. "Right now we are in the process of trying to put together the second half, and it is a monumental job. But I think it is going to be a remarkable film—not merely in its spectacle, but in the human relationships, too." When asked if the film was finally finished, JLM replied, "The company thinks so. I don't. Perhaps I am being over-anxious in wanting to do everything just right. I would like to go back and do some more, but they have a good reason why I shouldn't: They ran out of money."

278 "Waste in 'Cleo' Filming Is Cited by Zanuck; More Shooting Needed." *Hollywood Reporter* 29 Oct. 1962: 1+. DFZ's press conference cites *Cleopatra* budget concerns and his decision to consult JLM on retakes and additions.

279 Wing, William. "Zanuck Hints Caesar Tinsel Rubbed Off on Mankiewicz." *New York Herald Tribune* 27 Oct. 1962: 7. Zanuck press conference discusses his rift with Mankiewicz and gives details of JLM's salary package. DFZ refers to *Cleopatra* as "this monster hanging on my shoulder" since he inherited the film when he was, shortly before, named president of Fox. Notes that JLM will be off the picture once he finishes the dubbing he is currently working on in Paris. Zanuck also notes that while he intends to edit the film, he welcomes input from Mankiewicz.

280 "Zanuck Charges Mankiewicz's Method of Scripting 'Cleo' Added $7,500,000 to Prod'n Costs." *Variety* 29 Oct. 1962: 1+. Details of Zanuck's press conference wherein former Fox president Spyros Skouras and Mankiewicz are blamed for high cost of *Cleopatra*. Zanuck quotes from correspondence he and Mankiewicz exchanged following DFZ's viewing the rough cut. Zanuck concludes press conference by saying that he "personally produced and edited" JLM's earlier Fox successes, *A Letter to Three Wives* and *All About Eve*. (DFZ's memory slips: Sol C. Siegel produced *Letter.*)

281 "Zanuck Fires; Mankiewicz Ired." *Variety* [Daily] 25 Oct. 1962: 1+. The Zanuck-Mankiewicz feud in print. DFZ fires JLM during the editing process of *Cleopatra*. Zanuck intends to edit the film himself, and sacks JLM even though he has spent two years on the project. Mankiewicz pleads his side of the case to the press.

282 "Zanuck Says Door Has Been 'Left Open' to Mankiewicz." *Motion Picture Daily* 29 Oct. 1962: 1+. Zanuck's ego looms large over press conference held to substantiate his position that Mankiewicz is welcome to come back to *Cleopatra* after he (Zanuck) makes the next cut. Taking credit for JLM's Oscars ("His Awards were limited to films I produced and edited... that's not intended to take anything away from him. More people have won Academy Awards working on my pictures than on those of any other producer. And that includes Irving Thalberg. I do not intend to be immodest. It's simply a matter of record.") DFZ claims *Cleopatra* has cost more than $35 million to date and he, as president of 20th Century–Fox, with a proven track record, must see to its conclusion.

1963

283 Brodsky, Jack and Nathan Weiss. *The Cleopatra Papers: A Private Correspondence.* New York: Simon and Schuster, 1963. Diary entries by Weiss, 20th Century–Fox publicity manager, and Brodsky, assistant publicity manager.

284 Carmody, Jay. "Mr. M. and *Cleopatra* Are Parting Amicably." *Sunday Star* [Washington, D.C.] 30 June 1963: F1. Exhausted from the two and one-half years spent on *Cleopatra*, JLM remarks that he will take time off to read, play golf, and try to regain his sense of humor. "Right now, I find myself with no feeling of joy in getting back to work. I have always enjoyed my work. I'm sure I shall enjoy it again, but that will be after I have read all those unread books, played that unplayed golf and known the pleasure of not being under pressure, pressure, pressure."

285 Considine, Bob. "Zanuck Envisions 'Millions' from *Cleopatra*." *Philadelphia Inquirer* 3 Feb. 1963: 1+. Justifying himself as the new president of 20th Century–Fox, Zanuck claims that *Cleopatra* will make up for its losses once it hits the theaters in June. Regarding Mankiewicz, DFZ notes the reason he was fired was because, "I am the authority."

286 Curtis, Thomas Quinn. "Zanuck's 'Cleopatra' Finished at Last; Has Cost $37 Million." *New York Herald Tribune, Paris* 2–3 Mar. 1963: n. pag. Zanuck's point of view on the mammoth expense of *Cleopatra* and Mankiewicz's closeness to the film.

287 Gilbert, Joan. "Spotlight Interview: Phyllis Forman." *Plainview Herald* [NY] 24 Jan. 1963. n. pag. Totally erroneous article about a Phyllis Forman who supposedly wrote the original screenplay of *A Letter to Three Wives* and reportedly received thanks from JLM. The film premiered in 1949, yet this article states, "In 1950, she was hired by the story department of 20th Century–Fox. In this period, she wrote the first screen treatment of *Letters to Three Wives* [sic] which went on to win the Academy Award under the finished script of Joseph Mankiewicz. Phyllis proudly retains the original copy she wrote with a 'thank you' from the then unknown Mankiewicz." (Note: the story first appeared in Cosmopolitan as *A Letter to Five Wives* by John Klempner; an adaptation was written by Vera Caspary as *A Letter to Four Wives*; and JLM wrote *A Letter to Three Wives* for his 1949 film.)

288 Hopper, Hedda. "Mankiewicz Races Deadline on 'Cleo.'" *Los Angeles Times* 25 Mar. 1963, sec. IV: 10. An exhausted Mankiewicz, back on *Cleopatra* and facing a tight deadline of a June release, wonders if people care more about the gossip surrounding the film than the movie itself. "Maybe then somebody will write about what kind of picture 'Cleo' is—a helluva movie! It's been examined from every level—financial to moral (or unmoral), but never a word about the film itself."

289 Kurnitz, Harry. "The Antic Arts: Mankiewicz the Great." *Holiday* Jan. 1963: 93–98. Delightfully written homage to JLM by a fellow screenwriter who guides the reader through Mankiewicz's career from his early days at Paramount and MGM through *Cleopatra*. On the set of *Cleopatra*, JLM confesses, "Sometimes I feel like Alexander the Great, except that all he had to do was conquer the world. And he didn't have to conquer all day and go

back to his tent and work all night on the script. What's more, he had a horse who loved him."
290 Lewin, David. "It All Depends on Cleo." *Daily Mail* [London] 10 June 1963: n. pag. New 20th Century–Fox president, Darryl Zanuck comments on why film was a financial nightmare, noting that it was not Mankiewicz's fault. "I don't blame Joe... I blame the people at the top who were amateurs in producing and gave Skouras ... poor advice." Also lists some of the expensive oddities that fattened the budget. Characteristically, Mankiewicz was succinct about the film: "*Cleopatra* was conceived in a state of emergency, shot in hysteria and wound up in blind panic."
291 Lourcelles, Jacques and Michel Mourlet, eds. *Joseph L. Mankiewicz.* Spec. issue of *Présence du Cinéma* 18 (Nov. 1963): 1–56. Entire issue devoted to JLM. Articles by Lourcelles, Pierre Guinle, and John Houseman as well as reviews and illustrations.
292 MacDougall, Ranald. "Letters to the Editors." *Life* 10 May 1963: 19. Snide letter from one of the *Cleopatra* screenwriters who cites himself as the "author of the 'conventional' screenplay transformed by director Joseph L. Maniiewicz [sic]."
293 "Mankiewicz May Do 'Justine' for 20; Status of Walter Wanger Unclear." *Variety* 13 Feb. 1963: 3. Mankiewicz and Zanuck patch up their differences and are off to Spain to shoot added footage for *Cleopatra*. Contractual concerns surround JLM's "Justine" project.
294 McGrady, Mike. "*Cleopatra*: The Director's View." *Newsday* 10 June 1963: 3C. Two days before the New York premiere, JLM discusses the chance that he might never return to filmmaking. Regarding the editing process, "It had to open too quickly; we spent less time on the cutting of this film than on an average feature. The editing was a joint effort. The finished product is a compromise. I still feel strongly that it could use more time, more running time. Four hours was an arbitrary limit."
295 "Numb." *New Yorker* 15 June 1963: 27. JLM background as well as discussion of the problems on *Cleopatra*.
296 "People." *Time* 1 Mar. 1963: 32. Photo of Zanuck and Mankiewicz in Spain where they are finishing *Cleopatra* together.
297 Perrott, Roy. "Daylight on *Cleopatra*." *Observer* [London] 4 Aug. 1963: 13+. Extraordinarily detailed article chronicles the history of the film. First of a series of weekly articles.
298 Reid, John Howard. "Cleo's Joe, Part 1—The Typewriter Years." *Films and Filming* Aug. 1963: 44–48. Excellent coverage of JLM's early days at Paramount and MGM (film by film), with extensive quotes.
299 ____. "Cleo's Joe, Part 2—*All About Eve* and Others." *Films and Filming* Sept. 1963: 13–16. Continues the JLM story from his days at 20th Century–Fox to *Cleopatra*.
300 Sarris, Andrew. "The American Cinema." *Film Culture* Spring 1963: 1+. Precursor to Sarris' later book on filmmakers. Categorizing JLM as a "Fallen Idol" (in the company of Huston, Kazan, Lean, Mamoulian, Milestone, Reed, Wellman, Wilder, Wyler, and Zinnemann), Sarris attacks Mankiewicz for a lack of style.
301 Scheuer, Philip K. "*Cleopatra* Called Top Space-Grabber." *Los Angeles Times* 20 June 1963: n. pag. As the West Coast premier of *Cleopatra* looms, Scheuer

details the response the film has received since its release in New York a
week ago. Mankiewicz is quoted as being anxious to put the problems he
experienced while filming in the past.

302 Thompson, Howard. "Unveiling *Cleopatra*." *New York Times* 9 June 1963,
sec. X: 7. JLM interview describes his concept of the picture (two separate
films) and working with Taylor ("Basically, she's a lazy girl but a real professional in front of the camera.") Regarding the Zanuck dispute, JLM
speaks cautiously: "Well, let's say that of necessity six hours did have to be
trimmed down to approximately four. I'm still apprehensive about two
things, especially. There's emphasis, now on the Battle of Actium, which I
originally had used as background. And some deletions indicate now that
Antony broke with his generals deliberately because of Cleopatra. He did-
n't."

303 Wanger, Walter and Joe Hyams. *My Life with Cleopatra*. New York: Bantam, 1963. Diary-like book of production by producer, Wanger.

304 Winsten, Archer. Editorial. *New York Post* 10 June 1963: 37. JLM tells his
side of the story prior to the release of *Cleopatra*. Originally told he would
take over for a mere ten weeks, article tells how he and his colleagues (Sidney Buchman and Ranald MacDougall), tried to compose a character study
of Cleopatra. Included is an unusual quote about censorship and the film.
The censors viewed the film with preconceived notions that what had
occurred in public with Burton and Taylor had transferred to the screen, to
which JLM replied, "I've looked at the Sistine Chapel several times in my
life, and with reverence for the great art visible there, but when I do I don't
consider that Michelangelo was a pederast whose private life was the scandal of Rome."

305 Zunser, Jesse. "Hey, Ma, Cleo's Here!" *Cue* 8 June 1963: 15. Fascinating pre-
release article about some of the particulars behind the $39 million film.
JLM envisioned as "writer, director and 'deus ex machina' of the colossal
spectacular." JLM shot 120 miles of film for the four-hour *Cleopatra* of which
about 115 miles remained on the cutting room floor.

1964

306 Comolli, Jean-Louis. "*Cléopâtre*, le jeu, l'échec." *Cahiers du Cinéma* March
1964: 32–40. Close reading of *Cleopatra*. In French.

307 "Minding Our Own Business." *New Yorker* 25 July 1964: 60. Humorous ad
for *Business Week* magazine shows a rejection slip received from JLM regarding his subscription.

308 Narboni, Jean. "Mankiewicz à la troisième personne." *Cahiers du Cinéma*
March 1964: 27–31. Analysis of Mankiewicz's films. In French.

1965

309 Davis, Melton S. "Mankiewicz Looks at Lust in Rome." *New York Times* 5
Dec. 1965, sec. X: 13. Behind-the-scenes of "Anyone for Venice" (*The Honey
Pot*), JLM's first film since *Cleopatra*. Also includes reference to Mankie-
wicz's aversion to discussing *Cleopatra*. "I don't want to talk about it; I

consider it an experience rather than a movie—humiliating and not gratifying."

1966

310 Bontemps, Jacques and Richard Overstreet. "Mesure pour mesure." *Cahiers du Cinéma* May 1966: 36–51. Interview with JLM in French. (See *313* for English version.)

311 Brion, Patrick. "Biofilmographie de Joseph L. Mankiewicz." *Cahiers du Cinéma* May 1966: 52–57. Mankiewicz bio-filmography in French. (See *314* for English version.)

312 Johnson, Nunnally. "Joseph L. Mankiewicz." McDowall, Roddy. *Double Exposure*. New York: Delacorte Press, 1966. 196. Early collaborator, Johnson, writes brief bio of Mankiewicz for McDowall's picture book of film greats.

1967

313 Bontemps, Jacques and Richard Overstreet. "Measure for Measure: Interview with Joseph L. Mankiewicz." *Cahiers du Cinéma in English* Feb. 1967: 28–41. Extensive Q&A with JLM includes discussion of his style of writing and directing. Language is stilted because interview, conducted in English, was translated into French for the French publication, and then "retranslated" back into English for this publication. (See *311*.) References to JLM's varying participation in his early films; his themes; and his choice of actors. ("I try to choose very good actors and in particular intelligent actors. If the actor does not understand the role that he has to play, which I have to say and what I want to say, it is impossible for him to convey this thought to an audience.") Interview followed by detailed bio-filmography by Patrick Brion that includes foreign titles of JLM's films. (See *310* for French version.)

314 Brion, Patrick. "Bio-filmography of Joseph L. Mankiewicz." *Cahiers du Cinéma* in English Feb. 1967: 42–52. Excellent filmography with short biographical sketch preceding. Filmography reflects foreign language titles of JLM films and presents an interesting analysis of *House of Strangers* with its premakes and remakes. (See *312* for French version.)

315 _____. "La Tragédie de la réussite." *L'Avant Scène Cinéma* Mar. 1967: 6. Analysis of the Mankiewicz theme in *Contessa*. In French.

316 *La Comtesse Aux Pieds Nus. L'Avant Scène Cinéma* Mar. 1967: 1–60. Extended excerpts from the screenplay, photos, and JLM filmography highlight this publication on *The Barefoot Contessa*. In French.

317 "Film Buffs' Zeal Awes Mankiewicz at Paris Exhibition of His Pix." *Variety* [Weekly] 12 Apr. 1967: n. pag. JLM notes his interest in finding a film based predominantly on female characters. Also expresses awe at being so well received at Paris film festival where most of his films were shown without subtitles to adoring French fans.

318 Gelmis, Joseph. "Just Don't Call Him a Producer." *Newsday* 23 May 1967: 3A. The Mankiewicz perspective on why he dislikes being called a producer;

film criticism; today's youth; and his hopes of directing Duerrenmatt's *The Meteor* on Broadway.

319 "Joe on Aristocracy." *Sunday Telegraph* [England] 26 Mar. 1967: n. pag. Extensive quotes from JLM on his dislike of "pretenders."

320 "Laughing It Off." *Daily Mirror* [England] 13 Mar. 1967: 13. Brief quote from JLM about his preference for the genre of high comedy. "Comedy is the most effective way of making people see the truth."

321 Palmer, Alix. "A Time for Comedy." *Daily Express* [London] 13 Mar. 1967: n. pag. An article of Mankiewicz quotes on everything from violence in films to a reflection on his life in pictures. "I started working in films at 19. I think of myself as the oldest whore on the beat. I know the policemen, I know their footsteps, I know what is real, what is unreal, I have directed films, I have written them, I have directed for the Metropolitan Opera House in New York, I've done plays on Broadway. And when all this has happened to you everything comes full circle. That's when the weariness happens. But I am not bitter—just knowing. And I can still find excitement—especially in writing. Nothing is ever as perfect, for me, as when I first wrote it. That is a private joy."

322 Smith, Harrison H. "Joseph L. Mankiewicz, Native of City, Was Called 'Hollywood's Wonder Boy.'" *Wilkes-Barre Times Leader* [Pa.] 4 Mar. 1967: n. pag. Continues biography of native son. (See *323* for part one.)

323 _____. "Native Son of Wilkes-Barre Became Hollywood's Leading Film Producer." *Wilkes-Barre Times Leader* [Pa.] 25 Feb. 1967: n. pag. Family background from hometown newspaper. Includes photos of baby Joe with mother and siblings, and one of the family when children are grown. (Continued in *322*.)

324 Straram, Patrick. Rev. of *The Honey Pot*. *Take One* [Canada] June 1967: 30–31. Review of Mankiewicz's style as much as a critique of the film.

325 Walker, Alexander. "Four Women and a Mankiewicz." *Evening Standard* [London] 20 Mar. 1967: 7. Hailed as a filmmaker who writes "juicy" roles for women, Mankiewicz discusses his women characters in *The Honey Pot*.

1968

326 Legrand, Gérard. "Un Rire Jaun." *Positif* Mar. 1968: 17–21. Analysis of the Mankiewicz style in *The Honey Pot*. In French.

327 "Mankiewicz's W7 'Hang Up' to Be a 'Cynical Western.'" *Variety* [Daily] 19 Dec. 1968: n. pag. JLM discusses his return to Hollywood with a Warner–7 Arts product, "Hang Up" (later titled *There Was a Crooked Man*). Article refers to JLM's three-picture deal with W7 noting that he will soon work on "Couples" and "Will" (never realized).

1969

328 Scott, John. "Prison Springs Up in the Desert for Film 'Inmates.'" *Los Angeles Times* 5 May 1969, sec. IV: 1+. JLM's first Western gets attention during shooting. Calling it a "cynical Western" JLM based it "on the proposition that there's a bit of bad in every good man."

1970

329 French, Philip. "Concealed Rattlesnake of Arizona." *London Times* 30 Oct. 1970: 13C. Mixed review of *There Was a Crooked Man*. Reviewer cannot seem to determine whether it is a comedy or a drama. Useful JLM quote, however, helps understand why he undertook the Western genre. "I have no interest in the classic Western which shows good and bad in simplistic terms."

330 Gow, Gordon. "Cocking a Snook." *Films and Filming* Nov. 1970: 18+. Well-written discussion of Mankiewicz's work and background, in the guise of an interview. Direct quotes throughout seem secondary to Gow's analysis, although Mankiewicz does offer insights into his thematic and writing style. Presently at work on his first Western, *There Was a Crooked Man*, JLM discusses how he likes his tongue in cheek approach (cocking a snook) to the manners and mores films he makes. Article also corrects a mistake made in many JLM filmographies: *Three Godfathers*, the film written and produced by Mankiewicz and directed by Richard Boleslawsky, is not to be confused with the film by the same title directed by John Ford. Includes a filmography.

331 "J'aime les serpents, les crocodiles et aussi." *Paris Match* 3 Oct. 1970: 82. Review (in French) of *Le Reptile* (*There Was a Crooked Man*).

332 "A Little Bit of Bad...." *Evening Standard* [London] 29 Oct. 1970: n. pag. Review notes that *There Was a Crooked Man* was JLM's first film made in Hollywood in nearly 15 years.

333 Malcolm, Derek. "Old Joe, the Talk Man." *Arts Guardian* [England] 11 Aug. 1970: 8. Interview with 60-year-old Mankiewicz who sees himself as, "Old Joe, the talk man." JLM discusses the current trends in filmmaking, which he describes as "a frenzy of imagery and sound"; his early days in Hollywood, including the reference to himself as a "protégé" of Lubitsch; and his lack of financial compensation for *Applause* (the theatrical remake of *All About Eve*), as well as the television series based on *The Ghost and Mrs. Muir*.

334 Milne, Tom. "Crooked Fun Way Out West." *Sunday Observer* [London] 1 Nov. 1970: n. pag. Praise for *There Was a Crooked Man* includes reviewer's gratitude for JLM's sophisticated contribution to the Western—calling it a "Western comedy of manners."

335 Sarris, Andrew. "Mankiewicz of the Movies." *Show* Mar. 1970: 27+. Lengthy interview with JLM complete with editorial comments about JLM's liberalism and his adamancy to stick to his principles in filming complex, intelligent stories. Insights include a review of Mankiewicz's early works and the truth behind "Rosebud."

336 Török. Jean-Paul. "And He Lived Happy Ever After." *Positif* Nov. 1970: 1–7. Analysis of *There Was A Crooked Man* and the Mankiewicz style. In French.

337 Williams, John. "Mankiewicz in London." *Sight & Sound* Autumn 1970: 185–186. Commenting on the change in filmmaking from listening to looking at films, Mankiewicz claims young filmmakers today are paying more attention to optics and special effects than dialogue. "The spoken word is out temporarily.... I've always thought that if a director consciously comes between the screen and his audience, he's failed. When someone in a movie nudges his neighbor and says: 'Wonder how they did that?' you've lost them."

1971

338 Gilmour, Clyde. "Mankiewicz in the Wild West." *Toronto Telegram* 5 Feb. 1971: n. pag. JLM's first Western, *There Was a Crooked Man*, gets mixed review. Discussion of JLM's working style and affinity for working with good actors.

339 Gow, Gordon. "*There Was a Crooked Man....*" *Films and Filming* [London] Jan. 1971: 60. Review. Mankiewicz, as one of the old school of filmmakers, finds freedom in no longer having to deal with censorship in his adult-oriented films. "Despite the reactionary things Mankiewicz says nowadays about cinematic visuals getting out of hand, this latest film of his is an eyeful. The style is very trad, admittedly, but he keeps it brisk.... It almost seems as if he is saying to himself, 'So permissiveness is upon us, eh? All right, let's have a damned good wallow.'"

340 Gussow, Mel. *Don't Say Yes Until I Finish Talking: A Biography of Darryl F. Zanuck*. New York: Doubleday & Co., 1971. 154–195. Direct quotes from Mankiewicz about his relationship with Zanuck during his contract years at Fox.

341 Latham, Aaron. *Crazy Sundays: F. Scott Fitzgerald in Hollywood*. New York: Viking Press, 1971. 120–149. Extensive details of the Mankiewicz/Fitzgerald encounter on the film, *Three Comrades*.

342 Springer, John. "The Films of Joseph L. Mankiewicz." *Films in Review* Mar. 1971: 153–157. Filmography and commentary on JLM's contributions to his more well-known films.

1972

343 Blume, Mary. "The Art of Pretending and Joe Mankiewicz." *International Herald Tribune* 22–23 July 1972: n. pag. Better than usual newspaper interview. Theme of pretending permeates JLM's works. On the set of *Sleuth*, Mankiewicz talks about why he doesn't write any more (because audiences no longer come to listen to films). Includes references to early Hollywood and to his brother, Herman.

344 _____. "Joe Mankiewicz: Moralist with Bite of an 18th-Century Satirist." *Los Angeles Times* 20 Aug. 1972: 10+. Short rewrite of "The Art of Pretending...." (See *343*.)

345 Flythe, Starkey [sic], Jr. "It's Your Move, Larry." *Holiday* Nov.-Dec. 1972: 33+. Interplay between Olivier and Caine on set of *Sleuth* is focus of article. Brief mention of JLM's closing the set because of the surprise ending.

346 Zimmerman, Paul D. "All About Hollywood." *Newsweek* 4 Dec. 1972: 110+. More of a tribute to Mankiewicz's intelligence than a review of his book, *More About All About Eve*. Brief discussion of JLM's fascination with women characters.

1973

347 "Books." *Action* Mar.—Apr. 1973: 38–39. Extensive quotes from *More About All About Eve* with emphasis on directing. Includes references to early

Hollywood's "assembly-line approach to moviemaking," and his work as a "gun for hire" at the big studios.

348 Bourget, Jean-Loup. "Le dernier carre? (Houston, Mankiewicz, Cukor, Wilder.)" *Positif* April 1973: 1–13. Analysis of Hollywood's elder statesmen. In French.

349 Champlin, Charles. "All About 'Eve's' Mankiewicz." *Los Angeles Times* 4 May 1973, sec. IV: 1. Kudos for JLM's book. Review cites quotes about film as art, and the dilemma of the aging actress.

350 Ciment, Michel. "Cinéma: Mankiewicz parle." *L'Express* 14–20 May 1973: 122–123. Interview features Mankiewicz at his best in the Q&A format. In French.

351 _____. "Entretien avec Joseph L. Mankiewicz." *Positif* Sept. 1973: 31–45. Q&A with Mankiewicz for publication's lengthy analysis of his work. In French.

352 Garsault, Alain. "Le petit clown rouge." *Positif* Sept. 1973: 16–23. Analysis of the Mankiewicz style in *Sleuth*. In French.

353 Gilmour, Clyde. "'Watergate Gives Me Confidence in America.'" *Toronto Star* 7 July 1973: n. pag. Interview with JLM focuses on contemporary politics and early Hollywood.

354 Gottlieb, Morton. "Joe Mankiewicz: Forty Years and Eighty Movies Later, Still Going Strong." *Harper's Bazaar* Jan. 1973: 73+. *Sleuth* producer, Gottlieb, gives a behind the scenes account of JLM's directing.

355 Henry, Michael. "Un Labyrinthe pour tout un royaume." *Positif* Sept. 1973: 6–15. Overview of JLM films. In French.

356 Kaal, Ron. "Joseph Mankiewicz: 'De camera dient voor de leestekens.'" *Vry Nederland* [Holland] 8 Sept. 1973: 5. Lengthy question and answer interview with JLM at Arnhem [Holland] film festival. In Dutch.

357 Natkin, Jack. "*Sleuth* and the Mankiewicz Comedy of Manners." *Focus!* Spring 1973: 2+. Strange combination of concerns in this article which begins with an unflattering review of *Sleuth* and ends up defending Mankiewicz against Andrew Sarris' comments (that he falls into Sarris' category of directors he calls, "Less Than Meets the Eye"). Includes textual comparison of *All About Eve* with Sheridan's *School for Scandal*.

358 Schuster, Mel (comp.) "Mankiewicz, Joseph L." *Motion Picture Directors*. Metuchen, NJ: Scarecrow Press, 1973: 261–262. Bibliographic references in popular periodicals.

359 Segond, Jacques. "More About Joseph L. Mankiewicz." *Positif* Sept. 1973: 24–29. Reproduction of segment of Gary Carey's colloquy with JLM. In French.

360 Tallmer, Jerry. "Director Joseph Mankiewicz: Films Aren't Forever." *New York Post* 24 Feb. 1973: 15. Interview with lengthy quotes from Mankiewicz about his brother's involvement in *Citizen Kane*; working with Olivier; hating to be interviewed; critics who write for the benefit of other critics; his family; and his pet project—a book on the history of actresses.

1974

361 Corliss, Richard. *Talking Pictures: Screenwriters in the American Cinema 1927–1973*. Woodstock: Overlook Press, 1974. 236–246. Unflattering analysis

of JLM's writing style in *Letter*, *Eve*, and *Contessa*. Seen as flabby, theatrical dialogue, which Corliss likens to a point-counterpoint debate. Includes a brief filmography with assumptions of JLM contributions to scripts for which he received no writing credit.

362 Hochman, Stanley, comp. and ed. *A Library of Film Criticism: American Film Directors*. New York: Frederick Ungar Publishing Co., 1974. 313–323. Excellent assortment of difficult to find film reviews from foreign and US publications.

363 Porter, Bob. "Frank [sic] Mankiewicz." *Dallas Times Herald* 2 March 1974: G1. Despite the glaring error in the headline, indeed it was Joseph L. Mankiewicz (and not his nephew Frank) who addressed the USA Film Festival. Attempting to demythologize the Hollywood studio system, JLM reflects on the reality of the Hollywood product: "I've never read anything about that system that is really truthful. A lot of what you read is a result of the adulation of today. There have been a lot of attempts to remake an image to fit that. Roual [sic] Walsh was a work-a-day director who was given a script on a Saturday night and told to start shooting on Monday. I was expected to write and direct two films a day."

1975

364 Byrne, Bridget. "People Will Talk—Especially Joe." *Los Angeles Herald Examiner* 22 Oct. 1975: B1. San Francisco Film Festival. Noteworthy quotes include vague reference to Fitzgerald's screenplay of *Three Comrades*. "It's so fortunate for the Scott Fitzgerald cult that he looked like Wallace Reid and not Wallace Beery. He was a marvelous novelist but he wrote 'unspeakable' dialogue for the movies."

365 Frank, Gerold. *Judy*. New York: Harper & Row, 1975. 174–193. No direct quotes from Mankiewicz but helpful for a thorough discussion of the Mankiewicz-Garland relationship including his argument with Louis B. Mayer which resulted in Mankiewicz's departure from M-G-M.

366 Hartl, John. "Mankiewicz Likes 'Good Talk' in His Movies." *Seattle Times* [Wash.] 24 Oct. 1975: n. pag. A rare insight into why JLM agreed to take over *Cleopatra*. Having written a script of Lawrence Durrell's *Alexandria Quartet*, Mankiewicz looked forward to making the film. "I hoped it would be the definitive movie about a woman: four different versions, none of them true. 20th Century–Fox promised I could make the film, if only I'd do this job for them [*Cleopatra*]: production had been closed down on this epic with Elizabeth [Taylor], $6 million had already been used on footage that would be scrapped, and they wanted me to make it in a few weeks. I made two separate films, *Antony and Cleopatra* and *Caesar and Cleopatra*. They were taken over and butchered into the most beautiful and expensive banjo picks in the world. Well, after that debacle, I couldn't work with Fox again, and the 'Quartet' script has never been used. I am more bitter about that than about anything else that happened during *Cleopatra*."

367 Johnson, Charles. "A Defense of Good Writing." *Sacramento Bee* [Calif.] 7 Nov. 1975: B4. Strange article chastising Mankiewicz for tolerating bad acting (Bogart in *Contessa* and Taylor's final monologue in *Suddenly*) but praise

for his good writing. Complete with quotes from tribute at the San Francisco Film Festival.

368 Mahoney, John C. "Director Attacks Industry." *Hollywood Reporter* 21 Oct. 1975: 3. Derisive comments on the state of the film today prompt JLM to reminisce about early Hollywood. "I grew up with the Cohns, Mayers, Schenks, Warners and the like and hated them at the time for what I thought they were doing. Yet these largely semi-literate men did think that they were building something that would last forever. It was a place for the actor, writer and director to really learn his movie craft. I am afraid that in the latter respect the demise of the old studio structure has proved irreparable." On foreign filmmakers, Mankiewicz praises Bergman and Fellini; is bored by Antonioni; and dismisses Visconti as "the greatest set decorator of all time." Ever the wit, when asked about Ken Russell, JLM responded, "I'll let you know when he lands."

369 McClintock, John. "Talk Isn't Cheap for Mankiewicz." *Palo Alto Times* [Calif.] 20 Oct. 1975: n. pag. Extensive quotes in brief article from San Francisco Film Festival tribute to JLM. Commenting on actors, JLM remarked, "The best actor is the one who thinks and can project the author's meaning. But I don't want a creative actor in the sense of being a writing actor or a directing actor. My God, being an actor is achievement enough." On directors today: "Most young directors are directing lenses, not actors; effects, not content." On today's Hollywood: "Most creative decisions are made for commercial reasons but never has the American film industry been so single-mindedly devoted to a quick, hot, fast buck as it is today. I can't say honestly I'd rather be a young writer in today's Hollywood."

370 Michelson, Herb. "Frisco Hears Views of Mankie, Caine, Malle, Hackman, Kagan." *Variety* 29 Oct. 1975: 30. JLM defends literate film and sees himself as not fitting into the current mode of filmmaking. "I don't know how to write films today. I couldn't cope with all the visual violence that's expected. I believe in the word, that literacy may well be worth dramatizing. I don't think that grunts will ever replace talk. Good talk."

371 Miller, Jeanne. "Multi-talent Mankiewicz Stirs Fans." *San Francisco Examiner* 20 Oct. 1975: 27. San Francisco Film Festival. During a Q&A following a tribute to him, JLM shares his thematic concepts. "My thing is to develop characterizations, to direct actors instead of special effects. A recurrent theme in my films is how life louses up the script we write for ourselves each day."

372 Stone, Judy. "A Director's Spellbinding Reminiscences." *San Francisco Chronicle* 21 Oct. 1975: 42. San Francisco Film Festival. In a discussion following a tribute to him, JLM focuses on his career, films today, and the loyalty oath debate with C. B. DeMille. ("As I once said, Cecil B. DeMille had his finger up the pulse of the people.") Tired of apocalyptic visions on the screen today, JLM comments, "you're all being wrung out watching your own destruction.... Never in my experience has the American film industry been so dedicated to making the hot quick buck as today. Soon they'll be buying a bull-ring that seats 100,000 people, investing in an atom bomb and selling the seats for the picture, but you'll be happy because you'll be in on the ultimate destruction of yourself. Sure I'd make an apocalypse movie if I could find a

way to end them once and for all, but somebody would say, 'Let's make Apocalypse II.'"

373 Taylor, Robert. "Veteran Director Gossips About the Old Hollywood." *Oakland Tribune* [Calif.] 22 Oct. 1975: n. pag. When asked if he stereotyped women such as the Marilyn Monroe character in *All About Eve*, JLM replied, "I needed someone to play a girl that exists in the theater, as the screenplay says, 'a graduate of the Copacabana School of Dramatic Arts.' She's stupid, but not dumb. She is no more a stereotype than Margo Channing."

374 Truffaut, François. "Joseph Mankiewicz: *The Barefoot Contessa*." Trans. Leonard Mayhew. *The Films in My Life*. New York: Simon and Schuster, 1975. 129–132. Truffaut's cogent analysis of *The Barefoot Contessa* notes that the film is a "daring, novel, and most satisfying venture" in which Mankiewicz "uses it to settle scores with the Hollywood which condemned him to polishing furniture when he had dreamed of breaking down walls."

1976

375 Dardis, Tom. *Some Time in the Sun*. New York: Charles Scribner's Sons, 1973. 36–47. Excellent discussion of the tension between F. Scott Fitzgerald and Mankiewicz on the film, *Three Comrades*.

376 Parrish, Robert. *Growing Up in Hollywood*. Boston: Little, Brown and Co., 1976. 201–210. (According to RMM), JLM thought this the best account of the Screen Directors Guild confrontation between Mankiewicz and DeMille on the loyalty oath issue.

1977

377 Jorgens, Jack J. "Joseph Mankiewicz's *Julius Caesar*." *Shakespeare on Film*. Bloomington: Indiana UP, 1977. 92–105. Critical analysis on the film with emphasis on actors' portrayals.

378 Yacowar, Maurice. "*Suddenly, Last Summer* (1959)." *Tennessee Williams and Film*. New York: Frederick Ungar Pub., 1977. 49–59. Critical analysis of Mankiewicz's expansion of Williams' play.

1978

379 Geist, Kenneth. "Mankiewicz: The Thinking Man's Director." *American Film* Apr. 1978: 54–60. Brief condensation of Geist's book on Mankiewicz. "Oldest whore on the beat" concept is addressed at length.

380 ____. *Pictures Will Talk: The Life and Films of Joseph L. Mankiewicz*. New York: Charles Scribner's Sons, 1978. Good filmography highlights this gossipy biography.

381 Kissel, Howard. "The Mankiewicz Biography: No Mean Feat." *W* 8 Dec. 1978: n. pag. Biographer Geist shares the problems he faced in working on his book on JLM.

382 Meryman, Richard. *Mank: The Wit, World, and Life of Herman Mankiewicz*.

New York: William Morrow and Co., Inc., 1978. Biography of brother Herman and family.

1979

383 Ellis, Jack, Charles Derry, and Sharon Kern. *The Film Bibliography 1940–1975*. Metuchen, NJ: Scarecrow Press, Inc., 1979. Bio-bibliography entry on JLM.

384 Garfield, Kim. "All About Eavesdropping." *Advocate* 3 May 1979: n. pag. Interview with Kenneth L. Geist about his book on Mankiewicz. Includes reception of JLM's films in the gay community.

385 *The Ghost and Mrs. Muir. L'Avant Scène Cinéma* 1 Dec. 1979: 5–54. Publication dedicated to *The Ghost and Mrs. Muir*: includes screenplay, photos, and JLM and Tierney bio-filmographies. In French.

386 Katz, Ephraim. *The Film Encyclopedia*. New York: Thos. Y. Crowell Publishers, 1979: 771. Bio-sketch.

1980

387 Bernard, Jean-Jacques. "Joseph-Leo Mankiewicz." *Lumière du Cinéma*. Nov. 1980: 54–63. Lengthy interview in French includes many film photos.

388 Corliss, Richard. "Joseph L. Mankiewicz." *The Major Film-makers*. Vol. 2 of *Cinema: A Critical Dictionary*. Richard Roud, ed. New York: Viking Press, 1980. 663-664. Biographical sketch views JLM as a "screenplaywright."

389 Tesson, Charles. "All About Mankiewicz." *Cahiers du Cinéma* Oct. 1980: 41–44. Mankiewicz honored at Avignon festival. Overview of his work. In French.

390 Tierney, Gene with Mickey Herskowitz. *Self-Portrait*. New York: Berkley Books, 1980. 128-130. Tierney recalls her work on Mankiewicz's first film as a director, *Dragonwyck*, and how Ernst Lubitsch turned over the reigns to Mankiewicz.

1981

391 "Dossier—Auteur (1): Mankiewicz." *Cinéma* [France] June 1981: 7–46. Transcribed by Alain Carbonnier and Dominique Rabourdin. Mankiewicz at Avignon film festival. Lengthy Q&A. In French.

392 Ginsburg, Ina. "Joseph Mankiewicz." *Interview* Nov. 1981: 32–34. Bittersweet interview with JLM (who has not worked since *Sleuth*) about Hollywood writers, *All About Eve*, the Sarah Siddens award, MGM, and aging actresses.

393 "Joe Mankiewicz Harvest Nostalgia, but in New York." *Variety* [Weekly] 17 June 1981: 6+. JLM salute at MOMA garners praise from those who worked with him including Sidney Poitier who starred in *No Way Out*. Poitier credits JLM with giving him the break he needed to become a star "Mankiewicz was not only a liberal, he was a revolutionary. He molded me, he trained me. I owe it all to Joe."

394 "Joseph L. Mankiewicz." *Cinéma 81* [France] July-Aug. 1981: 83–106. Extended article includes excellent filmography. In French.

395 Lundegaard, Bob. "Joseph Mankiewicz: 'My Films Have to Be Listened To.'" *Minneapolis Tribune* 25 Jan. 1981: 1G+. Interview includes references to working with actors thought to be "difficult" (Bette Davis and Marlon Brando), casting in *All About Eve*, and commentary about today's audience. "Most of the audience for two generations now has grown up with its own projection room in the living room. When you're watching television, you think nothing of talking, you get up and go in the kitchen for a snack. When you go to the movies, the movie screen is nothing but a big television screen and you talk while the movie's on. Luckily, all those Popeyes and intergalactic warfares and intertwined sexual organs don't require that they be listened to."

1982

396 Milne, Tom. "All About Joseph." *Time Out* [England] 5 Aug. 1982: 24. A season of Mankiewicz films at the National Film Theatre prompts praise ("far ahead of his time") and an analysis of his work (including *Dragonwyck*). Calling him one of Hollywood's "most neglected film-makers," article reviews his style, dismissing the notion that he showed little interest in camerawork as "reminiscent of all those grumbles that the trouble with Picasso was that he simply couldn't paint...."

397 _____. "Tom Milne on 'Death Vengeance,' 'UndeRage' and Joseph L. Mankiewicz." *Observer* [London] 8 Aug. 1982: n. pag. Brief mention of JLM's literary film style. Considered by Milne to be "one of the cinema's great masters of the spoken word," along with Rohmer and Guitry.

398 O'Connor, John J. "TV: Drama of Country Music." *New York Times* 23 Nov. 1982: C15. A country and western musical version of *All About Eve* is reviewed and compared to the original. (*Country Gold* starring Loni Anderson.)

399 Sarris, Andrew. *The American Cinema: Directors and Directions 1929–1968*. New York: Octagon Books, 1982. 161–162. Calling Mankiewicz's films "a cinema of intelligence without inspiration," Sarris attacks what he calls "pedestrian" technique while, at the same time, praising *All About Eve* and *The Barefoot Contessa* as works of "a genuine auteur."

400 Shipman, David. "A Conversation with Joseph L. Mankiewicz." *Films and Filming* Nov. 1982: 9–15. Transcript of interview with JLM while at National Film Theatre to present the Guardian Lecture. Excellent discussion of *All About Eve*, *The Barefoot Contessa*, *Five Fingers*, Darryl Zanuck, Marlon Brando, and blacklisting in Hollywood.

401 Sinyard, Neil. "All About Mankiewicz." *National Film Theatre* [London] Aug. 1982: 2–8. Brief bio and filmography published to honor JLM as Guardian Lecturer during month-long film retrospective.

402 Turner, Adrian. "Ace in a Hole." *Movie Guardian* [England] 26 Aug. 1982: 9. Mankiewicz summary of where Hollywood went wrong.

1983

403 Belsey, Catherine. "Shakespeare and Film: A Question of Perspective." *Literature/Film Quarterly* XI: 3 (1983): 152–158. Scholarly, aesthetic criti-

cism of *Julius Caesar* and the plurality of Shakespearean texts on stage versus a fixed reading in film. Interesting analogy of JLM's *Julius Caesar* to a Western.

404 Dick, Bernard F. *Joseph L. Mankiewicz.* Boston: Twayne Publishers, 1983. Chronology, filmography, and analysis of films in this one and only scholarly book on JLM published by an American author. Limited bibliography.

405 Frank, Sam. "Rod Serling's Lost 'Christmas Carol.'" *Twilight Zone Magazine* Feb. 1983: 88–94. Background on the contemporary, highly political remake of *A Christmas Carol*, entitled, *Carol for Another Christmas*. Virtually a lost work, this made-for-television film was written by Serling and directed by Mankiewicz in 1964, in support of the United Nations. Article details the politics behind the production that was broadcast only once. Includes excerpts from national reviews.

406 Holdstein, Deborah H. "Men and Women: Voices in the Women's Picture." *Holding the Vision: Essays on Film. Proceedings of the First Annual Film Conference of Kent State U.* Ed. Douglas Radcliff-Umstead. [Ohio]: n.p., 1983. 8–15. Feminist analysis of *All About Eve* and *Mildred Pierce* as representative of the women's picture genre, yet defying stereotypical conventions.

407 Scott, Jay. "Mankiewicz Wit Barely Blunted by State of Films." *Globe and Mail* [Toronto]. 2 Nov. 1983: 17. JLM reflects on his films, contemporary films and television, censorship, film study, and his current work on the history of the performing woman. When he reflects on the present state of film he is often considered embittered. "I'm not bitter, I'm sad. I'm sad at the realization that television and the movies are trying to undercut each other."

408 Sherman, Eric. "Joseph L. Mankiewicz." *American Directors* Vol. 2. Ed. Jean-Pierre Coursodon with Pierre Sauvage. New York: McGraw-Hill, 1983. 228–232. Excellent scholarly analysis of Mankiewicz style, referring to his works as "films théâtraux" (films using theatrical effects).

409 Shuster, Aaron. "Joseph Mankiewicz." *Varsity* [University of Toronto student newspaper]. 11 Nov. 1983: 8–9. Q&A format. JLM responds to questions on his early works, cineastes, colorization, artistic innovations, location shooting, studio versus independent production, and audience expectations. Excellent for direct quotes.

1984

410 Farber, Stephen and Marc Green. "Family Plots: Writing and the Mankiewicz Clan." *Film Comment* July 1984: 68–77. Adaptation of Mankiewicz chapter of Farber and Green's *Hollywood Dynasties*. Full of quotes from JLM's sons Tom and Chris, this pop psychology take on the Mankiewicz family ranges from Herman and Joe's relationship with each other to their children's successes and failures.

411 ____. "House of Strangers: The Mankiewiczes." *Hollywood Dynasties*. New York: Delilah, 1984. 232–261. The writing Mankiewicz family dissected in Hollywood gossipy fashion.

412 Thomas, François. "*Chaînes conjugales* et 'Eve': L'intrigue mise en pièces." *Positif* Feb. 1984: 63–65. A second look at *A Letter to Three Wives* and *All About Eve*. In French.

1985

413 Fine, Richard. *Hollywood and the Profession of Authorship, 1928–1940*. Ann Arbor: UMI Research Press, 1985. 118–120. Small segment of book directed at the Fitzgerald-Mankiewicz writing confrontation on *Three Comrades*; includes a frustrated Fitzgerald's correspondence.

414 Heredero, Carlos. *Joseph L. Mankiewicz*. Madrid: Ediciones JC, 1985. Biography of JLM. In Spanish.

415 Margulies, Lee. "'3 Wives' Remake Accents Romance." *Los Angeles Times* 16 Dec. 1985, sec. VI: 9. Acknowledges the "real star" of the remake as JLM who wrote the original. Remake updated to change second story from radio to television writer. Critic slams current adaptation as lacking the "snap and crackle of the original, stressing romance over wit."

416 Robb, David. "Directors Guild Born Out of Fear 50 Years Ago." *Variety* 1+. Excellent, lengthy historical treatise on the Screen Directors Guild from its founding in the mid–1930s, through the turbulent era of blacklisting in the 1950s when Mankiewicz was its president, to today.

417 Rohmer, Eric. "Rediscovering America." *Cahiers du Cinéma The 1950s: Neo-Realism, Hollywood, New Wave*. Ed. Jim Hillier. Cambridge: Harvard UP, 1985. 88–93. Calls Mankiewicz an auteur.

1986

418 Attanasio, Paul. "Joseph Mankiewicz, Master of the Movies." *Washington Post* 1 June 1986: G1+. Detailed quotes in this excellent article in which Mankiewicz reflects on his career in films. "I have a lot to be sad about. Not bitter in any way. But I think it can be said fairly that I've been in on the beginning, the rise, peak, collapse and end of the talking picture."

419 Binh, N. T. *Mankiewicz*. Paris: Rivages, 1986. Biography of JLM. In French.

420 Bird, David. "'The Mankiewicz Story,' at Columbia." *New York Times* 16 Nov. 1986, sec. I: 42. Upon his acceptance of Columbia University's highest honor, the Alexander Hamilton Medal, alumnus Mankiewicz reflects on the state of contemporary film.

421 Clark, Randall. "Joseph L. Mankiewicz." *American Screenwriters 2*. Detroit: Gale Research, 1986. 215–222. Vol. 44 of *Dictionary of Literary Biography*. 161 Vols. 1978–. Brief bio and synopsis of his films. Daughter Alexandra is incorrectly identified as Alexander.

422 Fieschi, Jean-André. "Neo-neo-realism: *Bandits at Orgosolo*." *Cahiers du Cinéma 1960–1968: New Wave, New Cinema, Reevaluating Hollywood*. Ed. Jim Hillier. Cambridge: Harvard UP, 1986. 271–275. Recommends Mankiewicz as a topic for critical study.

423 Haun, Harry. "The Man Who Loved Words." *Daily News* [New York]15 June 1986: 3. JLM notes that *Cleopatra* is the only one of his 71 films for which he receives residuals. Also fears that audiences have "stopped listening" to films, and that the end of the era of literate filmmaking is near.

424 Natale, Richard. "For a Legend, It's Snowing in N.Y., Raining Honors in L.A." *Los Angeles Herald-Examiner* 7 Mar. 1986: 4. JLM believes his best job of directing was on his favorite film, *Julius Caesar*.

425 Sarris, Andrew. "Not Quite All About Mankiewicz." *Columbia* Nov. 1986: 40–41. In honor of Mankiewicz's receipt of the Alexander Hamilton Medal, fellow Columbia University alum, Sarris, highlights Mankiewicz' career and family history.

426 Sennett, Ted. "Joseph L. Mankiewicz." *Great Movie Directors*. New York: Harry N. Abrams Inc., 1986. 168–171. Brief critical overview of JLM's career and contribution to filmmaking. "The gifts he had as a writer—bringing to films a whiplash wit that reflected an amused concern with the foolish ways of people—and to some extent as a director are uncommon enough to stand out in the history of film."

1987

427 Cieply, Michael. "The Night They Dumped DeMille." *Los Angeles Times* 4 June 1987: sec. VI: 1+. Filmmaker Richard Brooks tells of his desire to make a film for Columbia about the Mankiewicz-DeMille feud over the Screen Directors Guild loyalty oath. Fears of retribution from those directors still living who were in attendance at the fiery meeting might hold up the project. (The film was never made.)

428 Ciment, Michel. "Joseph L. Mankiewicz." *Passeport pour Hollywood: entretiens avec Wilder, Huston, Mankiewicz, Polanski, Forman, Wenders*. Paris: Seuil, 1987. 143–225. Collection of interviews originally published in *Positif*, includes Ciment's 1973 interview with JLM. In French.

429 Darrigol, Jean. "Le Point de vue Mankiewicz: Aspects de l'oeuvre de Joseph L. Mankiewicz après 1946." Diss. U of Paris, 1987. Unpublished dissertation written under the direction of Jean-Paul Török and Claude Beylie at the Sorbonne, Institut d'art et d'archéologie, Département Cinéma et Audiovisuel. Includes limited bibliographic and filmography sections. In French.

430 Doniol-Valcroze, Jacques. "The Mankiewicz Touch." *La Cinémathèque Française* Sept. 1987: 3. Includes bibliography of French sources. In French.

431 Fano, Philippe. "Joseph L. Mankiewicz." *La Cinémathèque Française* Sept. 1987: 4–8. Analysis of Mankiewicz's style includes useful bibliography of foreign publications. In French.

432 Haun, Harry. "For Christmas, Follow the Yellow Brit Road." *Daily News* [New York] 17 Aug. 1987: n. pag. JLM recalls reading his obituary, which was mistakenly published by *New York Times* following the crash of a plane in which he was thought to be a passenger. Much to his dislike he was identified as a producer, a term, and job, he detested.

433 *L'Insospettabile Joseph L. Mankiewicz*. Venezia: La Biennale, 1987. Extraordinary book published in honor of the Mankiewicz retrospective at the 44th International Film Festival in Venice, Italy. Includes detailed filmography as well as previously published interviews and articles from around the world. In Italian.

434 Laitin, Joseph. "A Hollywood Sequel." *Washington Post* 18 Oct. 1987: D5. JLM called "probably the only intellectual in the movie industry with a respectful following among the riffraff because his pictures made money."

435 "Mankiewicz, Joseph L." *World Film Directors*. Ed. John Wakeman. Vol. 1.

New York: H. W. Wilson Co., 1987: 714–722. 2 vols. Excellent biographical sketch complete with quotes from JLM. Notes Mankiewicz fell in love with the theatre when he traveled to Berlin after college. Includes brief filmography and international bibliography.

436 Mérigeau, Pascal. "Joseph L. Mankiewicz—le maître du temps." *Studio Magazine* Nov. 1987: 68+. Includes lengthy interview, with studio photos and extensive filmography. In French.

437 Nocera, Robert. "A Horse Named Paul Revere: Damon Runyon on Film." *Transformations: From Literature to Film. Proceedings of the Fifth Annual Film Conference of Kent State U.* Ed. Douglas Radcliff-Umstead. [Ohio]: n.p., 1987. 75–82. Scholarly discussion of the transfer of the play *Guys and Dolls* to film. Includes behind-the-scenes information.

438 Walker, Michael. "Joseph L. Mankiewicz." *Film Dope* [England] Dec. 1987: 34–36. Useful bio-filmography entry with brief commentary about Mankiewicz style.

1988

439 Beuselink, James. "Mankiewicz's *Cleopatra.*" *Films in Review.* Jan. 1988: 2–17. Excellent speculation of what Mankiewicz's original conception of *Cleopatra* would have been if he had been allowed to make the final cut and release the project as two separate films. Beuselink draws his conclusions from copious research of publicity photographs of scenes cut from the final version as well as a final shooting script. This article is scholarly detective work at its finest, and serves to fill in the historical gaps evident in the four-hour version available on video.

440 "Mankiewicz, Joseph L." *Contemporary Theatre, Film, and Television.* Vol. 5. Detroit: Gale Research Co., 1988: 218–219. 17 Volumes. 1984–. Concise record of JLM's accomplishments. Includes references to films which he contributed to but for which he received no credit.

1989

441 Berg, A. Scott. *Goldwyn.* New York: Alfred A. Knopf, 1989. 469–474. Details of Goldwyn's vision of the film version of the Broadway hit, *Guys and Dolls*, and Mankiewicz's participation as writer-director.

442 Harwood, Jim. "Mankiewicz Lauds Women, Slams Writers at Tribute." *Variety* 20 Mar. 1989: 8. Extolling the virtues of writing about strong women, Mankiewicz also shares his views on the decline of American film at the Kurosawa Award ceremony honoring him for his lifetime achievement in film.

443 "Hollywood Disappoints." *Fort Lauderdale Sun-Sentinel* 18 Mar. 1989: n. pag. Small but succinct commentary from JLM on the state of American film today. "And I know—and I'm very sad—that American film has become, in my opinion, the major motivation for the American being as detested as he is throughout the world. All they see in American movies is variations on obscenity, boozing and [sex]."

444 Shulgasser, Barbara. "A Little Bit of Mankiewicz." *San Francisco Examiner*

16 Mar. 1989: C1. Puff piece with a quote or two from JLM, now aged 80, in town to receive Kurosawa Lifetime Achievement Award.

445 Sragow, Michael. "Movies and Mankiewicz." *San Francisco Examiner* 16 Mar. 1989: C1+. Mini-analysis of JLM films. Includes reference to JLM's screenwriting contribution to *The Philadelphia Story*.

446 Stack, Peter. "A Nervy, Humble Legend." *San Francisco Chronicle* 18 Mar. 1989: C3+. JLM dislikes Hollywood films today: "Somebody's got to stop looking at this crap, the men who once ran Hollywood, the Louis B. Mayers and the Daryl [*sic*] Zanucks, they were like the Medicis compared to the gangsters who are in charge today." Today's movies are gimmicky and full of punch lines: "The beauty of dialogue is that it represents the human being giving voice to feelings, and sometimes conflicts, to happiness and pain and dreams, and even to humor. These are things, shadings of life, you don't get when you just recite jokes."

447 Stone, Peter. "Hollywood Legend: All About Joe." *Interview* Aug. 1989: 70–75. Mankiewicz discusses his early years, his relationship with Lubitsch and his anger over being snubbed by film institutes and certain colleagues. "I have never been recognized by my own country for my body of work. All over the world, but not in my own country."

1990

448 Gardner, Ava. *Ava: My Story*. New York: Bantam Books, 1990. 194–200. The star of *The Barefoot Contessa* discusses her association with Mankiewicz while filming the picture, his first project as an independent writer-director-producer.

449 Haun, Harry. "A Man of 'Letter'—and Oscar." *Daily News* [New York] 8 Aug. 1990: 29. Bio-sketch with a few JLM quotes, including "art with a small 'a.'" Includes background on the making of the racially sensitive *No Way Out*. Regarding his reputation for making stars, JLM said the only person he ever made a star was critic, Judith Crist, because of the attention paid to her pan of *Cleopatra*.

450 Haun, Harry. "All About *All About Eve*." *Theater Week* 22 Oct. 1990: 13–19. Upon the fortieth anniversary of *All About Eve*, Haun discusses the film and notes that Mankiewicz "now confesses" that Eve was a lesbian. However, he does not quote Mankiewicz directly, making this revelation somewhat suspect.

451 _____. "Hollywood's All-Time Bitch Is Forty." *Hollywood Magazine* Oct.-Nov. 1990: 31+. A second look at *All About Eve* on its fortieth anniversary. Includes a detailed account of Mankiewicz's conception of the film; reference to its stage version, *Applause*, for which JLM received no credit; and JLM's meeting with Martina Laurence, the model for Eve in the Mary Orr short story.

452 Lyons, Donald. "All About Cicero." *Film Comment* Sept.-Oct. 1990: 59–63. High praise for *Five Fingers* in this analysis of the film and JLM's style. Mankiewicz seen as "the poet of ambition."

453 Smoodin, Eric. "Joseph L. Mankiewicz." *International Dictionary of Films and Filmmakers—2: Directors*. 2nd ed. Ed. Nicholas Thomas. Chicago: St. James Press, 1990. 548–550. Useful bio and bibliography.

1991

454 "All About 'Mank.'" *DGA News* Sept.-Oct. 1991: 6+. Q&A from session (11 May 1991) of DGA's "A Morning with Mankiewicz " program featuring his films and a discussion with the audience. Includes comments about his casting techniques and writing style.

455 Anderson, John. "All About Joe...." *Los Angeles Times* 6 May 1991: F1+. JLM reflects on his type of film: "films about the conflicts and arrangements and relationships and situations between human beings, and their effect upon each other in varying aspects of life...."

456 Arar, Yardena. "Academy Honors Mankiewicz." *Daily News* [Los Angeles] 8 May 1991, sec. LA Life: 20. Academy of Arts and Sciences Tribute. Actors who worked for Mankiewicz reveal his directorial style.

457 Haun, Harry. "A Producer in Spite of Himself." *Daily News* [New York] 19 Mar. 1991: 17. Reminiscing about being called a producer in his "obit" (published erroneously in 1958).

458 ____. *All About Eve. Films in Review* Mar.-Apr. 1991: 74+. Expansion of Haun's other articles on the fortieth anniversary of the film; the origin of the fictitious Sarah Siddens Society is explained as well as offscreen relationships during the filming.

459 Kornatowska, Maria and Witold Orzechowski. "The Last of the Greats." *Kosciuszko Foundation Newsletter* XLII.2 (1991): 8–9. Q&A with Polish film historian and director. Hepburn and Brando are discussed as is why JLM prefers to write about women.

460 Laffel, Jeff. "Joseph L. Mankiewicz: Part 1." *Films in Review* July-Aug. 1991: 238–244. Detailed interview includes original casting considerations for *Eve* and *Contessa*. Background on JLM's post-college days in Germany working for UFA. Dismisses today's films as pretending to be moral but sending a mixed message to young viewers: "Maybe the good guys win in the end... get to go home to the wives in the last reel... have destroyed the villain... but there have been ten reels in which the bad guys have had a ball."

461 ____. "Joseph L. Mankiewicz: Part 2." *Films in Review* Oct. 1991: 309+. JLM discusses *Julius Caesar* and *Cleopatra*. Emphasis on his themes (especially time), and the major disappointment of his career (the unrealized project "Justine"). Also comments on W. C. Fields, as well as actresses with whom he worked. Brief mention of whether or not the rumor is true that Eve (*All About Eve*), was a lesbian. "Yes, I've heard that. Look, sex has no emotional impact on Eve. It's nothing more than a bodily function. If she can use it, she'll use it. If it was to her advantage, Eve would hump a cat!"

462 McBride, Joseph. "Acad's Mankiewicz Salute Etched in Acid, Sentiment." *Variety* [Daily] 8 May 1991: 2+. Upon being presented with a life membership in the Academy, Mankiewicz (aged 82), called it "the longevity award," and further responded with: "At my age to be given a life membership in anything is small potatoes.... At least I keep telling myself, it's the sentiment that counts." Good for quotes from stars that worked for JLM, including Richard Widmark, Elizabeth Taylor, and Vincent Price.

1992

463 Canby, Vincent. "40 Years of Film Magic." *New York Times* 20 Nov. 1992: C1+. Analysis of JLM style and films for New York retrospective. JLM seen as a discreet, literate filmmaker whose films are "obsessed with society."

464 Carreno, Jose Maria. "Mankiewicz: un cine adulto." *El Mundo* [San Sebastian] 18 Sept. 1992: 4–5. Lengthy tribute to JLM's adult work. In Spanish.

465 Cuenca, José Ignacio. "Joseph L. Mankiewicz." *Interfilms Press* [San Sebastian] Sept. 1992: 28–31. Overview of JLM films. In Spanish.

466 Denke, Ron. "Mankiewicz al desnudo." *Moving Pictures International* 1[San Sebastian] 7 Sept. 1992: n. pag. All about Mankiewicz. In Spanish.

467 Ereñaga, Amaia. "La época dorada no disfruta con el cine actual." *Egin* [San Sebastian] 19 Sept. 1992: 67. JLM discusses the golden age of Hollywood versus films today. In Spanish.

468 Flaño, Teresa. "Mankiewicz impartió ayer una lección magistral de cine." *El Diario Vasco* [San Sebastian] 19 Sept. 1992: 67. JLM reminisces about his early years and regrets that movies no longer tell stories. In Spanish.

469 Garayalde, Ana. "Joseph L. Mankiewicz: Se ha dejado de retratar la intimidad humana." *El Mundo* [San Sebastian] 19 Sept. 1992: 7. Extensive Q&A with JLM during San Sebastian film festival. In Spanish.

470 Garmendia, Marisol. "Mankiewicz, el hecho cine." *Deia Zinemaldia* [San Sebastian] 19 Sept. 1992: 3. Mankiewicz explains why he retired from filmmaking. In Spanish.

471 Gelmis, Joseph. "All About 'Eve' and Mankiewicz." *Newsday* 20 Nov. 1992: 81. JLM discusses his motivation to take on *Cleopatra*: "It was, on my part, knowingly an act of whoredom. Hold your nose for fifteen weeks and get it over with," advised his agent, not knowing that it would take over two years to complete, *and* sully his reputation.

472 Gussow, Mel. "The Sometimes Bumpy Ride of Being Joseph Mankiewicz." *New York Times* 24 Nov. 1992: C13+. Biographical sketch accompanies this interview with the 83-year-old Mankiewicz. "I've lived without caring what anybody thought of me. I followed very few of the rules. I think I've written some good screenplays, gotten some good performances and made some good movies."

473 Haun, Harry. "The 3 Phases of 'Eve.'" *Daily News* [New York] 19 Nov. 1992: 43. Background on origin of *All About Eve*—from short story creator, Mary Orr, to the supposedly authentic personality upon whom Eve Harrington was based, actress Martina Laurence.

474 Heredero, Carlos F. "Joseph L. Mankiewicz." *Diario 16* [San Sebastian] 21 Sept. 1992. Q&A with Mankiewicz. In Spanish.

475 Norman, Barry. "Barry Norman On…." Editorial. *Radio Times* (England) 18–24 Jan. 1992: n. pag. Commentary on why Billy Wilder survived in Hollywood longer than Mankiewicz. "On the whole I think Wilder played the system better, or in any event more subtly…."

476 Shipman, David. *Judy Garland: The Secret Life of an American Legend.* New York: Hyperion, 1992. 140–146. Discussion of the Mankiewicz-Garland relationship, which includes direct quotes from JLM.

477 Tallmer, Jerry. "Now, All About Joe." *New York Post* 19 Nov. 1992: 33. Tribute to Mankiewicz at the New York Film Forum (four months before his

death), solicits comments from him on his style in an era of blatant sex on the screen. "I'm interested in the fragility of love, the fragility of human relations, the fragility of human beings." Saying he writes for the audiences "who come to listen to a film as well as look at it."

478   White, Patty and Hilton Als. "People Will Talk." *Village Voice* 1 Dec. 1992: 27–28. Calling *All About Eve* a "feminist camp thing," White and Als address homosexuality in the "cryptoqueerclassics," *All About Eve* and *Suddenly, Last Summer*, as well as discuss Mankiewicz's skill at writing for women.

1993

479   "Addio regista di ferro." *Corriere Adriatico* [Italy] 7 Feb. 1993: 33. Lengthy obituary of JLM. In Italian.

480   Amiel, Vincent. "Mankiewicz, ou le geste interdit." *Positif* [France] Apr. 1993: 66–67. Lengthy obituary of JLM. In French.

481   Behlmer, Rudy. *Memo from Darryl F. Zanuck:The Golden Years at 20th Century–Fox*. New York: Grove Press, 1993. Numerous letters and explanatory comments about the Zanuck-JLM association including confidential memo of 20 Dec. 1952, wherein DFZ refuses to take screen credit as producer of *People Will Talk*: "When you are both writer and director on a film the producer is inevitably subjected to a forgotten or completely secondary role." Zanuck finally did take credit for *People Will Talk*.

482   Butkiewicz, Joe. "Mankiewicz Proved He Was Nobody's Fool." *Times Leader* [Wilkes-Barre, Pa.] 9 Feb. 1993: 1B+. Hometown newspaper's obituary celebrates JLM's life and career with several references to brother Herman.

483   Cagle, Jess. "Joseph's Technicolor Dreamscape." *Entertainment Weekly* 19 Feb. 1993: 68. Useless obit but for the inclusion of the disturbing photo of JLM (bound and gagged), which was shot by French photographer, Catherine Cabrol, four days before his death.

484   Cantelli, Alfio. "Mankiewicz, il principale del set." *Giornale* [Italy] 7 Feb. 1993: 16. Lengthy obituary of JLM. In Italian.

485   Casiraghi, Ugo. "Vita e Oscar del professor Joseph Mankiewicz." *L'Unita* [Italy] 2 Feb. 1993: n. pag. Lengthy obituary of JLM. In Italian.

486   Chardiere, Bernard. "Fevrier en cinema." *Positif* [France] Apr. 1993: 68-69. Obit includes photo of JLM with daughter Alexandra. In French.

487   Ciment, Michel. "Mankiewicz un intello à Hollywood." *L'Événement du Jeudi* [France] 17 Feb. 1993: 111. Lengthy obituary of JLM. In French.

488   Cohn, Lawrence. "Joseph L. Mankiewicz." *Variety* 15 Feb. 1993: 99–100. Excellent, highly detailed obit reviewing JLM's career. Includes a rare reference to 1964 telefilm, *A Carol for Another Christmas*.

489   Colmant, Marie. "Mankiewicz, limier d'Hollywood." *Libération* [France] 8 Feb. 1993: 39+. Lengthy obituary of JLM. In French.

490   Crist, Judith. "Joe, *Cleopatra* and Me." *Columbia* Fall 1993: 39–41. Fellow Columbia University graduate Crist, with a love-hate relationship with JLM, discusses her claim to fame, the panning of *Cleopatra*, and subsequent relationship with Mankiewicz in the latter years of his life, which was a fine one as long as she never mentioned *Cleopatra* in his presence. She didn't.

491   Farber, Stephen and Marc Green. *Hollywood on the Couch: A Candid Look at*

the Overheated Love Affair between Psychiatrists and Moviemakers. New York: William Morrow and Co., Inc., 1993. An interesting examination of the fascination that many filmmakers have with psychoanalysis. Mankiewicz (along with many others) is discussed.

492 Fernández-Santos, Ángel. "Con Joseph Mankiewicz se aoaga una de las ultimas sombras del esplendor de Hollywood." *El País* [Spain]7 Feb. 1993: 35. Obituary of JLM. In Spanish.

493 "Film Auteur Joseph Mankiewicz Died at Age 83." Host Susan Stamberg. *Weekend Edition—Saturday*. Natl. Public Radio. 6 Feb. 1993. Transcript. 19 Sept. 1998. <http://www.elibrary>. Stamberg announces the death of Mankiewicz, and refers to a 1986 radio interview in which the director discusses how he visualizes what he writes when he works on a screenplay. He also discusses the candy scene in *All About Eve*.

494 "Final Credit for Sophisticate Who Gave Talkies Gift of the Bon Mot." *Observer* [England] 7 Feb. 1993: n. pag. Father and brother references in this obituary.

495 "Film Director Mankiewicz Dead at 83." Host Katie Davis. *All Things Considered*. Natl. Public Radio. 6 Feb. 1993. Transcript. 19 Sept. 1998. <http://www.elibrary>. In discussing the death of Mankiewicz, film critic, Bob Mondello, notes that if Mankiewicz had done nothing more than introduce Spencer Tracey to Katharine Hepburn, he would deserve a place in the Hollywood hall of fame, but that, indeed, he had accomplished much more. Frank Mankiewicz, nephew of the great filmmaker, is quoted within the transcript.

496 Flint, Peter B. "Joseph L. Mankiewicz, Literate Skeptic of the Cinema, Dies at 83." *New York Times* 6 Feb. 1993: A10. Calling Mankiewicz "elegant and epigrammatic," and "a meticulous craftsman who preferred words to images...." Lengthy obit details his early life; quotes from past *Times* reviews and highlights the difficulties he faced on *Cleopatra*.

497 Gross, Susanna. "Even He Couldn't Save 'Cleo.'" *Daily Mail* [London] 9 Feb. 1993: n. pag. "In recent years, Mankiewicz grew increasingly perturbed by the ascendancy of special effects over dialogue, and described most modern films as 'cartoons, with balloon dialogue for 14-year-old minds.'"

498 Heredero, Carlos F. "Muere Joseph L. Mankiewicz." *Diario* [Spain] 7 Feb. 1993: 33+. Lengthy obituary of JLM. In Spanish.

499 Hinckley, David. "For Film Icon, It's a Wrap." *Daily News* [New York] 6 Feb. 1993: n. pag. Pop-psychology obit (e.g. "The liberal son of a demanding scholar...."), with humorous reference to Burton-Taylor tryst on *Cleopatra*. ("Asked about a report that Taylor was infatuated with Mankiewicz and Burton was just a cover story, the director responded that actually he was in love with Burton and Taylor was the cover.")

500 Honeycutt, Kirk. "Joseph Mankiewicz, Filmmaker, Dies." *Hollywood Reporter* 8 Feb. 1993: 1+. Called "one of Hollywood's first 'hyphenates.'" Lengthy discussion of Screen Directors Guild feud with DeMille.

501 "Joseph Mankiewicz." *Current Biography* Apr. 1993: 59. Obituary.

502 "Joseph L. Mankiewicz 1909–1993." *New Yorker* 29 Mar. 1993: 9. Photo-obit of JLM in full-page GAP ad.

503 "Joseph L. Mankiewicz." *London Times* 8 Feb. 1993: 17A. Lengthy obituary with biography.

504 "Joseph L. Mankiewicz: de repente, el último suspiro." *Espectáculos* [Spain]
     6, Feb. 1993: 87. Lengthy obituary of JLM. In Spanish.
505 "Joseph Mankiewicz, el director mas culto de Hollywood, murio de un fallo
     cardiaco." *Sur* [Spain] 7 Feb. 1993: 61. Lengthy obituary of JLM. In Spanish.
506 "Joseph Mankiewicz." *Daily Telegraph* [London] 8 Feb. 1993: n. pag. Obit-
     uary includes in-depth biography with references to his very early works.
507 Kazan, Elia. "Joseph Mankiewicz en son ile d'Elbe." (trans. Michel Ciment
     and Yann Tobin). *Positif* [France] Apr. 1993: 64–65. This appreciation by
     Kazan includes photo of Kazan, Michel Ciment, and JLM.
508 Langton, James. "Death of Director Who Won Four Oscars." *Sunday Tele-
     graph* [England] 7 Feb. 1993: n. pag. Detailed obituary.
509 Malcolm, Derek. "A Film Man of His Word." *Guardian* [England] 8 Feb.
     1993: 13. Lengthy obit with quotes from past JLM interviews. Discusses the
     "black years" when working for Mayer at MGM, and how he followed his
     mentor Lubitsch to Fox so that he could direct. *Cleopatra* particulars noted.
510 Malcolm, Derek. "Film Man of His Word." *Guardian Weekly* [England] 14
     Feb. 1993: 9. Abbreviated version of early *Daily Guardian* obituary.
511 "Mankiewicz : l'art de la machination." *Cahiers du Cinéma* March 1993:
     40–41. Tribute to JLM. In French.
512 Mankiewicz, Frank. "Joe Mankiewicz, Leading the Way." *Washington Post* 8
     Feb. 1993: B1+. Warm tribute to JLM by Washington-insider and nephew
     (Herman's son). Includes personal reminiscences.
513 Mérigeau, Pascal. "Contre Hollywood, tout contre." *Cahiers du Cinéma*
     March 1993: 46–49. A look at Mankiewicz in Hollywood. In French.
514 Mérigeau, Pascal. *Mankiewicz.* Paris: Denoel, 1993. Biography in French.
515 Monroe, Robert. "Award-Winning Film Director Joseph Mankiewicz Dies
     at 83." *Independent on Sunday* [England]. 7 Feb. 1993: n. pag. AP wire story
     with references to the early days working with W. C. Fields, and Hepburn
     and Tracy.
516 Moullet, Luc. "Toujours plus loin." *Cahiers du Cinéma* March 1993: 42–45.
     Discussion of Mankiewicz's work and his influence on other directors. In
     French.
517 "Muere Mankiewicz, el maestro de los matices." *El Mundo* [Spain] 7 Feb.
     1993: 53. JLM obit. In Spanish.
518 Murat, Pierre. "All About Joseph." *Télérama* [France] 17 Feb. 1993: 28+.
     Lengthy obituary of JLM. In French.
519 Natale, Richard. "Pic Director Mankiewicz Dead at 83." *Variety* 8 Feb. 1993:
     1+. Perfunctory obit, notes critical acclaim and distraction. JLM seen as a
     "raconteur and bon vivant" who charmed the opposite sex.
520 Norman, Barry. "Barry Norman on the Late Joseph L. Mankiewicz, A Man
     Too Witty and Refined for Today's Hollywood." *Radio Times* [England]
     27 Feb.–5 Mar. 1993: 36. Appreciation for JLM's wit with a statement that
     Hollywood would not know what to do with such a talent now, "because
     Joe had long outlived his time, not simply because of age but because the
     movies don't want his kind any more."
521 Oliver, Myrna. "Joseph L. Mankiewicz; Writer, Director." *Los Angeles Times*
     6 Feb. 1993: A24. Lengthy obit with quotes from past interviews. "Don't
     make me out to be a nasty, irritable old snot who hates California and feels
     superior."

522 Parent, Denis. "Joseph L. Mankiewicz le rebelle d'Hollywood." *Studio Magazine* [France] Mar. 1993: 70–71. Obit includes Cabrol's unsettling photo (arms and feet bound with rope, tape over mouth), taken four days before his death. In French.

523 Shipman, David. "Joseph Mankiewicz." *Independent* [England] 8 Feb. 1993: 21. Excellent obit with more details than other obituaries. Reflects Shipman's personal knowledge of JLM; includes many quotes.

524 Siclier, Jacques. "Mankiewicz, l'intellectuel." *Le Monde* [France] 8 Feb. 1993: 1+. Lengthy obituary of JLM. In French.

525 Turan, Kenneth. "The Brothers Mankiewicz: A Gold Touch." *Los Angeles Times* 8 July 1993: F1+. UCLA film festival honors the Mankiewicz brothers. Biographical sketch of Herman and Joe with emphasis on the early years.

526 Wallach, George. "Mankiewicz of the Movies: A Memoriam." *DGA News* [Directors Guild of America] Aug.-Sept. 1993: 14+. Outstanding tribute to Mankiewicz includes the definitive answer to "the Rosebud question" (re: brother Herman and *Citizen Kane*). Lengthy quotes from Maggie Smith and Sidney Poitier as well as excerpts from the still-unpublished JLM chapbook.

527 Weil, Martin. "Joseph Mankiewicz, Movie Producer, Director, Screenwriter, Dies at 83." *Washington Post* 6 Feb. 1993: B4. Obit includes JLM's reference to movie theater owners as real estate operators; also notes Joe's relation to Frank Mankiewicz (his nephew).

528 Wiley, Mason. "A Small-Screen Tribute to Mankiewicz." *Daily News* [Los Angeles] 12 Mar. 1993: 47. Minitribute notes which Mankiewicz films are available on video.

529 "World-Wide. Died: Joseph Mankiewicz." *Wall Street Journal* 8 Feb. 1993: A1. Brief obituary of JLM.

530 Yeck, Joanne. "All About Joe." *Senior.* June 1993: n. pag. Lengthy obit with detailed quotes from Mankiewicz regarding the Screen Directors Guild loyalty oath controversy.

1994

531 Hazell, Ed. "Principle Role." *American Movie Classics Magazine* Nov. 1994: 14–15. Lightweight article about Mankiewicz with emphasis on his biting satire, as seen in *People Will Talk*.

1995

532 Grafe, Frieda. *The Ghost and Mrs. Muir*. London: BFI Publishing, 1995. Close reading of the film with extended analysis of Mankiewicz's style.

1996

533 Kurti, Jeff. *The Great Musical Trivia Book*. New York: Applause Books, 1996. 39–62. An abundance of miscellaneous information about Mankiewicz and his 1955 film, *Guys and Dolls*.

1997

534 Custen, George F. *Twentieth Century's Fox: Darryl F. Zanuck and the Culture of Hollywood*. New York: Basic Books, 1997. 329–342. Little new information in this discussion of the working relationship between Zanuck and Mankiewicz—from the Zanuck perspective.

535 Durang, Christopher. "'We Talked in Sentences Then!'" *Scenario* Fall 1997: 4+. Playwright Durang gives high praise to Mankiewicz for his clever dialogue in *All About Eve*: "But story on its own has a limited appeal—it's the way in which it's told, it's the way Mankiewicz's wise and wised-up sensibility informs the story, and it's the way that his writer's intelligence illuminates the characters who people the story. And so much of that illumination comes in how they *speak*, in their dialogue."

536 Lippy, Todd. "Celeste Holm: Acting in 'Eve.'" *Scenario* Fall 1997: 109+. Holm discusses how she got the part as Karen in *All About Eve* as well as Mankiewicz's style on the set.

537 ____. "Joseph L. Mankiewicz (1909–1993)." *Scenario* Fall 1997: 104–105. Biographical sketch of filmmaker.

538 ____. "Tom Mankiewicz: Remembering Joe." *Scenario* Fall 1997: 107+. Writer-director Tom Mankiewicz talks with pride about his father's talent and life in the film business.

539 Stone, Judy. *Eye on the World: Conversations with International Filmmakers*. Los Angeles: Silman-James Press, 1997. 723–725. Reprint of interview Mankiewicz gave to *San Francisco Chronicle* reporter Stone in 1975 while at the San Francisco Film Festival.

1998

540 Kamp, David. "When Liz Met Dick." *Vanity Fair* April 1998. 366+. Detailed background on the making of *Cleopatra* and the famous love affair between Elizabeth Taylor and Richard Burton that originated during the making of the film, and how Mankiewicz coped with the extensive media attention paid to the most expensive film ever made.

541 Mitchell, Greg. *Tricky Dick and the Pink Lady: Richard Nixon vs. Helen Gahagan Douglas*. New York: Random House, 1998. Sexual politics mingled with the Communist Red Scare of the 1950s includes a modern retelling of the battle in Hollywood between Mankiewicz and DeMille over the Screen Directors Guild loyalty oath.

542 ____. "Winning a Battle but Losing the War Over the Blacklist." *New York Times* 25 Jan. 1998: 13+. Adaptation of Mitchell's book, *Tricky Dick and the Pink Lady*, with an emphasis on the DeMille-Mankiewicz loyalty oath controversy.

1999

543 Archerd, Army. "Just for Variety." *Variety* 6 April 1999: 2. Interest in the Hollywood blacklisting days continues after Elia Kazan's receipt of controversial Oscar for lifetime achievement. Archerd recalls Mankiewicz's problems with DeMille over the loyalty oath controversy in 1950 and notes that Mankiewicz's nephew, Don Mankiewicz, is writing a screenplay for *Show-time* about this event.

544 Staggs, Sam. "Everything About Eve." *Vanity Fair* April 1999. 284+. Lengthy behind-the-scenes look at one of Hollywood's most honored films, *All About Eve*.

2000

545 Clarke, Gerald. *Get Happy: The Life of Judy Garland*. New York: Random House, 2000. 179–191. A brief look at Mankiewicz's role in Garland's life with an emphasis on his urging her into psychotherapy.

546 Staggs, Sam. *All About All About Eve*. New York: St. Martin's Press, 2000. A film fan's look behind the scenes of what he calls the "bitchiest" film ever made. Includes a preponderance of gossip and secondary source material. However, there is some interesting trivia, and a helpful glossary of many of the film's inside jokes and obscure references.

Filmography

In compiling this filmography, I relied predominantly on data gathered from the Mankiewicz personal papers. However, the script collections at AFI, USC, AMPAS, and UCLA were also very helpful. In addition, I turned to the following publications for assistance: *L'Insospettabile* (*433**) Walker (*438*), Taylor (*243*), Brion (*314*), Gow (*330*), Geist (*380*), Reid (*298*), and Springer (*342*). Unless it was absolutely necessary to confirm a discrepancy, sources on the Internet were not used because of the highly unreliable nature of the film databases to be found thereon.

As Titler

The Dummy (1929). Famous Players-Lasky-Paramount. Black and white. Director, Robert Milton; Supervisor, Hector Turnbull; Adaptation/Dialogue, Herman J. Mankiewicz; From play by Harvey J. O'Higgins and Harriet Ford; Titles (silent version), Joseph L. Mankiewicz. **Cast:** Ruth Chatterton, Fredric March, John Cromwell, Jack Oakie. Released March 9, 1929. 59 minutes.

Close Harmony (1929). Famous Players-Lasky-Paramount. Black and white. Director, A. Edward Sutherland; Dialogue, John V. A. Weaver and Percy Heath; Adaptation, Percy Heath; Story, Elsie Janis and Gene Markey; Songs, Richard A. Whiting and Leo Robin; Titles (silent version), Joseph L. Mankiewicz. **Cast:** Charles "Buddy" Rogers, Nancy Carroll, Harry Green, Jack Oakie, Richard "Skeets" Gallagher. Released Apr. 13, 1929. 67 minutes.

The Man I Love (1929). Famous Players-Lasky-Paramount. Black and white. Director, William A. Wellman; Associate Producer, David O. Selznick; Story, Herman J. Mankiewicz; Screen Play/Dialogue, Herman J. Mankiewicz; Titles (silent version), Joseph L. Mankiewicz. **Cast:** Richard Arlen, Mary Brian, Harry Green, Jack Oakie. Released May 25, 1929. 7 reels.

*Numbers in *italics* refer to sources listed in the Annotated Bibliography.

The Studio Murder Mystery (1929). Famous Players-Lasky-Paramount. Black and white. Director, Frank Tuttle; Screen Play, Frank Tuttle; From story by A. Channing Edington and Carmen Ballen Edington; Adaptation, Ethel Doherty; Titles (silent version), Joseph L. Mankiewicz. Cast: Doris Hill, Neil Hamilton, Fredric March, Warner Oland, Florence Eldridge, Chester Conklin. Released June 1, 1929. 66 minutes.

Thunderbolt (1929). Famous Players-Lasky-Paramount. Black and white. Director, Joseph von Sternberg; Associate Producer, B. P. Fineman; Screen Play, Jules Furthman; From story by Jules Furthman and Charles Furthman; Dialogue, Herman J. Mankiewicz; Titles (silent version), Joseph L. Mankiewicz. Cast: George Bancroft, Fay Wray, Richard Arlen, Tully Marshall. Released June 22, 1929. 8 reels, 91 minutes.

River of Romance (1929). Famous Players-Lasky-Paramount. Black and white. Director, Richard Wallace; Screen Play, Ethel Doherty; Adaptation, Dan Totheroh and John V. A. Weaver; From play by Booth Tarkington (*Magnolia*); Titles (silent version), Joseph L. Mankiewicz. Cast: Charles "Buddy" Rogers, Mary Brian, June Collyer, Henry B. Walthal, Wallace Beery. Released June 29, 1929. 8 reels, 78 minutes.

Dangerous Curves (1929). Famous Players-Lasky-Paramount. Black and white. Director, Lothar Mendes; Titles (silent version), Joseph L. Mankiewicz [and George Marion, Jr.]; Dialogue, Viola Brothers Shore; Adaptation, Donald Davis and Florence Ryerson; Based on story by Lester Cohen. Cast: Clara Bow, Richard Arlen, Kay Francis. Working title: "Pink Tights." Released July 13, 1929. 75 minutes. *Note: Previously published filmographies have excluded this film. However, Paramount script materials (file 00365) at AMPAS indicate Mankiewicz's contribution. (See 43.)*

The Mysterious Dr. Fu Manchu (1929). Famous Players-Lasky-Paramount. Black and white. Director, Rowland V. Lee; Screen Play, Florence Ryerson and Lloyd Corrigan; Dialogue, Florence Ryerson and Lloyd Corrigan; From story by Sax Rohmer; Comedic Dialogue, George Marion, Jr.; Titles (silent version), Joseph L. Mankiewicz. Cast: Warner Oland, Jean Arthur, Neil Hamilton. Released Oct. 26, 1929. 8 reels, 80 minutes.

The Saturday Night Kid (1929). Famous Players-Lasky-Paramount. Black and white. Director, A. Edward Sutherland; Adaptation, Lloyd Corrigan; From story by George Abbott and John V. A. Weaver ("Love 'Em and Leave 'Em"); Dialogue, Lloyd Corrigan and Edward E. Paramore, Jr.; Titles (silent version), Joseph L. Mankiewicz. Cast: Clara Bow, James Hall, Jean Arthur, Charles Sellon, Edna May Oliver, Jean Harlow. Shooting Schedule, July 27, 1929–Aug. 16, 1929. Released Oct. 29, 1929. 67 minutes. *Note: According to AMPAS script materials, Mankiewicz was paid $20 for his efforts. According to Gow, JLM worked on rejected versions only.*

The Virginian (1929). Famous Players-Lasky-Paramount. Black and white. Director, Victor Fleming; Screen Play, Howard Estabrook; From novel by Owen Wister and Kirk LaShelle; Adaptation, Grover Jones and Keene Thompson; Dialogue, Edward E. Paramore, Jr.; Photography, J. Roy Hunt; Titles (silent version), Joseph E. Mankiewicz [sic]. Cast: Gary Cooper, Walter Huston, Mary Brian, Richard

Arlen, Helen Ware, Chester Conklin, Eugene Pallette, Victor Potel, E. H. Calvert. Production schedule, May 20–June 15, 1929. Released Nov. 9, 1929. 9 reels, 95 minutes. *Note: As an indication that Mankiewicz's contribution extended beyond that of titler of silent versions, JLM notes in a letter to Gary Cooper, June 12, 1953: "The first writing I ever did for the screen, many years ago for both of us, was a love scene I wrote—at the request of Bud Lighton—for you and Mary Brian, in THE VIRGINIAN. It was a silly scene, as I remember, something about 'Why the hell didn't Romeo get a ladder, if he was so in love with the girl?'" (JLM unpublished correspondence.)*

As Screenwriter

Fast Company (1929). Famous Players-Lasky-Paramount. Black and white. Director, A. Edward Sutherland; Screen Play, Florence Ryerson, Patrick Kearney, and Walton Butterfield; Dialogue, Joseph L. Mankiewicz; Adaptation, Patrick Kearney and Walton Butterfield; From play by Ring Lardner and George M. Cohan (*Elmer the Great*). **Cast:** Jack Oakie, Evelyn Brent, Skeets Gallagher. Released Sept. 14, 1929. 70 minutes. *Note: Mankiewicz's first film for which he received complete credit. He was 20 years old.*

Slightly Scarlet (1930). Famous Players-Lasky-Paramount. Black and white. Directors, Louis Gasnier and Edwin H. Knopf; Screen Play/Dialogue, Howard Estabrook and Joseph Mankiewicz; Story, Percy Heath; Photography, Allen Siegler. **Cast:** Evelyn Brent, Clive Brook, Paul Lukas, Eugene Pallette, Helen Ware, Virginia Bruce, Henry Wadsworth, Claud Allister, Christiane Yves, Morgan Farley. Released Feb. 22, 1930. 72 minutes.

The Social Lion (1930). Paramount-Publix Corp. Black and white. Director, A. Edward Sutherland; Scenario, Agnes Brand Leahy; Story by Octavus Roy Cohen ("Marco Himself"); Adaptation, Joseph L. Mankiewicz; Dialogue, Joseph L. Mankiewicz; Photography, Allen Siegler. **Cast:** Jack Oakie, Mary Brian, Skeets Gallagher, Olive Borden, Charles Sellon, Cyril Ring, E. H. Calvert, James Gibson, Henry Roquemore, William Bechtel, Richard Cummings, Jack Byron. Working titles: "High Society," "Marco Himself." Released June 21, 1930. 60 minutes.

Only Saps Work (1930). Paramount-Publix Corp. Black and white. Directors, Cyril Gardner and Edwin H. Knopf; Adaptation, Sam Mintz and Percy Heath; Dialogue, Joseph L. Mankiewicz; From play by Owen Davis ("Easy Come, Easy Go"); Film Editor, Edward Dmytryk; Songs by Ballard MacDonald and Dave Dreyer; Photography, Rex Wimpy. **Cast:** Leon Errol, Richard Arlen, Mary Brian, Stuart Erwin, Anderson Lawler, Charles Grapewin. Working title: "Social Errors." Production schedule, July 21–Aug. 4, 1930. Released Dec. 6, 1930. 72 minutes.

The Gang Buster (1930/1931). Paramount-Publix Corp. Black and white. Director, A. Edward Sutherland; Story, Percy Heath; Dialogue, Joseph L. Mankiewicz; Photography, Harry Fishbeck; Film Editor, Jane Loring. **Cast:** Jack Oakie, Jean Arthur, William Boyd, Wynne Gibson, Tom Kennedy, William Morris, Albert

Conti, Francis McDonald, Pat Harmon, Constantin Romanoff, Harry Stubbs, Ernie Adams, Joseph Girard, Eddie Dunn. Working title: "On the Spot." Production schedule, Oct. 11–Nov. 1, 1930. Released Jan. 17, 1931. 68 minutes (6120 ft.).

Finn and Hattie (1931). Famous Players-Lasky-Paramount. Black and white. Directors, Norman Taurog and Norman Z. McLeod; Screen Play, Joseph L. Mankiewicz; Dialogue, Joseph L. Mankiewicz; Adaptation, Sam Mintz; Based on books by Donald Ogden Stewart; Photography, Dev Jennings. **Cast:** Leon Errol, ZaSu Pitts, Mitzi Green, Lilyan Tashman, Jackie Searl, Regis Toomey, Mack Swain, Ethel Sutherland, Syd Saylor, Harry Beresford. Working titles: "The Haddocks Abroad," "Finn and Hattie Abroad," "The Haddocks," "Mr. and Mrs. Haddock Abroad," and "Mr. and Mrs. Haddock in Paris France." Released Feb. 28, 1931. 76 minutes.

June Moon (1931). Paramount-Publix Corp. Black and white. Director, A. Edward Sutherland; Scenario, Keene Thompson and Joseph L. Mankiewicz; From play by Ring Lardner and George S. Kaufman; Dialogue, Keene Thompson, Joseph L. Mankiewicz, and Vincent Lawrence. **Cast:** Jack Oakie, Frances Dee, June McCloy, Ernest Wood, Wynne Gibson, Harry Akst, Sam Hardy. Production schedule, Dec. 18, 1930–Jan. 9, 1931. Released Mar. 21, 1931. 74 minutes.

Skippy (1931). Paramount-Publix Corp. Black and white. Director, Norman Taurog; Supervisor, Louis Lighton (uncredited); Scenario, Joseph L. Mankiewicz and Norman McLeod; Dialogue, Joseph L. Mankiewicz, Norman McLeod, and Don Marquis; Adaptation, Percy Crosby and Sam Mintz; From comic strip by Percy Crosby. **Cast:** Jackie Cooper, Robert Coogan, Mitzi Green, Jackie Searl, Enid Bennett, Willard Robertson, David Haines, Helen Jerome Eddy, Jack Clifford. Released Apr. 25, 1931. 80 minutes. *Note: JLM received his first Academy Award nomination for this film, for best screenplay.*

Forbidden Adventure / Newly Rich (1931). Paramount-Publix Corp. Black and white. Director, Norman Taurog; Scenario, Edward Paramore, Jr., Norman McLeod, Joseph L. Mankiewicz; From story by Sinclair Lewis ("Let's Play King"); Adaptation, Agnes Brand Leahy; Dialogue, Norman McLeod and Joseph L. Mankiewicz. **Cast:** Mitzie Green, Edna May Oliver, Louise Fazenda, Jackie Searl, Virginia Hammond, Bruce Line. Working title: "Newly Rich." Released July 5, 1931. 77 minutes. *Note: Retitled for release as* Forbidden Adventure.

Sooky (1931). Paramount-Publix Corp. Black and white. Director, Norman Taurog; Scenario/Dialogue, Sam Mintz, Joseph L. Mankiewicz, and Norman McLeod; Adapted from Percy Crosby's "Dear Sooky." **Cast:** Jackie Cooper, Bobby Coogan, Jackie Searl, Enid Bennett, Helen Jerome Eddy, Willard Robertson. Released Dec. 26, 1931. 85 minutes.

This Reckless Age (1932). Paramount-Publix Corp. Black and white. Director, Frank Tuttle; Scenario/Dialogue, Joseph L. Mankiewicz; Adaptation, Frank Tuttle; From play by Lewis Beach ("The Goose Hangs High"). **Cast:** Charles "Buddy" Rogers, Richard Bennett, Peggy Shannon, Charles Ruggles, Frances Dee, Frances Starr, Maude Eburne. Released Jan. 9, 1932. 80 minutes.

Sky Bride (1932). Paramount-Publix Corp. Black and white. Director, Stephen Roberts; Scenario/Dialogue, Joseph L. Mankiewicz, Agnes Brand Leahy, Grover

Jones; From story by Waldemar Young. **Cast:** Richard Arlen, Jack Oakie, Virginia Bruce, Robert Coogan, Charles Starrett, Louise Closser Hale, Tom Douglas, Harold Goodwin. Released Apr. 29, 1932. 78 minutes.

Million Dollar Legs (1932). Paramount-Publix Corp. Black and white. Director, Edward Cline; Supervisor, Herman J. Mankiewicz (uncredited); Scenario/Dialogue, Joseph L. Mankiewicz; From original story by Joseph L. Mankiewicz ("On Your Mark"); Photography, Arthur Todd. **Cast:** Jack Oakie, W. C. Fields, Andy Clyde, Lyda Roberti, Susan Fleming, Ben Turpin, George Barbier, Hugh Herbert, Dickie Moore, Billy Gilbert, Vernon Dent, Teddy Hart, John Sinclair, Sam Adams, Irving Bacon, Ben Taggart, Hank Mann, Chick Collins, Sid Saylor. Released July 8, 1932. 64 minutes. *Note: It is Geist who suggests that Herman Mankiewicz was an uncredited supervisor on this film.*

If I Had a Million (1932). Paramount-Publix Corp. Black and white. Multi-writer, multi-director film consisting of 8 episodes, prologue, and epilogue. Directors, Ernst Lubitsch (opening, "Clerk," and "Streetwalker"), Norman Taurog ("The Auto" or "Rollo and the Roadhogs"), Stephen Roberts ("The Forger"), Norman McCloud ("The Three Marines"), James Cruze ("The China Shop"), William A. Seiter ("Old Ladies' Home"), H. Bruce Humberstone ("The Condemned Man"); Story, Robert D. Andrews; Adaptations, Claude Binyon, Whitney Bolton, Malcolm Stuart Boylan, John Bright, Sidney Buchman, Lester Cole, Isabel Dawn, Boyce De Gaw, Walter De Leon, Oliver H. P. Garrett, Harvey Gates, Grover Jones, Ernst Lubitsch, Grover Jones, Lawton MacKall, Joseph L. Mankiewicz, William Slavens McNutt, Seton I. Miller, Tiffany Thayer. **Cast:** Gary Cooper, Wynne Gibson, George Raft, Charles Laughton, Richard Bennett, Jack Oakie, Frances Dee, Charles Ruggles, Alison Skipworth, W. C. Fields, Mary Boland, Roscoe Karns, May Robson, Gene Raymond, Lucien Littlefield. Released Dec. 2, 1932. 88 minutes. *Note: Mankiewicz holds certificates of authorship for the following episodes: "Henry Peabody and the China Shop," "The Prostitute," "Emily, Rollo and the Road Hogs," and "The Three Marines." Walker notes JLM also contributed to the linking story of the film.*

Diplomaniacs (1933). RKO. Black and white. Director, William A. Seiter; Producer, Sam Jaffe; Screen Play, Joseph L. Mankiewicz and Henry Myers; From original story by Joseph L. Mankiewicz ("In the Red"); Music, Max Steiner; Songs, Harry Akst, Edward Eliscu. **Cast:** Bert Wheeler, Robert Woolsey, Marjorie White, Phyllis Berry, Louis Calhern, Hugh Herbert, William Irving, Neely Edwards, Billy Bletcher, Teddy Hart. Released Apr. 29, 1933. 76 minutes.

Emergency Call (1933). RKO. Black and white. Director, Edward Cahn; Producer, Sam Jaffe; Screen Play, John B. Clymer and Joseph L. Mankiewicz; From story by John B. Clymer and James Ewens. **Cast:** Bill Boyd, Wynne Gibson, William Gargan, Betty Furness, Reginald Mason, Edwin Maxwell. Released June 24, 1933. 65 minutes.

Too Much Harmony (1933). Paramount. Black and white. Director, A. Edward Sutherland; Producer, William LeBaron; Scenario, Joseph L. Mankiewicz; Dialogue, Harry Ruskin; Music and lyrics, Arthur Johnston and Sam Coslow; Dance ensembles, Leroy Prinz; Photography, Theodor Sparkuhl. **Cast:** Bing

Crosby, Jack Oakie, Richard "Skeets" Gallagher, Harry Green, Judith Allen, Lilyan Tashman, Ned Sparks, Kitty Kelly, Grace Bradley, Mrs. Evelyn Offield Oakie. Released Sept. 23, 1933. 76 minutes.

Alice in Wonderland (1933). Paramount. Black and white. Director, Norman Z. McLeod; Producer, Louis L. Lighton; Screen Play, Joseph L. Mankiewicz and William Cameron Menzies; From novel by Lewis Carroll; Art Direction, William Cameron Menzies; Masks and costumes, Wally Westmore and Newt Jones; Setting, Robert Odell; Music, Dimitri Tiomkin; Technical effects, Gordon Jennings; Photography, Henry Sharp; Editor, Edward Hoagland. **Cast:** Charlotte Henry, Richard Arlen, Roscoe Ates, William Austin, Billy Barty, Billy Bevan, Gary Cooper, Leon Errol, Louise Fazenda, W. C. Fields, Richard "Skeets" Gallagher, Cary Grant, Ethel Griffies, Sterling Holloway, Edward Everett Horton, Roscoe Karns, Mae Marsh, Polly Moran, Jack Oakie, Edna May Oliver, May Robson, Charles Ruggles, Jackie Searl, Ned Sparks, Ford Sterling. Released Dec. 11, 1933. 90 minutes.

Manhattan Melodrama (1934). Metro-Goldwyn-Mayer. Black and white. Director, W. S. Van Dyke (and Jack Conway, uncredited); Producer, David O. Selznick; Screen Play, Oliver H. P. Garrett and Joseph L. Mankiewicz; From story by Arthur Caesar ("The Three Men"); Photography, James Wong Howe; Songs, Richard Rogers and Lorenz Hart; Editor, Ben Lewis; Special effects, Slavko Vorkapich. **Cast:** Clark Gable, William Powell, Myrna Loy, Leo Carillo, Nat Pendleton, George Sidney, Isabel Jewell, Murial Evans, Mickey Rooney. Production schedule, Mar. 12–Apr. 3, 1934. Released May 6, 1934. 93 minutes. *Note: It is Geist who notes Conway's contribution to direction of this film.*

Our Daily Bread (1934). A Viking Production/United Artists. Black and white. Producer/Writer/Director, King Vidor; Scenario, Elizabeth Hill Vidor; Dialogue, Joseph L. Mankiewicz; Photography, Robert Planck; Music, Alfred Newman; Editor, Lloyd Nossler. **Cast:** Karen Morley, Tom Kenne, John T. Qualen, Barbara Pepper. Released Oct. 2, 1934. 74 minutes. *Note: Title for Great Britain release, The Miracle of Life.*

Forsaking All Others (1934). Metro-Goldwyn-Mayer. Black and white. Director, W. S. Van Dyke; Producer, Bernard H. Hyman; Screen Play, Joseph L. Mankiewicz ; From play by Frank Morgan Cavett and Edward Barry Roberts; Musical Score, Dr. William Axt; Recording Director, Douglas Shearer; Art Direction, Cedric Gibbons; Associate, Edwin B. Willis; Gowns by Adrian; Photography, Gregg Toland and George Folsey; Film Editor, Tom Held. **Cast:** Joan Crawford, Clark Gable, Robert Montgomery, Charles Butterworth, Frances Drake, Billie Burke, Rosalind Russell. Released Dec. 25, 1934. 84 minutes.

I Live My Life (1935). Metro-Goldwyn-Mayer. Black and white. Director, W. S. Van Dyke; Producer, Bernard H. Hyman; Screen Play, Joseph L. Mankiewicz; From the story by A. Carter Goodloe ("Claustrophobia"); Adaptation, Gottfried Reinhardt and Ethel B. Borden; Photography, George Folsey; Music, Dimitri Tiomkin; Editor, Tom Held. **Cast:** Joan Crawford, Brian Aherne, Frank Morgan, Aline MacMahon, Eric Blore, Fred Keating, Jessie Ralph, Arthur Treacher. Production schedule, June 3–July 16, 1935. Released Oct. 14, 1935. 81 minutes.

Uncredited Work as Writer

The following are often cited in filmographies as uncredited work.

Paramount on Parade (1930). Paramount. Black and white. *L'Insospettabile Joseph Leo Mankiewicz* suggests that JLM wrote the dialogue for the Jack Oakie sequence (*433*). Paramount script materials at AMPAS offer no evidence of Mankiewicz's contribution. However, Mankiewicz told John Reid that he was assigned to write dialogue for Jack Oakie films, including *Paramount on Parade* (*298*).

Sap from Syracuse (1930). Paramount. Black and white. As in *Paramount on Parade*, *L'Insospettabile Joseph Leo Mankiewicz* suggests that JLM wrote the dialogue for the Jack Oakie sequence (*433*). Paramount script materials at AMPAS offer no evidence of Mankiewicz's contribution but see Reid for Mankiewicz's acknowledgment of his writing contribution (*298*).

Dude Ranch (1931). Paramount. Black and white. This film is often omitted from JLM filmographies. The AFI Film Catalog makes no mention of JLM's contribution to the film. Paramount file 839 at AMPAS indicates that Herman Mankiewicz contributed additional dialogue to the final script dated Feb. 13, 1931. There is no mention of Joseph Mankiewicz's contribution. However, the scenario budget in this same file indicates that both Joe and Herman received comparable salaries for their contribution to the film. Reid clears this up in his article, "Cleo's Joe: Part 1," noting that JLM worked on this project for just a few days before being reassigned to *Newly Rich* (*298*, 46).

Touchdown (1931). Paramount. Black and white. Paramount script files indicate no contribution from JLM. Reid notes that Mankiewicz added additional dialogue to Oakie's films (*298*). (See *Paramount on Parade*.) Additionally, JLM is cited in *L'Insospettabile Joseph Leo Mankiewicz* (*433*) as a contributor to this film.

College Humor (1933). Paramount. Black and white. Mankiewicz and Claude Binyon were responsible for the first treatment based on Dean Fales' story, "Bachelor of Arts," according to Paramount file 00305 at AMPAS. That was the extent of Mankiewicz's contribution to the project.

After Office Hours (1935). Metro-Goldwyn-Mayer. Black and white. Gow suggests JLM collaborated on the screenplay with brother Herman. No other evidence of JLM's contribution is evident.

As Producer

Three Godfathers (1936). Metro-Goldwyn-Mayer. Black and white. Director, Richard Boleslawski; Producer, Joseph L. Mankiewicz; Screen Play, Edward E. Paramore, Jr. and Manuel Seff; From the story by Peter B. Kyne; Photography, Joseph Ruttenberg; Musical Score, William Axt; Editor, Frank Sullivan. **Cast:** Chester Morris, Lewis Stone, Walter Brennan, Irene Hervey, Sidney Toler. Production schedule, Nov. 27, 1935–Jan. 3, 1936. Released Mar. 7, 1936. 82 minutes.

Fury (1936). Metro-Goldwyn-Mayer. Black and white. Director, Fritz Lang; Producer, Joseph L. Mankiewicz; Screen Play, Bartlett Cormack, Fritz Lang [Mankiewicz, uncredited]; From story by Norman Krasna [and Mankiewicz, uncredited]; Photography, Joseph Ruttenberg; Music, Franz Waxman; Editor, Frank Sullivan. **Cast:** Spencer Tracy, Sylvia Sidney, Walter Abel, Bruce Cabot, Edward Ellis, Walter Brennan, George Walcott, Frank Albertson. Working title: "Mob Rule." Production schedule, Feb. 20–Apr. 25, 1936. Released, May 22, 1936. 90 minutes. *Note: Anecdotal contradictions abound from Lang to Mankiewicz regarding Mankiewicz's involvement in the screenplay. However, significant story conference material exists at USC that indicates the extent of Mankiewicz's contribution to the story and screenplay.*

The Gorgeous Hussy (1936). Metro-Goldwyn-Mayer. Black and white. Director, Clarence Brown; Producer, Joseph L. Mankiewicz; Screen Play, Ainsworth Morgan and Stephen Morehouse Avery; From novel by Samuel Hopkins Adams; Photography, George Folsey; Film Editor, Blanche Sewell; Music, Herbert Stothart; Art Direction, Cedric Gibbons; Associates, William A. Horning and Edwin B. Willis; Dance staged by Val Raset; Gowns, Adrian. **Cast:** Joan Crawford, Lionel Barrymore, Franchot Tone, Robert Taylor, Melvyn Douglas, James Stewart, Beulah Bondi, Alison Skipworth, Sidney Toler, Gene Lockhart, Frank Conroy, Willard Robertson, Charles Trowbridge. Previewed Aug. 26, 1936. Released Sept. 1, 1936. 105 minutes.

Love on the Run (1936). Metro-Goldwyn-Mayer. Black and white. Director, W. S. Van Dyke; Producer, Joseph L. Mankiewicz; Screen Play, John Lee Mahin, Manuel Seff, and Gladys Hurlbut; From story by Alan Green and Julian Brodie ("Beauty and the Beast"); Photography, Oliver T. Marsh; Editor, Frank Sullivan. **Cast:** Joan Crawford, Clark Gable, Franchot Tone, Reginald Owen, Donald Meek. Production schedule, Aug. 19–Sept. 26, 1936. Released Nov. 26, 1936. 80 minutes.

The Bride Wore Red (1937). Metro-Goldwyn-Mayer. Black and white. Director, Dorothy Arzner; Producer, Joseph L. Mankiewicz; Screen Play, Tess Slesinger and Bradbury Foote; From play by Ferenc Molnár ("The Girl from Trieste"); Photography, George Folsey; Music, Franz Waxman; Lyrics, Gus Kahn; Editor, Adrienne Fazan. **Cast:** Joan Crawford, Franchot Tone, Robert Young, Billie Burke, Reginald Owen, George Zucco, Mary Phillips. Working titles: "The Girl from Trieste" and "Once There Was a Lady." Production schedule June 3–Aug. 10, 1937. Released Oct. 8, 1937. 80 minutes.

Double Wedding (1937). Metro-Goldwyn-Mayer. Black and white. Director, Richard Thorpe; Producer, Joseph L. Mankiewicz; Screen Play, Jo Swerling [and Waldo Salt, uncredited]; From play by Ferenc Molnár ("Great Love"); Photography, William Daniels; Music, Edward Ward; Editor, Frank Sullivan. **Cast:** William Powell, Myrna Loy, Florence Rice, John Beal, Jessie Ralph, Edgar Kennedy, Sidney Toler. Production schedule May 26–Aug. 12, 1937. Released Oct. 15, 1937. 80 minutes. *Note: It is Geist who names Waldo Salt as an uncredited contributor to the screenplay.*

Mannequin (1937). Metro-Goldwyn-Mayer. Black and white. Director, Frank Borzage; Producer, Joseph L. Mankiewicz; Screen Play, Lawrence Hazard; From original story by Katherine Brush; Photography, George Folsey; Assistant Director, Lew Borzage; Film Editor, Frederick Y. Smith; Music, Edward Ward; Recording Director, Douglas Shearer; Art Direction, Cedric Gibbons; Associates, Paul Groesse and Edwin B. Willis; Gowns, Adrian. **Cast:** Joan Crawford, Spencer Tracy, Alan Curtis, Ralph Morgan, Oscar O'Shea, Elizabeth Risdon, Leo Gorcey. Production schedule Sept. 7–Oct. 26, 1937. Previewed, Dec. 14, 1937. Released Jan. 20, 1938. 93 minutes.

Three Comrades (1938). Metro-Goldwyn-Mayer. Black and white. Director, Frank Borzage; Producer, Joseph L. Mankiewicz; Screen Play, F. Scott Fitzgerald and Edward E. Paramore; From novel by Erich Maria Remarque; Photography, Joseph Ruttenberg; Music, Franz Waxman; Songs, Bob Wright and Chet Forrest; Editor, Frank Sullivan; Montage, Slavko Vorkapich. **Cast:** Robert Taylor, Margaret Sullavan, Franchot Tone, Robert Young, Guy Kibbee, Lionel Atwill, Henry Hull, Charley Grapewin, Monty Woolley. Production schedule Feb. 4–Mar. 30, 1938. Released June 3, 1938. 100 minutes. *Note: Conference notes exist at USC that confirm Mankiewicz's involvement in reworking the final shooting script.*

The Shopworn Angel (1938). Metro-Goldwyn-Mayer. Black and white. Director, H. C. Potter; Producer, Joseph L. Mankiewicz; Screen Play, Waldo Salt; From story by Dana Burnet ("Private Pettigrew's Girl"); Photography, Joseph Ruttenberg; Music, Edward Ward; Editor, W. Don Hayes. **Cast:** Margaret Sullavan, James Stewart, Walter Pidgeon, Hattie McDaniel, Nat Pendleton, Alan Curtis, Sam Levene. Production schedule Mar. 28–May 6, 1938. Released July 15, 1938. 85 minutes.

The Shining Hour (1938). Metro-Goldwyn-Mayer. Black and white. Director, Frank Borzage; Producer, Joseph L. Mankiewicz; Screen Play, Jane Murfin and Ogden Nash; From play by Keith Winter; Photography, George Folsey; Music, Franz Waxman; Editor, Frank E. Hull. **Cast:** Joan Crawford, Margaret Sullavan, Robert Young, Melvyn Douglas, Fay Bainter, Allyn Joslyn, Hattie McDaniel. Production schedule Aug. 20–Oct. 3, 1938. Released Nov. 11, 1938. 80 minutes.

A Christmas Carol (1938). Metro-Goldwyn-Mayer. Black and white. Director, Edwin L. Marin; Producer, Joseph L. Mankiewicz; Screen Play, Hugo Butler; From novel by Charles Dickens; Photography, Sidney Wagner; Editor, George Boemer. **Cast:** Reginald Owen, Gene Lockhart, Kathleen Lockhart, Terry Kilburn, Barry Mackay, Lynne Carver, Leo G. Carroll, Lional Braham, Ann Rutherford, D'Arcy Corrigan. Production schedule Oct. 5–Nov. 3, 1938. Released Dec. 16, 1938. 69 minutes.

The Adventures of Huckleberry Finn / Huckleberry Finn (1939). Metro-Goldwyn-Mayer. Black and white. Director, Richard Thorpe; Producer, Joseph L. Mankiewicz; Screen Play, Hugo Butler; From novel by Mark Twain; Photography, John Seitz; Music, Franz Waxman; Editor, Frank E. Hull. **Cast:** Mickey Rooney, Walter Connolly, William Frawley, Rex Ingram, Lynne Carver, Jo Ann Sayers, Minor Watson, Elizabeth Risdon, Victor Kilian. Production schedule Nov. 20–Dec. 28, 1938. Released Feb. 10, 1939. 90 minutes. *Retitled:* Huckleberry Finn.

Strange Cargo (1940). Metro-Goldwyn-Mayer. Black and white. Director, Frank Borzage; Producer, Joseph L. Mankiewicz; Screen Play, Lawrence Hazard; From novel by Richard Sale (*Not Too Narrow, Not Too Deep*); Additional dialogue, Lesser Samuels; Photography, Robert Planck; Music, Franz Waxman; Editor, Robert J. Kern. **Cast:** Joan Crawford, Clark Gable, Ian Hunter, Peter Lorre, Paul Lukas, Albert Dekker, J. Edward Bromberg, Eduardo Cianelli, John Arledge. Working title: "Not Too Narrow Not Too Deep." Production schedule Oct. 19–Dec. 28, 1939. Previewed Feb. 28, 1940. Released Mar. 1, 1940. 105 minutes.

The Philadelphia Story (1940). Metro-Goldwyn-Mayer. Black and white. Director, George Cukor; Producer, Joseph L. Mankiewicz; From play by Philip Barry; Screen Play, Donald Ogden Stewart; Edited, Frank Sullivan; Photography, Joseph Ruttenberg; Music score, Franz Waxman; Recording Director, Douglas Shearer; Art Direction, Cedric Gibbons; Associate, Wade B. Rubottom; Set Decorations, Edwin B. Willis; Gowns, Adrian; Hair styles, Sydney Guilaroff. **Cast:** Cary Grant, Katharine Hepburn, James Stewart, Ruth Hussey, John Howard, Roland Young, John Halliday, Mary Nash, Virginia Weidler, Henry Daniell, Lionel Pape, Rex Evans. Production schedule July 5–Aug. 14, 1940. Previewed Dec. 4, 1940. Released, Dec. 26, 1940. 111 minutes. Awards: Academy Award nomination to Mankiewicz as producer of *The Philadelphia Story*. However, Donald Ogden Stewart won an Oscar for the best adapted screenplay: no mention was made of JLM's contribution. *Note: Mankiewicz illustrates the idiosyncrasies of Hollywood in a 1980 interview that explored his writing contribution to films for which he received no credit other than that of producer. Louis B. Mayer used JLM's negotiating prowess to acquire the screen rights to the successful Broadway play,* The Philadelphia Story, *from its owner Howard Hughes, who was also romantically involved with Katharine Hepburn. Hughes demanded that Hepburn star in the film, and that additionally, the film have two male stars to accompany her. However, the play had only one male lead and two minor male characters. Mankiewicz used his writing talents to appease the quirky Hughes. As he recalled, "I merged the two characters—the brother and the ex-husband, made one character out of it, and talked Cary Grant into playing it. The exciting part of the anecdote, if there is any excitement to it is (first of all I don't think George Cukor to this day knows what he really had wasn't like the screenplay), and I met Howard Hughes and I had to tell him my idea. And he said, 'Sounds good, I want to see it on paper.' Again, I wrote this treatment of 'Philadelphia Story,' and I remember having to go up to the top of Mullholland Drive, which is way up in the Hollywood Hills, get out of my car and walk to this limousine, (big, black limousine) in the back of which sat Howard Hughes. And I handed this thing into him. I didn't even get to sit with him, I just handed it in and he sat there and he read it. I walked up and down—you'd think I was waiting for a baby or something—sitting on top of this log—Howard was just sitting there, reading these 50 pages. Finally, his chauffeur called me and said, 'Mr. Hughes will see you.' And I walked in and sat in the back seat with Howard and he said, 'You've got it." (See 1980, Audio.)*

The Wild Man of Borneo (1941). Metro-Goldwyn-Mayer. Black and white. Director, Robert B. Sinclair; Producer, Joseph L. Mankiewicz; Screen Play, Waldo Salt and John McLain; From play by Marc Connelly and Herman J. Mankiewicz; Photography, Oliver T. Marsh; Editor, Frank Sullivan; Music, David Snell. **Cast:** Frank Morgan, Mary Howard, Billie Burke, Donald Meek, Marjorie Main, Connie Gilchrist, Bonita Granville, Dan Dailey, Jr., Andrew Tombes, Walter Catlett, Phil Silvers. Production schedule, Oct. 25–Nov. 20, 1940. Released Jan. 24, 1941. 78 minutes.

The Feminine Touch (1941). Metro-Goldwyn-Mayer. Black and white. Director, W. S. Van Dyke; Producer, Joseph L. Mankiewicz; Screen Play, George Oppenheimer, Edmund L. Hartmann, and Ogden Nash; Photography, Ray June; Music, Franz Waxman; Editor, Albert Akst. **Cast:** Rosalind Russell, Don Ameche, Kay Francis, Van Heflin, Donald Meek, Henry Daniell, Sidney Blackmer. Production schedule, June 30–July 29, 1941. Released Oct. 1941. 97 minutes.

Woman of the Year (1941/1942). Metro-Goldwyn-Mayer. Black and white. Director, George Stevens; Producer, Joseph L. Mankiewicz; Screen Play, Ring Lardner, Jr. and Michael Kanin; Photography, Joseph Ruttenberg; Film Editor, Frank Sullivan; Music, Franz Waxman; Art Direction, Cedric Gibbons and Randall Duell; Set decorations, Edwin B. Willis; Gowns, Adrian. **Cast:** Katharine Hepburn, Spencer Tracy, Fay Bainter, Minor Watson, William Bendix, Gladys Blake, Roscoe Karns, Dan Tobin, Reginald Owen, George Kezas, William Tannen, Ludwig Stossel, Jimmy Conlon, Joe Yule, Connie Gilchrist, Edith Evanson. Production schedule, Aug. 27–Oct. 25, 1941. Released Jan. 19, 1942. 112 minutes. *Note: JLM wrote the breakfast scene near the end of the film. (See 418.)*

Cairo (1942). Metro-Goldwyn-Mayer. Black and white. Director, Major W. S. Van Dyke II; Producer, Joseph L. Mankiewicz [uncredited]; Screen Play, John McClain; From idea by Ladislas Fodor; Photography Ray June; Music, Herbert Stothart and George Stoll; Songs, Arthur Schwartz, Harold Arlen, and E. Y. Harburg; Editor, James E. Newcom. **Cast:** Jeanette MacDonald, Robert Young, Ethel Waters, Reginald Owen, Grant Mitchell, Lionel Atwill, Edward Cianelli, Dooley Wilson. Working title: "Shadow of a Lady." Production schedule, Apr. 1–May 29, 1942. Released Aug. 17, 1942. 101 minutes. *Note: There is no mention of JLM's contribution (or that of any producer) in the press material at USC. Michael Walker notes in his filmography that Mankiewicz insisted his name be removed from the credits of this film because he was not pleased with the final product. Author John Reid offers another explanation as to why no producer's name appears on the credits— that Mankiewicz was asked to "supervise" Cairo: "This is equivalent to saying that he acted as a sort of executive producer. He controlled the film's budget from the front office and did not actually appear on the set. This nutty arrangement was Louis B. Mayer's way of expressing trust and friendship for his favourite Director, WS Van Dyke." However, Mankiewicz's role as producer is confirmed in the MGM Eddie Mannix ledger at AMPAS.*

Reunion in France (1942). Metro-Goldwyn-Mayer. Black and white. Director, Jules Dassin; Producer, Joseph L. Mankiewicz; Screen Play, Jan Lustig, Marvin Borowsky, and Marc Connelly; From original story by Ladislas Bus-Fekete; Photography, Robert Planck; Music, Franz Waxman; Recording Director, Douglas Shearer; Art Direction, Cedric Gibbons; Associate, Daniel B. Cathcart; Set Decorations, Edwin B. Willis; Special Photographic Effects, Warren Newcombe; Gowns, Irene; Film Editor, Elmo Veron. **Cast:** Joan Crawford, John Wayne, Philip Dorn, Reginald Owen, Albert Bassermann, John Carradine, Ann Ayars, J. Edward Bromberg, Moroni Olsen, Henry Daniell, Howard da Silva, Charles Arnt, Morris Ankrum, Edith Evanson, Ernest Dorian, Margaret Laurence, Odette Myrtil, Peter Whitney. Working title: "Reunion." Production schedule, June 29–Sept. 4, 1942. Released Dec. 2, 1942. 104 minutes. *Note: USC script materials indicate Mankiewicz also contributed to the screenplay. L'Insospettabile also cites JLM* *as an uncredited contributor to the screenplay (433). Released in Great Britain as* Mademoiselle France.

The Keys of the Kingdom (1944). 20th Century–Fox. Black and white. Director, John Stahl; Producer, Joseph L. Mankiewicz; Screen Play, Joseph L. Mankiewicz; From novel by A. J. Cronin; Photography, Arthur Miller; Music, Alfred Newman; Orchestral Arrangements, Edward Powell; Art Direction, James Basevi and William Darling; Set Decorations, Thomas Little; Associate, Frank E. Hughes; Film Editor, James B. Clark; Costumes, Bonnie Cashin; Makeup Artist, Guy Pearce; Special Photographic Effects, Fred Sersen; Sound, Eugene Grossman and Roger Heman. **Cast:** Gregory Peck, Thomas Mitchell, Vincent Price, Rosa Stradner, Roddy McDowall, Edmund Gwenn, Sir Cedric Hardwicke, Peggy Ann Garner, Jane Ball, James Gleason, Anne Revere, Ruth Nelson, Bensen Fong, Leonard Strong, Philip Ahn, Arthur Shields, Edith Barrett, Sara Allgood, Richard Loo, Ruth Ford, Kevin O'Shea, H. T. Tsiang, Si-Lan Chen, Eunice Soo-Hoo, Dennis Hoey, Ethel Griffies, Terry Kilburn, Lumsden Hare, J. Anthony Hughes, Abner Bierman, George Nokes. Final script, Jan. 28, 1944. Production schedule, Feb. 1–May 20, 1944. Released Dec. 15, 1944. 137 minutes.

As Director

Includes detailed cast listings.

Dragonwyck (1946). 20th Century–Fox. Black and white. Executive Producer, Darryl F. Zanuck; Director, Joseph L. Mankiewicz; Producer, Ernst Lubitsch [uncredited]; Screen Play, Joseph L. Mankiewicz; From novel by Anya Seton; Music, Alfred Newman; Director of Photography, Arthur Miller, A.S.C.; Orchestral Arrangements, Edward B. Powell; Art Direction, Lyle Wheeler and Russell Spencer; Set Decorations, Thomas Little; Associate, Paul S. Fox; Film Editor, Dorothy Spencer; Costumes, Rene Hubert; Makeup Artist, Ben Nye; Special Photographic Effects, Fred Sersen; Dances staged by Arthur Appel; Sound, W. D. Flick and Roger Heman. **Cast:** Gene Tierney (Miranda Wells); Walter Huston (Ephraim Wells); Vincent Price (Nicholas Van Ryn); Glenn Langan (Dr. Jeff Turner); Anne Revere (Abigail Wells); Spring Byington (Magda); Connie Marshall (Katrina Van Ryn); Henry Morgan* (Klaus Bleecker); Vivienne Osborne (Johanna Van Ryn); Jessica Tandy (Peggy O'Malley); Trudy Marshall (Elizabeth Van Borden); Reinhold Schunzel (Count de Grenier); Jane Nigh (Tabitha); Ruth Ford (Cornelia Van Borden). Final Script, Feb. 8, 1945. Production schedule, Feb. 12–May 4, 1945. Released Apr. 10, 1946. 103 minutes (9,176 feet). *Adding to the ongoing confusion for actor Harry Morgan (Dragnet, M*A*S*H) is that he is listed on-screen as "Henry" Morgan.*

Somewhere in the Night (1946). 20th Century–Fox. Black and white. Director, Joseph L. Mankiewicz; Producer, Anderson Lawler; Screen Play, Howard Dimsdale and Joseph L. Mankiewicz; Adaptation, Lee Strasberg; From story by Marvin Borowsky; Director of Photography, Norbert Brodine, A.S.C.; Art Direction, James Basevi and Maurice Ransford; Set Decorations, Thomas Little; Associate, Ernest Lansing; Editorial Supervision, James B. Clark; Costumes, Kay Nelson;

Music, David Buttolph; Musical Direction, Emil Newman; Orchestral Arrangements, Arthur Morton; Makeup Artist, Ben Nye; Special Photographic Effects, Fred Sersen; Sound, Eugene Grossman and Harry M. Leonard. **Cast:** John Hodiak (George Taylor); Nancy Guild (Christy); Lloyd Nolan (Lt. Kendall); Richard Conte (Mel Phillips); Josephine Hutchinson (Elizabeth); Fritz Kortner (Anzelmo); Margo Woode (Phyllis); Sheldon Leonard (Sam); Lou Nova (Hubert); Houseley Stevenson (Conroy); Charles Arnt (Little Man); Phil Van Zandt (Navy Doctor); John Kellogg (Medical Attendant); Forbes Murray (Executive); Whitner Bissell (Bartender); Jeff Corey (Bank Teller); Paula Reid (Nurse); John Russell (Marine Captain); Al Sparlis (Cab Driver); Richard Benedict (Technical Sargent); Mary Currier (Miss Jones); Sam Flint (Bank Guard); Henry Morgan (Swede); Charles Marsh (Hotel Clerk); Nancy Cooper (Attendant); Jack Davis (Dr. Grant); Louis Mason (Brother Williams); Henri DeSoto (Headwaiter); Harry Tyler (Baggage Clerk). Working title: "Lonely Journey." Final script, Nov. 14, 1945. Production schedule, Nov. 21, 1945–Jan. 24, 1946. Press preview Apr. 30, 1946. Released May 2, 1946. 109 minutes (9,926 feet).

The Late George Apley (1947). 20th Century–Fox. Black and white. Director, Joseph L. Mankiewicz; Producer, Fred Kohlmar; Screen Play, Philip Dunne; From play by John P. Marquand and George S. Kaufman; Based on novel by John P. Marquand; Music Direction, Alfred Newman; Director of Photography, Joseph LaShelle, A.S.C.; Art Direction, James Basevi and J. Russell Spencer; Set Decorations, Thomas Little; Associate, Paul S. Fox; Editorial Supervision, James B. Clark; Music, Cyril J. Mockridge; Orchestral Arrangements, Maurice de Packh; Costumes, Rene Hubert; Makeup Artist, Ben Nye; Special Photographic Effects, Fred Sersen; Sound, Bernard Freericks and Roger Heman. **Cast:** Ronald Colman (George Apley); Vanessa Brown (Agnes Willing); Peggy Cummins (Eleanor Apley); Richard Haydn (Horatio Willing); Charles Russell (Howard Boulder); Richard Ney (John Apley); Percy Waram (Roger Newcombe); Mildred Natwick (Amelia Newcombe); Edna Best (Catherine); Nydia Westman (Jane Willing); Francis Pierlot (Wilson, butler); Kathleen Howard (Margaret, maid); Paul Harvey (Julian Dole); Helen Dickson (Governess); Frank Dawson (Charles, waiter); Clancy Cooper (Irish Cop); also with Theresa Lyon, William Moran, Clifford Brooke, Ottola Nesmith. Production schedule June 24–Aug. 22, 1946. Previewed Jan. 30, 1947. Premiere Feb. 13, 1947 (London: Leicester Square Cinema). Released Mar. 20, 1947 (NY: Music Hall). 98 minutes (12,375 feet).

The Ghost and Mrs. Muir (1947). 20th Century–Fox. Black and white. Director, Joseph L. Mankiewicz; Producer, Fred Kohlmar; Screen Play, Philip Dunne; From novel by R. A. Dick; Music, Bernard Herrmann; Director of Photography, Charles Lang, Jr., A.S.C.; Art Direction, Richard Day and George Davis; Set Decorations, Thomas Little and Stewart Reiss; Film Editor, Dorothy Spencer; Wardrobe Direction, Charles Le Maire; Costumes, Eleanor Behm; Costumes for Tierney designed by Oleg Cassini; Makeup Artist, Ben Nye; Special Photographic Effects, Fred Sersen; Sound, Bernard Freericks and Roger Heman. **Cast:** Gene Tierney (Lucy Muir); Rex Harrison (Ghost of Captain Gregg); George Sanders (Miles Fairley); Edna Best (Martha); Vanessa Brown (Anna Muir); Anna Lee (Mrs. Miles Fairley); Robert Coote (Coombe); Natalie Wood (Anna as child); Isobel Elsom (Angelica); Victoria Horne (Eva); Whitford Kane (Sproule); William Stelling (Bill); David Thursby (Scroggins); also with Heather Wilde, Houseley

Stevenson, Will Stanton, Stuart Holmes. Rev. final script, Nov. 21, 1946. Production schedule, Nov. 29, 1946–Feb. 13, 1947. Released June 26, 1947. 104 min. (9,375 feet). *Note: Fox legal materials at UCLA indicate that here, once again, Mankiewicz was a hands-on contributor to a screenplay that he did not author. JLM added revisions to final versions of Dunne's screenplay. Television remake: US television series based on the film starred Edward Mulhare and Hope Lange; 50 half-hour episodes were produced for NBC-TV (1968) and ABC-TV (1968).*

Escape (1948). 20th Century–Fox. Black and white. Director, Joseph L. Mankiewicz; Producer, William Perlberg; Screen Play, Philip Dunne; From play by John Galsworthy; Director of Photography, Frederick A. Young; Editors, Alan L. Jaggs and Kenneth Heeley-Ray; Art Direction, Alex Vetchinsky; Music Composed by William Alwyn; Music Direction, Muir Mathieson. **Cast:** Rex Harrison (Matt Denant); Peggy Cummins (Dora Winton); William Hartnell (Inspector Harris); Norman Wooland (Parson); Jill Esmond (Grace Winton); Cyril Cusack (Rodgers); Frederick Piper (Brownie); Marjorie Rhodes (Mrs. Pinkem); Betty Ann Davies (Girl in Park); John Slater (Car Salesman); Frank Pettingell (Village Constable); Michael Golden (Plain Clothes Man); Frederick Leister (Judge); Walter Hudd (Defense Counsel); Maurice Denham (Crown Counsel); Jacqueline Clarke (Phyllis); Frank Tickle (Mr. Pinkem); Peter Croft (Titch); George Woodbridge (Farmer Browning); Stuart Lindsell (Sir James); Patrick Troughton (Shepherd); Ian Russell (Car Driver); Cyril Smith (Policeman). Filmed in England (Denham Studio). Revised final script, Sept. 15, 1947. Production schedule, Sept. 15–Dec. 18, 1947. Premiere March 28 (Easter Sunday), 1948 (London: Gaumont Marble Arch). Released May 17, 1948. 78 minutes. *Note: Fox legal materials at UCLA indicate that Mankiewicz was a contributor to the revised final screenplay.*

A Letter to Three Wives (1948/49). 20th Century–Fox. Black and white. Director, Joseph L. Mankiewicz; Producer, Sol C. Siegel; Screen Play, Joseph L. Mankiewicz; Adapted by Vera Caspary from a *Cosmopolitan Magazine* novel by John Klempner; Music, Alfred Newman; Director of Photography, Arthur Miller, A.S.C.; Art Direction, Lyle Wheeler and J. Russell Spencer; Set Decorations, Thomas Little and Walter M. Scott; Film Editor, J. Watson Webb, Jr.; Wardrobe Direction, Charles LeMaire; Costume Design, Kay Nelson; Orchestral Arrangements, Edward Powell; Makeup Artist, Ben Nye; Special Photographic Effects, Fred Sersen; Sound, Arthur L. Kirbach and Roger Heman. **Cast:** Jeanne Crain (Deborah Bishop); Linda Darnell (Lora Mae Hollingsway); Ann Sothern (Rita Phipps); Kirk Douglas (George Phipps); Paul Douglas (Porter Hollingsway); Barbara Lawrence (Babe); Jeffery Lynn (Brad Bishop); Connie Gilchrist (Mrs. Finney); Florence Bates (Mrs. Manleigh); Hobart Cavanaugh (Mr. Manleigh); Patti Brady (Kathleen); Ruth Vivian (Miss Hawkins); Thelma Ritter (Sadie); Stuart Holmes (Old Man); George Offerman Jr.(Nick); Ralph Brooks (Character); James Adamson (Butler); Joe Bautista (Thomasino); John Davidson (Waiter); Carl Switzer (Messenger); Celeste Holm (voice of Addie Ross, uncredited). Production schedule, June 3–Aug. 9, 1948. Released Jan. 20, 1949. 103 minutes (9,266 feet). Awards: Academy Awards (1949): Best Director (Mankiewicz); Screen Play (Mankiewicz). Academy Award nominations: Best picture. Directors Guild of America Quarterly Awards (1948-49): Mankiewicz. Directors Guild of America Annual Award (1949): Joseph L. Mankiewicz. *Television remake: Fox*

Television remade film Dec. 16, 1985 starring Loni Anderson as Laura Mae [sic]; Michelle Lee (Rita); and Stephanie Zimbalist (Debra). Directed by Larry Elikann. This adaptation by Sally Robinson did not credit Mankiewicz on its first showing. After complaints from JLM, the rerun noted: "Based on the screenplay, A Letter to Three Wives *by Joseph L. Mankiewicz."*

House of Strangers (1949). 20th Century–Fox. Black and white. Director, Joseph L. Mankiewicz; Producer, Sol C. Siegel; Screen Play, Philip Yordan (with extensive revisions by Joseph L. Mankiewicz); From novel by Jerome Weidman; Music, Daniele Amfitheatrof; Director of Photography, Milton Krasner, A.S.C.; Editor, Harmon Jones; Art Direction, Lyle Wheeler and George W. Davis; Set Decorations, Thomas Little, Walter M. Scott; Wardrobe Direction, Charles LeMaire; Orchestration, Maurice de Packh; Recording "Largo Al Factotum" by Lawrence Tibbett*; Makeup Artist, Ben Nye; Special Photographic Effects, Fred Sersen; Sound, W. D. Flick, Roger Heman. **Cast:** Edward G. Robinson (Gino Monetti); Susan Hayward (Irene Bennett); Richard Conte (Max Monetti); Luther Adler (Joe Monetti); Paul Valentine (Pietro Monetti); Efrem Zimbalist, Jr. (Tony Monetti); Debra Paget (Maria Domenico); Hope Emerson (Helena Domenico); Esther Minciotti (Theresa Monetti); Diana Douglas (Elaine Monetti); Tito Vuolo (Lucca); Albert Morin (Victoro); Sid Tomack (Waiter); Thomas Browne Henry (Judge); David Wolfe (Prosecutor); John Kellogg (Danny); Ann Morrison (Woman juror). Working titles: "East Side Story" and "Never Go There Any More." Shooting final script, Dec.20, 1948. Production schedule, Dec. 21, 1948–Feb. 22, 1949. Released July 30, 1949. 101 minutes. Awards: Cannes Film Festival (1949): Best Actor (Robinson). *Note: UCLA files indicate that Mankiewicz contributed to retakes of the screenplay. However, story conference material at USC indicates that JLM came up with a new ending for the film. DGA News also cites Mankiewicz as coscreenwriter with Yordan. *The recording title is incorrectly listed in the credits. The aria sung by Tibbett is "M'appari" from the opera* Martha *by von Flotow.*

No Way Out (1950). 20th Century–Fox. Black and white. Director, Joseph L. Mankiewicz; Producer, Darryl F. Zanuck; Screenplay, Joseph L. Mankiewicz and Lesser Samuels; Music, Alfred Newman; Orchestration, Edward Powell; Director of Photography, Milton Krasner, A.S.C.; Art Direction, Lyle Wheeler and George W. Davis; Set Decorations, Thomas Little and Stuart Reiss; Film Editor, Barbara McLean; Wardrobe Direction, Charles LeMaire; Costumes, Travilla; Makeup Artist, Ben Nye; Special Photographic Effects, Fred Sersen; Sound, Bernard Freericks and Roger Heman. **Cast:** Richard Widmark (Ray Biddle); Linda Darnell (Edie Johnson); Stephen McNally (Dr. Wharton); Sidney Poitier (Dr. Luther Brooks); Mildred Joanne Smith (Cora Brooks); Harry Bellaver (George Biddle); Stanley Ridges (Dr. Moreland); Dots Johnson (Lefty); Amanda Randolph (Gladys); Bill Walker (Mathew Tompkins); Ruby Dee (Connie); Ossie Davis (John); Ken Christy (Kowalski); Frank Richards (Mac); George Tyne (Whitey); Robert Adler (Assistant deputy); Bert Freed (Rocky); Jim Toney (Deputy sheriff); Maude Simmons (Luther's mother); Ray Teal (Day deputy); Will Wright (Dr. Cheney); Harry Lauter, Harry Carter, Don Kohler, and Ray Hyke (Orderlies); Wade Dumas (Jonah); Fred Graham (Ambulance driver); William Pullen (Ambulance doctor); Jasper Weldon (Henry); Ruben Wendorf (Polish husband); Laiola Wendorf (Polish wife); Ernest Anderson (School teacher); Victor Kilian, Sr. (Father); Mack Williams (Husband); Dick Paxton (Johnny Biddle); Eleanor Audley (Wife); Doris Kemper (Wife); Stan Johnson and Frank Overton (Interns); Kitty O'Neil (Landlady); Phil Tully (Sergeant); J. Louis Johnson (Elderly Negro); Ian Wolfe (Watkins); Emmett Smith (Joe); Ralph Dunn (Sam); Ruth Warren (Sam's wife); Robert Davis (Hoodlum); Ann Morrison, Eda Reis Merin, and Ann Tyrrell (Nurses); Kathryn Sheldon (Mother); Ralph Hodges (Terry); Thomas Ingersoll (Priest). Final script, July 6, 1949. Production schedule, Oct. 28–Dec. 20, 1949. Released Aug. 16, 1950. 106 minutes (9,590 feet). Awards: National Board of Review: One of the 10 best films of 1950. Academy Award nomination: Best original story and screenplay. *Note: Mankiewicz believed he should have received full credit for the screenplay, and requested a review from the Screen Writers Guild. Fox story conference materials in the Zanuck collection at USC indicate the original story treatment was by Lesser Samuels but that he had no further contact with the screenplay. Mankiewicz documents indicate he was assigned as writer Apr. 27, 1949. He sought arbitration for complete screenplay credit from the Screen Writers Guild on Nov. 12, 1949. He was distressed that he did not receive full credit for the screenplay and felt embarrassed that he had to ask them to reconsider. As an indication of the extent to which he felt he deserved full credit, Mankiewicz explains in a letter to the arbitration committee: "I have written a script based upon an excellent original story. I have utilized those elements of the original, which I considered proper, and I have supplemented them by contributions of my own in great number. The script structure is mine, the script characterizations are mine and certainly, with the exception of technical phrases and street addresses and perhaps a dozen odd lines, the dialogue is all mine. If ever I wrote a screenplay, gentlemen, I wrote the screenplay of NO WAY OUT." The committee declined his petition and the screen credits read: "Written by Joseph L. Mankiewicz and Lesser Samuels." (JLM papers)*

All About Eve (1950). 20th Century–Fox. Black and white. Director, Joseph L. Mankiewicz; Producer, Darryl F. Zanuck; Screenplay, Joseph L. Mankiewicz from story by Mary Orr ("The Wisdom of Eve" in *Cosmopolitan*); Music, Alfred Newman; Director of Photography, Milton Krasner, A.S.C.; Art Direction, Lyle Wheeler and George W. Davis; Set Decorations, Thomas Little and Walter M. Scott; Film Editor, Barbara McLean; Costume Direction, Charles LeMaire; Costumes of Bette Davis, Edith Head; Orchestration, Edward Powell; Makeup Artist, Ben Nye; Special Photographic Effects, Fred Sersen; Sound, W. D. Flick and Roger Heman; Assistant Director, Gaston Glass. **Cast:** Bette Davis (Margo Channing); Anne Baxter (Eve Harrington); George Sanders (Addison DeWitt); Celeste Holm (Karen Richards); Gary Merrill (Bill Sampson); Hugh Marlowe (Lloyd Richards); Gregory Ratoff (Max Fabian); Thelma Ritter (Birdie Coonan); Marilyn Monroe (Miss Caswell); Barbara Bates (Phoebe); Walter Hampden (Aged Actor); Randy Stuart (Girl); Craig Hill (Leading Man); Leland Harris (Doorman); Barbara White (Autograph Seeker); Eddie Fisher (Stage Manager); William Pullen (Clerk); Claude Stroud (Pianist); Eugene Borden (Frenchman); Helen Mowery (Reporter); Steve Geray (Captain of Waiters). Production schedule, Apr. 11–June 7, 1950. Released Oct. 13, 1950. 130 minutes (12,531 feet). Awards: Academy Awards: Best Film (1950); Director (Mankiewicz); Screenplay (Mankiewicz); Supporting Actor (Sanders); Sound Recording; Costume Design (Head and LeMaire). Academy Award Nominations: Actress (Baxter and Davis); Supporting Actress (Holm and Ritter); Cinematography; Art Direction/Set Decoration; Score; Film Editing. British Academy Awards: Best Film. Cannes Film Festival (1951): Best Film (Mankiewicz); Best Female Performance (Davis); Special Jury Prize (Mankiewicz). Directors Guild of America (Quarterly and Annual Awards): Joseph L. Mankiewicz. Golden Globe (1950): Best Screenplay (Mankiewicz). New York Film Critics Circle: Best Picture; Best Actress (Davis); Best Director (Mankiewicz). National Board of Review: Best American Films of 1950 (*All About Eve* and *No Way Out* two of the ten best American films*). Note: Two errors occur in the on-screen cast credits: Gary Merrill is listed as Bill "Simpson" rather than Sampson, and Marilyn Monroe's character is misspelled as "Casswell," even though the script notes the correct spelling as "Caswell."*

People Will Talk (1951). 20th Century–Fox. Black and white. Director, Joseph L. Mankiewicz; Producer, Darryl F. Zanuck; Screen Play, Joseph L. Mankiewicz; From play by Curt Goetz (*Dr. Praetorius*); Music conducted by Alfred Newman; Director of Photography, Milton Krasner, A.S.C.; Art Direction, Lyle Wheeler and George W. Davis; Set Directions, Thomas Little and Walter M. Scott; Film Editor, Barbara McLean, A.C.E.; Wardrobe Direction, Charles LeMaire; Makeup Artist, Ben Nye; Special Photographic Effects, Fred Sersen; Sound, W. D. Flick and Roger Heman; Orchestration, Edward Powell. **Cast:** Cary Grant (Dr. Noah Praetorius); Jeanne Crain (Deborah Higgins); Finlay Currie (Shunderson); Hume Cronyn (Prof. Elwell); Walter Slezak (Prof. Barker); Sidney Blackmer (Arthur Higgins); Basil Ruysdael (Dean Brockwell); Katherine Locke (Miss James); Will Wright (John Higgins); Margaret Hamilton (Miss Pickett); Esther Somers (Mrs. Pegwhistle); Carleton Young (Technician); Larry Dobkin (Business manager); Ray Montgomery (Doctor); Jo Gilbert (Nurse); Ann Morrison (Dietitian); Julia Dean (Old lady); Gail Bonney (Secretary); William Klein (Student manager); George Offerman (Haskins); Adele Longmire (Mabel); Billy House (Coonan); Kay Lavelle (Bella); Maude Wallace (Night Matron); Joyce Mackenzie (Gussie); Parley Baer (Toy Salesman); Irene Seidner (Cook). Working title: "Dr. Praetorius." First draft screenplay, Dec.29, 1950–Feb. 9, 1951. Production schedule, Mar. 20–May 5, 1951. Released Aug. 29, 1951. 110 minutes.

Five Fingers (1952). 20th Century–Fox. Black and white. Director, Joseph L. Mankiewicz; Producer, Otto Lang; Screen Play, Michael Wilson; From book by L. C. Moyzisch (*Operation Cicero*); Dialogue, Joseph L. Mankiewicz [uncredited*]; Music, Bernard Herrmann; Director of Photography, Norbert Brodine, A.S.C.; Editor, James B. Clark; Art Direction, Lyle Wheeler and George W. Davis; Set Decorations, Thomas Little, Walter M. Scott; Film Editor, James B. Clark, A.C.E.; Wardrobe Direction, Charles LeMaire; Makeup Artist, Ben Nye; Special Photographic Effects, Ray Kellogg; Sound, W. D. Flick, Roger Heman. **Cast:** James Mason (Diello/Cicero); Danielle Darrieux (Countess Staviska); Michael Rennie (Colin Travers); Walter Hampden (Sir Frederic); Oscar Karlweis (Moyzisch); Herbert Berghof (Col. von Richter); John Wengraf (von Papen); A. Ben Astar (Siebert); Roger Plowden (MacFadden); Michael Pate (Morrison); Ivan Triesault (Steuben); David Wolfe (DaCosta); Larry Dobkin (Santos). Filmed in Turkey. Rev. final script, Aug. 4, 1951. Production schedule, Aug. 17–Oct. 23, 1951. Released Feb. 22, 1952. 108 minutes. Awards: Academy Award nominations (1952): Best Director (Mankiewicz); Screenplay (Wilson); Directors Guild of America (Quarterly Awards): Mankiewicz. Golden Globe: Screenplay (Wilson). Mystery Writers of America (1952): Edgar Allen Poe Award for outstanding mystery motion picture of the year. National Board of Review: "One of the 10 Best American Films of 1952." *While JLM received no screen credit for his contribution to the revised final script, 135 pages of his rewritten dialogue exists in the Mankiewicz papers. Additionally, Zanuck acknowledged Mankiewicz's contribution to the dialogue in a memo to JLM dated March 18, 1952 (JLM papers).*

Julius Caesar (1953). Metro-Goldwyn-Mayer. Black and white. Director, Joseph L. Mankiewicz; Producer, John Houseman; Music, Miklos Rozsa; Director of Photography, Joseph Ruttenberg, A.S.C.; Art Directors, Cedric Gibbons and Edward Carfagno; Film Editor, John Dunning, A.C.E.; Assistant Director, Howard W. Koch; Recording supervisor, Douglas Shearer; Set Decorations, Edwin B. Willis and Hugh Hunt; Special Effects, Warren Newcombe; Costumes, Herschel McCoy; Hair Styles, Sydney Guilaroff; Make-Up Artist, William Tuttle; Technical Advisor, P. M. Pasinetti. **Cast:** Marlon Brando (Mark Antony); James Mason (Brutus); John Gielgud (Cassius); Louis Calhern (Julius Caesar); Edmond O'Brien (Casca); Greer Garson (Calpurnia); Deborah Kerr (Portia); George Macready (Marullus); Michael Pate (Flavius); Richard Hale (Soothsayer); Alan Napier (Cicero); John Hoyt (Decius Brutus); Tom Powers (Metellus Cimber); William Cottrell (Cinna); Jack Raine (Trebonius); Ian Wolfe (Ligarius); Morgan Farley (Artemidorus); Bill Phipps (Servant to Antony); Douglas Watson (Octavius Caesar); Douglass Dumbrille (Lepidus); Rhys Williams (Lucilius); Michael Ansara (Pindarus); Dayton Lummis (Messala); Edmund Purdom (Strato); John Hardy (Lucius); Lumsden Hare (Publius); Victor Perry (Popilius Lena); O. Z. Whitehead (Cinna, a poet); Michael Tolan (Officer to Octavius); John Lupton (Varro); Preston Hanson (Claudius); John Parrish (Titinius); Joe Waring (Clitus); Stephen Roberts (Dardanius); Thomas Browne Henry (Volumnius); John Doucette (Carpenter and Second Citizen); Ned Glass (Cobbler); Chester Hayes (Roman Soldier); Chester Stratton (Servant to Caesar); Paul Guilfoyle (First Citizen); Lawrence Dobkin (Third Citizen); Jo Gilbert (Fourth Citizen); David Bond, Ann Tyrrell, John O'Malley, Oliver Blake, Alvin Hurwitz, Donald Elson (Citizens of Rome). Production schedule, Aug. 15–Oct. 13, 1953. World premiere May 8, 1953 (Sydney, Australia: Liberty Theatre). Released June 4, 1953. 121 minutes. Awards: Academy Award (1953): Art Direction/black and white (Gibbons). Academy Award nominations: Best Picture; Best Actor (Brando); Cinematography/black and white (Ruttenberg). British Academy Awards: Best Actor/British (Gielgud); Best Actor/Foreign (Brando). National Board of Review: Best American Film Picture of 1953; Best Actor (Mason). *Also known as "William Shakespeare's Julius Caesar."*

The Barefoot Contessa (1954). Figaro Inc./United Artists. Technicolor. Director, Joseph L. Mankiewicz; Producer, Joseph L. Mankiewicz; Screenplay, Joseph L. Mankiewicz; Manager of Production, Forrest E. Johnston; Photography, Jack Cardiff; Editor, William Hornbeck, A.C.E.; Music, Mario Nascimbene; Assistant Director, Pietro Mussetta; Settings, Arrigo Equini; Sound, Charles Knott; Costumes, Fontana; Production Associates, Franco Magli and Michael Waszynski. **Cast:** Humphrey Bogart (Harry Dawes); Ava Gardner (Maria Vargas); Edmond O'Brien (Oscar Muldoon); Marius Goring (Alberto Bravano); Valentina Cortesa (Eleanora Torlato-Favrini); Rossano Brazzi (Vincenzo Torlato-Favrini); Elizabeth Sellars (Jerry); Warren Stevens (Kirk Edwards); Franco Interlenghi (Pedro); Mari Aldon (Myrna); Bessie Love (Mrs. Eubanks); Diana Decker

(Drunken blonde); Bill Fraser (J. Montague Brown); Alberto Rabagliati (Proprietor); Enzo Staiola (Busboy); Maria Zanoli (Maria's mother); Renato Chiantoni (Maria's father); John Parrish (Mr. Black); Jim Gerald (Mr. Blue); Riccardo Rioli (Gypsy dancer); Tonio Selwart (Pretender); Margaret Anderson (Pretender's Wife); Gertrude Flynn (Lulu McGee); John Horne (Hector Eubanks); Robert Christopher (Eddie Blake); Anna Maria Paduan (Chambermaid); Carlo Dale (Chauffeur). Produced in Italy, at the Studio of Cinecittà, in association with Angelo Rizzoli and Robert Haggiag. Production schedule, Jan. 11–Mar. 29, 1954. World premiere Sept. 29, 1954 (NY: Capitol Theatre). Released Sept. 29, 1954. 128 minutes. Awards: Academy Award (1954): Best Supporting Actor (O'Brien). Academy Award nominations: Best story and screenplay (Mankiewicz). Golden Globe: Supporting Actor (O'Brien).

Guys and Dolls (1955). Samuel Goldwyn/Metro-Goldwyn-Mayer. Technicolor. Director, Joseph L. Mankiewicz; Producer, Samuel Goldwyn; Screenplay, Joseph L. Mankiewicz; Based on Play with book by Jo Swerling and Abe Burrows from the story "The Idyll of Miss Sarah Brown" by Damon Runyon produced on the stage by Cy Feuer and Ernest H. Martin; Music and Lyrics, Frank Loesser; Director of Photography, Harry Stradling, A.S.C.; Dances and Musical Numbers staged by Michael Kidd; Production Design, Oliver Smith; Costumes, Irene Sharaff; Music supervised and conducted by Jay Blackton; Background Music, Cyril J. Mockridge; Orchestrations, Skip Martin, Alexander Courage, Nelson Riddle, Al Sendrey; Film Editor, Daniel Mandell; Color Consultant, Alvord L. Eisecombe; Special Photographic Effects, Warren Newcombe; Sound, Fred Lau, Roger Heman, Vinton Vernon; Assistant Director, Arthur S. Black, Jr.; Art Director, Joseph Wright; Set Decoration, Howard Bristol; Make-up, Ben Lane; Hair Stylist, Annabell. **Cast:** Marlon Brando (Sky Masterson); Jean Simmons (Sarah Brown); Frank Sinatra (Nathan Detroit); Vivian Blaine (Miss Adelaide); Robert Keith (Lt. Brannigan); Stubby Kaye (Nicely-Nicely Johnson); Johnny Silver (Benny Southstreet); Regis Toomey (Arvid Abernathy); B. S. Pully (Big Julie); Sheldon Leonard (Harry The Horse); Dan Dayton (Rusty Charlie); George E. Stone (Society Max); Kathryn Givney (General Cartwright); Veda Ann Borg (Laverne); Mary Alan Hokanson (Agatha); Joe McTurk (Angie the Ox); Kay Kuter (Calvin); Stapleton Kent (Mission Member); Renee Renor (Cuban Singer); The Goldwyn Girls (Dancers). Photographed at Samuel Goldwyn Studios, Hollywood. Premiere Nov. 3, 1955 (NY: Capitol Theatre). Released Nov. 3, 1955. 149 minutes. Awards: *Boxoffice*: Best Picture of the Month (January 1958). Golden Globe: Best Picture (Comedy/ Musical); Best Actress (Comedy/Musical) Jean Simmons. Screen Writers' Annual Award: Nomination for Writing Achievement to Joseph L. Mankiewicz.

The Quiet American (1958). Figaro Inc./United Artists. Black and white. Director, Joseph L. Mankiewicz; Producer, Joseph L. Mankiewicz; Screenplay, Joseph L. Mankiewicz; Based on novel by Graham Greene; Settings, Rino Mondellini; Music, Mario Nascimbene conducted by Franco Ferrara; Editor, William Hornbeck, A.C.E.; Photography, Robert Krasker, B.S.C.; Production Manager, Forrest E. Johnston; Assistant Director, Pietro Mussetta; Sound Recording, Basil Fenton-Smith; Camera Operator, John Harris; Set Dressing, Dario Simoni; Make-Up, George Frost; Continuity, Elaine Schreyeck; Special Effects, Rocky Cline; Production Associates, Michele Waszynski, Vinh Noan; Production

Assistant, Rosemary Matthews; Second Assistant Director, Colin Brewer; Third Assistant Director, Giorgio Gentili; Camera Assistants, Ronald Maasz and Godfrey Randall; Boom Operator, Bryan Coates; Sound Recordist, Al Thorne; Sound Maintenance, Fred Hughesdon; Assistant Art Direction, Pierre Guffrey; Wardrobe, Gloria Mussetta; Hairdresser, Ida Mills; Assistant Special Effects, George Schlicker. **Cast:** Audie Murphy (The American); Michael Redgrave (Fowler); Claude Dauphin (Inspector Vigot); Giorgia Moll (Phuong); Kerima (Miss Hei); Bruce Cabot (Bill Granger); Fred Sadoff (Dominguez); Richard Loo (Mister Heng); Peter Trent (Eliot Wilkins); Georges Brehat (French Colonel); Yoko Tani (Hostess); Clinton Andersen (Joe Morton); Sonia Moser (Yvette); Phung Thi Nghiep (Isabelle); Vo Doan Chau (Commandant); Le Van Le (Deputy); Le Quynh (Masked Man). Shot on location in Saigon, Vietnam, and at the Cinecittà Studios, Rome. Production schedule, Jan. 27–June 5, 1957. Premiere Jan 22, 1958 (Washington D.C.: The Playhouse, as a benefit for "American Friends of Viet-Nam"). Released Feb. 5, 1958. 120 minutes.

Suddenly, Last Summer (1959). Horizon Pictures/Columbia Pictures. Black and white. Director, Joseph L. Mankiewicz; Producer, Sam Spiegel; Screenplay, Gore Vidal and Tennessee Williams; Adapted from the play by Tennessee Williams; Director of Photography, Jack Hildyard, B.S.C.; Production Design, Oliver Messel; Art Direction, William Kellner; Production Supervisor, Bill Kirby; Set Decorations, Scott Slimon; Editorial Consultant, William W. Hornbeck, A.C.E.; Editor, Thomas G. Stanford; Sound Editor, Peter Thornton; Assembly Editor, John Jympson; Special Photographic Effects, Tom Howard; Camera Operator, Gerry Fisher; Assistant Director, Bluey Hill; Construction Manager, Peter Dukelow; Sound, A. G. Ambler and John Cox; Continuity, Elaine Schreyeck; Costumes, Oliver Messel; Costumes (Taylor), Jean Louis; Costumes (Hepburn), Norman Hartnell; Associate Costume Design, Joan Ellacott; Makeup, David Aylott; Hairdresser, Joan White; Music Composed by Buxton Orr and Malcolm Arnold, Conducted by Buxton Orr. **Cast:** Elizabeth Taylor (Catherine Holly); Montgomery Clift (Dr. Cukrowicz); Katharine Hepburn (Mrs. Venable); Albert Dekker (Dr. Hockstade); Mercedes McCambridge (Mrs. Holly); Gary Raymond (George Holly); Mavis Villiers (Miss Foxhill); Patricia Marmont (Nurse Benson); Joan Young (Sister Felicity); Maria Britneva (Lucy); Sheila Robbins (Dr. Hockstader's Secretary); David Cameron (Young Blond Intern). Shoot location: Shepperton Studios, England, and Spain [exteriors]. Preview Dec. 21, 1959 (NY: Criterion Theatre). Released Dec. 22, 1959. 112 minutes. Awards: Academy Awards (1959): Best Actress nominations (Katharine Hepburn and Elizabeth Taylor). Golden Globe: Best Actress (Drama): Elizabeth Taylor. National Board of Review: One of the 10 Best films of 1959.

Cleopatra (1961-63). 20th Century–Fox. DeLuxe Color-Todd-AO. Director, Joseph L. Mankiewicz; Producer, Walter Wanger; Screenplay, Joseph L. Mankiewicz, Ranald MacDougall, and Sidney Buchman based upon histories by Plutarch, Suetonius, Appian, and other ancient sources, and *The Life and Times of Cleopatra* by Charles Marie Franzero (London 1957); Music Composed & Conducted by Alex North; Choreography, Hermes Pan; Costumes for Taylor, Irene Sharaff; Director of Photography, Leon Shamroy, A.S.C.; Art Direction, Jack Martin Smith, Hilyard M. Brown, Herman A. Blumenthal, Elven Webb, Maurice Pelling, Boris Juraga; Production Design, John DeCuir; Set Decorations,

Walter M. Scott, Paul S. Fox, Ray Moyer; Men's Costumes, Vittorio Nino Novarese; Women's Costumes, Renie; Film Editors, Dorothy Spencer and Elmo Williams; Special Photographic Effects, L. B. Abbott, A.S.C., Emil Kosa, Jr.; Sound Recording Supervisors, Fred Hynes and James Corcoran; Sound Recorded by Bernard Freericks, Murray Spivack; Assistant Director, Fred R. Simpson; Production Managers, Forrest E. Johnston and C. O. Erickson; Casting Consultant, Stuart Lyons; Makeup, Alberto DeRossi, Robert J. Schiffer, Vivienne Walker; Taylor's Hairstylist, Vivienne Zavitz; Color Consultant, Leonard Doss; Second Unit Directors, Ray Kellogg and Andrew Marton; Second Unit Photography, Claude Renoir; Second Unit Production Manager, Saul Wurtzel; Associate Music Conductor, Lionel Newman; DeLuxe Color-Todd-AO, Pietro Portalupi. **Cast:** Elizabeth Taylor (Cleopatra); Richard Burton (Mark Antony); Rex Harrison (Julius Caesar); Pamela Brown (High Priestess); George Cole (Flavius); Hume Cronyn (Sosigenes); Cesare Danova (Apollodorus); Kenneth Haigh (Brutus); Andrew Keir (Agrippa); Martin Landau (Rufio); Roddy McDowall (Octavius); Robert Stephens (Germanicus); Francesca Annis (Eiras); Gregoire Aslan (Pothinus); Martin Benson (Ramos); Herbert Berghof (Theodotus); John Cairney (Phoebus); Jacqui Chan (Lotos); Isabelle Cooley (Charmian); John Doucette (Achillas); Andrew Faulds (Candidus); Michael Gwynn (Cimber); Michael Hordern (Cicero); John Hoyt (Cassius); Marne Maitland (Euphranor); Carroll O'Connor (Casca); Richard O'Sullivan (Ptolemy); Gwen Watford (Calpurnia); Douglas Wilmer (Decimus); Loris Loddi (Caesarion, age 3); Del Russei (Caesarion, age 7); Kenneth Nash (Caesarion, age 11); Finlay Currie (Titus); Gin Mart (Marcellus); Laurence Naismith (Archesilaus); Marina Berti (Queen at Tarsus); Llewelyn Rees (Senator); Jean Marsh (Octavia); Furio Meniconi (Mithridates); John Karlsen (High Priest); Dafydd Havard (Scrawny Guard); Gabrielle D'Olive (Roman Mother); Edwin Richfield (Courier); Patrick Troughton (Drunk Legionnaire); Bernard Goldman (Very Fat Potentate); Georgia Simmons (Old Hag, market); John Colin (Smokestained Officer); Eric Corrie (Young Officer); Desmond Llewelyn, Alan Browning (Senators); Desmond Llewelyn (Domitius); Alan Browning (Publius); John Stacey (Bacchus); Marie Devereux (Cleopatra's double); Robert Gardette (Caesar's double); Luciano Doria (Antony's double). Shoot locations: Cinecittà Studios (Rome); Ischia, Italy and Alexandria [exteriors]. Production schedule, Sept. 25, 1961–July 28, 1962. World premiere June 12, 1963 (NY: Rivoli Theatre). Released June 12, 1963. 243 minutes. Awards: Academy Awards (1963): Cinematography/Color (Shamroy); Art Direction/Color (DeCuir and nine others); Costume Design/Color (Sharaff, Novarese, Renie); Special Visual Effects. Academy Awards nominations: Best Picture; Best Actor (Harrison). National Board of Review: Actor (Harrison). Writers' Guild of America: Screenwriter Award (Mankiewicz).

The Honey Pot (1967). Charles K. Feldman/Famous Artists Productions/United Artists. Technicolor. Director, Joseph L. Mankiewicz; Producer, Joseph L. Mankiewicz; Screenplay, Joseph L. Mankiewicz; Based upon a Play by Frederick Knott, a Novel by Thomas Sterling, and a Play, *Volpone*, by Ben Jonson); Production Designer, John De Cuir; Art Director, Boris Juraga; Set Dressings, Paul Fox and Kenneth Muggleston; Director of Photography, Gianni Di Venanzo; Wardrobe Design, Rolf Gérard, executed by Annamode; Jewelry and Silver, Bulgari, Rome; Assistant Director, Gus Agosti; Second Assistant, Franco Cerino;

Unit Manager, Angelo Binarelli; Script Continuity, Yvonne Axworthy; Make Up, Amato Garbini; Hairdressing, Gabriella Borzini; Sound Recording, David Hildyard, Len Shilton; Sound Editor, Jim Groom; Film Editor, David Bretherton; Production Associate, Attilio d'Onofrio; Camera Associate, Pasquale de Santis; Choreography, Lee Theodore; Music Composed and Conducted, John Addison. **Cast:** Rex Harrison (Cecil Fox); Susan Hayward (Lone-Star Crockett Sheridan); Cliff Robertson (William McFly); Capucine (Princess Dominique); Edie Adams (Merle McGill); Maggie Smith (Sarah Watkins); Adolfo Celi (Inspector Rizzi); Hugh Manning (Volpone); David Dodimead (Mosca); Herschel Bernardi (Oscar Ludwig); Cy Grant (Revenue Agent); Frank Latimore (Revenue Agent); Luigi Scavran (Massimo); Mimmo Poli (Cook); Antonio Corevi (Tailor); Carlos Valles (Assistant Taylor). Working titles: "Time of the Fox," "Tale of the Fox," "The Man Who Took It with Him," "Anyone for Venice" and "It Comes Up Murder." Shooting locations, Cinecittà Studios (Rome), Venice (exteriors). Production schedule, Sept. 20, 1965–Feb. 26, 1966. Premiere May 21, 1967 (London and NY: Trans Lux West Theatre). Released May 22, 1967. 131 minutes.

There Was a Crooked Man... (1969-70). Warner Brothers–Seven Arts, Inc. Technicolor. Panavision. Director, Joseph L. Mankiewicz; Producer, Joseph L. Mankiewicz; Executive producer, C. O. Erickson; Screenplay, David Newman and Robert Benton; Director of Photography, Harry Stradling, Jr., A.S.C.; Production Decorator, Edward Carrere; Costumes, Anna Hill Johnstone; Makeup, Perc Westmore; Makeup Supervisor, Gordon Bau, S.M.A.; Hair Stylist, Annabell Levy; Supervising Hair Stylist, Jean Burt Reilly, C.H.S.; Film Editor, Gene Milford; Sound, Al Overton, Jr.; Aerial Photography with Tyler Camera Systems; Main Title Design, Wayne Fitzgerald; Assistant to the Producer, Sidney Ganis; Production Supervisor, Peter V. Herald; Assistant Director, Don Kranze; Music Supervisor, Sonny Burke; Music, Charles Strouse; Title Song, Charles Strouse, Lee Adams, Sung by Trini Lopez. **Cast:** Kirk Douglas (Paris Pitman, Jr.); Henry Fonda (Woodward Lopeman); Hume Cronyn (Dudley Whinner); Warren Oates (Floyd Moon); Burgess Meredith (Missouri Kid); Lee Grant (Mrs. Bullard); Arthur O'Connell (Mr. Lomax); Martin Gabel (Warden LeGoff); John Randolph (Cyrus McNutt); Michael Blodgett (Coy Cavendish); Claudia McNeil (Madame); Alan Hale (Tobaccy); Victor French (Whiskey); Jeanne Cooper (Prostitute); C. K. Yang (Ah-Ping); Bert Freed (Skinner); Gene Evans (Col. Wolff); Barbara Rhoades (Miss Brundige); Pamela Hensley (Edwina); J. Edward McKinley; Karl Lukas; Larry D. Mann; Ann Doran; Paul Prokop; Bart Burns. Working titles: "Hang Up" and "The Prison Story." Production schedule, Mar. 5–July 3, 1969. Released Dec. 25, 1970. 125 minutes.

Sleuth (1972). Palomar Pictures International/20th Century–Fox. Technicolor. Director, Joseph L. Mankiewicz; Executive Producer, Edgar J. Scherick; Producer, Morton Gottlieb; Screenplay, Anthony Shaffer (based on his play); Associate Producer, David Middlemas; Assistant Director, Kip Gowans; Production Manager, Frank Ernst; Production Design, Ken Adam; Production Executive, Allan B. Schwartz; Art Decorator, Peter Lamont; Set Decorator, John Jarvis; Costume Designer, John Furniss; Hairdresser, Joan White; Director of Photography, Oswald Morris, B.S.C.; Camera Operator, Jimmy Turrell; Sound Editor, Don Sharpe; Assistant Editor, Mary Kessel; Sound Recordist, John Mitchell, Ken Barker; Special Effects, Leslie Hillman; Make-up, Tom Smith; Continuity,

Elaine Schreyeck; Words and Music to "Just One of Those Things," "You Do Something to Me," and "Anything Goes," Cole Porter; Editor, Richard Marden; Music Composed, Conducted and Arranged by John Addison. **Cast:** Laurence Olivier (Andrew Wyke); Michael Caine (Milo Tindle*). Shooting locations, Pinewood Studios (England), the County of Dorset (exteriors). Released Dec. 10, 1972. 139 minutes. Awards: Academy Award nominations (1972): Best Actor (Caine); Best Actor (Olivier); Best Director; Original Dramatic Score (Addison). All-American Press Association (1973): Best Movie Award (non-musical). New York Film Critics Circle: Actor (Olivier). *Note: There are only two actors in this film even though the following fallacious credits also exist: Alec Cawthorne (Inspector Doppler); Eve Channing (Marguerite); John Matthews (Sergeant Tarrant); Teddy Martin (Constable Higgs); Karen Minfort-Jones (Teya).*

Other Works

Mankiewicz as Actor

Woman Trap (1929). Paramount. Black and white. Director, William Wellman; Story, Edwin Burke; Dialogue, Bartlett Cormack; Adaptation, Louise Long; Photography, Henry Gerard. **Cast:** Hal Skelly (Dan Malone); Chester Morris (Ray Malone); Evelyn Brent (Kitty Evans); William Davidson (Watts); Effie Ellsler (Mrs. Malone); Guy Oliver (Mr. Evans); Leslie Fenton (Eddie Evans); Charles Giblyn (Smith); Joseph Mankiewicz (Reporter); Wilson Hummell (Detective). 82 minutes.

Filmic Contribution

King: A Filmed Record, Montgomery to Memphis (1970). Martin Luther King Film Project, Inc. Conceived and Produced by Ely Landau; Directors, Joseph L. Mankiewicz and Sidney Lumet. 153 minutes. *Note: This documentary credits JLM as "contributing talent." Walker notes that Mankiewicz was responsible for the connecting sequences that were codirected with Sidney Lumet.*

George Stevens: A Filmmaker's Journey (1988). ABC Television. Producer, George Stevens, Jr.; Director, George Stevens, Jr. Televised nationally, 25 Aug. 1988, now available on videotape. *Note: Mankiewicz discusses the SDG loyalty oath controversy.*

Opera

La Bohème (1952-53 season). Metropolitan Opera. Based on "La Vie de Bohème" by Henri Murger. Opera in Four Acts. Libretto, Giuseppe Giacosa and Luigi Illia; New English version, Howard Dietz; Music, Giacomo Puccini; Conductor, Alberto Erede; Staging, Joseph L. Mankiewicz; Decor and Costumes, Rolf Gerard; Chorus Master, Kurt Adler. First performance, Dec. 27, 1952 (Benefit, Institute for Crippled and Disabled). *Note: Cast members for Jan. 1, Jan. 7, Jan. 12 with alternating programs in English and Italian.* Richard Tucker, Eugene Conley, Jan Peerce (Rodolfo); Robert Merrill, Frank Guarrera (Marcello); Clifford Harvuote (Schaunard); Jerome Hines, Nicola Moscona (Colline); Nadine Conner, Hilde Gueden, Victoria de los Angeles (Mimi); Patrice Munsel. (Dec. 27, 1952, benefit): Brenda Lewis, Regina Resnik (Musetta); Lawrence Davidson (Parpignol); Paul Franke (Alcindoro); Alessio De Paolis (Alcindoro); Algerd Brazis (A Sergeant*).* *Note: Mankiewicz staged the first version in English at the Met. He also staged the alternating Italian version but was not involved in the television broadcast version. The Met wanted him back in 1967 and 1972 but he declined because of his film schedule (JLM files).*

Television

Carol for Another Christmas (1964). ABC-TV/Telsun Foundation Inc. Black and white. Director, Joseph L. Mankiewicz; Producer, Joseph L. Mankiewicz; Teleplay, Rod Serling; Music, Henry Mancini; Director of Photography, Arthur J. Ornitz; Production design, Gene Callahan; Costumes, Anna Hill Johnstone; Supervising Film Editor, Robert Lawrence; Production manager, Jim Di Gangi. For the Telsun Foundation: Associate Producer, C. O. Erickson; Executive Producer, Edgar Rosenberg; Assistant Director, Dan Eriksen. **Cast:** Sterling Hayden (Daniel Grudge); Ben Gazzara (Fred); Peter Sellers (Imperial Me); Steve Lawrence (Ghost of Christmas Past); Pat Hingle (Ghost of Christmas Present); Robert Shaw (Ghost of Christmas Future); Barbara Ann Tee (Ruby); Percy Rodriguez (Charles); Eva Marie Saint (Wave); James Shigeta (Doctor); Britt Ekland (Mother). Preview, Dec. 20, 1964 (Washington, D.C.: U.S. State Department gala hosted by Secretary of State Dean Rusk). Televised, Dec. 28, 1964, 9:30–11:00 P.M. Awards: Emmy nomination (1964–65). *Note: This commercial-free television production in support of the United Nations aired only once.*

Documentaries About Mankiewicz

All About Mankiewicz (1983). Janus Film/Filmedis [France]. Directors, Luc Beraud and Michel Ciment; Producer, Klaus Hellwig; Writers, Luc Beraud and Michel Ciment; Photography, Tom Hurwitz and Michael Teutsch; Sound, Peter Miller and Christian Moldt; Editor, Juliette Welfrig; Interviewer, Michel Ciment. 104 minutes (two segments of 52 minutes each). *Note: Excellent interview with lengthy movie clips detailing JLM's life in films. Part I "His Life and His Films"; Part II "Working in Hollywood." In French with JLM's responses to questions in English (with French subtitles).*

Anyone for Venice (1966). France. Director, Charles Chabaud; Interviewer, Richard Overstreet. Interview date, 14 Nov. 1965 (Venice, Europa Hotel). Televised, 8 Feb. 1966 (France). 29 minutes. *Note: French television documentary on the making of* The Honey Pot. *In French.*

Mankiewicz à Avignon (1981). France. Directors, Pierre-André Boutang and Jean Douchet. Televised: Part I, 28 Feb. 1981; Part II, 17 Oct. 1981. 38 minutes each (two parts). *Note: French television documentary on Mankiewicz at Avignon film festival. In French.*

Other Audio and Audiovisual Interviews*

Popular Arts Project: Joseph L. Mankiewicz (1958). Oral history conducted by Mr. and Mrs. Robert C. Franklin. New York: Columbia University Oral History Research Department. 24 Oct. 1958. Audiotape transcribed by Oral History Research Office. 55 pages. *JLM discusses his life in the film industry following his graduation from Columbia University.*

Tonight (1959). Interview produced by Alistair Milne. BBC, London. 15 May 1959.

Omnibus: Humphrey Bogart (1971). Interview produced by Michael Houldey. BBC–1, London. 27 Dec. 1971.

Cinema Showcase: Joseph L. Mankiewicz (1974). Interview with Jim Whaley. WETV, Atlanta, GA. 23 May 1974. Executive Producer/Director, Danny Royal. Televised locally in two segments: Part I, 23 May 1974; Part II, 30 May 1974. *Lengthy interview for broadcast on local public television in Atlanta, Georgia.*

Hollywood Greats. Programme 3: Spencer Tracy (1977). Interview with Barry Norman. Producer, Barry Brown. BBC–1, London. 18 Aug. 1978.

Hollywood Greats. Programme 4: Judy Garland (1978). Interview with Barry Norman. Producer, Barry Brown. BBC–1, London. 24 Aug. 1978.

Joseph Mankiewicz' Hollywood (1978). Interview with Dick Cavett. Center for Cassette Studies #38939 Audiotape. 128 minutes. *Originally broadcast on Cavett's television program.*

Hollywood Greats. Programme 5: Marilyn Monroe (1978). Interview with Barry Norman. Producer, Barry Brown. BBC–1, London. 24 Aug. 1978.

Saturday Night at the Movies (1980). Interview with Elwy Yost. TV Ontario, Toronto, Canada. 11 Nov. 1980. Producer, Richard Johnson. 90 minutes. *Excellent discussion of JLM's writing contribution to those films that he produced.*

Talking Pictures (1985). Interview produced by Judy Lindsay. BBC–1. 12 July 1985.

CBS Morning Program (1987). Interview with Mariette Hartley on the anniversary of the death of Marilyn Monroe. CBS. Nationally televised, 3 Aug. 1987.

Classical Hollywood: Joseph L. Mankiewicz (1991). New York Center for Visual History. Videotape. Interviewer, Lawrence Pitkethly. Recorded, 12 July 1991. Televised in part, "American Cinema" Series, PBS. Transcript of interview, Center for Visual History, 79 pages. *Lengthy interview wherein Mankiewicz discusses the studio system and individual films.*

Mankiewicz also made guest appearances on many popular television shows including The Dick Cavett Show, What's My Line? *and* I've Got a Secret.

Appendix A.
Miscellaneous
and Unrealized
Mankiewicz Projects

Miscellaneous Projects

Finnish Relief Fund (1940). Chairman, Motion Picture Division. *While at MGM, Mankiewicz briefly served as the head of a fund raising drive.*

Screen Directors Guild (1950). President. *Ironically, Cecil B. DeMille, the man who eventually initiated a recall of JLM's presidency over the loyalty oath controversy, nominated Mankiewicz. Mankiewicz served one term and later declined to accept his unanimous reelection.*

Figaro, Inc. (1953–60). Founder/Owner. *Independent production company based in New York. Fifty percent of the company was sold to NBC in 1956. In 1961, Figaro, Inc. was sold to 20th Century–Fox.*

National Arts Foundation (1963). "Concerning S.165 and S.1316—A Statement by Joseph L. Mankiewicz." 15 November 1963, 13 pages. *Mankiewicz was invited to reply to Sen. Claiborne Pell's request for input regarding the establishment of a National Arts Foundation. Mankiewicz replied that he did not think legislation was needed, fearing an imposition of bureaucratic structure on the arts.*

"The Performing Woman" (1973–). *Mankiewicz begins collecting research for book on history of actresses. Little progress made.*

Epcot (1978). "A Suggested Concept for an Extraordinary Project." 11 November 1978, 38 pages. *Mankiewicz contracted to write a project description for the "Mankind" Pavilion and an overall concept for the Epcot project.*

Yale University (1979–). Associate Fellow. *In response to a petition from students of the Ezra Stiles College, Mankiewicz is appointed Associate Fellow of Yale University.*

Actors' Studio, Playwrights'/Directors' Unit [New York] (1982–). *Mankiewicz participates in weekly discussion with prospective playwrights.*

Unrealized Projects*

"The Pirate" (1943). MGM film. Original screenplay, Joseph L. Mankiewicz. *JLM work completed: First script (29 Mar. 1943, 106 pages); Temporary complete script (4 Aug. 1943, 126 pages). Mankiewicz soon left MGM for Fox. Project never materialized.*

"Captain from Castile" (1945). Film. Based on novel by Samuel Shellabarger. *JLM work completed: Screenplay treatment (16 July 1945, 19 pages).*

"Berkeley Square" (1946–51). Film. Working titles: "The House on Berkeley Square" and "The House on the Square." *JLM work completed: Screenplay (22 Apr. 1946, 123 pages).*

"The Bright Promise" (1947). Film. Based on novel by Richard Sherman. *JLM work completed: First draft screenplay (19 May 1947, 37 pages).*

"Jefferson Selleck" (1952–53). MGM film. Working titles: "All the Livelong Day" and "The Great American Heart Attack." Based on novel by Carl Jonas. Spencer Tracy vehicle. *JLM film work completed: Final shooting script (30 Jan. 1953, 157 pages). Film project canceled February 1953. Later pursued as a Broadway play, "All the Livelong Day."*

"Maiden Voyage" (1955). Play. Playwright, Paul Osborne. Director, Joseph L. Mankiewicz. Producer, Billy Rose. *One month away from the beginning of rehearsals, play is canceled because of lack of theatre space on Broadway.*

"All the Livelong Day" (1958). Play. Working title: "Jefferson Selleck." Based on novel by Carl Jonas. Writer/director, Joseph L. Mankiewicz. Producer, David Merrick. Henry Fonda vehicle. *JLM work completed: First draft of play (Sept. 1958, 164 pages). Rosa Stradner Mankiewicz died 27 Sept. 1958. Project canceled.*

"John Brown's Body" (1959–60). Film. Property of 20th Century-Fox. Based on narrative poem by Stephen Vincent Benét. Writer/director, Joseph L. Mankiewicz. Projected release, April 1961 (100th anniversary of firing on Fort Sumter). *JLM work completed: Essential plot outline (13 Jan. 1960, 41 pages); Preliminary screenplay outline (23 Mar. 1960, 53 pages). Project canceled due to writers' strike of 1960. JLM moves on to "Justine" project.*

"Justine" (1960). Film. Property of Twentieth Century–Fox. Based on "The Alexandria Quartet," a tetralogy by Lawrence Durrell. *JLM work completed: Treatment and screenplay outline (14 Sept. 1960, 151 pages); First draft screenplay (no date [late 1960], 674 pages). History of an ill-fated project: (1960) Writers' strike inter-*

*All works among the Mankiewicz papers.

rupts project; (Feb. 1961) Fox postpones project as JLM takes on Cleopatra; *(1963) JLM refuses to work for Fox after* Cleopatra; *(1969) Fox releases George Cukor's film version of* Justine *based on book (not JLM's screenplay); (1991) Producer Steven Haft (*Dead Poets Society*) writes to JLM wanting to produce film. JLM sends him script. Nothing materializes.*

"The Meteor" (1967–68). Play. Intended as Mankiewicz's Broadway debut. Based on German play by Friedrich Durrenmatt. Writer, Joseph L. Mankiewicz. Producer, David Merrick. *JLM work completed: First draft of play (10 Jan. 1967, 136 pages); Second draft (no date [1967–68], 127 pages). Film commitments interfere. Project canceled.*

"The Last One Left" (1967–68). Film. Based on novel by John D. MacDonald. Writer/director, Joseph L. Mankiewicz. *JLM work completed: Screenplay treatment #1 (24 Aug. 1967, 28 pages); Screenplay treatment #2 (31 Aug. 1967, 34 pages). Sold to United Artists for $1.00 on 13 Feb. 1968.*

"Couples" (1968–69). Film. Based on novel by John Updike. Writer/director, Joseph L. Mankiewicz. David L. Wolper Productions/United Artists. *JLM work completed: Screenplay (no date [mid–1968], 293 pages). Contract dissolved through mutual release of services June 4, 1969.*

"Jane" (1974–). Film. Based on novel by Dee Wells. Screenplay, Joseph L. Mankiewicz. *JLM work completed: First draft (budget) screenplay (9 Sept. 1974, 410 pages); Draft screenplay (27 June 1975, 202 pages). Mankiewicz began this project in May of 1974 and continued to work on it for the remainder of his life.*

"Madonna Red" (1979–80). Film. Based on novel by James Carroll. Writer/director, Joseph L. Mankiewicz. Production company, Ladd Company. Paul Newman vehicle. *JLM work completed: Screenplay précis (Nov. 1979, 152 pages); Draft screenplay (Apr. 1980, 148 pages). Some believe that this project did not materialize because production company feared Irish terrorism.*

Appendix B.
Film Festivals
Honoring Mankiewicz

British Film Festival [London] (1960). "A Season of Mankiewicz Films."

Cinémathèque Française [Paris] (1967). "Hommage-Rétrospective."

Shakespeare Film Festival [England] (1972). Mankiewicz on lecture series.

Arnhem Film Festival [Holland] (1973). *Sleuth* premieres at Mankiewicz retrospective.

Ontario Film Institute [Canada] (1973). Tribute to Mankiewicz.

U.S.A. Film Festival [Dallas, TX] (1974). Great Director of the Year: Tribute to Mankiewicz.

San Francisco 29th Annual International Film Festival [California] (1975). Tribute to Joseph L. Mankiewicz.

Festival d'Avignon [France] (1980). "Hommage-Rétrospective."

Deauville Film Festival [France] (1981). "Hommage-Rétrospective."

Minneapolis Film Festival [Minnesota] (1981). Director's Tribute Series.

British Film Institute [London] (1982). Second retrospective-tribute to Mankiewicz who delivered the Guardian Lecture at National Film Theatre.

Berlin Film Festival [Germany] (1983). Mankiewicz Tribute. *JLM served as copresident of the festival jury with Jeanne Moreau.*

Rotterdam Festival [Holland] (1984). Mankiewicz Retrospective.

Internacional de Cine de Valladolid [Madrid] (1985). Tribute to Mankiewicz.

Cinémathèque Française [Paris] (1987). "Hommage-Rétrospective."

Cinémathèque Luxembourg (1987). Mankiewicz Retrospective.

Swedish Film Institute [Stockholm] (1988). Mankiewicz Retrospective.

Museum of Modern Art Department of Film [New York] (1990). Tribute to Mankiewicz in conjunction with The Academy of Arts and Sciences.

Academy of Motion Picture Arts and Sciences [Los Angeles] (1991). Tribute to Joseph L. Mankiewicz.

Berkshire Film Society [Great Barrington, MA] (1991). Salutes the Director: Joseph L. Mankiewicz.

Film Forum 2 [New York] (1992). "All About Mankiewicz."

Institut Lumiére [Lyon, France] (1992). Mankiewicz Tribute.

San Sebastian International Film Festival [Spain] (1992). Film Retrospective-Tribute.

Director's View Film Festival [Stamford, CT] (2000). The Joseph L. Mankiewicz Award for Excellence in Film is established.

Appendix C. Awards

Academy Awards (1949): Best Screenplay (*A Letter to Three Wives*); Best Director (*A Letter to Three Wives*).

Screen Directors Guild Award (1949): Best Directorial Achievement (*A Letter to Three Wives*); Best American Comedy (*A Letter to Three Wives*).

Academy Awards (1950): Best Screenplay (*All About Eve*); Best Director (*All About Eve*).

B'nai B'rith Annual Award (1950): For direction and coauthorship of *No Way Out*.

British Film Academy (1950): Best Film (*All About Eve*); Best Director (*All About Eve*).

Film Daily (1950): Director of the Year; Writer of the Year.

Holiday Magazine **Motion Picture Award** (1950): "Hollywood's Man of the Year" (for *No Way Out* and *All About Eve*).

Motion Picture Herald Achievement Award (1950): "A Champion Director for 1950–51."

Screen Directors Guild Award (1950): Best American Comedy (*All About Eve*); Best Directorial Achievement (*All About Eve*).

Cannes Film Festival (1951): Special Jury Prize (*All About Eve*).

Columbia University (1951): Class of 1928 Award.

New York Film Critics Award (1951): Best Direction (*All About Eve*).

Mystery Writers of America (1952). Edgar Allan Poe Awards: Best Mystery Film of the Year (*Five Fingers*); Best Director (*Five Fingers*).

Writers Guild of America (1963): Laurel Award for Achievement.

Republic of Italy (1965): Commander in the Order of Merit of the Republic. *Mankiewicz was the first American director to receive this honor.*

International Film Importers and Distributors of America (1971): Great Filmmaker Award.

Directors Guild of America (1981): Honorary Life Membership Award.

City of Rotterdam [Holland] (1984): Erasmus Award. *Mankiewicz was the first filmmaker to receive this honor bestowed on distinguished visitors to Rotterdam.*

Columbia University (1986): Alexander Hamilton Medal.

Directors Guild of America (1986): 50th Anniversary Tribute Salute to Mankiewicz. *Museum of Modern Art hosted salute to Mankiewicz with screening of* The Ghost and Mrs. Muir *followed by reception in his honor.*

Venice Film Festival (1987): "Leone d'Oro alla Carriera." *Mankiewicz is awarded Golden Lion Award for Lifetime Achievement.*

Republic of France (1988): "Chevalier de la Legion d'Honneur." *Mankiewicz is made a member of the Legion of Honor.*

San Francisco International Film Festival (1989): Akira Kurosawa Award for Lifetime Achievement. *Mankiewicz was the first American to receive this honor.*

Academy of Motion Picture Arts and Sciences (1991): Lifetime Membership.

Directors Guild of America (1991): D. W. Griffith Award for Outstanding Lifetime Achievement in Film Direction.

San Sebastian International Film Festival [Spain] (1992): Award for Lifetime Achievement.

Index

Photographs are noted with the letter p following the page number. Alternate names and spellings are in parentheses beside the name most widely used. **Boldface** indicates major essays.

271